CW01023705

The Handbook of Corporate Financial Risk Management

The Handbook of Corporate Financial Risk Management

---

by Stanley Myint and Fabrice Famery

Published by Risk Books, a Division of Incisive Media Investments Ltd

Incisive Media
32–34 Broadwick Street
London W1A 2HG
Tel: +44(0) 20 7316 9000
E-mail: books@incisivemedia.com
Sites: www.riskbooks.com
www.incisivemedia.com

ISBN 978-1-906348-92-2

British Library Cataloguing in Publication Data
A catalogue record for this book is available from the British Library

Publisher: Nick Carver
Commissioning Editor: Sarah Hastings
Managing Editor: Lewis O'Sullivan
Editorial Development: Alice Levick
Designer: Lisa Ling
Copy-edited and typeset by T&T Productions Ltd, London

Printed and bound in the UK by Berforts Group

For

Sarah, Marko, Nora and Milica

Sandrine, Edouard, Elisa and Victoria

BNP PARIBAS CORPORATE & INVESTMENT BANKING

BNP Paribas Corporate & Investment Banking is one of the world's pre-eminent investment banks, with expertise spanning fixed income, structured finance, global equities, commodity derivatives and corporate finance. We are part of a global banking group that, in the first half of 2012, generated a net income of EUR 4.7 billion on EUR 20.0 billion of revenue, demonstrating persistent strength despite a challenging economic environment.

The fixed income division boasts world-class research and strategy, debt capital markets and corporate solutions teams offering, among others, risk management solutions across interest rates and foreign exchange, as well as debt management strategies.

It is one of the world's leading partners for bond issuers and investors: for EUR-currency bond issues, BNP Paribas Corporate & Investment Banking has been ranked "No. 1 Lead Manager" by volume every year since 2009, while, for corporate EMEA bond issues (all currencies), it ranked no. 1 in 2009, 2010 and 2012 to date (Thomson Reuters).

The Corporate Solutions Group is a team comprising 25 professionals, whose mandate is to assist key corporate clients of BNP Paribas on strategic issues related to funding and risk management.

INDUSTRY ACCOLADES

Euromoney Interest Rates Survey 2012

No.1 EUR Derivatives for Corporates

EuroWeek Awards 2012

Best Bank for:
Corporate DCM in EUR (1st)
Corporate DCM in USD (3rd)

Euromoney Awards for Excellence 2012

Best Debt House in Western Europe
Best Bank in Western Europe

Contents

About the Authors xiii

Foreword xv

Preface xvii

Introduction xix

PART I FUNDING 1

Funding 3

1 How to Obtain a Credit Rating 9

2 The Intermediated Exchange 19

3 Cash Tender Offer 27

4 Optimal Debt Duration via Merton's Model 33

5 Funding Cost Drivers 41

PART II INTEREST RATE AND INFLATION RISKS 51

Interest Rate and Inflation Risks 53

6 How to Develop an Interest Rate Hedging Policy 57

7 How to Improve Your Fixed–Floating Mix and Duration 69

8 Impact of Fixed–Floating Policy on Company Valuation 93

9 Do You Need Inflation-Linked Debt? 107

10 Prehedging Interest Rate Risk 117

11 When to Prehedge 127

12 Constrained Maturity Optimisation 141

13 Asset and Liability Management 147

14 Pension Fund Asset and Liability Management 159

PART III CURRENCY RISK 167

Currency Risk 169

15 How to Develop a Foreign Exchange Hedging Policy 175

16 Netting Foreign Exchange Risks 185

17 Managing the Risk from Emerging Market Currencies 199

18 Currency Risk on Covenants 207

19 How to Manage Translation Risk 215

20 Managing Foreign Exchange Risk with a Dynamic Option Strategy 227

PART IV CREDIT RISK 239

Credit Risk 241

21 Counterparty Risk Methodology 245

22 Counterparty Risk Protection 255

23 Optimal Deposit Composition 263

24 Prehedging Credit Risk 277

PART V M&A-RELATED RISKS 285

M&A-Related Risks 287

25 Rating Impact of an Acquisition 293

26 Risk Management for M&A 299

27 Amendments to Bond Documentation 313

28 Monetising Deferred Consideration 317

29 Hedging Uncertain Exposures 323

PART VI COMMODITY RISK 337

Commodity Risk 339

30 Managing Commodity-Linked Revenues and Currency Risk 345

31 Managing Commodity-Linked Costs and Currency Risk 353

References 360

Index 363

About the Authors

Stanley Myint heads the risk management advisory team at BNP Paribas and has 18 years of experience in this field. The mandate of the team is to advise key corporate clients of BNP Paribas on issues related to financial risk management, particularly with regards to interest rate, currency, inflation and credit risk. His approach is a mixture of quantitative finance and corporate finance. Prior to BNP Paribas, Stanley worked at The Royal Bank of Scotland, McKinsey & Company and Canadian Imperial Bank of Commerce, always in the field of risk management. He has published several articles in Risk Books publications and *Risk* magazine. Stanley has a PhD in physics from Boston University and a BSc in physics from Belgrade University (Serbia).

Fabrice Famery is head of rates and FX corporate sales for Western Europe at BNP Paribas. His group provides corporate clients with hedging solutions across interest rate and foreign exchange asset classes. Corporate risk management has been the focus of Fabrice's professional path for the past 24 years. He spent the first seven years of his career in the treasury department of the energy company ELF, then, in 1996, joined Paribas (now BNP Paribas), where he occupied various positions including FX derivative marketer, head of the FX advisory group and head of the fixed income corporate solutions group. Fabrice has published articles in *Finance Director Europe* and *Risk* magazine. He has a Master's degree in international affairs from Dauphine University (France).

Foreword

The Handbook of Corporate Financial Risk Management has the rare quality of delivering exactly what its title promises.

Over the years, managing financial risks has represented an ever-increasing share of the workload of any chief financial officer (CFO), and this is unlikely to reverse any time soon. Our world has become more risky and more complex. This is a fact.

To highlight one example of various financial risks, the figure below illustrates the performance of copper, freight, short-term interest rates and the EURUSD exchange rate, since 1994:

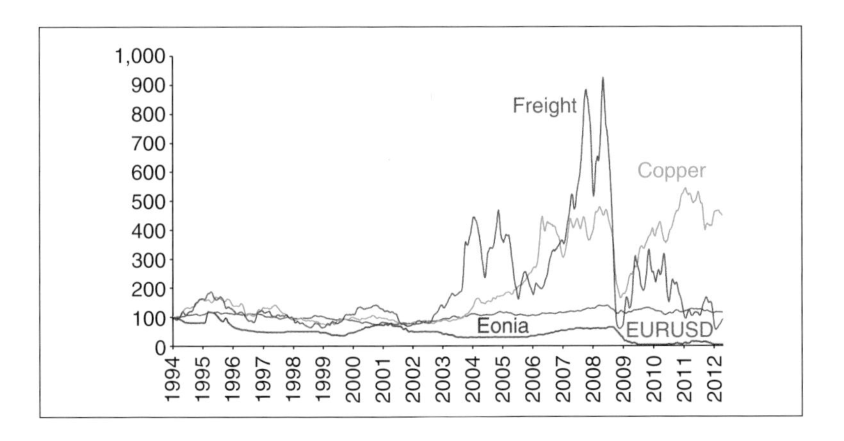

Companies around the world are affected by these and numerous other market variables, and risk managers have to tackle them all in order to lessen their impacts on financial results and the financial position of their firm.

Among the many sins closely associated with bankers, one of the most frequently cited is opacity. This book will encourage you to revisit this cliché. Stanley Myint and Fabrice Famery have conducted a thorough analysis of the many financial risks facing companies and, most importantly, of how to identify, measure, reduce or eliminate them. Some are obvious, such as interest risk; some are more intricate, such as the risk of deferred consideration in an M&A transaction, or counterparty risk.

Having spent thousands of days thinking about how to help companies address financial risks that they sometimes have not even identified, about how to present solutions in a clear way that is easy to understand, and about how to outsmart the competition and win advisory mandates from clients, Stanley and Fabrice are now able to deliver this handbook, ie, a book that presents issues and solutions. All are example based and very pragmatic. No chapter is complete before a recommendations paragraph being included.

Stanley and Fabrice are successful in business because their clients continue to appreciate their ideas. They have the ability to identify areas of academic research that can be of use for solving new problems or opening new fields such as optimal debt duration or the impact of fixed–floating policy on company valuation. To these problems they apply academic rigour and often advanced analytical techniques, eg, Monte Carlo simulations or efficient frontier methodology.

The end result is very clear and readable, and I have no doubt that financial managers, once they have read this book, will keep it close at hand, as I myself did with previous unpublished versions when I was working as an M&A specialist. Advanced finance students will discover an intellectually challenging world in which there are so many different situations that boredom is never an issue. They may even be tempted to start their professional careers in this expanding field.

Enjoy this handbook; it is likely to be one of your best investments ever!

Pascal Quiry
BNP Paribas Professor of Finance at HEC Paris
September 2012

Preface

Risk. Human life is uncertain, and risk arguably defines the human condition, but as individuals or groups we do everything in our power to predict and reduce it; yet in the context of the world's most turbulent peacetime financial outlook in something like 80 years, risk now seems intensely heightened for many global corporations and financial institutions. Assumptions have been turned upside down, models and paradigms undermined or even abandoned; flagship companies have foundered, and confidence in major institutions has been weakened and in some cases shattered.

In our business, in the businesses of those we seek to serve, the name of the game is financial risk. Where risk is excessive, or not approached with sufficient prudence and rigour, or simply misunderstood, share prices fall, pensions suffer, people suffer; in the most extreme cases, international stability is weakened and nation states themselves can be shaken.

It is therefore ironic, surely, that corporate risk is not more written about and better understood. This book has come about because the authors feel there is a gap in the published analysis of corporate risk. In the introduction to the book we detail the existing literature on the subject (and indeed we hope this book will be read alongside good existing material, to create a broad understanding of the issues, and to that end we have provided an outline of what existing literature is in our opinion likely to prove valuable to professional risk managers); nevertheless, we believe that, while much literature exists covering risk management in the financial sector, there is relatively little covering risk in the corporate sector. And while risk is certainly well understood in many large companies, the same does not hold true for many smaller, privately held companies.

Into this space, we offer our analysis. It is based not on remote, abstract or esoteric dimensions of risk, but on several years' detailed analysis, by practitioners, of hundreds of real-life risk situations faced by many of the world's top corporations. If there is one main message of the book, it is this: financial risks, no matter how serious, can be analysed and managed using a systematic quantitative approach, described in these pages. We hope it is not arrogant for us to suggest that a practical, rigorous, thoroughly researched and, we hope, clearly written guide may illuminate the subject of risk for anyone who is touched by the issue of corporate risk management. If, in these troubled times, we have helped clarify and even reduce financial risk for just a few of our readers, we will feel our efforts have been worthwhile.

Introduction

> Every day I know what my sales are, what my profit margin is and what my debt is. Anything I do not know, I hedge.
>
> CFO of a Swiss multinational company

MOTIVATION FOR THIS BOOK

This book is wholly based on real-life client discussions we had in the corporate solutions group at BNP Paribas between 2005 and 2012. During this period, we noticed that corporate treasurers and chief financial officers (CFOs) often have similar questions on risk management, and that these questions are rarely addressed in the existing literature.

This situation can and should lead to a fruitful collaboration between companies and their banks. Companies often come up with the best ideas, but do not have the resources to test them. Leading banks, on the other hand, have strong computational resources, a broader sector perspective and extensive experience in internal risk management, so if they make an effort to understand a client's problem in depth, they may be able to add considerable value.

This book is the result of such an effort, lasting seven years and covering several hundred of the largest European corporations from all industrial sectors.[1] Its subject is corporate financial risk management, ie, the management of financial risks for non-financial corporations.

While there are many papers on this topic, they are generally written by academics and rarely by practitioners. If we contrast this with the subject of risk management for banks, on which many books have been written from the practitioners' perspective, we notice a significant gap. Perhaps this is because financial risk is clearly a more central part of business among banks and asset managers than in non-financial corporations. But, even if this is true, it does not mean that financial risk is only important for banks and asset managers. Let us look at one example.

Consider a large European automotive company, with an operating margin of 10%. More than half of its sales are outside Europe, while its production is predominantly in EUR. This exposes the company to currency risk. Annual currency volatility is of the order of 15%; therefore, if the foreign currencies fall by 15%, this can almost wipe out the net profits.[2] Clearly, an important question for this company is how to manage the currency risk.

Another example: a European investment grade telecom operator has EUR 10 billion in total debt. Annual interest cost for this company can easily exceed 5% of its debt, ie, EUR 500 million per year. As the interest rate curves are normally upward-sloping, the company has a choice of fixing the debt, which normally results in a higher interest rate, or leaving the debt floating, in which case the interest rate risk is higher. The choice, normally referred to as the fixed–floating proportion, is not an easy one, and again is evidently important for the company.

Another reason why corporate risk management has so far attracted relatively little attention in the literature is that, even though the questions asked are often simple (eg, "Should I hedge the translation risk?") the answers are rarely simple, and in many cases there is no generally accepted methodology on how to deal with these issues.

So where does the company treasurer go to find answers to these kinds of questions? General corporate finance books are usually very shy when it comes to discussing risk management. Two famous examples of such books devote only 20–30 pages to managing financial risk, out of almost 1,000 pages in total.

This does not mean that the subject of corporate risk management has been entirely neglected in the literature. There are a couple of books (and many articles) which cover this topic and we will now briefly review some of them.

OVERVIEW OF THE LITERATURE

We are aware of five books on corporate financial risk management (CFRM) in English (for details see the bibliography). In addition, there are many academic articles, and we apologise to their authors and our readers that space prevents us from listing them all here, but we will mention some of them in the text.

The literature on CFRM takes one of the following four formats.

1. **Theory of CFRM:** conditions under which risk management adds value in companies (ie, when it reduces the tax or probability of financial distress or when it improves company's investment decisions); how much risk should a company have and similar issues.
2. **Practice of CFRM:** how specific techniques and products (for instance, credit derivatives or interest rate swaps) are used in companies to manage financial risks.
3. **Surveys of CFRM:** periodic surveys performed by academic institutions, in which a sample of companies is asked multiple-choice questions about various aspects of their risk management practice.
4. **Case studies:** concrete examples of how companies manage their financial risks.

First, there are three book-length compilations of articles, which have mostly been published previously in various journals:

1. Brown and Chew (1999) covers all four areas.
2. Jameson (1997) focuses on practice.
3. Culp and Miller (1999) is devoted to theory and practice (with a particular focus on the Metallgesellschaft derivative loss from 1993).

In addition to these anthologies, there are two books which are based on original material:

1. Triana (2006) focuses on practical uses of derivatives among corporations.
2. Leautier (2007) focuses on the theory, particularly of risk capital.[3]

SCOPE OF THE BOOK

So how does the present volume fit within the existing literature? Our book is entirely devoted to real-life case studies of companies managing financial risk, but also provides our views on the best way to deal with those situations. So the book is partly descriptive, but largely prescriptive. The reader will find here answers to the most commonly asked practical questions about financial risk. Some of the situations will be brief (eg, how to obtain a credit rating) and some will require a significant amount of thought and detailed quantitative analysis (eg, how to improve your fixed–floating mix and duration), but all are real-life situations that our clients have faced over the years.

The focus of the book is management of financial risks, ie, primarily currency, interest rates, inflation, credit and commodity risks. We do not cover non-financial risks (eg, business and operational risks), which are normally outside of the scope of the financial department. We do not talk about insurance contracts; nor do we focus on equity derivatives, since they are outside the day-to-day experience of most financial treasuries. The reader interested in the use of equity derivatives for corporate risk management should consult Ramirez (2011).

Finally, we do not spend a lot of time explaining the details of financial derivatives, for two reasons. First, most corporate treasurers and CFOs are familiar with few basic types of financial derivatives, which tend to get a hedge accounting treatment under IAS 39. These are FX forwards and options, interest rate and cross-currency swaps, interest rate caps and collars. There are many books which extol the virtues of more complex derivatives, but in our experience the latter are rarely used by companies, for a variety of reasons including the inability to price and risk-manage them, unfavourable accounting treatment and relative illiquidity in comparison with the basic products. This does not mean that structured products should be excluded from the toolbox of a corporate risk manager, but (as we discuss in Chapter 6 on "How to Develop an Interest Rate Hedging Policy"), they should always be compared with simpler products. Only if the simpler product does not satisfy the same genuine purpose as the structured one should the latter's use be considered. Second, this book is primarily about corporate problems and how to solve them. Most of the time, we noticed that the key question is not what kind of product (whether it is a derivative or a cash instrument) is used, but how it is used. For us, derivatives are just one of the means by which a corporate risk can be reduced, but nothing more.

CORPORATE GOVERNANCE

There are several well documented cases in which a company did not manage its financial risks properly and ended up losing a lot of money as a result. Some of the earlier ones are described in Culp and Miller (1999) and Triana (2006), but even today, and probably in the future, there will be similar misuses of derivatives that attract public attention for the wrong reason.

We strongly feel that these situations should be put into perspective. Most companies manage their financial risks prudently, and this is never reported. The only time that financial risk management gets media attention is when there is a significant loss. This is similar to the bias in reporting of airline safety; every incident is publicised and scrutinised, while millions of uneventful flights are never mentioned, because they are, well, uneventful.

Perhaps this is normal, and extreme aversion to corporate risk is understandable and can be explained by the general public's lack of understanding of this field coupled with the fear we all have of the things we don't understand.

Nevertheless, we should probably say a few words about why derivatives scandals (yes, they normally have to do with derivatives!) are thankfully so rare, and how these incidents can be avoided as much as possible.

First, large public companies who manage their financial risk using derivatives tend to have well-designed risk management processes, which codify the applicable policies and provide strict guidance on the use of derivatives. We talk more about how to develop interest rate and FX hedging policies in Chapters 6 and 15, but the main purpose of these policies is to give the financial department sufficient freedom to implement the risk management policy while not giving them "too much freedom".

Second, in our experience, corporate treasurers, CFOs and other risk management professionals in large companies normally tend to be very experienced and equipped with a significant amount of common sense when it comes to dissecting more adventurous risk management ideas. They will very rarely accept a proposal that they do not understand. Even if they are convinced that a given solution genuinely reduces the company's financial risk profile, they will only propose it to their boards if they are convinced that they can explain it to them.

Unfortunately, the same process does not always hold in small, privately held companies (even though in some of them we met first class risk managers and financial decision-makers).

BENCHMARKING RISK MANAGEMENT PERFORMANCE

One of the questions that is not asked as often as it should be is: "how do we know whether what we are doing is right?" This can be in regards to any kind of corporate policy, but in the context of this book the two most obvious areas of examination are the interest rate and currency risk management policies.

Why do we think that this question should be asked more often?

First, in most companies we know, the financial department can have more impact than any other department, generally with minimal resources. We have illustrated how big this impact can be in the two examples at the beginning of this introduction. So then, it is natural to ask the question for the benefit of both the financial department and other key decision-makers in the company.

Second, company policy normally evolves over time, and if the existing policy is not appropriate, it should be changed, but this can be done only if the policy is in some way contrasted to its alternatives.

In any case, many financial treasurers and CFOs talk to their peers at other companies and already have a sense of how their policy is different. The point of benchmarking is simply to formalise this process and provide an independent objective comparison that can be used for review and performance measurement.

So how do we go about constructing a benchmark? Now that we have argued that benchmarking is necessary, we have to admit that it is not easy or obvious how to create a good benchmark. We mention this in the two chapters on risk management policy, but in our experience there are several pitfalls.

- The benchmark has to be risk adjusted. For instance, if one company has a policy to float most of its debt, while another leaves its debt largely fixed, the expected interest cost of the two cannot be compared directly. A fixed interest rate policy is generally more expensive, but also less risky (for more details, see Chapter 7).
- Back-testing of corporate policies is a tricky business. For example, a policy to hedge currency exposure to EURJPY can be benchmarked in terms of the average rate achieved over a given period. However, the conclusions will very much depend on the period in question. A company treasurer once asked our views on how to benchmark their actual historical

cost of funding. When we compared it with the average market cost of funding over several years, the company cost turned out to be much higher. Upon careful inspection, we noticed that it was strongly affected by a single bond issuance in early 2009, which was much more costly than the other bonds of that company. But, at that time, in the immediate aftermath of the Lehman Brothers default, corporate liquidity was severely limited, and this company had correctly decided to reduce its refinancing risk by issuing a bond at whatever cost would be achievable.

- Every benchmark has to incorporate the limitations of the existing risk management policy and can only measure the skills of the financial team within that policy. For example, if the company policy is to keep between 60% and 80% of total debt fixed for more than three years and the rest floating, then a reasonable benchmark interest cost would be an average three-year swap rate weighted with 70%[4] plus average Euribor weighted with 30%. When the actual interest cost (excluding the credit spread) is compared against this benchmark, it tells us how successful the treasury was in deciding on its position within the allowed bounds over a given period of time.

MATHEMATICAL ASSUMPTIONS AND REQUIRED KNOWLEDGE

Corporate treasurers and CFOs have to be familiar with many areas in order to manage financial risk. The three main ones are corporate finance, financial derivatives and accounting.

We assume a basic knowledge of corporate finance at the level taught in a typical MBA course, including a familiarity with the concept of the "efficient frontier". Another important concept to which we refer many times is value-at-risk (VaR), or earnings-at-risk (EaR). For more details on these, readers can consult Jorion (2006) or Dowd (1998).

In some chapters we refer to specific financial products, especially foreign exchange derivatives. Unlike the solutions and situations, which are specific to client situations we describe, these derivatives are fairly standard and we assume that the reader is familiar with them. If not, the standard reference is Hull (2011), which also provides a good initial overview of Monte Carlo simulations, to which we refer many times. For a much more comprehensive overview of this technique, see Jäckel (2002).

We do not assume any specialised accounting knowledge, but there are many cases when we refer to the accounting treatment under the relevant accounting standards (IAS 39 and IFRS).[5] While detailed knowledge of the accounting framework is not necessary in order to understand most of the ideas in the book, it will certainly help in applying them to the corporate framework. For specific applications to corporate risk management, see Ramirez (2007).

A technically minded reader will notice that we do not always assume a risk-neutral distribution, but in fact rely on a historical distribution in many cases. This will particularly be the case in Part II, on interest rate risk.

LIMITATIONS OF VALUE-AT-RISK OR EARNINGS-AT-RISK METHODOLOGY

Since we often refer to VaR or EaR in the text, we should explain what the limitations of this technology are.

Computation of value-at-risk, cash-flow-at-risk or earnings-at-risk analysis (here commonly called "VaR"), started as a technology used by banks to assess their financial risk exposure. Nowadays, this technique is also used by many corporate treasurers to assist in the quantification and formulation of their risk management procedures. VaR is a statement of potential loss. It does not say that such and such a loss will happen, but rather represents the potential for loss in particular circumstances.

The main advantage of using VaR is its ability to present the exposure as a single monetary value; it may be helpful for communication to have a single figure which represents the potential for loss.

However, it is a well-accepted fact that the VaR model is not a fail-safe. The model's deficiencies surface in times of major crisis or during extreme volatility (such as that experienced in 2008–9). It is also dependent upon an accurate initial assessment of the firm's position. VaR does not accurately capture extreme scenarios and is therefore liable to significantly underestimate rare events. For example, if VaR is computed at the 95th percentile confidence interval, it gives an estimate of the exposure in 19 out of 20 cases. However, in the 20th case, the value can exceed the VaR by a significant amount.

In addition, there are many existing methodologies for computing VaR, and different methods are likely to lead to different results. In particular, our VaR numbers are generally centred on the forward curve, which is by no means the most likely outcome. Among others, we could choose to centre the distribution on the spot or various economic forecasts.

The most useful aspect of the VaR is that the monetary figure makes for easy comparison across different portfolios and risks. So it should be used for relative comparison of risk of different portfolios, but not for their absolute size. The most useful comparisons are:

- comparing VaR across different types of risk, for instance, currency VaR against interest rate VaR for a given company;
- comparing VaR across different companies in the same sector;
- comparing the impact on VaR of different hedging strategies.

This is how we will be using VaR numbers whenever they appear in the book.

WHERE DO WE GO FROM HERE?

Since the 2008 crisis, there have been a host of regulatory initiatives aimed at both banks and non-financial companies which will affect corporate risk management practices. At the time of writing in 2012, these initiatives have not been confirmed in detail, so it is not possible to predict exactly what their final impact will be, but we can make an educated guess as to the rough outline of the final regulation.

Most Basel III proposals are focused on financial institutions. Consequently, most Basel III proposals will not affect corporates directly, but there will be a secondary effect of banks' higher overall "cost of doing business", due to a significantly higher capital requirement for banks and therefore a higher cost of providing liquidity.

A direct impact of Basel III is the increase in the credit valuation adjustment (CVA) charge, which is due to come into force from the start of 2013. This is due to increase the cost of uncollateralised long-dated derivatives, such as FX forwards or cross-currency swaps. As a result, many companies in the "real economy" will find that hedging currency risk for longer maturities becomes prohibitively expensive. This is an unfortunate and obviously unintended consequence of the new Basel III rules, which were supposed to make the world a "safer place".

Other current regulatory reforms such as the Dodd–Frank Act, European Market Infrastructure Regulation (EMIR), Markets in Financial Instruments Directive (MiFID) Review, etc, could potentially have important implications for how corporates manage and finance their businesses and in particular the potential requirement to clear derivatives. However, at the time of writing, it seems that the general corporate hedging (in particular, of currency and interest rate risks) will be excluded from the mandatory clearing requirement, which is a good thing, as it will allow companies to decide for themselves how or whether they want to manage their counterparty risk.

Another impact will be from the change of accounting standards under IFRS 9, which is expected from 2015. It is likely that hedge accounting will be simplified (and in particular the 80–125% effectiveness testing requirement may be scrapped). The other main proposed changes include a more friendly treatment of options, simplified hedging documentation, allowed hedging portions of risk of non-financial items and a more friendly treatment of dynamic hedging.

So, what do all these changes mean for corporate risk management practice? We expect that in the future treasurers will have to be more prudent about their counterparty exposure as well as about the utilisation of their banks' credit through long-dated uncollateralised derivatives. One way to deal with this is through an increased use of options, which we describe in Chapter 20, on "Managing Foreign Exchange Risk with a Dynamic Option Strategy".

OVERVIEW OF TOPICS COVERED

Our case studies fall into six parts, according to the main situation that they are designed to address. Each starts with an introduction to the kind of risk covered, followed by a range of cases related to it. Since every company's situation is different, these examples are not meant to exhaust all possible issues a company may face, but rather to illustrate the kinds of techniques for solving them. We find that a systematic approach to any problem is a necessary first step, so in many chapters we start by giving a detailed process chart, which lists the necessary steps to arrive at an answer.

Part I deals with a variety of issues related to corporate funding via fixed income instruments, with a particular focus on unsecured debt. The cases in this section are intended to help companies who plan to either issue debt or borrow in the loan market, with guidance given from the initial stages (eg, obtaining a credit rating) up to liability management and optimisation of debt duration for companies with existing debt.

Part II deals with the next set of issues once the corporate debt structure is in place. At this point, the interest rate risks are introduced and must be managed. The first seven chapters focus on the interest rate risk on the debt side of the balance sheet, while the last two chapters look at both assets and liabilities.

Part III is devoted to the management of currency risk, which is the most common risk affecting companies. We gather here a variety of topics ranging from management of translation risk to a development of a dynamic option strategy, which reduces the credit charge under Basel III.

Part IV covers credit risk, ie, the risk of default by counterparties. This kind of risk rose to the forefront of corporate attention since the credit crisis in 2008–9 and again as a result of the European sovereign crisis in 2010–11. Examples in this part of the book should help companies to manage their credit and counterparty risk.

In Part V we talk about risk management within the context of mergers and acquisitions (M&A). In such situations companies often focus on the deal execution first and funding second, while the risk management is the last priority. In the examples discussed here we show how risk management can be an important part of the overall M&A process and how to go about implementing it.

Part VI is devoted to commodity risk management. As we explain in the introduction to this part of the book, management of commodity risk is fundamentally not too different from the management of currency risk; we therefore focus only on the key differences.

HOW TO NAVIGATE THIS BOOK

Depending on your interest, you can read this book either by part or by topic covered, or simply dip into individual chapters in any order.

Since the chapters are based on real client problems, many of them cover more than one kind of situation. For example, Chapter 26 on "Risk Management for M&A" could be in the part on "Currency Risk" or in the one on "M&A-Related Risks". We have decided to place it in "M&A", since this is the main focus of the chapter. But it could also be of interest to someone who is primarily interested in currency risk.

We hope that you will find this diverse collection of corporate stories stimulating and useful. If you have a question regarding an issue that is not described in the book, we would be very interested to hear about it.

ACKNOWLEDGEMENTS

We would like to thank our colleagues for contributing the following parts: Tom Cant for chapters on credit ratings; Stephanie Sfakianos for chapters on liability management; Valerio Pace for the chapters on "Monetising Deferred Consideration" and "Prehedging Credit Risk".

We also thank the following colleagues and friends for useful discussions, as well as their input and help at various stages and in different ways: Bradley Anderson, Harald Nieder, Adi Shafir, Yann Ait-Mokhtar, Adil Belmejdoub, Michael Kalouche, Manoj Agarwal, Jay Horacek, Martin Buckley, Hann Ho, Adrian Thomas, Ligia Torres, Dominique Leca, Christopher Marks, Anthony Bryson and Tim Drayson.

Iakovos Kakouris and Dean Demellweek have been very helpful in preparing the illustrations in this book.

For their editorial help, useful suggestions and above all infinite patience, many thanks go to Alice Levick, Lewis O'Sullivan and Nick Carver from Risk Books.

Finally, by far the biggest thanks go to our corporate clients (too many to mention here), who have provided the idea for all the cases discussed in this book, and without whom this book would never have been written. In order to protect their confidentiality, we have changed the client names and financial information in all cases. In most cases, we also changed the industrial sector, except where the sector is key to the situation described.

All factual errors remain the responsibility of the authors. The views expressed in this book are the authors' own and do not necessarily reflect the views of our employer, BNP Paribas.

1 For the sake of concreteness, most examples in this book are based on European companies, but the ideas and concepts apply to companies in any territory. We assume International Financial Reporting Standards (IFRS) as the relevant accounting treatment.

2. Assuming that the costs have not changed, and that all other lines in the income statement are unchanged, the impact on it would be to reduce the net profit by a factor of four.
3. See Merton *et al* (1993).
4. That is, the midpoint between 60% and 80%.
5. See International Accounting Standards Board (2003) and Deloitte (2011).

Part I

Funding

Funding

The *sine qua non* of every business and personal endeavour is the necessary funding. No matter how great the business idea or how brilliant its people, companies cannot exist if nobody will invest in them. Witness the political and economic debate about how to jump start the world economy at the moment of deep crisis we are witnessing in 2012 and you will notice how funding has become intricately linked to growth. So the first and arguably most important source of risk for every company is lack of funding.

Let us start with a bold statement: "It is impossible to talk about corporate risk management without first discussing funding". Before we explain why we think this, let us define the terms. Funding, in the broadest sense of the word, means provision of monetary resources for a project or a company. Funding can take many forms, and this chapter focuses on two main sources of unsecured fixed-income funding (or simply "debt"), ie, bonds and loans. Bonds are financial instruments through which a company borrows money from investors for a fixed period of time, normally up to 30 years, and in most cases they carry a fixed coupon or a floating coupon linked to a Libor (or Euribor) rate. Loans are extended to a company by banks either bilaterally or through syndication among several lenders, and typically they pay a floating coupon and have a maturity of up to five years.

Since the focus of this book is risk management, and not funding on its own (as well as for obvious reasons of space), we decided to focus on debt at the cost of all other potential sources of funding. This excludes such important topics as equity, convertibles and other hybrid instruments, secured bonds, and many other kinds of rare and structured products. One could write a whole book about each one of these topics and in fact, many books have been written.[1]

The question of how much debt a company should have (known as "optimal capital structure") has been extensively studied.[2] The two traditional competing schools of thought are the trade-off theory and the pecking-order theory. Trade-off theory tends to determine the optimal debt amount as that point beyond which the tax benefits are outweighed by the disadvantages of higher leverage (eg, potential bankruptcy costs). Pecking-order theory posits that the amount of debt a company has comes as a result of the ability of the firm to generate cash. In Part I, we shall assume that the firm has decided on the amount of debt it wants to have.

Now that we have clarified the scope of this part of the book, let us explain the link between corporate funding and risk management and why we think it is so important. In our view, corporate funding and risk management are intricately connected in the following way. Every funding structure imposes certain risks upon the company, but a careful choice of the funding structure can also reduce the company risks.

Let us give two examples, which will clarify this.

Our first example has to do with interest rate risk. When a company decides how much of its debt should be split between fixed coupon bonds and floating bonds or loans, its decision directly affects the amount and type of interest rate risk it will have.[3] Having, for instance, a single bond with fixed coupons reduces the "cashflow" risk on the bonds, which we define as the variability of the interest cost of the company. On the other hand, if the bond is floating and linked to Euribor, the cashflow risk is much higher, since the interest cost will depend directly on the evolution of Euribor rates. However, in this case, the company "fair value" or "mark-to-market" risk will be reduced, as we shall see in Part II ("Interest Rate and Inflation Risks").

Another example would be the currency risk, which can be introduced by a currency composition of debt. If a company has half of its revenues, assets and free cashflows generated in USD and EUR, it would be natural to match that split with an equal split of debt by currency. Choosing a different split of debt would introduce various risks upon the company, in particular, cashflow, translation or leverage risks, as we shall discuss in Part III ("Currency Risk").

But, for now, enough about risks, and let us focus our attention on debt. In the spirit of practicality, which we hope to maintain throughout this book, we do not attempt to cover all the potential issues that may arise related to debt. Instead, we cover only the most common questions that corporate treasurers, financial directors and chief financial officers (CFOs) tend to ask when they think about their company's debt.

The first question is "How can I obtain debt funding for my company?" For a large publicly listed company, which has a good track record of borrowing, unsecured debt comes in two main forms: bonds and loans. The choice between the two depends on many factors, including

- availability (how much do investors or banks want to lend to the company?),
- the range of maturities and currencies available in the market at the time,
- price (ie, the credit spread and other transaction costs linked to debt issuance),
- restrictions imposed by lenders in terms of covenants, ratings and similar,
- the flexibility to subsequently manage liabilities, ie, to restructure the existing debt.

Generally, bank debt is more restrictive and, before the Basel III capital rules, was often cheaper. As a result of more stringent capital rules under Basel III, banks will most likely be forced to increase the credit margins on unsecured corporate loans. Also, as a company grows, it often decides to diversify sources of funding beyond bank debt into the public debt sphere. But investors in public debt often require the company to obtain an external rating from one of the main rating agencies. The process of obtaining a credit rating is explored in the first chapter in this part of the book: "How to Obtain a Credit Rating".

Once the debt is issued, a company may leave it in place until it matures, or, in some cases, may decide either to buy it back before maturity or to extend its maturity. These two situations, commonly known as "liability management", are the subjects of Chapters 2 and 3: "The Intermediated Exchange" and "Cash Tender Offer".

Chapter 4 discusses the issue of debt duration and how it affects company valuation. Traditional theory of capital structure (see, for example, Quiry *et al* (2011)) states that the company debt structure should not affect its valuation, ie, the value of the company's assets is independent of how the company funds those assets. However, this theory is based on a number of strong assumptions, which are almost never satisfied in real life, such as the absence of taxes, the absence of bankruptcy costs and open and stable capital markets. As those simplifying assumptions are relaxed, a much more complex but also more realistic picture emerges, and it is one with which companies are faced every day. In the full picture, not only the amount of debt, but also its duration or currency can be important drivers of company valuation.[4] In this chapter we approach the issue of debt duration from a quantitative angle, based on the option pricing model, but also briefly touch upon other considerations that companies take into account when determining the ideal duration of their debt.

Finally, in the last chapter of this part, "Funding Cost Drivers", we explore how the credit spread of the company is determined as a function of market and balance-sheet parameters. Credit spread is the excess over the reference rates, ie, Treasury, Libor or swap rates, which the company has to pay on its debt. It reflects a relative return that investors require as compensation for the company's default risk compared with the reference government or bank risk. Therefore, the higher the risk, the higher the credit spread. The credit spread is the subject of many discussions, and sometimes heated negotiations between companies and their lenders, but it is never possible to fully explain how it is reached for every company, because, at the end of the day, it is determined by the investors' consensus. In other words, there are as many different views among debt investors on the appropriate credit spread as there are different views among shareholders on the "correct" share price. However, there are a few obvious factors which we can look at when trying to understand how to determine the credit spread. One of them is the leverage of the company, measured by a variety of metrics,[5] for example, total debt/EBITDA.[6] Consider an investor who compares two companies that are identical in every respect, but one of them has a leverage of two times EBITDA and the other has a leverage of six times EBITDA. A rational investor will conclude that the likelihood of the debt being repaid is higher with a company with a lower leverage since that company can use a larger part of EBITDA to pay off the debt. Therefore, if all else is kept the same, higher leverage means a higher default probability, and this in turn means a higher credit spread. In the real world, of course, no two companies are the same, but we can use statistical techniques to extract the main drivers of the funding cost among the companies in the same sector.

We shall return to the subject of funding many times throughout the book. In particular, we shall talk about fixed versus floating and inflation-linked debt in Part II and about the currency composition of debt in Part III. We shall explore credit risk linked to debt in Part IV and the role of debt in acquisitions in Part V, which will also give us a chance to come back to the topic of credit rating, with which this book starts.

1 See for example, Quiry *et al* (2011) for a general overview, or Woodson (2002) for convertible bonds.

2 For details, see Brealey *et al* (2010) or Quiry *et al* (2011) and the articles listed therein. An interesting recent contribution is Van Binsbergen *et al* (2011). A recent overview of the whole capital structure topic is given in Baker and Martin (2011).

3 We distinguish between "cashflow" and "fair value" or "mark-to-market" risk, which will be defined as we go along.

4 Of course, the impact of debt on the company valuation depends on its leverage. For a company with a very small amount of debt compared with company size, the actual debt characteristics will not affect the valuation significantly.

5 Another choice would be EBITDA/interest cost or total debt/equity.

6 "EBITDA" stands for earnings before interest, taxes, depreciation and amortisation.

1

How to Obtain a Credit Rating

There are two main sources of debt financing in the capital markets: bank lending and issuance of bonds to investors. As a result of increased capital requirements under Basel III, banks have reduced the amount of lending to companies and this has been reflected in increased credit spreads on their loans. Companies that require a lot of debt usually fund themselves mostly through bond issuance, since the price is generally more attractive, they can reach more investors that way and the potential maturity is longer. However, at the time of writing, bond investors usually require the issuer to obtain a credit rating from one of the three major credit rating agencies, eg, Moody's, Standard & Poor's or Fitch.

This case describes the typical steps through which a bond issuer goes in order to obtain a first credit rating. As time goes on, the rating may change and, to a certain extent, the ongoing communication with rating agencies would follow similar lines as during the initial credit rating.

BACKGROUND

The Middle Eastern Holding Company (MEHC) has a number of majority owned and diverse operating businesses both in the Middle East and outside the region. In addition, MEHC has a very significant investment portfolio, both strategic and financial, well diversified by business, type of investment and location.

MEHC has grown strongly since the early 2000s and further significant growth is forecast. It is also nearing the end of a major strategic review of its entire business operation, a key component of which is its financing strategy. Having initially relied on bilateral arrangements with local and international banks, MEHC first diversified its funding via the international syndicated loan market. Following the assignment of a credit rating from a regional rating agency, MEHC then accessed the local capital markets with domestic currency bond issues.

To date, MEHC's funding has remained concentrated on bank lines, but market conditions (pressure on banking partners' capital ratios and rising provisioning levels) have the following impacts:

- the capacity of existing banks to roll over maturing lines has been limited;
- the appetite of existing lenders to provide new money has been constrained;
- the supply of new committed lines from potential new lenders has been limited;
- the cost of debt has increased and this has led to more stringent terms and conditions for rolled over commitments and (where available) new credit lines.

Although the maturity profile of committed bank lines is still adequate, MEHC decided to implement a risk-reduction strategy to improve its liquidity position and reduce its refinancing risks via accessing the international bond markets. The proceeds will be used to refinance a proportion of its bank lines. For MEHC, the first step in this process is to obtain credit ratings from international credit rating agencies (hereafter "agencies").

MEHC decided to appoint a rating advisor to lead this process, and the rest of this case is told from their point of view.

COMPANY OBJECTIVES

- To assist MEHC in obtaining optimal credit ratings from one or more of the agencies.
- To facilitate MEHC's access to the international capital markets.

Figure 1.1 Credit rating process: step by step

ANALYSIS

While MEHC was very keen to engage the rating agencies as soon as possible, we believed it was important, before engaging any of the agencies, to structure the approach through the following three steps (Figure 1.1).

Table 1.1 MEHC business classification

	Business characteristics	Analytical approach taken by the rating agency
Investment holding company	• Typically very diversified portfolio of minority stakes in listed equities • Can also include diversified holdings in unlisted subsidiaries • Aim to increase shareholder value by buying and selling assets and realising capital gains • Large pool of liquid investments	• Focus on: – diversification of investments – portfolio liquidity • Volatility of investments • Asset coverage of debt • Debt service at holding company • Capacity and willingness to sell assets at short notice
Operating holding company	• More limited portfolio diversification but often a concentration in a few core holdings • Often a mix of minority and majority/wholly owned companies • Often represented on the board of their subsidiaries • Typically not committed to keeping core holdings for the long term: businesses are bought and sold over time	• S&P: combines investment holding company and conglomerate analytical approach. This includes credit assessment of main subsidiaries and an assessment of the group's financial flexibility and asset coverage • Moody's: considers the financial profile of issuers on the basis of: (i) the holding company plus the full consolidation of the majority owned subsidiaries; (ii) a "sum of the parts" assessment assigning estimated ratings for each of the main entities of the group

Table 1.1 Continued

	Business characteristics	Analytical approach taken by the rating agency
Industrial conglomerate	• A few large investments, typically in several industry sectors • Typically full control of subsidiaries and direct involvement in management • Aim to increase shareholder value by driving profits and cashflows from their industrial activities	• "Sum of the parts" credit assessment of the constituent operating businesses

STEP 1: FORMING INITIAL RATING EXPECTATIONS

The first step was for us to determine the most likely rating that could be achieved from the agencies. Ratings assigned by agencies often differ from those assigned by relationship banks and may well be markedly different from management expectations. Given the different methodologies applied by the agencies, it is also quite common for rating differences to arise between the agencies themselves. Hence, it was particularly important that management should be given a realistic expectation of likely ratings before deciding to proceed.

Prior to entering into the credit rating process, it was critical that MEHC's management should have a realistic expectation of the likely rating outcome. In order to obtain this, we performed a detailed credit analysis of MEHC, applying the same rating methodologies that would be used by the agencies themselves. We now give a brief overview of the type of analysis undertaken.

The analytical approach taken by agencies begins with classifying MEHC's business, as shown in Table 1.1.

Having done this, the next step is to analyse MEHC's business and financial profile. The business profile is the primary rating driver. It determines the level of financial risk appropriate for any rating category (Table 1.2).

The next step is to analyse the financial profile (see Table 1.3), which helps to refine the rating level.

Table 1.2 MEHC business profile

Key strengths	Possible concerns
Significant sector diversification within the region	Current weak market conditions and negative outlook
Favourable business environment	Limited geographic diversification, the bulk of the profits coming from the Middle East
Good track record at managing businesses	Exposure to GCC countries whose strong economies largely depend on crude oil exports
Very experienced management	Exposure to financial institutions, which typically attract higher ratings
Hidden value in subsidiary/associate companies	High exposure to local stock exchange
Strong shareholder group	Continued losses in one specialist division
	Potential volatility of oil and gas, real estate and building materials industries
	Control over strategic investments unclear

We then assess how MEHC compares to its peers. In Table 1.4, we show three of the closest rated peers of MEHC, together with their main financial metrics, and the credit metrics that are normally used by the rating agencies to determine the financial strength of the company. Based on the analysis above we provided MEHC with our estimate that the agencies would rate the group in the BBB range.

STEP 2: INTRODUCTORY AGENCY MEETINGS

Once MEHC management was happy with the estimated ratings, the next stage was for them to meet together with the rating advisor all three agencies on an informal basis. The purpose of these meetings was to introduce the relevant personnel and obtain initial feedback from the analysts from each agency who would actually cover the company. Having obtained an outline confirmation of our preliminary analysis, we advised MEHC to move forward to the next stage.

Table 1.3 MEHC financial profile

Key strengths	Possible concerns
High investment returns	High portfolio leverage
Continued dividends since establishment	Weak interest coverage ratios
Good liquidity: listed holdings make about half of the portfolio	Track record in selling large stakes unclear
Conservative valuation policies	Low turnover on stock exchanges in GCC countries
Strong capital base	
Group focus on reducing the short-term component of debt	

Once MEHC management was satisfied with the expected rating outcome, we set up introductory meetings with all three credit rating agencies. The rationale for holding such meetings is as follows:

- to establish an initial rapport with key analysts;
- the meetings allow for informal discussion on approach, methodology and industry outlook;
- to help to ensure all key issues are identified before the management presentation;
- the meetings have proved successful in helping to achieve an optimal rating outcome in the past.

Prior to committing to seek a rating we recommend that MEHC together with the rating advisor, hold informal meetings with key agency analysts, with the following agenda.

1. Introduction.
2. MEHC plans for ratings.
3. Rating timetable.
4. Rating confidentiality.
5. Rating agency initial views on:
    - rating methodology to be applied;
    - key issues for MEHC;
    - peer group and relative positioning.

6. Initial thoughts on rating.
7. Rating fees.
8. Any other business.

It is essential that the rating advisor has extensive experience working with all three agencies. That experience, together with debt funding plans, targeted rating levels and agency methodologies are all considered, in addition to information obtained at the introductory meetings, in coming to a final decision with which agencies engage.

Table 1.4 Peer group analysis

	MEHC	Peer ABC
Key financial parameters:		
Rating range	—	BBB
Total investment portfolio (estimated value (USD m))	2,537	2,040
Market cap of listed holding (USD m)	1,326	1,812
No of stocks of core holdings	3	4
Three largest holdings/investment portfolio (%)	17.2	79
Majority owned company, as % of investment portfolio	6.1	37
Portfolio diversification	Moderate	Moderate
Liquidity	Moderate	Weak/moderate
Asset quality	Average	Average
Dividends received (USD m)	21	46
Net adjusted (USD m) debt	1,235	755
Shareholders' equity (USD m)	2,307	533
Key credit metrics:		
FFO/net adjusted debt (%)	46.9	—
Net debt/investment portfolio (%)	48.7	37.0
Net debt/investment portfolio of listed holdings (%)	93.2	41.7
Net debt ceiling as % of investment portfolio	Not disclosed	—
Cash interest cover	1.6×	1.7×
Cash cover of interest plus expenses	—	1.3×
(EBITDA + dividend)/interest	12×	—
Dividend interest cover	0.4×	—

Table 1.4 Continued

	Peer DEF	Peer GHK
Key financial parameters:		
Rating range	BBB	BBB
Total investment portfolio (estimated value (USD m))	3,250	6,026
Market cap of listed holding (USD m)	1,504	413
No of stocks of core holdings	3	5
Three largest holdings/investment portfolio (%)	75	85
Majority owned company, as % of investment portfolio	77	—
Portfolio diversification	Weak	Strong
Liquidity	Moderate	Weak
Asset quality	Average	Good
Dividends received (USD m)	48	—
Net adjusted (USD m) debt	469	1,169
Shareholders' equity (USD m)	1,905	1,334
Key credit metrics:		
FFO/net adjusted debt (%)	52.0	—
Net debt/investment portfolio (%)	14.4	19
Net debt/investment portfolio of listed holdings (%)	31.2	283
Net debt ceiling as % of investment portfolio	40	30
Cash interest cover	23.1×	—
Cash cover of interest plus expenses	—	—
(EBITDA + dividend)/interest	24×	—
Dividend interest cover	1.2×	—

Following these meetings, the MEHC, together with their rating advisor, finalised the rating strategy and engaged two agencies. Once the agencies were engaged by MEHC, there was no further contact between the agencies and MEHC until the management presentation.

STEP 3: PREPARING FOR MANAGEMENT PRESENTATION

We recommended to MEHC that they formally engage two agencies. We then worked with the project team to produce a background information document and a thorough management presentation which clearly explained MEHC's credit story. As we progressed, following the receipt of more detailed and confidential information, we continually reassessed our initial rating expectations to ensure they were still valid.

Prior to meeting again with the agencies, we performed a full dress rehearsal for the senior management team, including detailed "Q&A". We also advised shareholders of the agencies' unique perspective, and ensured they met with the agencies as part of the rating process.

Following the selection of the agencies to rate MEHC, the focus then turned to preparing background documentation and more importantly, the management presentation. This document was intended to fully describe MEHC's business and financial position as well as future strategy and forecasts, and included the following:

- historical development, current business and market position;
- business organisation, structure of management and shareholders;
- detailed strategic discussion;
- a full asset breakdown and review of performance of core subsidiaries, strategic investments and financial investments;
- a full review of historical financial performance including acquisitions/disposals, full debt and liquidity analysis, risk management policies, etc;
- detailed forecast information for the next three years.

Following completion of the presentation document, but prior to meeting with the agencies, MEHC management attended a full dress rehearsal, with their rating advisor taking the place of the agencies. This was a critical step in the rating process for the following reasons:

- to provide senior management with an opportunity to present MEHC and receive feedback on their presentation performance;
- to allow MEHC management to answer likely agency questions and increase their awareness of the agencies' perspectives;
- to ensure that management presented a complete and consistent credit story to the agencies.

RECOMMENDATIONS

Following due diligence, introductory meetings with the agencies, preparation of a detailed management presentation and a full dress rehearsal, MEHC met with the selected agencies and presented their credit story. As rating advisor, we helped to ensure that MEHC should

- minimise the extent of senior management's involvement in the process,
- benefit from an efficient and focused rating process,
- obtain significant reductions in fees (compared with published fee schedules),
- deliver a comprehensive and consistent management presentation,
- achieve the targeted rating levels from two international credit rating agencies,
- be well prepared to take forward their own agency relationships.

MEHC has already tapped the international capital markets with a very successful inaugural issue.

CONCLUSION

In this chapter, we described the process of obtaining a credit rating from the perspective of a bond issuer and their rating advisor. The process inevitably differs from company to company and in some cases is much more complicated than that described here. We covered the main stages of the initial rating process, which should give the reader an idea of what to expect in a similar situation.

2

The Intermediated Exchange

As the company issues bonds in capital markets, over time it becomes faced with a number of upcoming maturities, ie, dates when the outstanding bonds need to be repaid. A prudent company will monitor these dates and pay particular attention to the investor's appetite for refinancing the debt. As the investor's sentiment changes, the conditions under which the debt will be refinanced will vary as well, in terms of possible size, maturity and cost. This variability is called the refinancing risk, and many companies manage it actively, by refinancing the outstanding bonds before their maturity. This can be done by issuing new debt before the maturity of the existing bond, and then keeping the issue proceeds until the maturity of the old debt. At maturity the proceeds of the new debt will be used to repay the principal of the old bond. Another way is via liability management, ie, by repurchasing the old bond from the existing investors prior to maturity, and in some cases offering a new, longer-dated bond in exchange. The following case deals with one such situation.

BACKGROUND

UMC is a manufacturing company that funds itself principally in the debt capital markets, where at the time of writing it would be faced with a significant maturity spike in its debt profile. Within the next two years, bonds in EUR, GBP and USD, totalling EUR 2 billion equivalent, or about 20% of UMC's total outstanding debt were due to mature (Figure 2.1).

UMC actively manages its refinancing risk, and adopted a treasury policy of maintaining an average debt maturity of no shorter than three years. A liability management strategy was needed to avoid any breach of this policy.

Figure 2.1 UMC debt maturity profile

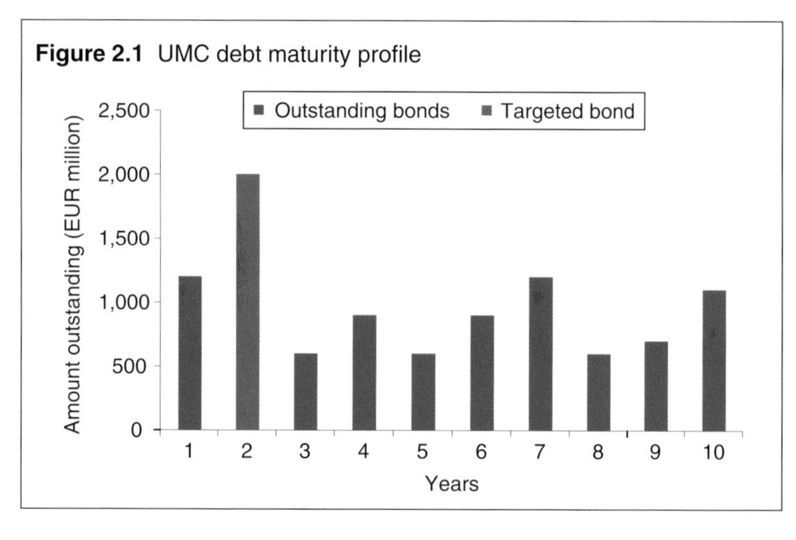

COMPANY OBJECTIVES

- To take full advantage of the market conditions characterised by low spreads and yields to lock-in longer term financing, in support of the company's general treasury policy.
- To refinance not more than EUR 750 million in a single transaction, in order to avoid creating a new peak in the company's maturity profile.
- To avoid incurring a sizeable charge to the profit and loss account (P&L) in respect of the premium over par at which the bonds were trading, when redeeming the old bonds early.
- To avoid the addition of the accrued coupon payment in the year in which the bonds are redeemed.

MARKET BACKGROUND

At the time of writing, the market environment was highly favourable for a new issue by UMC. Both low credit spread and the low level of swap rates meant that coupon on a new issue would be low. The old notes, which the company was thinking about buying back, were issued at a spread of 300 basis points (bp) over the reference midswap rate, and had tightened to mid-swaps plus 100bp by the time of the liability management exercise (Figure 2.2). Although higher than their all-time lows, the absolute level of interest rates was also considered to be attractive compared with historical levels.

Figure 2.2 Spread versus mid-swaps for UMC's old notes

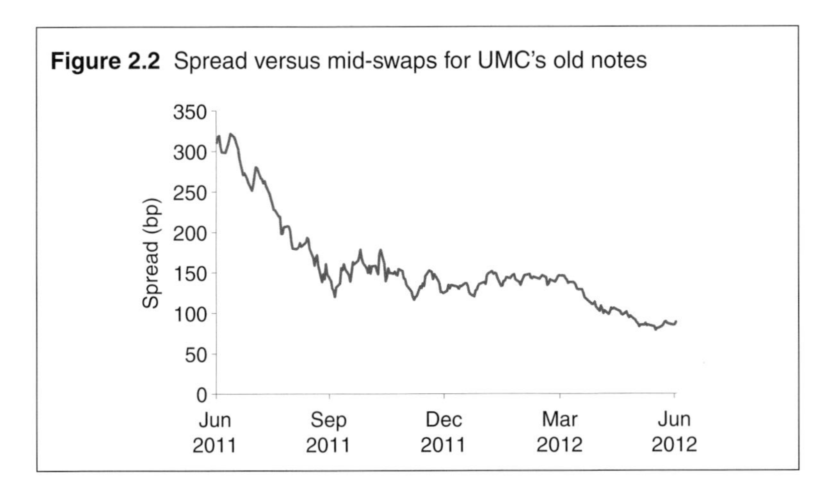

However, because of rate decrease since the old notes were launched, five years previously, the old notes were trading at a premium to par, leading to a potential charge to UMC's P&L if they were to be redeemed early.

SOLUTION

Three possible options were considered.

1. **Do nothing:** waiting until maturity had the benefit of simplicity, but would not address either the impending breach of UMC's policy on average debt maturity being always longer than three years or the market risk involved in refinancing EUR 2 billion of old debt.

2. **Pre-financing:** UMC had the option of locking in current attractive spreads by tapping the new issue market. However, doing so would imply a negative cost of carry on the pre-financed amount until maturity of the old notes.

3. **Early refinancing:** this would be an opportunity to lengthen UMC's average debt duration while keeping the overall level of debt constant, smooth its maturity profile and bring down its interest costs.

Based on UMC's objectives, option 3 was clearly optimal, assuming that the company's preferred accounting treatment (ie, exchange accounting; see Table 2.1 for details) could be achieved.

Table 2.1 Principal benefits

Exchange offer	Cash tender offer plus new issue
Accounting treatment: if the transaction qualifies for "exchange accounting" treatment (agreed by the issuer's auditors), the company is allowed to amortise any buy-back premium over the life of the new bond.	Investor behaviour: a cash offer is simple for investors to understand, since it is broadly comparable to a secondary market sale. Investors have complete flexibility in how they reinvest their cash.
Investor behaviour: by offering investors bonds rather than cash, an exchange tackles reinvestment risk, which is a big concern in a low-yield environment where new issues are several times oversubscribed.	Execution considerations: information on any liability management transaction is sent to investors via the clearing systems and a chain of custodians. An offer has to be open, on the basis of fixed spreads for not less than four business days, to accommodate the two-way flow of information. There is significantly less risk in fixing the spread on the bond being bought back, which is typically short dated and illiquid.[1]
	Pricing and allocation: the new issue is launched, priced and allocated in the normal way, typically intra-day. The issuer targets the optimal holders for the new issue and can allocate to strategically important investors who are diversified by sector and geography.[2]

PROS AND CONS OF DIFFERENT APPROACHES

Having concluded that the early refinancing (ie, option 3) was most likely to meet UMC's transaction criteria, the sub-options were considered. The two principal liability management strategies for early refinancing are

- an exchange offer, whereby holders of the old bonds are invited to exchange their bonds for a new longer dated EUR bond, or

- a cash tender offer plus new issue, in which holders are invited to sell their old bonds for cash. They have an option of reinvesting in the new longer-dated bond that is simultaneously issued to finance the cash tender (both of which are illustrated in Table 2.1).

RECOMMENDATIONS

We devised a structure that combined the benefits of both types of strategies, within a single "intermediated exchange". The transaction was structured to accommodate the preferences of investors concerned about reinvestment risk, as well as those who wanted the simplicity of cash, and was executed through a carefully coordinated three-step process (Figure 2.3).

Figure 2.3 Step-by-step transaction structure

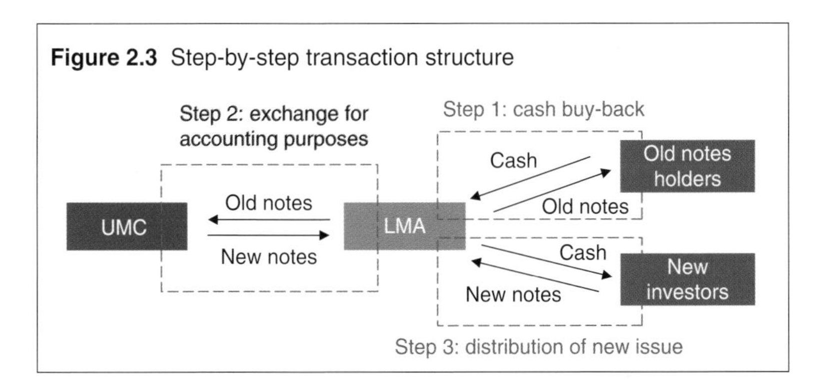

1. The liability management advisor (LMA), acting as principal, undertook a cash tender for up to EUR 750 million of the old notes. Holders of old notes were offered the option of having an allocation of new longer dated securities, to be issued by UMC to refinance the purchase of existing bonds, in a nominal amount equal to their current holding.
2. As the holder of the old notes, the LMA entered into a private exchange with UMC, for new longer-dated securities.
3. The new securities were placed by the LMA with holders who had requested an allocation, with the balance placed into the market to investors identified during a marketing/roadshow process.

EXECUTION OF THE OPERATION

On the launch date, LMA announced its offer to purchase for "any and all" of UMC's outstanding EUR 1 billion old notes, with notes purchased pursuant to the tender to be exchanged with UMC for longer dated securities. Simultaneously, UMC announced its intention to finance the cash tender via the issue of new notes with a 10-year maturity.

The tender was launched on the fixed spread basis of mid-swaps plus 130bp, a premium versus pre-launch trading levels of 30bp. The pricing reflected UMC's preference for achieving a hit rate of approximately 50%.

RESULTS

By the tender expiration, which lasted about three days, EUR 500 million of bonds had been validly tendered, of which approximately half was from holders who also wanted an allocation of the new issue. The new issue book opened on the morning of the tender's expiration: in just over four hours, the order book was five times oversubscribed at the initial price guidance of mid-swaps plus 140bp, enabling the company to achieve tighter pricing of mid-swaps plus 135bp.

CONCLUSION

Using this innovative structure, UMC was able to do the following.

- Capitalise on current market conditions to extend their EUR curve by three years at a favourable rate and without incurring unnecessary cost of carry.
- Optimise new issue pricing: the new issue spread was only fixed on the morning of pricing. Given the volatile market conditions in the week of pricing and the ability to dynamically react to investors' positive response to the new issue, UMC were able to save between 5 and 7bp on the new issue (versus if the transaction was structured as a straight exchange).
- Amortise the P&L cost of the whole transaction across a 10-year period.

1 This compares with the exchange offer, where both the buy-back and new issue spreads must be fixed.

2 This compares with the exchange offer, where secondary market purchases during the offer period can result in highly concentrated holdings of the old bond and hence of the new issue following the exchange.

3

Cash Tender Offer

The situation described in this chapter is another example of a liability management exercise, described in Chapter 2. The main difference here is that, at the time when this project took place, the company was awash with cash, and did not need to issue new debt in order to retire an existing bond. The company was concerned about the low rate of return that it was receiving on its cash deposits, and needed to find a more attractive return, albeit with limited risk. Buying back its own debt is equivalent to investing cash in its own bonds, and thereby realising the return which is equal to the yield of the outstanding bond, and higher than the deposit rate on offer.

BACKGROUND

Orion is one of the world's leading international retailers with more than 3,000 shops around the world and a market share of around 25% in the UK. It employs over 150,000 people worldwide.

In early 2009, refinancing risk became a key concern for corporate treasurers in the face of exceptionally weak conditions in the loan and capital markets, resulting from the global financial crisis. Taking advantage of its position as a frequent and favoured name with bond investors, Orion issued approximately EUR 1.25 billion of new notes in March 2009 to cover refinancing obligations in the near future and to extend the company's debt maturity profile (Figure 3.1).

As 2009 progressed, the market situation started to normalise (Figure 3.2). A strong market rally, with consequent dramatic spread tightening in the second half of 2009, gave rise to opportunities for the company to use some of the cash raised as a result of its pre-financing exercise more efficiently. Orion had indicated that EUR 750 million were available on its free cash balances invested in short-term deposits via money market funds. Market movements since 2009 gave Orion a favourable opportunity to redeem early a proportion of the notes by "investing" in its own bonds instead.

Figure 3.1 Orion debt maturity profile

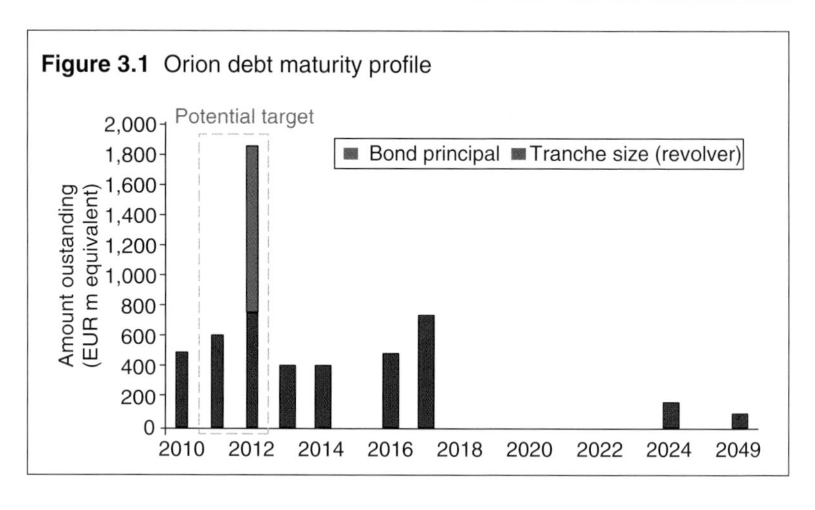

Figure 3.2 Short-dated EUR Orion bond yield and three-month Euribor for 2009

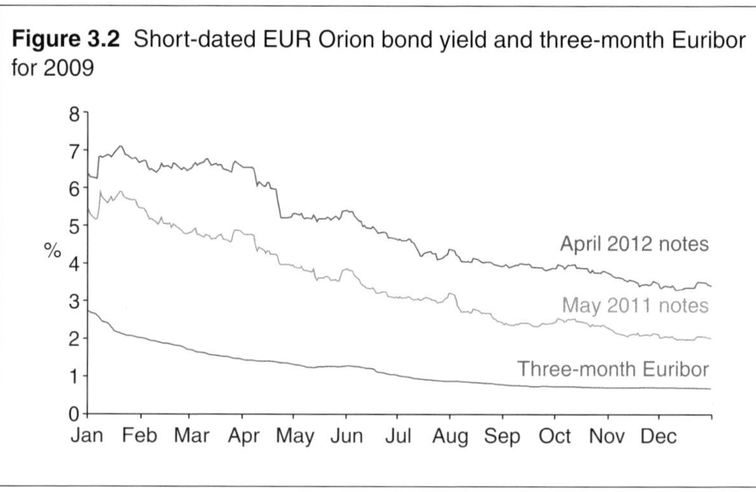

COMPANY OBJECTIVES

- To utilise excess cash.
- To reduce carry between assets and liabilities.
- To reduce refinancing risk in 2011–12.
- To minimise the P&L cost of the operation.
- To maximise the overall net present value (NPV) gain.
- To maintain smooth investor relations by avoiding pro-ration.[1]

MARKET BACKGROUND

Orion first issued public bonds in mid-March 2009, locking[2] excellent market conditions to launch three benchmark bonds across the spectrum of currency, maturity and coupon types with an aggregate nominal value of EUR 1.25 billion equivalent.

In order to take advantage of the market conditions, Orion decided to redeem short-to-medium-dated EUR bonds yielding 2.00–3.40%, while conditions on the deposit market remained unattractive.

Furthermore, the rate environment meant that cost of carry considerations[3] would persist for some time.

SOLUTION

Orion has two options to use the cash efficiently.

1. Continue to invest in short-term deposits via money market funds at an interest rate of around 1%.
2. "Invest" in its own bonds (given a buy-back yield of 3.40% on the 2012 EUR bonds and 2.00% on the 2011 EUR bonds) via cash tender offer. Orion would launch a public offer for one or more of its outstanding bonds at a premium of between 5bp and 15bp versus current offer yields.

    - Orion can enter into a so-called "any and all" offer, where investors have certainty as to the amount they will receive. However, there is a risk that participation exceeds Orion's liquidity constraints, ie, the amount of cash available for bond purchases.
    - Orion can alternatively put a cap on this offer and pro rate acceptances above a certain level yet to be determined.
    - If Orion wants to buy back up to 100% of an issue, a so-called squeeze-out consent solicitation can be used to ask bondholders to vote in favour of inserting a call option into the documentation.

Orion was willing to spend EUR 500–750 million to buy back short to medium term debt and wished to minimise the aggregate P&L impact of a restructuring transaction.

Orion's April 2012 bond would have a limited P&L impact while generating the greatest NPV gain from a tender relative to the 2011 bond. A so-called waterfall acceptance structure[4] will allow Orion to prioritise buying back any and all of the April 2012 bond: all offers to tender the April 2012 bond will be accepted in full and offers to tender the 2011 bond will be accepted on a pro rata basis, subject to a cap of EUR 750 million aggregate nominal value of bonds accepted for tender.

Some advantages of this structure are as follows.

- Prioritising the buy back of any and all of the April 2012 bond enables Orion to minimise overall P&L impact and maximise NPV gain.
- This flexible structure ensures that it meets Orion's aggregate target debt reduction, by building in explicit flexibility to increase acceptances above target if needed. This also satisfies investors by avoiding pro-ration (defined in endnote 1).
- Targeting to repurchase EUR 750 million with an EUR 1.35 billion offer basket allows Orion to offer a low tender premium of 6–8bp.

SUMMARY OF THE STRUCTURE

The cash tender offer involved two short-dated EUR bonds with a waterfall acceptance structure (determined according to the P&L impact of repurchasing the target bonds) that prioritised the repurchase of

- any and all of its EUR 750 million notes due 2012,
- certain amounts of its EUR 600 million notes due 2011.

The aggregate acceptance levels were based on a target acceptance amount of EUR 750 million and a maximum acceptance amount equal to the 2012 notes validly offered for sale or the target acceptance amount (whichever is the higher). Orion reserved the flexibility to raise the target acceptance amount at any time to avoid pro-rating tenders where feasible.

PRICING AND EXECUTION

Tender pricing was fixed at launch as follows.

- **2011 notes:** mid-swaps plus 60bp (~8bp lower than the pre-trading levels).

- **2012 notes:** mid-swaps plus 110bp (~10bp lower than the pre-trading levels).

The tender premiums offered were lower than the market average for tender offers, as

(i) the bonds were already trading exceptionally tight,

(ii) the tender offer was opportunistic and participation was purely voluntary, and

(iii) only a low hit-rate of 55% relative to the basket size was desired, due to the limited amount of cash available for the tender offer.

The offer period lasted six business days, slightly longer than the five-day market average for stand-alone tender offers, in order to account for the expected high percentage of retail investors (who take longer to receive information and submit participation instructions), which were successfully identified in the two bonds.

RESULTS

Over EUR 820 million in aggregate nominal amount of bonds were validly tendered during the offer period – EUR 480 million of the 2012s and EUR 340 million of the 2011s – exceeding the original target acceptance amount.

In response to the positive reaction to the offer, Orion decided to raise the overall acceptance amount to EUR 820 million so as to accept all tenders of the 2011 and 2012 notes.

CONCLUSION

By using free cash balances opportunistically to retire early a portion of its short-dated outstanding debt, Orion achieved a higher return on investment by "investing" in its own bonds.

The transaction also met Orion's secondary objectives:

- to minimise the P&L cost of the operation;
- to maximise the overall NPV gain;
- to maintain smooth investor relations by avoiding pro-ration.

1 "Pro-ration" is a mechanism by which each investor willing to sell back the bond buy a reduced amount of bonds, proportional to the amount accepted in the overall cash tender offer.

2 That is, being able to capture the low credit spread to issue a new bond.

3 That is, the negative difference between the rate earned on deposits and coupon Orion had to pay on their bonds.

4 That is, the precise mechanism that defines the order in which different bond maturities are bought back.

4

Optimal Debt Duration via Merton's Model

In a 2002 study based on a Survey of 392 CFOs from the Fortune 500 Company list,[1] one of the questions was: "How do you decide on the debt maturity?" Possible answers were divided into three categories.

1. Cashflow profile: matching maturity of assets and liabilities, underinvestment concerns and asset substitution concerns.
2. Risk appetite: avoiding market instability or avoiding potential changes in credit rating.
3. Interest cost: optimising cost of borrowing, and view on long-term rates.

One thing was very clear from the study: companies use a variety of considerations in order to decide on their debt maturity.

In practice, companies rarely use advanced analytical techniques similar to the one described below in order to optimise their debt. One of the reasons for this is that the conclusions reached based on quantitative analyses depend to a certain extent on the underlying mathematical assumptions. Another reason is the practical limitation of many companies in terms of possible debt maturities and amounts. A simpler method is to project the expected generated free cashflows into the future, and then match the duration of debt so that the debt matures at the time when the cashflows are sufficient to pay it.[2] In the case below, we show an alternative method which is based on the option valuation techniques.

Traditional theory regarding the optimal corporate debt structure (see, for example, Quiry *et al* (2011) for a general overview) postulates that the maturity of debt should match the maturity of the assets of the company in question. Any mismatch introduces the risk of either refinancing or reinvestment, depending on the relative maturities of company's debt and assets. For instance, let us assume that the company's single asset is a factory with an expected lifetime of 10 years. After 10 years the company value will amortise to zero. At time zero, the company finances the factory by issuing a single bond with a 10-year maturity. Proceeds from the bond are used to finance the construction of the factory and the operating expenses for the next 10 years. Subsequent income generated by the factory is accumulated until the bond maturity. At that point the process is repeated. In this case, there is no risk, since the maturity of the financing (bond) and the asset (factory) are the same.

Now we consider a case when the period of financing is shorter than the duration of the related assets. Let us assume that, at time zero, the company finances the same project with a single bond but with a shorter maturity of five years. Initial proceeds are again used to finance the construction of the factory and operating costs, while the income generated by the factory is used to pay the bond at maturity. The first problem is that the amount of income may no longer be sufficient to pay back the bond, since we shall only have five years of accumulated income at the bond maturity. The second and more fundamental problem is the refinancing risk. At time zero, we do not know what the cost of refinancing the bond would be in five years' time, when the bond matures. This will depend on a variety of factors, including the profitability of the company in years 1 to 5, based on which the bond investors will analyse the creditworthiness of the company and decide which credit spread to apply at refinancing. Also, the refinancing cost will depend on the interest rates at the time, general credit appetite and a variety of other factors.

Similarly, if the bond has longer maturity than the factory, let us say 12 years compared to 10, the company is exposed to the reinvestment risk in years 10–12.

Therefore, intuitively, it makes sense to match the duration of debt and assets in order to reduce refinancing or reinvestment risk. Of course, in real life, a company has many assets with various durations, and there are limitations to the range of debt maturities acceptable by the market at any one time. However, the intuitive picture still holds, although with many real-life constraints.

Corporate finance theory puts the question of optimal debt maturity on a much more analytical footing. In particular, the work of Merton and subsequent researchers evaluates the impact of credit on the company valuation.[3] The following case describes how a manufacturer based in the Middle East used Merton's model in order to optimise its debt maturity.

BACKGROUND

Al Hambra is a manufacturer based in the Middle East, with most of its assets and revenues in the local market. In the past Al Hambra has funded its assets largely through local bank loans, which have an average maturity of 20 months. As some of the loans come close to maturity, Al Hambra has been considering what maturity would best fit with its assets. The company's credit rating (A+) allows it to consider maturities of up to 10 years in the USD public bond market. At the same time, the owner of the company is planning a cash injection to support Al Hambra's current credit rating, and would like to know how much cash is required for this purpose.

COMPANY OBJECTIVES

- To develop a method by which Al Hambra can analyse the impact of various debt durations on its equity valuation.
- To apply the method to Al Hambra's balance sheet in order to determine the optimal refinancing maturity.
- To evaluate the impact of refinancing on the 10-year default probability and the required cash injection to retain a single A+ credit rating.

ANALYSIS

Merton's model and its generalisation

The impact of debt structure on company valuation is based on Merton's model for valuing the equity of a company, based on the relation between its equity, its assets and its debt

$$\text{equity} = \max(\text{assets} - \text{debt}, 0)$$

Merton observed that the payout is option-like; therefore, equity holders have a call option on the company's assets struck at the market value of its debt. If the debt of the company is a single zero-coupon bond, we can use the Black–Scholes formula to evaluate the equity value. For any other debt structure we need to calculate the equity value by a numerical procedure.

Cenci and Gheno (2005) showed how to generalise the Merton result for an arbitrary debt structure, based on this numerical procedure. The KMV corporation developed an application of the Merton model[4] to determine the expected default probability of a company at any moment in time if we assume a given probability distribution for the company's assets:

- if the assets are less than the debt, the company defaults;
- if assets are more than the debt, the assets continue to grow.

This model is, among others, used by Moody's rating agency to estimate the default probabilities of companies. A detailed discussion of Merton's model, the KMV application and the subsequent generalisation by Cenci and Gheno is beyond the scope of this book. However, for the sake of clarity and completeness, here we give the main ideas, while the rigorous derivation can be found in the original articles.

Merton's model approximates the debt structure by a single zero-coupon bond with the same total amount and the average duration as the original debt. The equity value can then be computed as the call option embedded in the company, using the Black–Scholes options pricing formula (Merton 1974).

Cenci and Gheno generalise this to an arbitrary debt structure, but the price they had to pay is that the Black–Scholes formula can no longer be used for company valuation, and has to be replaced by a numerical procedure. We start from the company balance sheet, defined by total assets and current or the targeted debt structure. From the historical volatility of the share price and of the funding cost, we can estimate the asset volatility. We shall assume that asset return is normally distributed with the risk-free rate growth and the estimated historical volatility. We shall then simulate numerically the evolution of the asset price until the last debt payment date. At each debt or coupon payment date we subtract the payment from the assets. If the assets fall below zero, or below a certain threshold, the company defaults. We continue the procedure at a given time frequency, eg, quarterly, and find the future asset distribution after the last debt payment. We use this distribution to compute the discounted present value of the assets minus debt. The discounted expectation of assets minus debt is the current equity value. This also allows us to compute the probability of default at any point in time (Figure 4.1).

Figure 4.1 Illustration of Merton's model

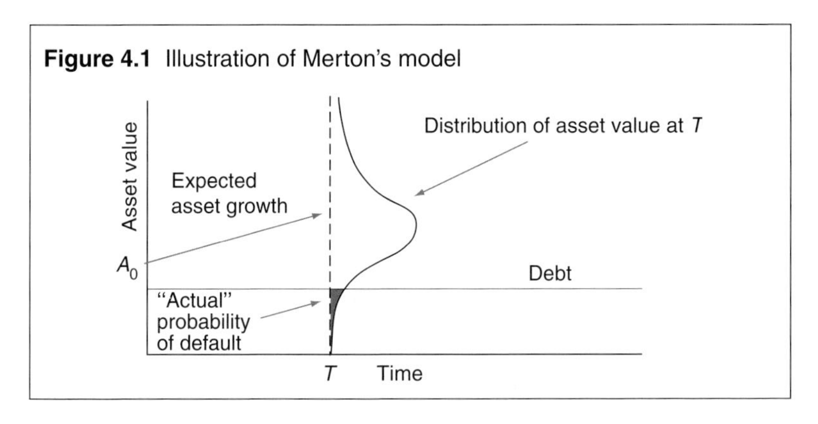

Using the model to analyse the debt structure

We analyse the impact of two refinancing alternatives for Al Hambra: issuance of USD 2 billion bonds for either five or ten years. The current debt structure of Al Hambra is based on short-dated debt (average maturity is only 20 months). This short maturity exposes Al Hambra to refinancing risk. Equity investors and analysts cannot be certain what the future funding cost will be, and this uncertainty affects the equity valuation. On the other hand, if the company extends the maturity of its debt by refinancing, then uncertainty decreases, and this increases the equity value of the company. This follows from the option pricing theory.

A well-known consequence of the Black–Scholes pricing formula is that, as we increase the call option maturity, the value of the option grows, as long as all the other parameters (strike, spot, forward and volatility) are kept constant. Similarly, if we increase the maturity of the debt in Merton's model, the equity valuation will increase.

However, longer term debt is normally issued at a higher annual cost. This is to be expected, as investors want to be compensated for leaving their money with the company for longer. This factor is called the "carry impact", and it reduces the equity valuation if the debt maturity is increased. Based on the credit curve as of August 2012 (Figure 4.2), we estimate that the extra carry of new five-year debt is about 25bp per year compared with the debt maturity (at 2012) of 20 months. Ten-year debt would cost 50bp more than the 20-month debt. We apply this to the amount of new debt of USD 1 billion and annualise over a period of 10 years to obtain the carry impact of two alternatives of USD 50 million and USD 100 million, respectively.

Figure 4.2 Al Hambra's credit curve

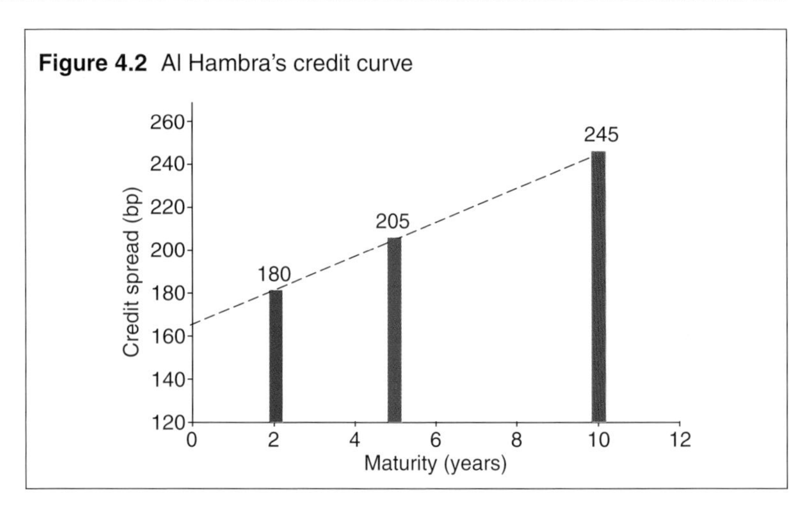

The net impact depends on the relative impact of the two factors. For Al Hambra, based on the current low rate situation and high asset volatility, the two options increase the equity value at the currently favourable market conditions despite a negative carry impact, as summarised in Table 4.1. In addition, the required cash injection consistent with the default probability according to the Standard & Poor's migration matrix for a company starting at an A+ rating reduces with longer maturity of debt.[5]

Table 4.1 Impact of refinancing on the Al Hambra's valuation

	Duration (y)	Equity value (USD m) excl. carry[6]	Refinancing impact excl. carry (USD m)
Currently	1.7	5,200–5,400	—
Option 1	2.4 (+40%)	5,400–5,700	+(200–300) = +(4–6%)
Option 2	3.3 (+92%)	5,600–6,200	+(400–800) = +(7–14%)

	Carry impact over 10y (USD m)	Net refinancing impact incl. carry (USD m)	Cash injection required (USD bn)
Currently	—	—	10
Option 1	−50	+(150–300) = +(3–6%)	5
Option 2	−100	+(300–700) = +(6–12%)	1

Note: Option 1, USD 2 billion 5-year bond. Option 2, USD 2 billion 10-year bond.

RECOMMENDATIONS

Given the significant appetite of investors for Al Hambra's debt and its high credit rating, the credit curve of Al Hambra is not too steep. The company can benefit from this by issuing longer-dated debt. An initial bond issuance of USD 2 billion equivalent would increase the equity value by 6–12%, depending on whether we use Cenci and Gheno's numerical procedure or Merton's model, net of the carry cost. This will also improve the creditworthiness of the company, so that a smaller cash injection is required in order for it to maintain the A+ credit rating.

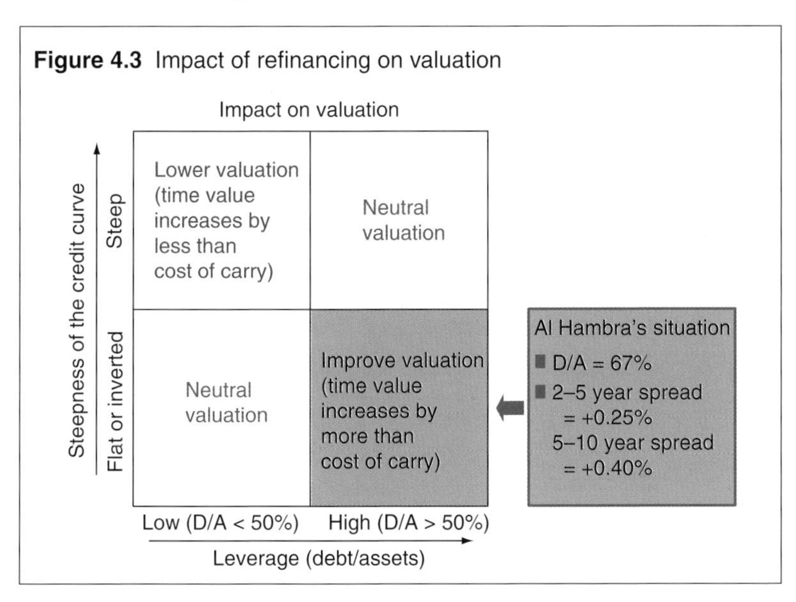

Figure 4.3 Impact of refinancing on valuation

An obvious question is why there is a net positive impact of refinancing on the Al Hambra valuation. In Figure 4.3, we illustrate this as the interplay between the time value improvement and extra cost of carry. Al Hambra is in a lucky situation where its leverage is higher than average but its credit curve is relatively flat. Therefore, the improvement of the time value through Merton's model more than compensates for the higher cost of carry due to longer debt. In addition, longer maturities reduce the refinancing risk.

CONCLUSION

In this chapter, we have discussed how the duration of debt can affect the company valuation. For this we used Merton's model and its extensions by Cecci and Gheno. Longer debt duration tends to improve the value of the company, as the refinancing risk is reduced. However, the valuation is reduced by the higher carry implicit in longer debt maturities. The relative size of these two effects depends on the company leverage, but the first effect is dominant for investment-grade companies.

1 See Graham and Harvey (2002).

2 In practice, this is not as simple as it sounds; cashflows are not entirely predictable, and therefore a significant margin for risk needs to be built in to these forecasts.

3 See Merton (1974) for zero-coupon bonds and Cenci and Gheno (2005) for subsequent generalisation for coupon bonds.

4 This model is often called the KMV–Merton model. KMV stands for Kealhofer, McQuown and Vasicek, the three founders of the corporation.

5 Obviously, the actual rating given is determined by the rating agencies, based on a variety of quantitative and qualitative criteria. Here we focus on the default probability, which is just one aspect of the overall analysis.

6 The number on the left is computed using the procedure in Cenci and Gheno's model; the number on the right is computed using Merton's model.

5

Funding Cost Drivers

This chapter covers an important and often discussed topic. When a company decides to issue a new bond, it must address three main questions.

1. Is there investor appetite to buy any new debt issued by our company?
2. If yes, what are the possible sizes and maturities?
3. What is the coupon we shall have to pay?

In this chapter we attempt to answer the third question.[1]

Let us assume for the sake of concreteness that a company decides to issue an EUR 1,000 million bond, paying a fixed coupon for a period of five years. The company has in the past issued bonds in EUR, and now tries to find out the coupon that it will have to pay on the new bond. The company approaches the debt capital markets (DCM) desk of an investment bank and is given an estimate of credit spread of 200bp. This estimate is normally referred to as the Z-spread, or spread over five-year swap rates. The total coupon on the bond, assuming that it is issued at par, is going to be given by the sum of the Z-spread and the five-year swap rate at the time of issuance. The company can then decide whether or not the resulting coupon is acceptable, and therefore whether to go ahead with the bond issuance or to postpone it for a later date.

In practice, of course, the discussions are more complicated, and require negotiations about a whole range of parameters, including bond currency, maturity, Z-spread, potential embedded call and put options and a host of other parameters that define the bond. The DCM desk serves an essential purpose in providing an indication of market sentiment towards the particular bond issuer at that point in time, while other parts of the bank provide other services, such as the actual distribution of the bond to investors, secondary trading and fundamental research on the issuer.

BACKGROUND

Electra is a large electrical utility, based in a core European market. In this chapter "core" means one of the less indebted countries of the Eurozone that have, through the sovereign debt crisis, been labelled as core by the media, as opposed to the "peripheral" countries,[2] which, as a result of higher indebtedness and other problems, have struggled with high refinancing costs, in some instances exceeding 7%. The main operation of Electra is the provision of electrical power to retail and business customers in their home market, but in the past Electra acquired limited assets in foreign jurisdictions. The assets have predominantly been funded through medium- to long-dated public bonds. This has generally been easy, given Electra's high credit rating. Among the reasons for the high rating, agencies have in the past noted a "conservative financial policy", "large proportion of regulated business", "dominant position in the domestic market" and "high likelihood of state support".

Electra has observed its funding cost at the time of issuance over the past five-years, and has noticed a significant volatility over time. Moreover, several benchmark issues of Electra are regularly traded on the secondary market and the company has also been able to observe those prices. Electra is a large and highly cash generative company, with a high operating margin. At the time of writing, Electra has been considering various strategic options, including deleveraging or tactically acquiring cheap foreign assets, if they become available for sale.

COMPANY OBJECTIVES

- To understand the main drivers of its funding cost and how changes to those drivers would affect the funding cost.
- To find out if there are any short-term dislocations in the market, which would benefit Electra if it decides to issue new debt.
- To analyse the two main strategic options: deleveraging or acquisitions in view of the funding cost drivers.

ANALYSIS

We perform a statistical analysis of the funding cost of Electra. For simplicity, in this chapter we shall focus on the five-year Z-spread in EUR, but in fact the analysis covers multiple maturities and currencies. We shall look at two kinds of analysis:

(i) historical analysis, ie, how did the funding cost of Electra and their peers vary over time;

(ii) peer group analysis, ie, how at a single point in time did the funding cost of Electra and their peers vary as a function of key corporate parameters.

The approach follows the four steps in Figure 5.1.

Figure 5.1 Funding cost drivers: step by step

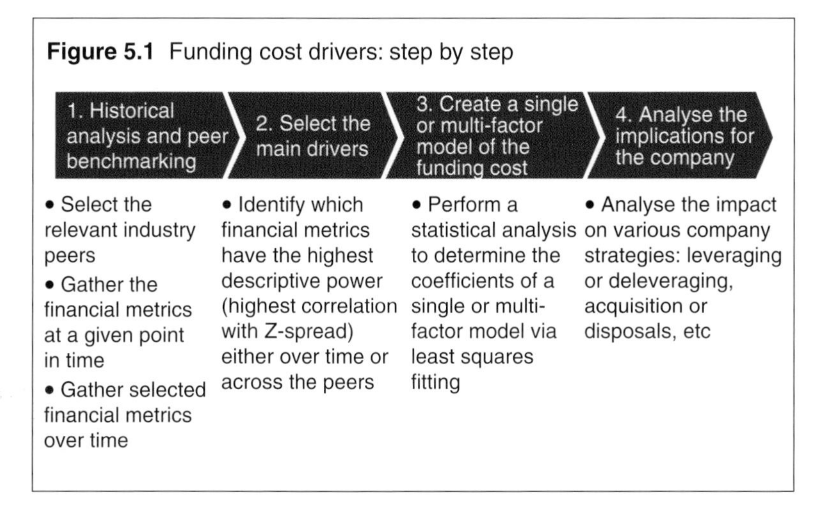

STEP 1: HISTORICAL ANALYSIS AND PEER BENCHMARKING

We start by comparing the two main components of Electra's five-year cost of funding at the time of writing with their historical distribution in the period of the previous six years (Figure 5.2):

- the five-year EUR swap rate was almost at the historical minimum;
- Electra's five-year Z-spread was lower only in about 10% of the cases in the past.

As we can see from Figure 5.2, the cost of funding of Electra is low due to both a low swap rate and low credit spread compared with the previous six years.

At the time of writing in spring 2012, many of Electra's peers from peripheral European countries have credit spreads that have

Figure 5.2 Historical funding cost of Electra

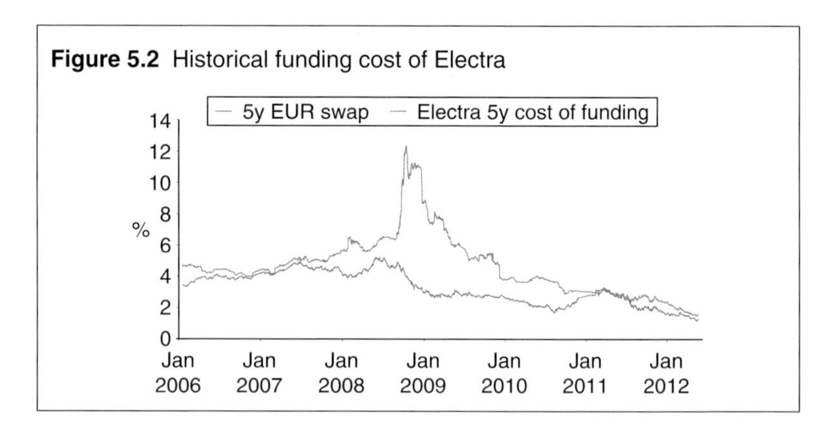

Figure 5.3 Credit ratings versus five-year Z-spread

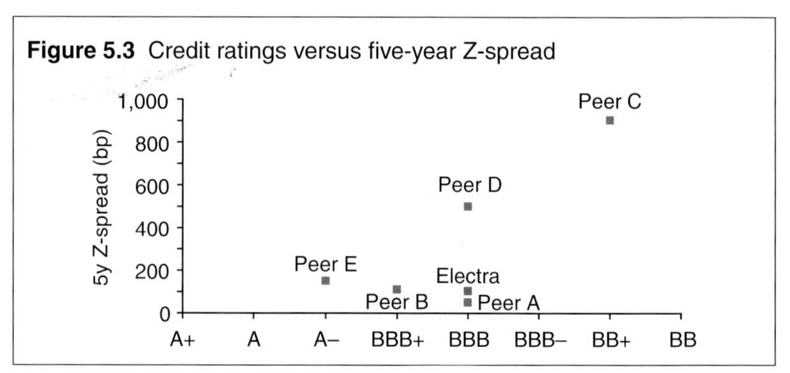

considerably widened compared to the past. Figure 5.3 shows the funding cost, measured by the five-year Z-spread of Electra and five of their closest peers against their credit rating at the time.

Peers A and B are from core European countries, while C, D and E are from the periphery. Under normal circumstances, we would expect to have a rough alignment of the credit rating with the funding cost, but, at the time of writing, the market seems to apply a premium in terms of the Z-spread to the utilities in European peripheral markets. We call this premium the "sovereign premium". For instance, Electra and its peer "A" have the same credit rating as peer D, whose funding cost is almost 500bp wider. So the markets disagree with the credit rating and penalise peripheral European utilities with a higher funding cost. This reflects the concern of the markets about the economic situation in the European peripheral countries, and about the will and ability of these sovereign states to support their utilities in the case of default.

How did this discrepancy develop? Has it always been there or is it a recent phenomenon? In Figures 5.4 and 5.5 we show the correlation between the sovereign credit default swap (CDS) of two European countries and their utilities funding costs over the same six-year period as before.

Figure 5.4 Core European sovereign five-year credit default swap versus Electra's five-year funding cost

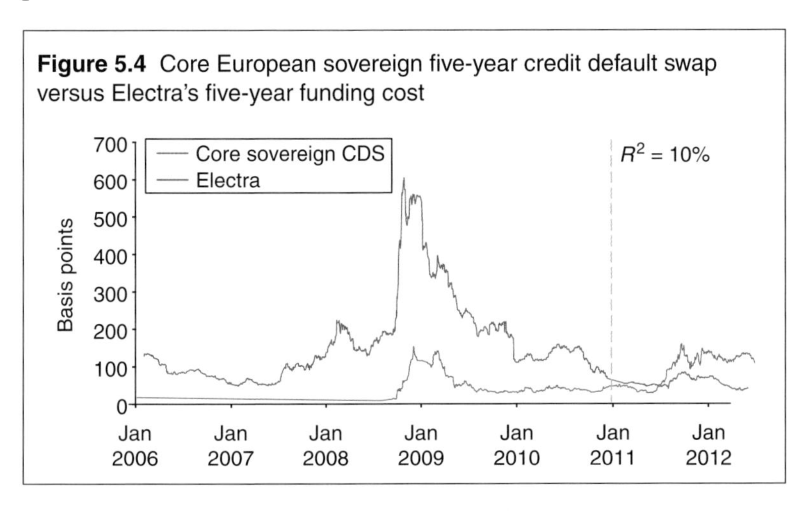

Figure 5.5 Peripheral European sovereign five-year credit default swap versus peer D's five-year funding cost

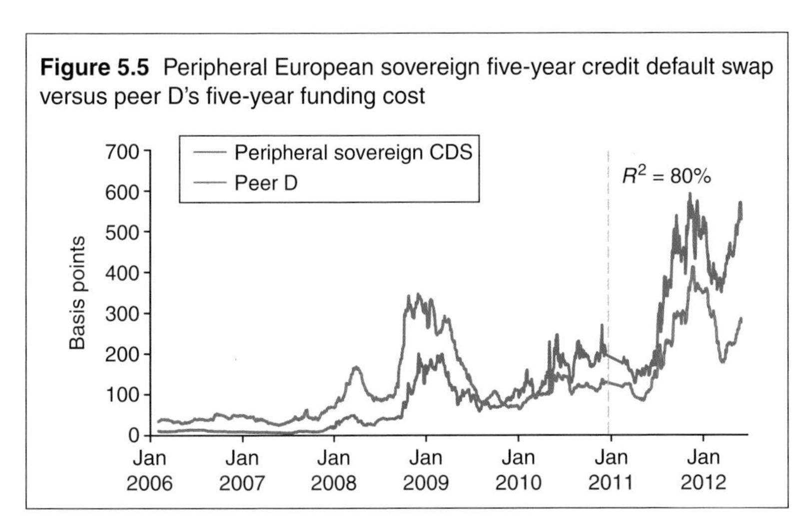

When we compare Figures 5.4 and 5.5, we notice that there are two separate regimes. Prior to 2011, both companies' funding costs were relatively similar and uncorrelated to their sovereign CDS. However, since 2011, the fate of peer D has been closely linked to its sovereign, as evidenced by the correlation squared of 80%, while

Electra has barely shown any correlation with its sovereign CDS (with a correlation squared of 10%).

This completes the historical analysis, and we now focus our attention on the comparison across the peer group at a single point of time. The first step is to gather all the possible financial parameters for the peer group at that moment. By this we mean all the financial parameters as of the end of a given reporting period.

STEP 2: SELECT THE MAIN DRIVERS

From the peer group parameters, we can compute various financial metrics. In order to select the main drivers of the funding cost, we compute the correlations of each individual metric with the five-year Z-spread of our universe of companies. Selected metrics should each describe a different aspect of the company. For the utility sector, we chose four main aspects of the company: country risk, leverage, size and profitability. (Later on we shall see how well this choice describes the actual funding cost.) We required the chosen metrics to be as independent from each other as possible, in order to avoid describing the funding cost with two or more highly correlated factors. So, for example, as a size metric, we should not take into account both sales and assets, as they would be highly correlated.

In Table 5.1 we list the four metrics that were drivers of the funding cost among European utilities at the time of writing.

Table 5.1 Chosen drivers of funding cost for European utilities

Area	Metric	Units	Coeff.	Correlation with Z-spread squared (%)
Country risk	Sovereign 5y CDS	bp	+0.5	80
Leverage	Net debt/EBITDA	—	+1.5	10
Size	log(sales/average sales)	—	−40.0	7
Profitability	EBITDA margin	%	−2.0	5

From the correlation in the last column, we can see that the main driver of the funding cost is the country risk (measured by either CDS or the equity risk premium). This is not surprising, given the sovereign crisis at the time of writing (ongoing since 2011), and we expect that this driver will be less important as the sovereign crisis abates.

STEP 3: CREATE A SINGLE OR MULTI-FACTOR MODEL OF THE FUNDING COST

When we run the multi-linear regression of the Z-spread against the four metrics from Table 5.1, we obtain our multi-factor model for the European utility sector

$$\begin{aligned}\text{Z-spread 5y} = {} & 40 + (0.5 \times \text{country CDS}) + (1.5 \times \text{leverage}) \\ & - (40.0 \times \text{size}) - (2.0 \times \text{EBITDA margin (\%)}) \\ & + \text{error}\end{aligned}$$

For example, if we use this model for Electra, we obtain

$$\begin{aligned}\text{Z-spread 5y} &= 40 + (0.5 \times 100) + (1.5 \times 6.0) \\ &\quad - (40.0 \times 0.6) - (2.0 \times 10.0) + \text{error} \\ &= 55 + \text{error}\end{aligned}$$

This is to be compared with the actual value of 35bp at the time of writing, so the error is −20bp for Electra. This error is due to all the other factors, which we do not take into account in our analysis, as well as the inaccuracy of the statistical analysis.[3]

In Figure 5.6 we compare the forecasted funding costs across the whole sector, which consists of 12 electrical utilities.

The correlation squared between the estimated and actual funding cost is 98%, and the maximal error is −64bp, which shows that the impact of all the other factors is small compared with the factors we have chosen.

STEP 4: ANALYSE THE IMPLICATIONS FOR THE COMPANY

In Figures 5.7 and 5.8 we show the estimated funding cost for Electra based on the model above, compared to the average of the peer group. We can see that, compared to its peers, Electra has similar leverage, size and profitability. So what differentiates it from the average peer is its country risk, which is three times lower at 50bp, compared to 150bp.

We also performed the same analysis for a different point in time, before the sovereign crisis of 2011, and found that the correlation of the funding cost with the country risk was greatly diminished

Figure 5.6 Actual versus estimated funding costs (basis points)

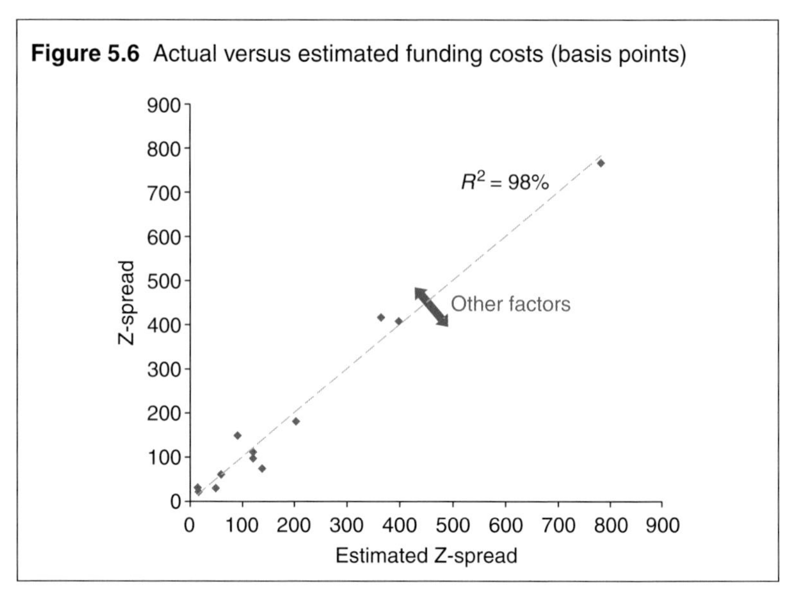

Figure 5.7 Five-year funding cost for the average of the peer group

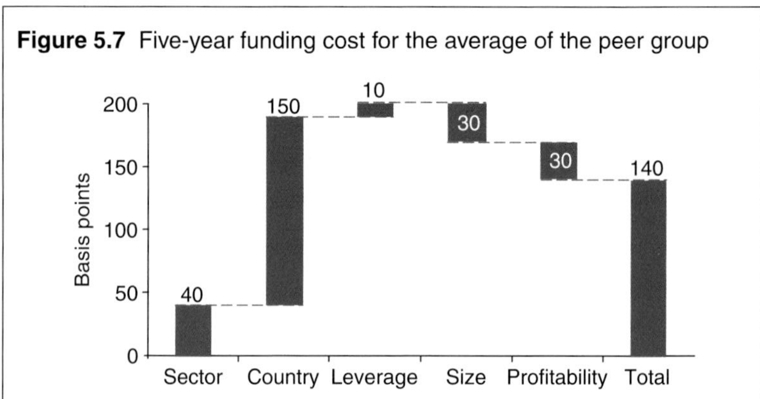

then, while the correlation of company-specific drivers such as leverage, size and profitability was increased. In other words, before the sovereign crisis, markets were more focused on fundamentals than on the country risk.

RECOMMENDATIONS

Due to sovereign problems, markets at the time of writing were penalising peripheral European companies with a higher funding cost and rewarding the core European companies with a lower funding cost. Electra has benefited from this current market bias. Its debt

Figure 5.8 Five-year funding cost for Electra

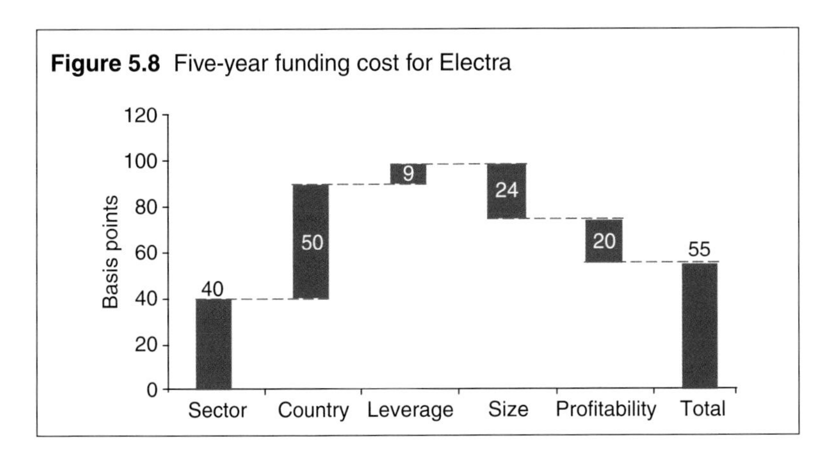

was trading at a tighter credit spread than that of its peers, adjusted for the country risk, leverage, size and profitability. This is consistent with the sovereign premium and results of our historical analysis and indicates that the market was greatly concerned about the credit of peripheral European companies.

Electra can benefit from this temporal dislocation by temporarily moderately increasing its leverage. Since the leverage factor in our model is not significant, this will not affect its funding cost. Alternatively, Electra can refinance its short-term debt and extend its debt maturity (see Chapter 2). If there are acquisition targets available, Electra can benefit from both the funding cost differential and the likely depressed equity valuation of the potential target to expand by acquiring cheap assets in the peripheral European countries. Deleveraging at this point in time is not advised for Electra, since it would be a defensive move, which does not take account of the situation at the time.

CONCLUSION

In this chapter, we analysed the main drivers of the funding cost among European utilities. At the time of writing, these were the country risk, leverage, size and profitability, but this will change over time and sectors. This kind of analysis helps companies to understand whether the market is pricing them "fairly" compared to their history and to their peers and further allows them to create strategies to reap the benefit from dislocations in the market, such as the one during the sovereign crisis of 2011–12.

1 The other two questions are, for the moment, too difficult to answer in a systematic quantitative framework which we try to follow for most chapters in this book. Questions of investor appetite, sizes and maturities vary greatly from one day to another based on the investor sentiment towards a particular company or sector and tend to be driven by many factors, including global macroeconomic ones.

2 Italy, Greece, Portugal, Ireland and Spain.

3 The accuracy of the statistical analysis can be measured by the correlation between the expected and actual funding costs.

Part II

Interest Rate and Inflation Risks

Interest Rate and Inflation Risks

When we get in debt, we can start to worry about interest rates, and for many people the interest rate paid on their loans and mortgages is one of the most important financial concerns. Though it is an important factor for individuals, the risk can be even higher for companies or states. During the financial crisis of 2011–12, the mistrust of investors in certain countries was manifested by an increase of the sovereign cost of debt, and when this reached an unsustainable level the country had to be bailed out. Another economic risk that is often talked about is inflation, which determines how much more things will cost tomorrow than today. Inflation can be good because it reduces the value of our debt in real terms, but it can also be bad if our earnings are not rising fast enough to offset it. The interplay between these two groups of variables is complex and requires careful consideration for anyone who has debt.

Companies are exposed to interest rate risk through the rates they pay on their debt and the rates they receive on their deposits and other financial assets. The first seven chapters in this part of the book focus on the interest rate risk on the debt side of the balance sheet, while the last two chapters look at both assets and liabilities.

So, let us talk about debt.

In Part I, we described several important decisions that companies have to make in order to decide on their debt structure. Once the company is fully funded, the interest rate risks are introduced and must be managed. In Chapter 13, on asset and liability management (ALM), we define the interest rate risks and clarify the difference between two kinds of interest rate risk: cashflow and fair-value risk, which is particularly important for ALM issues. For now, let us define the interest rate risk as the cashflow risk only, ie, risks to company cashflows due to the variability of interest rates. As long as the company does not intend to repay their debt before maturity, this definition will suffice, and is the one that most companies care about.

In Chapter 6, "How to Develop an Interest Rate Hedging Policy", we start by discussing qualitative aspects of interest rate risk management. These are usually codified in a policy document outlining the main principles and implementation details of the risk management process. We shall see which aspects of the policy are documented (eg, allowed instruments, limits on size and counterparties, and other organisational and process-related issues). Policies often include an important quantitative parameter, which is the targeted fixed proportion of debt.

The optimal proportion of fixed debt is the subject of Chapter 7, "How to Improve Your Fixed–Floating Mix and Duration". This topic is frequently discussed within companies, and companies tend to choose among two kinds of policies: a dynamic or a static one. An example of a dynamic policy is defined by a target fixed–floating range (eg, 40–60% fixed debt), which matches the long-term risk appetite of the company, and then the company position is adjusted within this range as a function of market movements, company risk and other factors.

Let us look at the example of Vodafone's risk management policy from their 2012 annual report:

> Under the Group's interest rate management policy, interest rates on monetary assets and liabilities denominated in euros, US dollars and sterling are maintained on a floating-rate basis except for periods up to six years where interest rate fixing has to be undertaken in accordance with treasury policy. Where assets and liabilities are denominated in other currencies interest rates may also be fixed. In addition, fixing is undertaken for longer periods when interest rates are statistically low.

So Vodafone's policy essentially says that the debt in three main currencies is always floating, or fixed up to six years unless the interest rates are low compared to history. In such a case, the company may decide to fix the rates for longer. What is the reason for such a policy? We shall see the main principles and reasons for such a policy in Chapter 7.

An example of a static policy would be a company choosing a level of fixed debt, which is kept constant over time. These levels are normally based on round numbers, most often 100% or 50%. There are several reasons why a company decides to choose a static fixed proportion of debt. The company may decide that the interest rate cost (and therefore risk) is so insignificant that it is simply not worthwhile spending too much time on dynamically adjusting the policy. Another reason could be organisational, for instance if the company simply does not have the resources and capacity to tackle the issue of optimising the fixed proportion in detail, and so it chooses by default a round number, since it believes that it "can't go wrong" with a 50% fixed proportion, or it believes that "100% means that all is safe", etc.

In many cases, we do not consider these beliefs satisfactory, and we urge our readers to think about their fixed-rate policy more carefully. How much difference can the fixed-rate policy make? Chapter 8, "Impact of Fixed–Floating Policy on Company Valuation", attempts to answer this question. We say "attempts", since it is not clear to what extent, if at all, the actual company share price would change as a result of changes in its fixed–floating policy. What we are talking about here instead is an impact on the intrinsic valuation of a company, as determined through a discounted cashflow (DCF) model. The key idea is that the weighted average cost of capital (WACC) can be affected by the proportion of fixed debt.[1] As shown in Chapter 7, floating debt is generally cheaper than fixed, and so changing the proportion of fixed to floating debt is statistically likely to affect the actual cost of debt. On the other hand, floating debt is more risky for a company, and one of the questions we discuss in this chapter is how to incorporate this effect into the DCF calculation.

In a similar vein, the company can decide whether to buy or issue any other kind of debt. For instance, an oil company could in theory issue bonds whose coupon and principal are linked to the price of oil.[2] This would partly hedge the company's profits in case of the oil price going down. An airline, which is normally exposed to the opposite risk (of oil prices rising), could then buy those bonds, as they would reduce the risk of rising oil prices.

In practice, structured debt issued by companies for hedging their liabilities is not common[3]. One of the main types of such debt is inflation-linked debt and it is discussed in Chapter 9.[4]

Chapters 10 and 11 are devoted to the issue of prehedging bond issuance.[5] The former, on "prehedging interest rate risk", describes the prehedging process from the perspective of a company that is planning to issue a bond in several months' time. The coupon of the bond will be partly linked to the swap rate at the time of issuance, and so prehedging interest rates can allow the company to manage this risk. The latter, "when to prehedge" is devoted to the question of when to manage this risk. We perform a statistical analysis of the good moments to prehedge the interest rate risk for bonds of various maturities and use that analysis to forecast moments when prehedging interest rate risk was more likely to reduce the issuance cost.

Chapter 12, "constrained maturity optimisation" explains how to manage interest rate risk in the presence of financial constraints. The situation described therein is based on a company whose year-to-year interest rate cost was restricted to rise by not more than 5% at a 95th percentile confidence interval.

Chapters 13 and 14, on "asset and liability management" and "pension fund ALM", introduce the risks from the asset side of the balance sheet. In Chapter 13, the assets are short-term financial assets that the company has received as a result of a sale of a business. In Chapter 14, we are talking about assets in company's pension fund. In both cases, the introduction of assets totally changes the picture, as these can offset the interest rate risk on the liability side (to the extent that the currency, size and maturities of assets are similar to the liabilities).

In conclusion, we find the subject of interest rate risk management to be a complex topic, and one that can have a huge impact on any company which has debt. We have chosen a variety of cases in this part of the book, to illustrate the most commonly discussed areas of interest rate risk management.

1 This would not be the case if we assumed lack of arbitrage, since then the fixed debt would be expected to cost the same as the floating debt, but it is possible if we base our analysis on the historical distribution.

2 This is assuming that there are investors who are interested in buying such a bond.

3 See Smithson and Chew (1992)

4 This topic is also discussed in Benaben (2005, pp. 227–46).

5 Use of the prefix "pre" is redundant, as clearly hedging has to happen before the risk affects the company. Nevertheless, use of the word "prehedging" is retained here, as it is accepted practice when it comes to bond issuance.

6

How to Develop an Interest Rate Hedging Policy

In this chapter we introduce several important qualitative aspects of an interest rate hedging policy. There are a large number of choices to be made in derivation of such a policy, and most companies formalise these choices in a risk management policy document. The purpose of such a document is to provide a balance between operational freedom and company oversight and control. The document has to specify the risk management parameters in sufficient detail that it protects the company against unauthorised use of derivatives, while not paralysing the treasury, who have to implement the policy often quickly and against volatile market conditions.

BACKGROUND

A European media company, Media Corporation, is seeking to grow through external acquisitions. The company's policy has historically been to grow organically but management has now decided to pursue a more aggressive expansion policy.

The change in policy will lead the company to issue more debt. The treasury department of Media Corporation is faced with an increased exposure to interest rate risk and therefore plans to put in place a state-of-the-art interest rate risk management framework.

Media Corporation needs our help in the development of their interest rate risk management procedures.

COMPANY OBJECTIVES

- To perform a peer group analysis.
- To determine the proper interest rate risk management procedure.

ANALYSIS

Methodology

The approach chosen follows the steps in Figure 6.1. In the rest of this chapter we focus on step 2: "best practice".

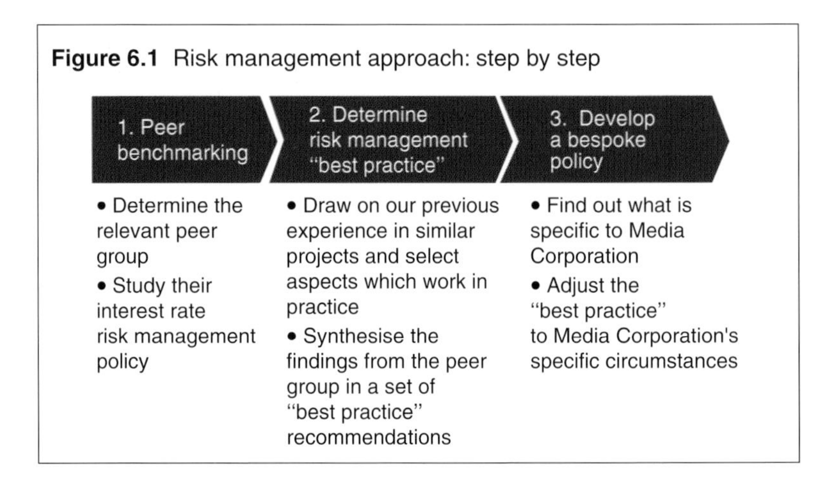

Figure 6.1 Risk management approach: step by step

Summary

We arrive at bespoke recommendations for Media Corporation via a synthesis of sector specific risk management practices ("sector case studies") and general principles of prudent risk management ("best practice"), applied to the specific circumstances of Media Corporation.

Sector case studies

We look at the European media sector and summarise the business and risk management information as published by some of Media Corporation's peers. The peers covered are chosen according to their similarity in size and availability of information. We also want the scope of peers to range from strongly domestically focused companies to geographically more diversified companies.

We classify the respective approach to risk management according to the following broad scheme.

- **Conservative approach:** this is characterised by a low level of risk appetite. One aim is to avoid possible losses due to market fluctuation through a total hedging of the exposure, while minimising the cost of such operations. The potential benefit from favourable market movements is not targeted. Another objective is to minimise the accounting variability as much as possible. Therefore, all hedges should aim to qualify for hedge accounting under international financial reporting standards (IFRS), as far as it is possible. Instruments used offer only a linear payout, ie, a forward or a swap. This approach was most common when the IFRS were first put in place, but is being increasingly replaced by the dynamic approach.

- **Aggressive approach:** this is characterised by a high level of risk appetite. The aim is to realise favourable market levels by actively trading positions. The treasury's objective is to produce profits from the trading activity. Limitation of the accounting variability is not an explicit objective, and therefore most positions entered into do not have to qualify for hedge accounting under IFRS. Instruments used can include leveraged structured strategies with unlimited downside to the corporation. This approach has very rarely been taken by corporations, especially since the introduction of IFRS.
- **Dynamic approach:** this is a compromise between the conservative and aggressive approaches that has an intermediate level of risk appetite. The objective is not to exclusively minimise the impact of unfavourable market movements, but to partly benefit from positive variable changes while minimising the overall risk and the cost of such strategies. This approach requires dynamic management focused on constant market trend monitoring, which allows the capture of market opportunities by partial repositioning of a hedging portfolio. Instruments used can include swaptions and collars. Most instruments satisfy hedge accounting, with a small and controlled proportion being kept in a marked-to-market (MTM) portfolio.

Before defining the entire approach, we define the primary objectives of risk management for Media Corporation, as follows:

(i) to reduce economic variability through hedging strategies to defend the corporate business plan, ie, reduce the impact of market movements on the economic model and key financial variables, financial ratios, financial targets (both internal and external) and covenants;

(ii) to minimise the costs of the hedging strategies, as long as this does not endanger the first objective;

(iii) to reduce the accounting variability introduced by the hedging programme according to the accounting methodologies indicated by the accounting standards (both local and international), as long as this does not endanger our first two objectives.

Risk management must be based on the best industry practices and prudent management of the compromise between the downside risks, the potential for upside rewards (eg, the possibility of participation in favourable market movements) and the expected payout on the overall portfolio basis.

Now that we have defined the objectives, the next step is to create the hedging portfolio, with a composition that would best satisfy the objectives. Our portfolio can be divided into three parts, as shown in Table 6.1.

PROCESSES AND ORGANISATION

Two important aspects of a risk management policy are the processes to be followed and the organisation that supports these processes. In most of this book, we follow a structured approach to risk management, and such an approach can be followed in risk management processes, from establishment of the risk management policy to its implementation, monitoring and periodic review. Whereas the basic principles are the same, details vary from one company to the next. In Figure 6.2, we show the organisation of the risk management function at Media Corporation and the roles and responsibilities each participant undertakes.

DERIVATIVES RISKS

The purpose of the use of derivatives is management of market risk; however, the use of derivatives exposes Media Corporation to the following additional risks.

- **Valuation risk:** the risk of changes in the level of derivative prices due to changes in interest rates, foreign exchange rates, commodity prices or other factors that relate to market volatility of the underlying rate.

- **Liquidity risk:** changes in the ability to sell or novate[1] the derivative. Derivatives bear the additional risk that a lack of market liquidity or willing counterparties may make it difficult to close out the derivative or enter into an offsetting contract.
- **Counterparty risk:** the risk that a counterparty will not settle an obligation for full value either when due or at any time thereafter.
- **Settlement risk:** the risk that one side of a transaction will be settled without value being received from the counterparty.

Figure 6.2 Risk management roles and responsibilities

Planning

Board of Directors

- Establishes risk philosophy
- Approves objectives and guidelines
- Reviews and approves changes to policy

CEO

- Approves significant deviation from limits
- Delegates execution to CFO
- Receives periodic reporting on execution

Risk Management Committee

- Defines guidelines for hedging strategy
- Recommends risk limits
- Reviews RM reports
- Suggests changes to policy

CFO

- Responsible for RM committee
- Oversees implementation
- Informs CEO and board about RM

Implementation

Financial Director

- Responsible for implementation
- Responsible for financial planning
- Supports the CFO in presenting RM policy
- Reviews implementation

Treasury

- Responsible for quantification of exposures
- Performs execution
- Measures risk
- Prepares documentation and confirmations

Accounting

- Verifies accounting provided by treasury
- Reconciles accounting flows with cashflows

Internal audit

- Responsible for ensuring policies and procedures are being implemented

Table 6.1 Composition of the hedging portfolio

Part of portfolio	Description	Accounting treatment	Guidance on use
Hedge accounting portfolio	**Derivatives that qualify for hedge accounting** in accordance with IFRS. These positions allow Media Corporation to reduce the economic variability of its financial results due to market movements without increasing the accounting variability. In some circumstances, IFRS allows offsetting of the variability of the hedging instrument against the variability of the underlying ("hedge accounting"), thereby reducing the accounting variability. This is the case in limited conditions when the exposure being hedged can be clearly identified, and the hedging instruments are very simple. The objective of risk management is to maximise the hedge accounting portfolio. However, this policy recognises that it is not always possible to reconcile the economic hedging requirements with the hedge accounting ones. In those cases, economic requirements take precedence, and positions are taken that do not satisfy hedge accounting.	The income statement is not affected by market volatility except for the ineffective part of the hedges.	Target a large proportion of the portfolio.

WAYS OF MITIGATION

To mitigate these risks, derivatives used by Media Corporation must have the following characteristics:

- easy to price and measure;
- easy to unwind;
- liquid in the sizes needed;
- have an acceptable worst-case scenario.

Table 6.1 Continued

Part of portfolio	Description	Accounting treatment	Guidance on use
Dynamic hedging portfolio	**Derivatives that do not qualify for hedge accounting** in accordance with IFRS. Therefore, the impact of fair value changes in the value of derivatives is recognised in the income statement. These positions encompass a wider variety of hedging strategies and deliver a higher level of flexibility in managing risks. Risk exposure is minimised by a prudent choice of instruments in the portfolio. These positions are only entered into when the economic goals cannot be achieved through the hedge accounting instruments.	Income statement is affected by market volatility.	Use only when it is not possible to achieve the same economic goals with the hedge accounting portfolio.
Un-hedged portfolio	**Part of the portfolio that is exposed to the market volatility.** Normally positions are left unhedged only when required by market illiquidity, prohibitively high cost of hedging, or specific market considerations.	Income statement affected by market volatility.	Use only when required by illiquidity, prohibitively high hedging cost, or specific market considerations.

Media Corporation must clearly state to all stakeholders that the objective of risk management is to provide a prudent management of the market risk and therefore the use of derivatives is intended to add the level of flexibility in risk management and not as an endorsement of trading activity. For all derivatives, the following limits must be in place:

- limits on authorised instruments (eg, swaps, forwards and at-the-money options);
- instrument exposure limits (notional, maturity, etc);
- limits on financial counterparties[2] (credit rating, CDS, concentration);

- timing limits (on how long the exposure can be left unhedged, etc);
- aggregate portfolio limits (sensitivity to market moves, value-at-risk, cashflows-at-risk).

As an example, we show here the limits which Media Corporation adopted.

1. Exposure limits by type:
   (a) hedge accounting, 50–70%;
   (b) dynamic hedging, 20–25%;
   (c) unhedged, 5–30%.
2. Delegated authority for interest rate hedging by notional:
   (a) Treasurer, up to EUR 100 million;
   (b) Financial director, up to EUR 250 million;
   (c) CFO, up to EUR 500 million;
   (d) CEO, above EUR 500 million.
3. Hedge timing:
   (a) hedge accounting to be implemented within three months of the decision;
   (b) dynamic hedging to be implemented within one month of the decision.

In addition, Media Corporation specified limits on the counterparty risk, which we shall review in Part IV.

Limits on dynamic hedging

As dynamic hedging transactions introduce additional variability on the income statement due to the absence of hedge accounting treatment, there are additional limits on these transactions. The maximum accounting loss is defined in any given period as a given percentage (base case = 5%) of the earnings at risk at 95% confidence interval. Maximum accounting loss expresses the potential negative impact of the dynamic hedging portfolio on the income statement in a 95% worst case scenario of market moves. Maximum accounting loss is checked periodically by comparing the VaR of the dynamic hedging portfolio against maximum loss.

In case of a material breach of policy, processes must be put in place to escalate the incident up the reporting chain, investigate the reasons for the breach and agree remedial action.

PERFORMANCE MEASURES

The company will periodically assess and report the results of the interest rate risk hedging programme:

- evolution of interest risk exposure according to budget and business plan scenarios;
- assessment of the effectiveness of the risk management strategy compared with the benchmark rates;
- compliance with the covenants of the financial model and/or any internal financial targets;
- accounting volatility introduced by the dynamic hedging portfolio;
- sensitivity analysis of the market movements.

The quantitative measure of performance is reflected in the P&L, which results principally from the activity of the market risk exposure. The main indicators are:

- the net exposure to market risk and percentage of hedging by portfolio type;
- the gross and net hedging costs of interest rate risk exposure;
- the effectiveness of the interest rate risk management strategy compared with the benchmark interest rates;
- the net cashflows;
- compliance with financial covenants and any internal financial targets;
- the performance measurement and the definition of specific benchmarks, which are one of the tasks of the risk management committee.

BENCHMARKING

Companies define the benchmark interest rate in many ways.

- **Forecast rate:** from one institution, a consensus rate or some other combination.
- **Forward rate:** the implied future rate from the swap curve.
- **Blended rate:** a combination of short-term (spot) rate and the long-term (swap) rate weighted according to the target fixed–floating mix.
- **External benchmark:** comparison against an external benchmark, eg, peer group.

Each approach has a downside. Forecast rates are notoriously unreliable, while forward rates tend to overestimate the evolution of short-term rates. This makes the blended rate unreliable. In any case, when benchmarking a company's risk management strategy against alternatives, it is important to do so in a risk-adjusted way, ie, how well Media Corporation could perform with another strategy, but with the same amount of risk. There is no point in comparing the rate against a better one that is realised with a much more aggressive risk management strategy.

OPTIMUM FIXED–FLOATING MIX

When defining the fixed–floating mix it is necessary to define precisely the part of the overall debt to which the required proportion applies. In the case of Media Corporation, it includes bank debt, bond issues and financial leases minus the surplus projected cash.

We compared the fixed–floating mix for the peer group of Media Corporation. We noted that the higher leverage generally leads to a lower proportion of floating debt. In addition, a smaller amount of total debt seems to imply a higher proportion of floating debt, irrespective of EBITDA.

A possible allocation consistent with peer group data corresponds to 35% floating and 65% fixed. Expected deleveraging in the future (due to high EBITDA growth and more conservative financial policy) may expose Media Corporation to significant interest rate risk on the fixed portion. Therefore, the fixed–floating mix may need to be rebalanced in the future.

However, we stressed to the company that, in general, the fixed–floating mix is an oversimplification of company position for several reasons:

- it ignores duration (is a one-year fixed-coupon bond really fixed?);
- it ignores currency composition (how much you should fix depends on the currency);
- it ignores other derivative strategies (caps, collars, etc).

Our conclusion is that the peer comparison should be used only as an indication, and the optimal fixed–floating mix should be reached through other means. Moreover, there is a wide spread of fixed–floating mix among the peers, as there are other aspects which affect it. For instance, all of the following reasons would imply a higher fixed proportion:

- the company's perceived financial risk (higher than usual);
- interest rates and shape of the yield curve (flat and low-yield curve);
- the company's rate expectations (interest rate rise expected);
- cyclicality of the company's earnings (less cyclical industries).

Figure 6.3 Towards the optimal liability structure: step by step

1. Optimal fixed–floating mix	2. Optimal duration	3. Optimal maturity
• A good starting point for determining the debt composition • An easy way to benchmark against peer group • Allows us to quickly compare the cashflows at risk (high for floating) and fair value-at-risk (high for fixed) • Significant limitations	• Used by some peers as a more precise indicator of interest rate risk • Allows us to overcome an arbitrary distinction between fixed and floating • A natural estimate of sensitivity to interest rate risk	• Much closer to the way financial institutions manage risk, but also more complex • Requires a good view of the yield curve environment • Used only by the most sophisticated industrial companies with billions of EUR in debt

As part of its interest rate policy, Media Corporation should select a fixed–floating policy. If Media Corporation were to be around 35%

floating (in line with its peers), that would put it in a similar situation to other similar companies. However, due to expected deleveraging over the next couple of years, Media Corporation is exposed to a potential fair-value risk (ie, potential cost of unwinding the fixed part of debt). On the other hand, floating part of the debt exposes Media Corporation to cashflow risk. It is possible to quantify and compare these two risks and help to determine the mix which is best overall. In any case, determining the optimal fixed–floating mix is just a first step towards defining the optimal liability structure (Figure 6.3). For more details, see other chapters in Part II.

RECOMMENDATIONS

After performing the peer group comparison and analysing the best practices in risk management and how they apply to Media Corporation, we came up with the following recommendations:

- a dynamic hedging approach should be adopted;
- the fixed–floating mix of debt should be further studied in order to determine the appropriate policy for Media Corporation's risk appetite;
- as an initial guess, a floating proportion of debt should be targeted around 35%, to be increased in line with the planned deleveraging.

CONCLUSION

In this chapter, we reviewed main qualitative aspects of the interest rate risk management policy. It is important to stress that all companies have a slightly different set of priorities when it comes to managing risk, and that therefore what we have shown in this case is just a sample of one such study. At the end of the chapter we briefly touched upon the subject of the optimal fixed–floating mix and duration, which are discussed in more detail in Chapter 7.

1 Novation is a process by which a company "A" exits a derivative position with Bank "B" by finding another counterparty, normally a Bank "C", that will take A's position with B. In order for novation to happen, a payment may be needed between A, B and C.

2 See Chapter 21.

7

How to Improve Your Fixed–Floating Mix and Duration

In Chapter 4, we discussed how to determine the optimal duration of debt. Once the debt is in place, the company in question still has the freedom to adjust the debt structure via interest rate derivatives. For instance, the company can decide to swap all the bonds into floating, or all the loans into fixed coupons. More often than not, the company will swap part of the debt of a given maturity and currency into floating.

There are two separate but closely linked issues here: how much debt should be fixed and floating, and the duration of the interest rate fixing period. We shall analyse both questions in turn in the case that follows.

BACKGROUND

JSCOM is an EUR-based investment-grade telecom operator. It has issued a significant amount of long-term debt, and has kept 80% of it in fixed rates to avoid the earnings volatility. JSCOM has been using the low interest rate environment to review its high fixed policy, and has requested our help.

This chapter is the first of two case studies dealing with JSCOM's duration analysis. Here we focus on the improved duration profile and the expected interest cost savings, while in Chapter 8 we shall assess the impact this duration change may have on the valuation of JSCOM.

COMPANY OBJECTIVES

- To create a framework for assessing the optimal duration for JSCOM debt after derivatives from the perspective of risk versus reward.

- To improve the duration and fixed–floating mix of JSCOM's debt portfolio, based on this framework.

ANALYSIS

We perform a historical analysis of the cost of fixing, and apply it to the case of JSCOM. The main assumption here is that the future dynamic of interest rates will not be fundamentally different from the past. This is the key limitation of this analysis and, to the extent that it is violated, our findings will become invalid. However, certain aspects of the interest rate dynamic (eg, predominance of the upwards-sloping yield curve) seem to be remarkably stable and largely independent of the currency or period of time observed.

The approach follows the four steps in Figure 7.1.

Figure 7.1 Duration optimisation approach: step by step

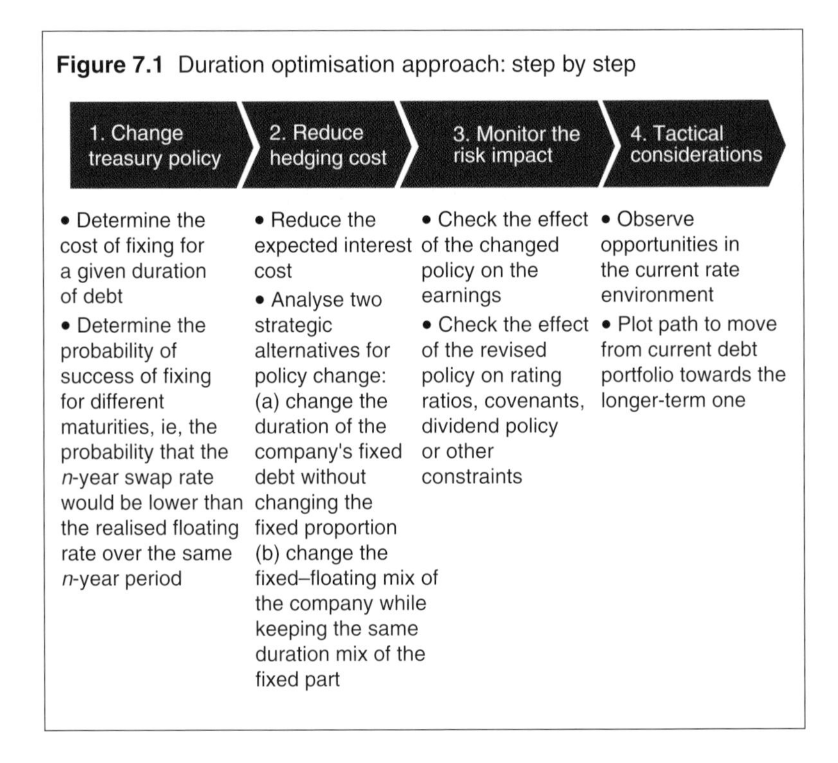

STEP 1: CHANGE TREASURY POLICY

Table 7.1 shows JSCOM's portfolio; all bonds are denominated in EUR and paid annually.

Table 7.1 JSCOM bonds

Notional (EUR million)	Maturity (y)	Coupon (%)
400	5	4.0
500	8	5.0
1,000	11	5.5
300	15	5.8

In addition, JSCOM has the bank loans shown in Table 7.2 in place. All loans are floating, paying a quarterly coupon of three-month Euribor plus spread. Finally, JSCOM has entered into the pay fixed/receive floating swap contracts shown in Table 7.3. JSCOM's duration profile is shown in Figure 7.2. Including bonds, loans and swaps, JSCOM's fixed proportion is 80% and the average duration of fixing is 7.5 years.

Table 7.2 JSCOM loans

Notional (EUR million)	Maturity (y)	Spread over Euribor (%)
200	5	0.22
200	6	0.50
400	7	0.70

Table 7.3 JSCOM swap contracts

Notional (EUR million)	Maturity (y)	Fixed leg (%)	Frequency
100	5	4.2	Quarterly
100	6	4.9	Quarterly

The cost of fixing

Our first step was to try to understand better the cost of hedging. We did this by comparing, for every seven-year period, the seven-year swap rate set at the start of the period as opposed to what the company would have paid had it decided to leave the debt floating

Figure 7.2 Duration profile of the portfolio

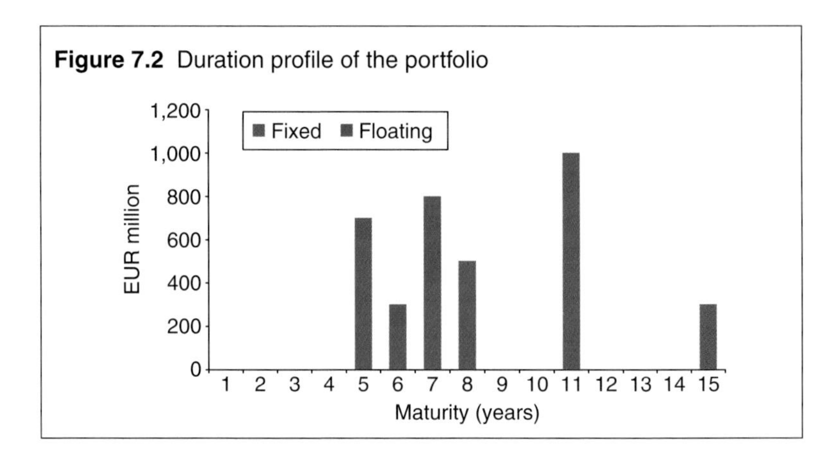

over this period. The results are shown in Figure 7.3. For the seven-year periods starting from 1989 to 2002, it would have been better to be floating than fixed for seven years in EUR in 96% of the cases (the remaining 4% are before 1990).[1] In Figure 7.3, the blue line is the seven-year swap rate and the purple line is the average Euribor during the same seven years, computed at the end of the period. We define the difference between the two as the "swap premium". It is important to note that we can only determine the swap premium at the end of the period.

Figure 7.3 Swap premium for seven years in EUR

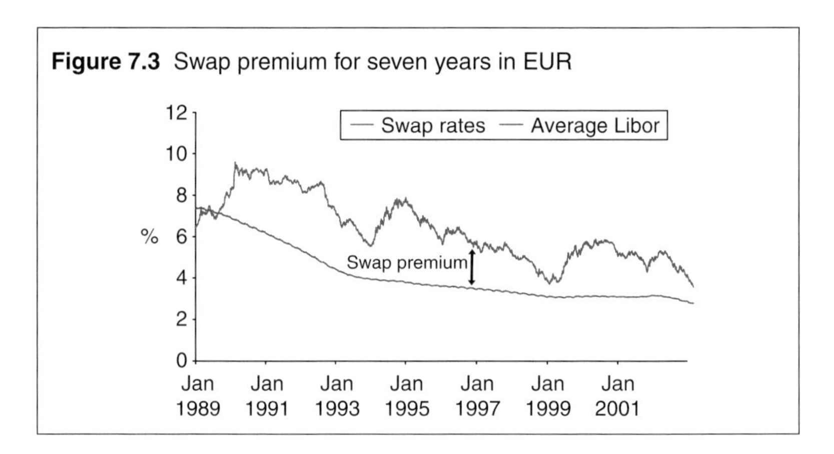

We then compared our results with a common method for estimating the swap premium via the yield curve steepness. When deciding on whether to fix the rates, corporations often consider the "cost of carry" (ie, the difference between the swap and the Libor rate) to be indicative of the hedging cost. Therefore, there is an implicit assumption that it is cheaper to fix rates when the curve is flat. Instead of the single Euribor rate, we use the average actual realised Euribor rate and obtain quite different results.

Figure 7.4 Correlation (=1%) between seven-year carry and seven-year swap premium in EUR (%)

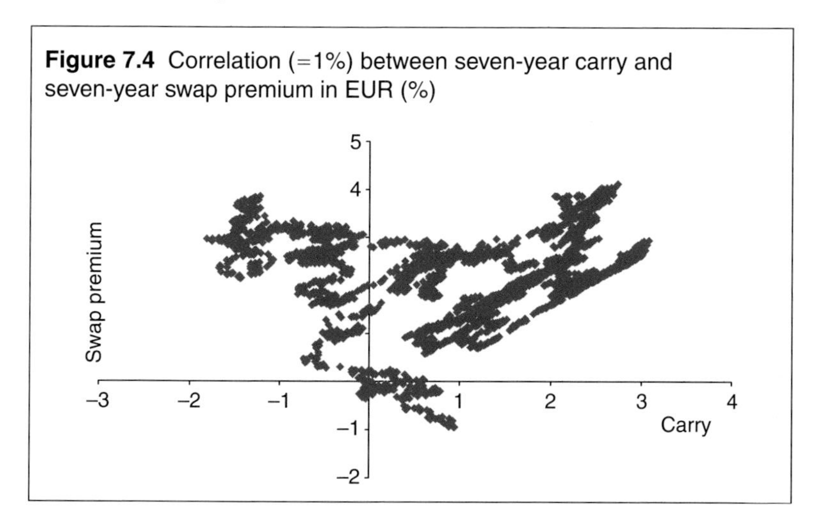

From Figure 7.4, it is evident that we cannot use carry to determine the actual cost of hedging, since the correlation between the two is extremely low (less than 1%).

What are the possible ways to reduce the hedging costs?

Reducing the fixed proportion

We calculate the seven-year swap premium for every day over the period from 1989 to 2002. The distribution of these swap premiums is shown in Figure 7.5.

As can be seen from Figures 7.3 and 7.5, distribution of the swap premiums is sharply skewed to the positive. In fact, as mentioned before, the swap premium is negative (ie, the swap saves money) only in about 4% of the cases. The average seven-year swap premium is 2.22%.

The swap premium can also be used to estimate the historical average saving from changing the fixed proportion, since, for a given maturity, the swap premium is proportional to the amount of fixed debt. For example, by moving from having 80% of its debt fixed to 20% fixed over seven years, JSCOM could save on average 1.34% per year

$$2.22\% \times (80\% - 20\%) = (1.78\% - 0.44\%)$$

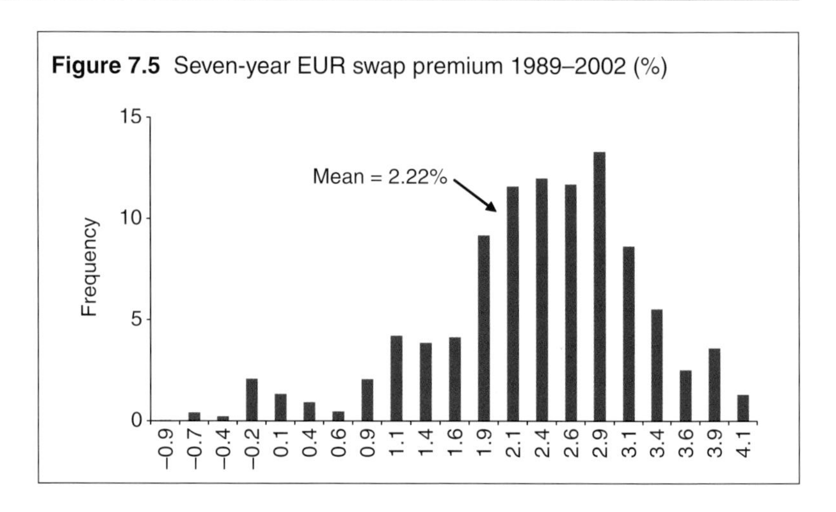

Figure 7.5 Seven-year EUR swap premium 1989–2002 (%)

Table 7.4 Seven-year EUR swap premium for different fixed proportions

Fixed proportion (%)	Average cost of hedging (%)
100	2.22
80	1.78
60	1.33
40	0.89
20	0.44
0	0.00

as shown in Table 7.4.

Reducing the duration

Next, we analyse the swap premium for different tenors. The swap premium is found to increase with the duration of the fixed part, as shown in Figure 7.6. We do not calculate the swap premium for duration longer than 10 years, due to lack of data. This is because the latest swap premium that can be calculated for a 20-year swap, for example, would at the time of writing in 2012 be for a swap that started in 1992, which would not leave us enough recent statistical data to obtain a distribution of swap premiums. In the following, we make the conservative assumption that swap premiums for durations longer than 10 years are the same as for the 10-year swap premium.[2]

Figure 7.6 EUR historical swap premiums for different durations (from 1989 to 2009)

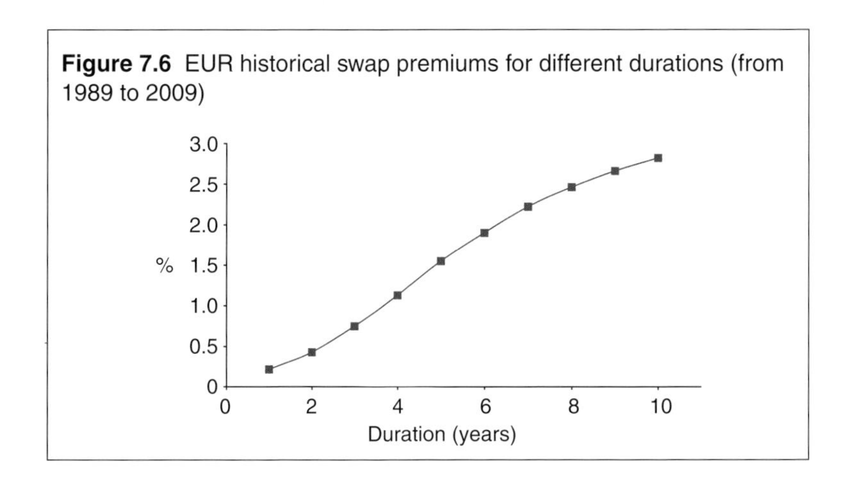

Table 7.5 EUR historical swap premiums for different durations (from 1989 to 2009)

Duration (y)	Swap premium (%)
1	0.22
2	0.43
3	0.75
4	1.13
5	1.55
6	1.90
7	2.22
8	2.46
9	2.66
10+	2.82

Table 7.5 is useful, as it allows us to evaluate the impact on the company over the observation period if it changed the duration of its fixed rate. For example, using the swap premiums from Table 7.5, we observe that moving from a seven-year duration to a two-year duration would save JSCOM on average 1.79% = 2.22% – 0.43% per year.

Increasing the probability of saving

Finally, we looked at the percentage of time that fixing the rates was successful, ie, that the swap premium was negative. The results are given in Figure 7.7 and Table 7.6.

Figure 7.7 Percentage of time when fixing EUR rates saved money (1989 to present)

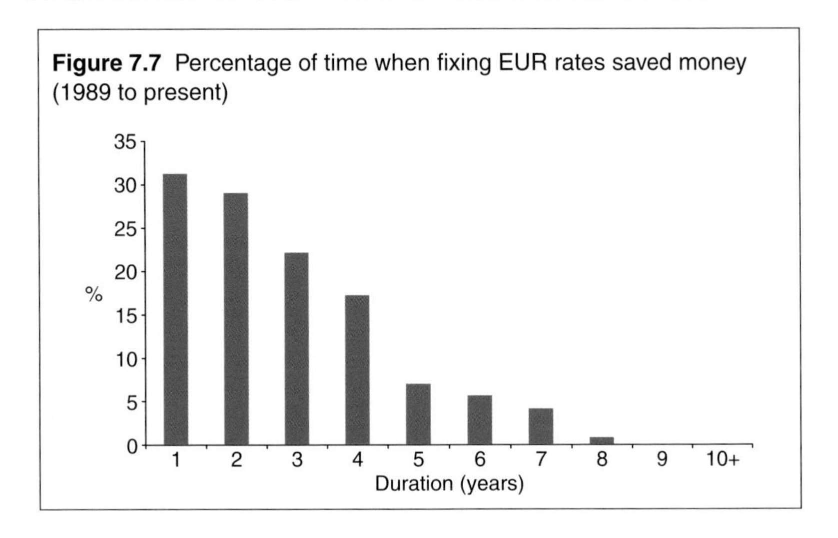

Table 7.6 Percentage of time when fixing EUR rates saved money (1989 to present)

Duration (y)	Amount of time (%)
1	31.2
2	29.0
3	22.1
4	17.2
5	7.0
6	5.6
7	4.1
8	0.8
9	0.0
10+	0.0
Sum	117.0

As expected, we can see that the chances of success for shorter duration are higher than to fix rates for longer duration. This can be explained by the lower swap premium for the lower duration, which means that rates do not have to move that much to make fixing successful. Furthermore, it is easier to forecast floating rates for a short period of time, and therefore short swap rates are a more accurate descriptor of expected interest rate moves than the long swap rates. Note that the total, at 117%, is greater than 100% due to the overlaps. For example, there are many dates when it makes sense to fix for one year and for two years at the same time.

STEP 2: REDUCE HEDGING COST

Simplified strategy

As we just illustrated, there is a better chance for the rate fixing to save money if the rates are fixed for a lower duration. However, it is impossible to guess in advance the conditions under which fixing rates for any particular duration would be successful. The other possible course of action is to fix each year for duration N, a sum proportional to the probability of success of fixing for N years (Figure 7.8). This approximation is obviously not equivalent to finding the optimal fixing time, but allows us to bias fixing in favour of the tenors where there is a higher probability of saving rather than tenors where there is little or no probability of saving. In the text that follows, we shall analyse how well the simplified strategy has performed in the past.

Figure 7.8 Simplified strategy

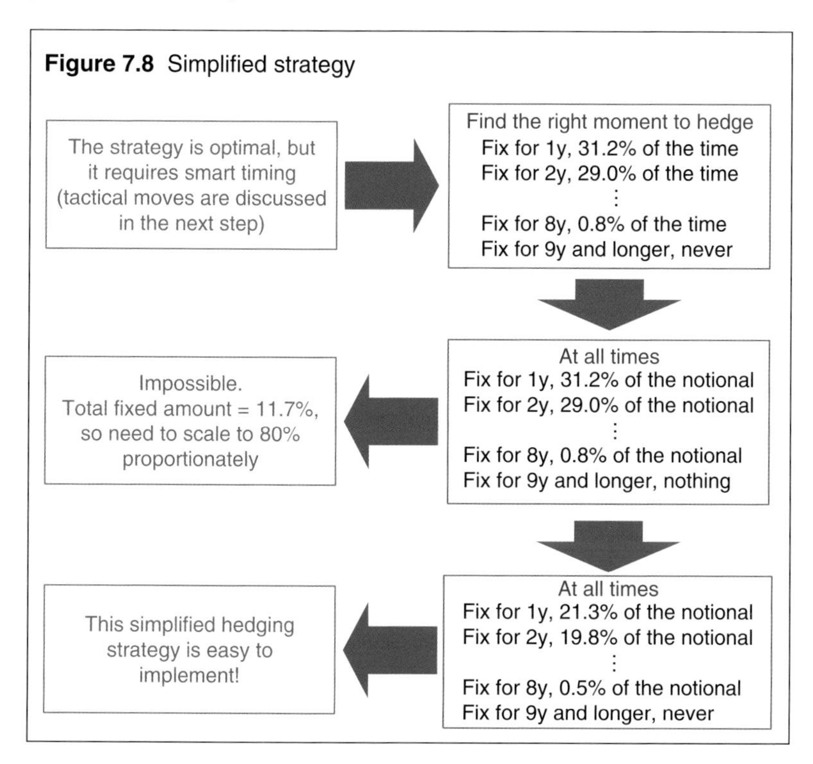

Impact on JSCOM – option (a): reduced duration strategy

We show below the effect of implementing the above strategy on JSCOM's debt. We do this by calculating the weighted swap premium that JSCOM would pay under the strategy above, as opposed to the weighted swap premium under JSCOM's current strategy. We calculate the weighted swap premium for the strategy as the average of all the swap premiums, weighted by the percentage of debt fixed for a given duration. For example, if the company has fixed 16.7% of their debt for five years, and the swap premium for five years is 1.55%, then the premium that they will pay for this part of their debt is 16.7% × 1.55% = 0.26%. We define the swap premium of the strategy as the sum of all the contributions from the different durations, and present the results in Table 7.7.

The reduced duration strategy (Figure 7.9 and Table 7.7) is defined as the strategy with the same fixed proportion as the original JSCOM strategy, but with weighting for each duration proportional to the probability of success of fixing the rates for that duration.

The allocations to the different durations in the reduced duration strategy are calculated by making sure that the total fixed amount is still 80% (original fixed proportion of JSCOM), but the duration mix is proportional to the probability of success of the different durations. For example, since the probability of success for fixing rates for one year is 31.2% (see above), and the sum of all probabilities is 117%, the allocation to the one-year duration is 31.2% × 80%/117% = 21.3%.

Figure 7.9 Current versus reduced duration strategy

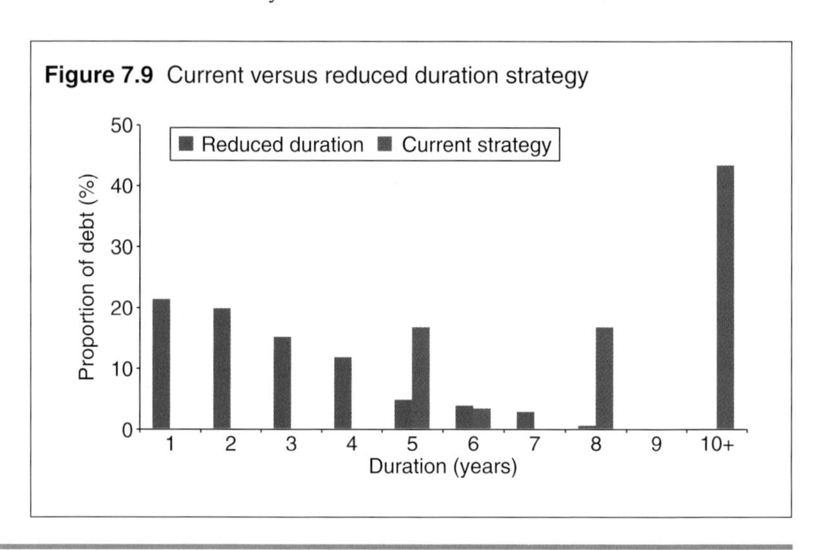

If we implement this strategy, we can reduce JSCOM's duration from 7.5 years to 2.2 years without reducing the fixed proportion, as shown in Figure 7.9.

Table 7.7 Reduced duration strategy

Duration (y)	A (%)	B (%)	C (%)	D (%)	E (%)
1	0.22	0.0	0.00	21.3	0.05
2	0.43	0.0	0.00	19.8	0.09
3	0.75	0.0	0.00	15.1	0.11
4	1.13	0.0	0.00	11.8	0.13
5	**1.55**	**16.7**	**0.26**	**4.8**	**0.07**
6	1.90	3.3	0.06	3.8	0.07
7	2.22	0.0	0.00	2.8	0.06
8	2.46	16.7	0.41	0.5	0.01
9	2.66	0.0	0.00	0.0	0.00
10+	2.82	43.3	1.22	0.0	0.00
Sum		80.0	1.95	80.0	0.60

Note: A, swap premium; B, current portfolio; C (= A × B), premium for current portfolio; D, reduced duration portfolio; E (= A × D), premium for reduced duration portfolio.

If previous swap premiums are an accurate estimator of the future, then this strategy would, on average over time, lead to an interest cost saving of 1.95% – 0.60% = 1.35% per year.

Impact on JSCOM – option(b): reduced fixed proportion strategy

Reducing the duration while keeping the overall fixed proportion the same is one option, but JSCOM can get similar a saving by reducing the overall fixed proportion from 80% to 24% while leaving the duration profile the same. This is presented in Figure 7.10 and Table 7.8.

In this case, the duration of the portfolio will be reduced from 7.5 years to 2.3 years, and the saving would again be 1.35%

STEP 3: MONITOR THE RISK IMPACT

So far, we have shown that reducing JSCOM's weighted debt duration saves it money. The downside is that this would also increase

Figure 7.10 Current versus reduced fixed strategy

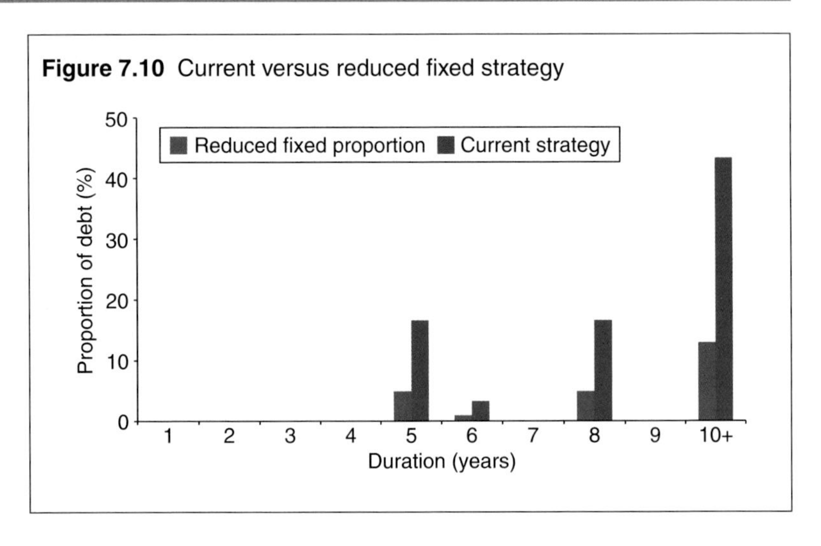

Table 7.8 Reduced fixed proportion strategy

Duration (y)	A (%)	B (%)	C (%)	D (%)	E (%)
1	0.22	0.0	0.00	0.0	0.00
2	0.43	0.0	0.00	0.0	0.00
3	0.75	0.0	0.00	0.0	0.00
4	1.13	0.0	0.00	0.0	0.00
5	**1.55**	**16.7**	**0.26**	**5.0**	**0.08**
6	1.90	3.3	0.06	1.0	0.02
7	2.22	0.0	0.00	0.0	0.00
8	2.46	16.7	0.41	5.0	0.12
9	2.66	0.0	0.00	0.0	0.00
10+*	2.82	43.3	1.22	13.0	0.37
Sum		80.0	1.95	24.0	0.60

Note: A, swap premium; B, current portfolio; C (= A × B), premium for current portfolio; D, reduced fixed portfolio; E (= A × D), premium for reduced fixed portfolio.

the interest cost risk, since a lower fixed proportion or lower duration would leave a larger part of JSCOM's debt floating. We shall now quantify this risk by back-testing.

Back-testing

We start our risk analysis of by comparing the historical long-term performance of the current strategy and the two improved options (reduced duration and reduced fixed proportion) above. In order to do this, we compare the suggested strategies over 10-year periods, starting every day from 1989 to 1999.[3] For each period, we assume that the company enters into the tested strategy on the first day, and refinances any maturing swap until the end of the period. We then calculate the average interest rate for the period, and compare it to the similar interest rate paid using the current strategy.

The distribution of the differences is shown for both of our strategies in Figure 7.11 and Table 7.9, which show the saving by moving to the reduced duration strategy.

Figure 7.11 Distribution of savings for option (a) (reduced duration) versus JSCOM's current strategy (%)

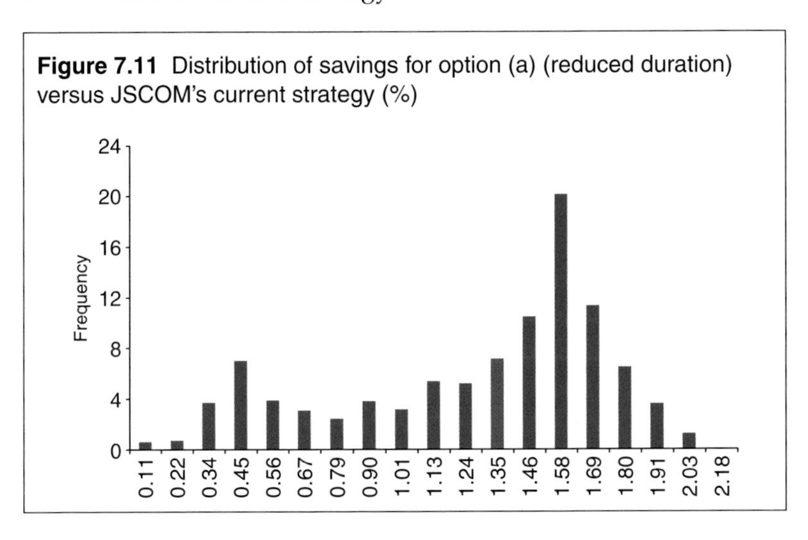

Table 7.9 Distribution of savings for option (a) (reduced duration) versus JSCOM's current strategy

Percentile (%)	IC* difference (%)
5	0.45
10	0.52
25	1.00
Average	1.33
75	1.68
90	1.82
95	1.91

Note: * IC, interest cost.

For example, in Figure 7.11 we notice that the average saving of option (a) over the current strategy was 1.33%, which is consistent with what we showed earlier.[4] There is a 5% probability that the saving was less than 0.45% and 95% probability that the saving was less than 1.91%.

Similarly, in Figure 7.12 and Table 7.10 we show the savings for option (b): reduced fixed proportion strategy.

Figure 7.12 Distribution of savings for option (b) (reduced fixed proportion) versus JSCOM's current strategy (%)

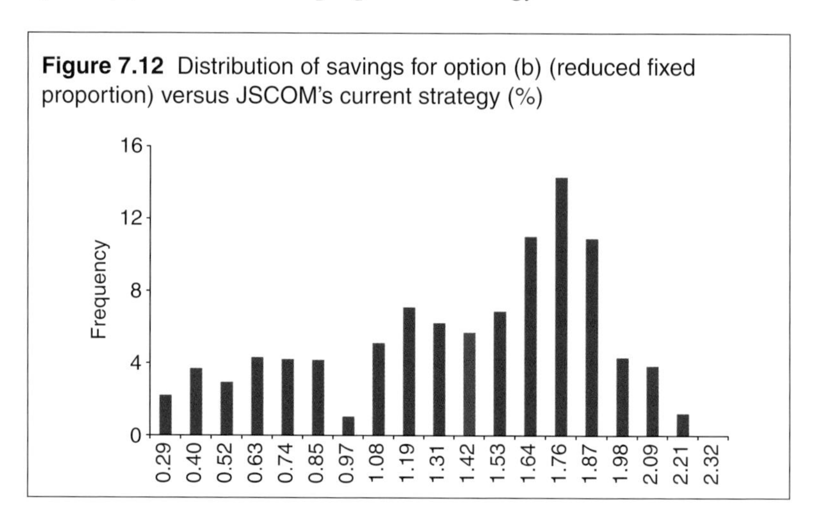

Table 7.10 Distribution of savings for option (b) (reduced fixed proportion) versus JSCOM's current strategy

Percentile (%)	IC difference (%)
5	0.48
10	0.66
25	1.16
Average	1.44
75	1.84
90	1.97
95	2.10

As can be seen, there were no 10-year periods over the last 20 years when the proposed strategies (options (a) and (b)) did worse than the current strategy.

Impact on JSCOM's earnings

In Figure 7.13 we show JSCOM's EBITDA since 2000 Q2. In addition, we show the interest cost it would have incurred from a 100% floating

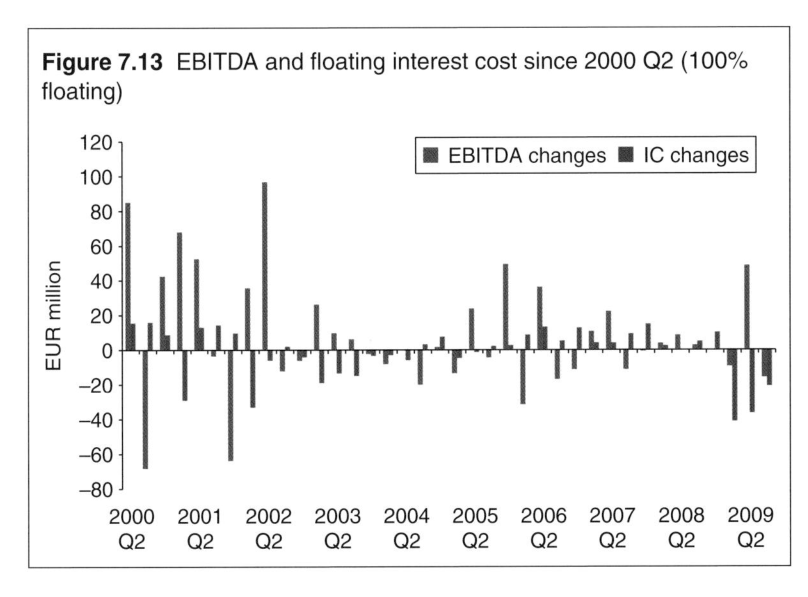

Figure 7.13 EBITDA and floating interest cost since 2000 Q2 (100% floating)

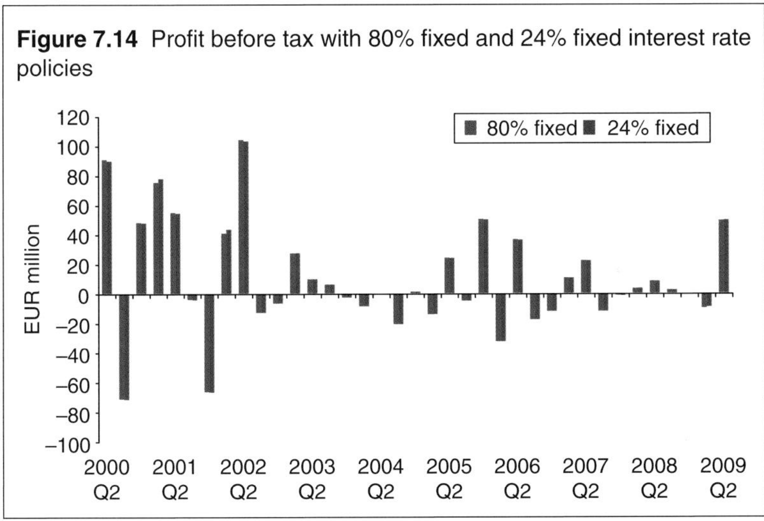

Figure 7.14 Profit before tax with 80% fixed and 24% fixed interest rate policies

interest rate policy, assuming the actual amount of debt JSCOM had at the time of writing and the actual floating rates over the period. We calculated the interest cost using the Euribor at the beginning of the quarter and added an average spread (CDS plus basis spread) of 0.60% for all years.

We note that the annual volatility of EBITDA is 69%, which is much higher than the annual volatility of the interest cost at 30%. This shows that the volatility of earnings is dominated by the EBITDA changes, and the effect of interest rate volatility should not cause significant changes. This is quite intuitive, since for most investment-grade companies the primary cause of risk is the business risk, not the interest rate risk.

To quantify the change in volatility, we must find a company metric which includes the impact of interest cost. To that effect, we shall consider the profit before tax (PBT) of JSCOM (Figure 7.14). Volatility of PBT assuming an 80% fixed proportion is 73.6% per year, while the volatility in the 24% fixed (option (b)) is 73.7%, a minimal increase in volatility! This means that an investor would in all likelihood not notice extra volatility to JSCOM's profits from a lower fixed debt proportion.

STEP 4: TACTICAL CONSIDERATIONS

Finally we examine the current market conditions and discuss how JSCOM can take advantage of the low interest rate regimes at the time of writing to implement the optimal fixed floating policy.

- We start by determining the value of timing, ie, how important is it to find the right time to change from fixed to floating. We estimate this effect by computing how much could theoretically be saved if the company knew exactly when to fix and when to float.
- We analyse previous periods when the rates were near the local minimum. In these periods, it was beneficial to fix rates for shorter periods of time (eg, for two years or similar maturities). However, fixing rates for longer periods of time (eg, for five years or similar) usually yielded much smaller savings.

The value of perfect timing

We show below a highly optimised tactical solution which would have been impossible to implement in practice. If at any point in time JSCOM knew all the future interest rates, this solution would have given a saving of 0.86% per year over the floating rate since January 3, 1989. Our solution is defined by the following algorithm (see Figure 7.15 for a schematic presentation).

1. **Start:** start at January 3, 1989 (the starting point for most our data).

Figure 7.15 Perfect hindsight solution: algorithm

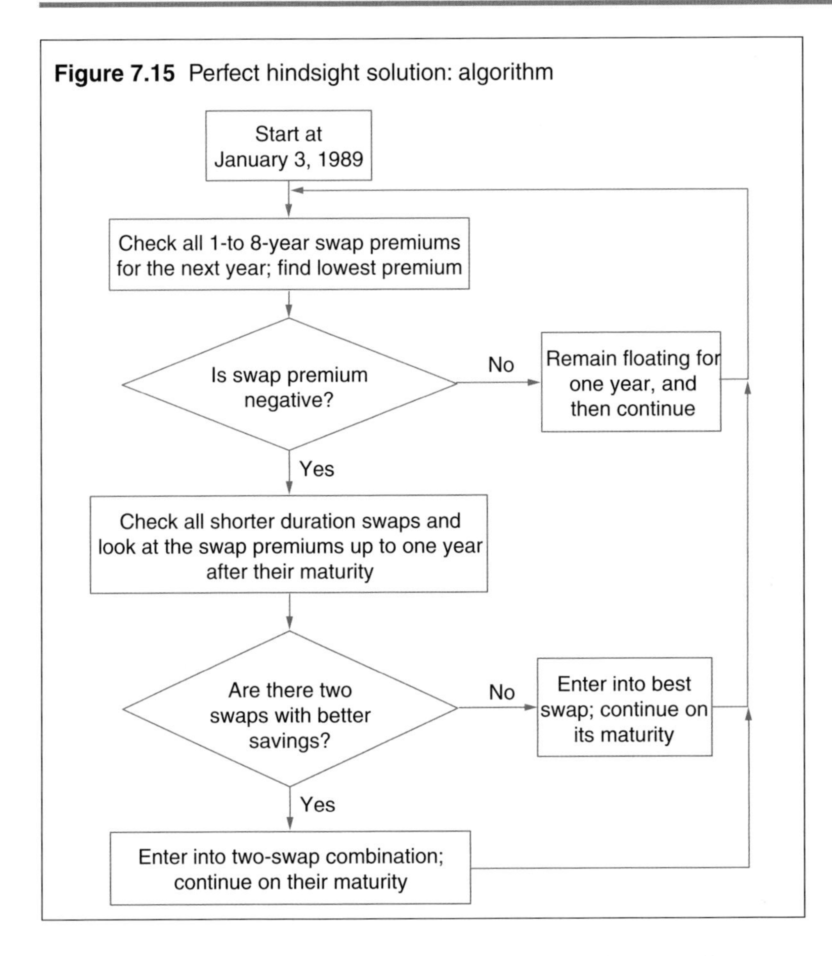

2. **Decide whether to fix and for how long:** observe all 1- to 8-year swap premiums for swaps starting every day of the next year. Find the date and swap tenor with the highest overall saving (equal to the tenor multiplied by the swap premium) within the next year. If none is found, remain floating for one year and repeat the check.
3. **Improve the duration:** try to find a set of shorter swaps which have a total similar maturity (within one year) to the highest saving swap from the previous step but with a combined better saving. If one is found, replace the swap from stage 2 with this set.
4. **Repeat:** when the swaps mature, repeat the algorithm in stages 2 and 3 until the present date.

Obviously, this solution is impossible to implement in practice since no one can predict the future Euribor or swap rates. However, we can use this theoretical concept to illustrate the value of perfect timing. The results of the algorithm, showing the perfect hindsight solution are shown in Figure 7.16 and Table 7.11.

Figure 7.16 Perfect hindsight solution

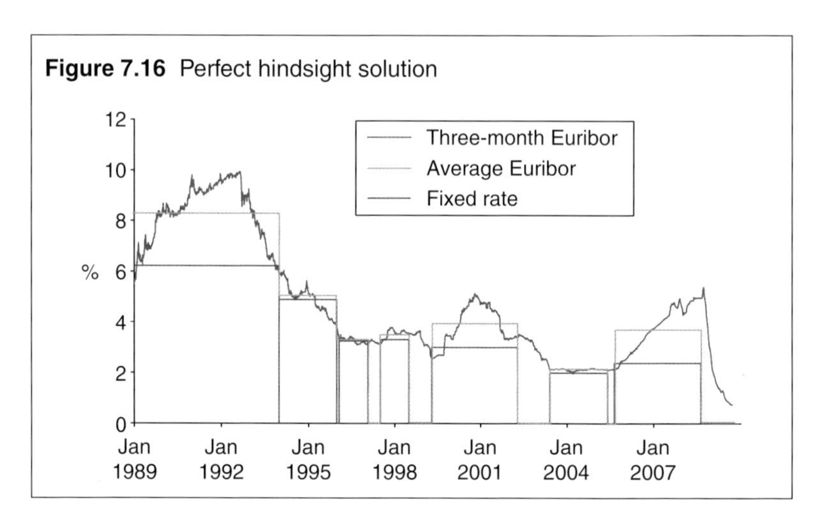

The average fixed proportion is 82%, and the average duration is 2.5 years. Even though the perfect hindsight solution is not possible to implement in practice, it is shown to illustrate the power of good timing, ie, fixing at low rates for JSCOM in Figure 7.17.

Figure 7.17 Interest cost premium over floating

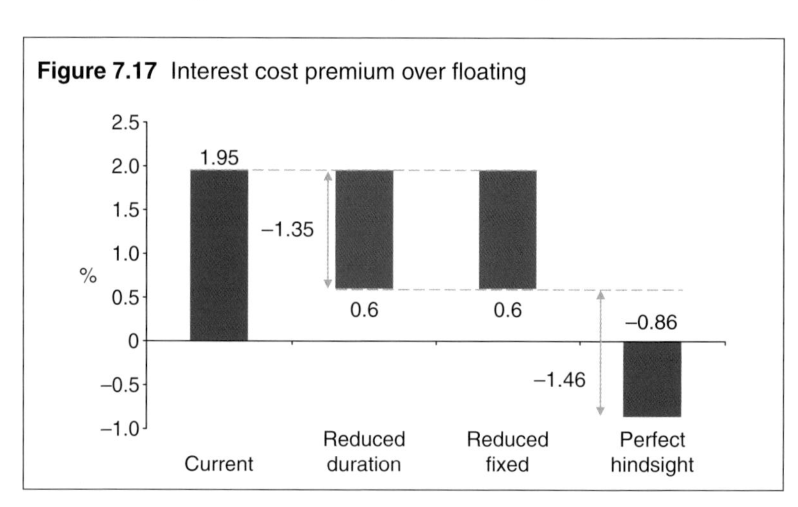

Table 7.11 Perfect hindsight solution

	Perfect hindsight solution		
Date	**Fixing tenor (y)**	**Rate (%)**	**Savings (%)**
03/01/1989	5	6.22	2.09
03/01/1994	2	4.89	0.17
01/02/1996	1	3.25	0.03
09/07/1997	1	3.30	0.18
27/04/1999	3	3.00	0.92
13/06/2003	2	1.99	0.14
05/09/2005	3	2.38	1.30
Remaining	Floating		0.00
Average saving			0.86

	Premiums at the time (%)							
Date	**1y**	**2y**	**3y**	**4y**	**5y**	**6y**	**7y**	**8y**
03/01/1989	−0.98	−1.63	−2.09	−2.34	−2.09	−1.50	−0.94	−0.34
03/01/1994	−0.18	−0.17	0.38	0.84	1.07	1.46	1.62	1.73
01/02/1996	−0.03	0.40	0.85	1.46	1.67	1.85	2.16	2.52
09/07/1997	−0.18	0.26	0.66	0.67	1.00	1.41	1.87	2.22
27/04/1999	−0.35	−1.03	−0.92	−0.53	−0.03	0.39	0.71	0.86
13/06/2003	−0.20	−0.14	0.02	−0.04	−0.21	−0.12	0.00	0.00
05/09/2005	−0.39	−0.89	−1.30	−0.97	0.00	0.00	0.00	0.00
Remaining	−0.98	−1.63	−2.09	−2.34	−2.09	−1.50	−0.94	−0.34
Average saving	−0.18	−0.17	0.38	0.84	1.07	1.46	1.62	1.73

When is it good to fix rates?

In the past, strong minimums were good fixing times for shorter maturities: this is quite intuitive, since the average Euribor is quite slow to change, while the swap rates are more volatile. Therefore, when the swap rates are low, it should be a good time to hedge. This can be seen in Figure 7.18 (see also Table 7.12).

We now try to see the effect of higher duration on the savings at the strong minimums. As expected, for longer duration the savings are substantially reduced, even at very strong minimums. This too is quite intuitive, since for long durations the average swap premium increases considerably, and therefore only extremely low swap rates can give any saving. This is shown in Figure 7.19 (see also Table 7.13).

Figure 7.18 EUR two-year swap rates versus actual realised rates

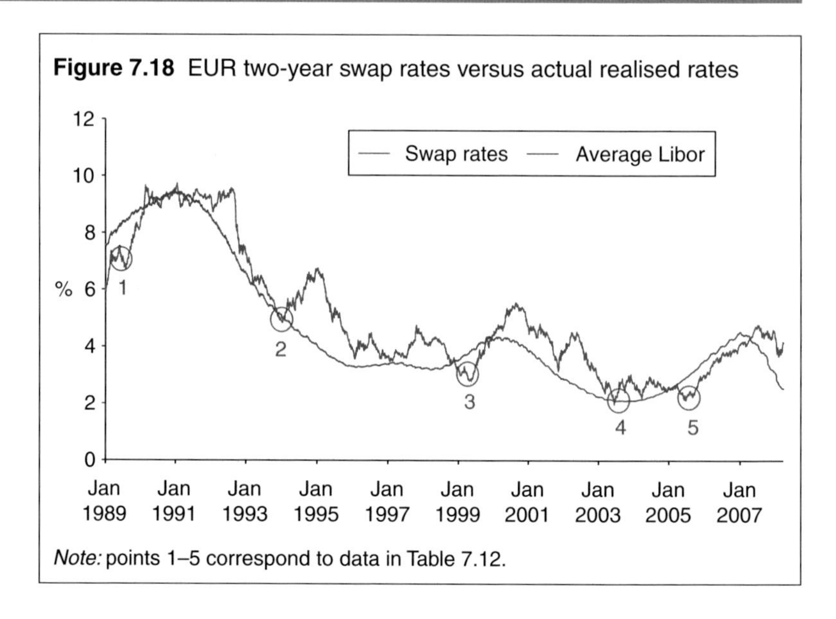

Note: points 1–5 correspond to data in Table 7.12.

Table 7.12 EUR two-year swap rates versus actual realised rates (%) shown in Figure 7.18

Point	Date	Saving (%)
1	02/08/1989	1.7
2	07/01/1994	0.2
3	13/05/1999	1.1
4	13/06/2003	0.1
5	27/0620005	0.8

Table 7.13 EUR five-year swap rates versus actual realised rates (%) shown in Figure 7.19

Point	Date	Saving (%)
1	31/07/1989	1.5
2	07/01/1994	−1.1
3	29/04/1999	0.0
4	13/06/2003	0.2
5	25/03/2005	0.2

If this is the case, it looks reasonable to hedge only at strong minimums, and only for lower durations.

Figure 7.19 EUR five-year swap rates versus actual realised rates

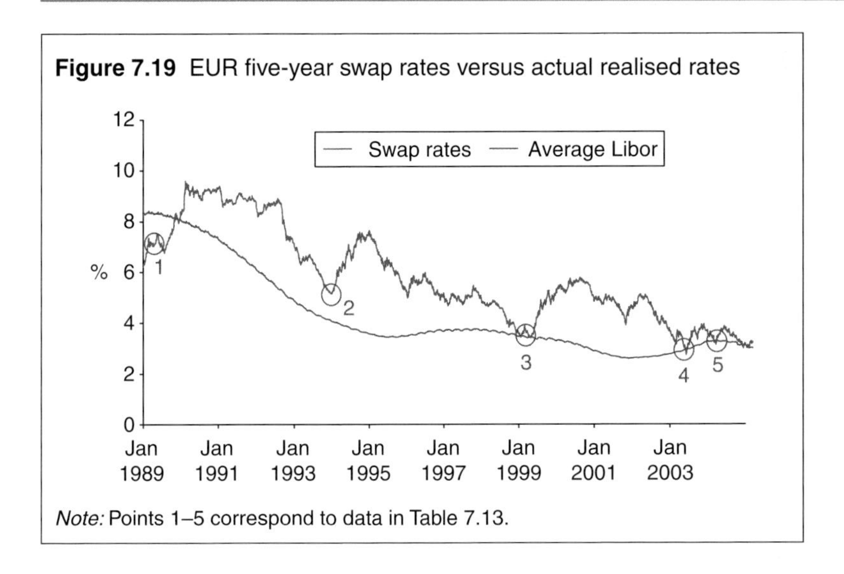

Note: Points 1–5 correspond to data in Table 7.13.

RECOMMENDATIONS

We suggested two alternatives to JSCOM (Figures 7.20 and 7.21), which use the current short-term rates by doing the following.

Figure 7.20 Swapping into shorter term fixing

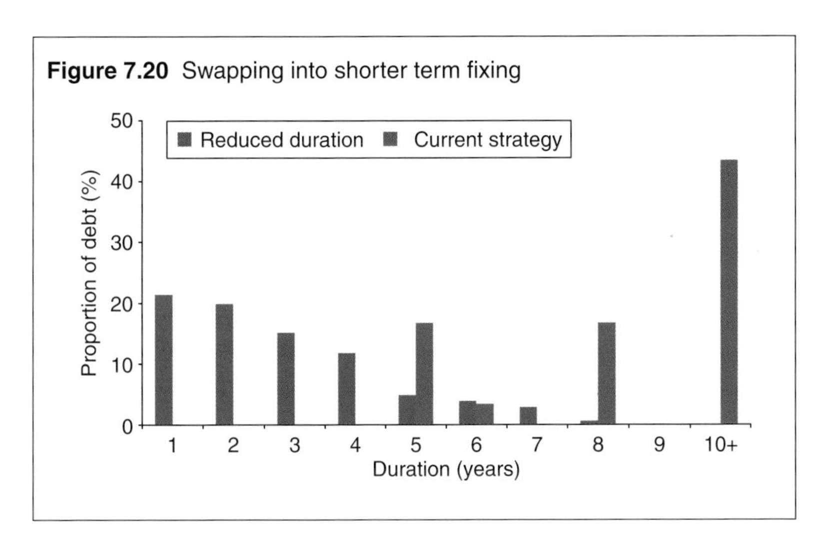

Swap JSCOM's debt into lower duration

1. Swap JSCOM's long-term fixed debt into floating debt, in order to stop paying the high expected carry on it.

Figure 7.21 Swaption strategy

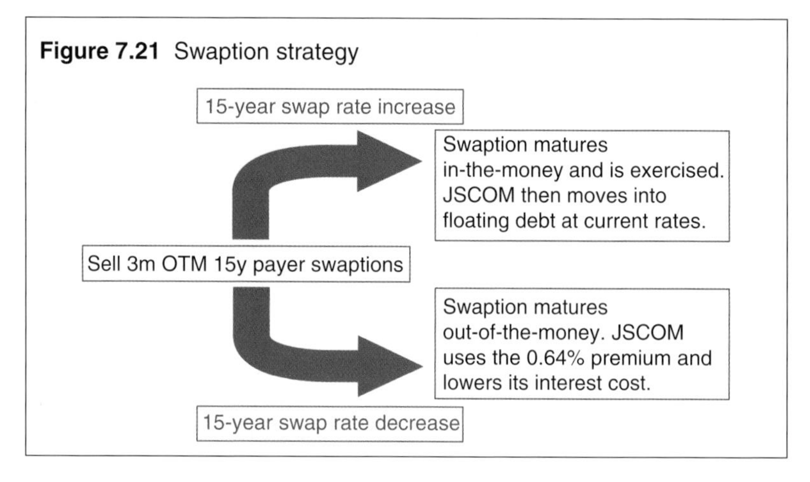

2. Swap the resulting floating debt into shorter term fixed debt now, in order to benefit from the current historically low rate environment.
3. Leave JSCOM's medium term fixed debt as it is, as over time this will become the short-term fixed debt.

Use swaptions in order to float JSCOM's debt

An alternative for moving JSCOM's fixed debt into floating is by selling short-dated (under three months) out-of-the-money (OTM) payer swaptions on long duration swap. This process would allow JSCOM to monetise their move to a floating rate in the following way.

1. JSCOM sells a short-dated receiver swaption, with the underlying swap duration of its longer maturity debt (15 years). The options are struck out of the money, at 4.00%, where at the time of writing the current 3-month into 15-year forward swap rate was 3.78%. This would allow JSCOM to receive an upfront premium of 0.64%.
2. There are two possibilities.

    (a) If the 15-year rates are above the strike at the maturity date, the option buyer will exercise the option and move JSCOM's debt into floating. Since it is our strategic recommendation for JSCOM to reduce its duration, this will fit nicely with the strategy, but will also allow JSCOM to benefit from the option premium.

(b) If the 15-year rates are below the strike at the maturity date, then the option expires worthless. JSCOM then just pockets the premium for the option, and may do the same thing again.

The reasons why the swaptions are short dated are to

- give JSCOM an option to actively manage the transition to floating, and
- avoid designation as non-hedge accounting.

Since JSCOM reports its earnings quarterly, it does not have to have any earning volatility if the swaptions are sold and expire within the quarter.

The options are struck OTM so that the transition is slow. In this way, as the swap rates rise, more and more of JSCOM's debt will move to floating, and perhaps be swapped back into shorter maturities. The change, however, will not be sudden. Moreover, swapping the debt into floating when rates rise will allow JSCOM to lock in a better spread over floating for its debt.

JSCOM was interested in executing the recommendations above, but asked us for further information on the effect this would have on its share price. This further analysis is presented in Chapter 8, on the effect of the duration policy on company valuation.

CONCLUSION

In this chapter we discussed one of the questions most often raised by companies: "What is the optimal fixed floating composition of our debt?". We proposed measuring the cost of fixing via the concept of the "swap premium" and analysed this parameter over history for various swap maturities.[5] Shorter maturities seem to offer a better risk–return profile, and we used this in order to obtain the optimal proportion of debt fixed for various maturities. In the next chapter we shall look into the risk and compare the risk increase with the reduction in interest cost.

1 Using swap rates and Euribor rates from January 3, 1989, to January 5, 2010. Data before the introduction of the EUR is based on Deutschmark rates.

2 This is because the premium for higher tenors is difficult to calculate due to insufficient data.

3 For example, the first 10-year period starts on January 1, 1989, and ends on January 1, 1999. The second period starts on January 2, 1989, and ends on January 2, 1999, and so on. The last period starts on January 1, 1999, and ends on January 1, 2009.

4 There is a small difference here between the saving shown earlier of 1.35% and the value of 1.35% in Table 7.9. This is due to slightly different observation periods.

5 Even though in this chapter we have focused on the EUR rates, we have performed the same analysis for companies in USD, GBP and AUD, and obtained very similar results.

8

Impact of Fixed–Floating Policy on Company Valuation

This is the second of two chapters relating to JSCOM. In Chapter 7 we answered JSCOM's questions about how to optimise the fixed–floating and duration policies (from now on we call the two "interest rate risk policy") and JSCOM took on board our recommendations. The next question that JSCOM management asked was "What (if any) impact would a new fixed–floating mix have on the equity valuation of our company?".

The question of the impact of interest rate hedging on the company valuation is not normally asked. Most companies assume that their share price does not depend on their derivatives portfolio, and in generally this is a correct assumption (unless there is a very serious problem with the derivatives portfolio blowing up). However, it is necessary to differentiate here between the actual market valuation of the company, as measured by its market capitalisation, and the "internal" (or "theoretical") valuation, which the company or analysts calculate to be the true value. Over long periods of time, the two valuations should match, as long as the same assumptions are used by the investors on the one hand and everyone who values the company, ie, equity analysts and the company itself, on the other. In practice, of course, the assumptions vary between different observers of the company, and therefore the actual share price differs from the brokers' consensus or the company's own valuation.

In this chapter we talk about the theoretical or fundamental valuation, as opposed to the market valuation. Many books are dedicated to the subject of company valuation[1] and many analysts spend their days estimating the "true value" of various companies. In addition to that, there are many valuation techniques, and arriving at correct assumptions about the company valuation is more of an art than a science. This is evidenced by the wide discrepancy of values that can be observed when comparing brokers' reports on the world's biggest companies. (This is in sharp contrast with the valuation of financial derivatives, which follows a much more consensual approach between different valuers.)

Our purpose in this chapter is neither to give an overview of different valuation techniques, which is well outside the scope of this book, nor to argue for benefits of a certain approach over the others. We aim instead to estimate the relative impact of the interest rate risk policy on the company valuation. The key word here is "relative", and what we mean by it is the change in the company valuation resulting from a change in the interest rate risk policy.

BACKGROUND

JSCOM is an EUR-based investment-grade telecom operator. It has issued a significant amount of long-term debt, and has kept 80% of it in fixed rates to avoid the earnings volatility. JSCOM has been using the current low rate environment to review its high fixed policy, which it suspects to be suboptimal.

In Chapter 7, we showed two strategies to improve JSCOM's debt duration. Before accepting our recommendations, JSCOM's management wanted us to estimate if there would be any impact on their theoretical valuation. In this chapter we use the discounted cashflow (DCF) model and weighted average cost of capital (WACC) to evaluate the impact on the theoretical (ie, "model" or "true") valuation. In order for a similar change to be reflected in the actual share price of JSCOM, analysts and investors would have to factor in the expected changes in the interest cost and risk in their valuation.[2]

COMPANY OBJECTIVES

- Create a framework to analyse the effect of a changed duration structure on the company valuation.
- Apply the framework to the case of JSCOM.

ANALYSIS

We perform a valuation based on the DCF model, described below, and develop a methodology to include the increased risk in the valuation by changing the beta of the company.

The approach follows the steps shown in Figure 8.1.

Figure 8.1 Duration effect on the share price: step by step

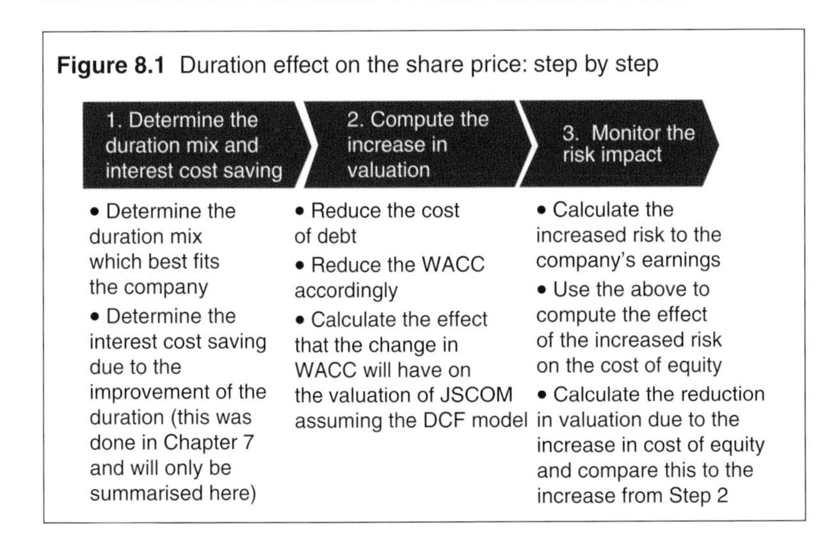

STEP 1: DETERMINE THE DURATION MIX AND INTEREST COST SAVING

We include below a reminder of the main results from Chapter 7, including JSCOM's portfolio and change in interest cost. These will be used later in our analysis.

Figure 8.2 Current versus suggested strategies

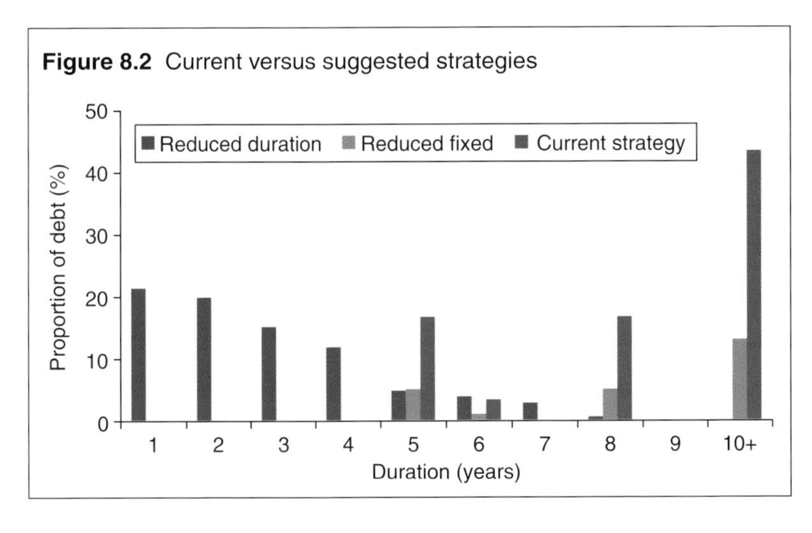

We suggested two possible strategies for JSCOM.

(a) Reduce JSCOM's duration from 7.5 to 2.2 years while leaving the fixed proportion unchanged at 80%. In this option, we suggested that JSCOM should fix more of its debt for durations with higher probabilities of success, and never fix any debt for longer than eight years.

(b) Reduce the fixed proportion to 24%, while leaving the duration profile as it is.

Both of these strategies would give, on average over the long term, a saving of 1.35% per year in JSCOM's total interest cost. The strategies are presented in Figure 8.2 and their impact on the swap premium is illustrated in Table 8.1.

Table 8.1 Current versus suggested strategies

Duration (y)	A (%)	B (%)	C (%)	D (%)	E (%)	F (%)	G (%)
1	0.22	0.0	0.00	21.3	0.05	0.0	0.00
2	0.43	0.0	0.00	19.8	0.09	0.0	0.00
3	0.75	0.0	0.00	15.1	0.11	0.0	0.00
4	1.13	0.0	0.00	11.8	0.13	0.0	0.00
5	**1.55**	**16.7**	**0.26**	**4.8**	**0.07**	**5.0**	**0.08**
6	1.90	3.3	0.06	3.8	0.07	1.0	0.02
7	2.22	0.0	0.00	2.8	0.06	0.0	0.00
8	2.46	16.7	0.41	0.5	0.01	5.0	0.12
9	2.66	0.0	0.00	0.0	0.00	0.0	0.00
10+	2.82	43.3	1.22	0.0	0.00	13.0	0.37
Sum		80.0	1.95	80.0	0.60	24.0	0.60

Note: A, swap premium; B, current portfolio; C (= A × B), premium for current portfolio; D, reduced duration portfolio (option (a)); E (= A × D), premium for reduced duration portfolio; F, reduced fixed portfolio (option (b)); G (= A × F), premium for reduced fixed portfolio. We assume that the swap premium for all durations over 10 years is the same as the 10-year duration. This is because data for higher tenors is difficult to calculate due to insufficient data

STEP 2: COMPUTE THE INCREASE IN VALUATION

Discounted cashflow methodology

The equity value of a company can be computed as its enterprise value (EV) minus the value of its debt. The EV is defined as the market value of the whole company. The value of its debt can easily be approximated using the price of the company's bonds.

We compute the EV by using the DCF methodology.[3] This method consists in four steps.

1. Forecast free cashflows

$$\text{FCF} = \text{EBITDA} - \text{CAPEX} - \text{change in working capital} - (\text{EBIT} - \text{interest}) \times \text{tax rate}$$

   This gives us an estimate of the cash that can be used to service the debt of the company or paid as dividend to its equity holders.

2. Calculate the weighted average cost of capital

$$\text{WACC} = \frac{E}{E+D} \times K_e + \frac{D}{E+D} \times K_d$$

   where E is the market value of equity, D is the market value of debt, K_e is the cost of equity, calculated as

$$K_e = \text{risk-free rate} + (\text{beta} \times \text{market risk premium})$$

   (this gives an estimate of the risk that investors are attributing to JSCOM, as well as the required return on their equity), beta is the risk coefficient which is equal to the covariance of the market risk return with JSCOM return, divided by the variance of the market risk return; the market risk premium is the difference between the market risk return of the stock index and the risk-free rate; K_d is the after-tax cost of debt, computed as

$$K_d = [(1 - \text{tax}) \times \text{pre-tax cost of debt}]$$

3. Obtain EV in years 1 to N by discounting the FCFs at WACC

$$\text{EV} = \sum_{m+1}^{n} \left[\frac{\text{FCF}}{(1 + \text{WACC})^n} \right]$$

4. Add the terminal value, eg, last year's FCF discounted by WACC growth, computed through the Gordon–Shapiro formula as

$$\text{TV} = \frac{\text{FCF}(\text{year } N)}{\text{WACC} - \text{growth}}$$

The theoretical share price

$$S = \frac{\text{EV} - \text{market value of debt}}{\text{number of shares}}$$

The DCF method is used because it allows us to evaluate both the reduction in cost of debt and the extra risk to corporate earnings (through the equity risk premium).

Consensus forecasts for JSCOM

We used several analyst reports to obtain a consensus for the future cashflows. The estimates show a slow increase in the expected earnings, but a relative stability in free cashflows. The consensus forecasts are presented in Table 8.2.

Table 8.2 Forecasts for JSCOM (EUR million)

	Year			
	1	2	3	4
Revenues	5,552	5,555	5,558	5,587
EBIT	1,001	1,007	1,029	1,066
+ depreciation	207	226	230	216
− capital expenditure	202	207	239	234
− change in working capital	61	60	54	54
− tax	187	190	201	208
Free cashflows	759	776	765	786

WACC calculation

We estimate the WACC based on the company balance sheet at the last reporting date. JSCOM's funding is mostly based on equity (57%), and it has a beta close to 1. In total, its WACC is 6.72%.

If JSCOM changes its debt duration according to the above strategies, its average cost of debt should reduce by 1.35% per year as shown before. This reduction will reduce JSCOM's WACC, as shown in Table 8.3.

Therefore, reducing the expected interest cost by 1.35% would reduce the WACC by 0.44%, excluding the risk impact, with which we deal later.

Valuation

We use the free cashflows that we estimated above to calculate the enterprise value of JSCOM. We assume that the free cashflows after year 4 remain constant. We look first at the current strategy, and calculate the enterprise value of the company using the above cashflows and WACC.

In order to value the company, we also need to subtract the market value of debt. We calculate this by using the prices of JSCOM's

Table 8.3 Weighted average cost of capital for JSCOM

	Current strategy (%)	Reduced interest cost (%)	Change (%)
Market value of equity	57.00	57.00	
Market value of debt	43.00	43.00	
Cost of equity	9.28	9.28	
Pre-tax cost of debt	4.46	3.11	−1.35
Tax rate	26.00	26.00	
Risk free rate	3.28	3.28	
Beta	88.00	88.00	
Market risk premium	6.82	6.82	
WACC	6.72	6.28	−0.44

bonds in the market, and the mark-to-market of any relevant derivative contracts. The market value of the debt according to all these is EUR 3,150 million. This is used in Table 8.4 to arrive at the valuation for JSCOM using the original strategy.

Table 8.4 Valuation for JSCOM using the original strategy, WACC at 6.72% (EUR million)

	Year					
	1	2	3	4	5+	Total
Free cashflows (undiscounted)	759	776	765	786	786 pa	
Free cashflows discounted at WACC = 6.72%	711	681	630	606		2,628
Sum of later year cashflows discounted at 6.72%					8,453	8,453
Cash at start of period	300					300
Enterprise value						11,381
Market value of debt						3,150
Valuation						8,231

The valuation of the company under these parameters fits their market capitalisation at the time of writing.

We now repeat the calculation for the case of a reduced WACC of 6.28%. These results are presented in Table 8.5.

Table 8.5 Valuation for JSCOM using suggested strategies: WACC at 6.28% (EUR million)

	Year					
	1	2	3	4	5+	Total
Free cashflows (undiscounted)	759	776	765	786	786 pa	
Free cashflows discounted at WACC = 6.28%	714	687	637	616		2,654
Sum of later year cashflows discounted at 6.28%					9,221	9,221
Cash at start of period	300					300
Enterprise value						12,175
Market value of debt						3,150
Valuation						9,025 (+9.7%)

So a reduction in the duration of debt can increase the DCF valuation of the company by 9.7%. This increase is due to the reduction of the cost of debt, which reduces the overall WACC of the company.

Back-testing

We re-run a historical analysis described in the previous chapter, when we compared the original strategy of JSCOM to the new strategies. We compare the suggested strategies over overlapping 10-year periods,[4] starting every day from January 1989 to January 1999. For each 10-year period, we assume that the company enters into the tested strategy on the first day, and refinances any maturing swap until the end of the period. We then calculate the average interest rate for the period and compare it to the similar interest rate paid using the current strategy. The interest rate increase also implies an increase in valuation, so this distribution also implies a distribution of valuation, as shown in Tables 8.6 and 8.7.

As we showed earlier, there were no 10-year periods within the 20-year period from 1989 to 2009 when the proposed strategies (options (a) and (b)) did worse than the current strategy. At a 95% confidence level, the share price may increase between 3.1% and 14.6% in strategy (a) and between 3.3% and 15.6% in strategy (b).

Table 8.6 Distribution of savings for option (a) (reduced duration) versus JSCOM's current strategy

Percentile (%)	IC difference (%)	Valuation increase (%)
5	0.45	3.1
10	0.52	3.6
25	1.00	7.0
Average	1.33	9.5
75	1.68	12.2
90	1.82	13.3
95	1.91	14.0

Table 8.7 Distribution of savings for option (b) (reduced fixed proportion) versus JSCOM's current strategy

Percentile (%)	IC difference (%)	Valuation increase (%)
5	0.48	3.3
10	0.66	4.5
25	1.16	8.2
Average	1.44	10.3
75	1.84	13.5
90	1.97	14.5
95	2.10	15.6

STEP 3: MONITOR THE RISK IMPACT

So far we have focused on the reduction of expected interest cost through the optimised interest rate strategy. This reduces the WACC. However, there is also an impact of increased risk, which will increase the WACC.

There are two ways that increased risk can affect the WACC:

1. higher cost of debt, through a higher credit spread;
2. higher cost of equity, through a higher beta.

JSCOM is an investment-grade company, and therefore their credit spread is a relatively low proportion of the cost of debt. Moreover, for such companies, credit spread is mostly driven by country risk, leverage and other parameters (see the Chapter "Funding cost drivers") and not the interest cost volatility. Therefore, we shall disregard the first effect in our calculation and focus on the higher cost of equity.

Higher cost of equity

Our final step requires us to estimate the impact of higher risk on the cost of equity. We shall do this by using the capital asset pricing model (CAPM),[5] and making strong assumptions on how the parameters change as a result of increased risk. In practice, things are not so simple. Investors and analysts will in all likelihood not be able to directly notice a higher volatility of interest cost that is due to the new interest rate risk policy, because it will be masked by changes in the debt structure of the company, changes of underlying interest rates, credit and basis spreads and many other parameters that affect the interest cost of a company. However, what they notice are the key financial parameters of the company after the interest cost has been taken into account. The key point here is that for investment-grade companies the actual interest rate risk is relatively small compared with all the other risks, both business and financial, that the company faces. Therefore, the impact of changes to the interest rate structure will necessarily increase the risk only by a small proportion.

Beta in the CAPM model is a measure of the non-diversifiable risk in JSCOM's share price. In order to estimate the effect of higher risk on higher cost of equity, we shall make two big assumptions:

1. the beta is proportional to the volatility of corporate earnings (Figure 8.3), since this risk essentially drives the risk to JSCOM's share price;
2. the increase in risk from the changed fixed–floating mix and duration is all non-diversifiable, ie, can all be attributed to beta.

Therefore, the increase in beta should be proportional to the increase in the volatility of JSCOMs profit before tax (PBT) between the original strategy and the proposed strategies.

In order to calculate the volatility of earnings, we referred to the calculation of the changes in PBT from Chapter 7. We did this by taking the EBITDA, depreciation and amortisation and total debt numbers from the quarterly reports of JSCOM from 2000 to 2009, and then calculated the PBT of JSCOM assuming either the current 80% fixed proportion or the 24% fixed proportion from option (b) (reduced fixed–floating mix).[6]

Figure 8.3 Assumed dependence of beta on earning volatility

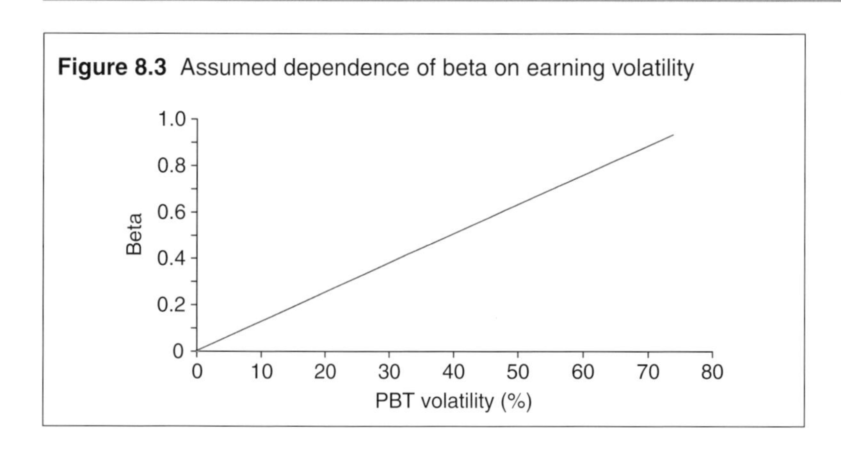

As mentioned before, the volatility of JSCOM's profit before tax, assuming an 80% fixed proportion, is 73.6%. If the fixed proportion is reduced to 24% (option (b)), the volatility increases by 0.07% in relative terms, ie, to 73.7%, which is only a marginal increase, as expected.

Under our assumption for the dependence of beta on the earnings volatility, the beta of JSCOM should also increase by a relative factor of 0.07% due to the increase in interest rate risk. Therefore, the new WACC would be that given in Table 8.8.

Table 8.8 Weighted average cost of capital for JSCOM

	Current strategy (%)	Reduced interest cost with increased risk (%)	Change (%)
Market value of equity	57.00	57.00	
Market value of debt	43.00	43.00	
Cost of equity	9.28	9.29	+0.01
Pre-tax cost of debt	4.46	3.11	−1.35
Tax rate	26.00	26.00	
Risk free rate	3.28	3.28	
Beta	88.00	88.06	+0.06
Market risk premium	6.82	6.82	
WACC	6.72	6.29	−0.43

The reduction in WACC is now slightly lower, at 0.43%. The valuation therefore becomes that in Table 8.9.

Table 8.9 Valuation for JSCOM using suggested strategies: WACC at 6.29% and beta increased by 0.07% (EUR millions)

	Year					
	1	2	3	4	5+	Total
Free cashflows (undiscounted)	759	776	765	786	786 pa	
Free cashflows discounted at WACC = 6.28%	714	687	637	616		2,654
Sum of later year cashflows discounted at 6.28%					9,217	9,217
Cash at start of period	300					300
Enterprise value						12,171
Market value of debt						3,150
Valuation						9,021 (+9.6%)

Therefore, taking into account both the risk and the interest rate saving, JSCOM's valuation should increase by 9.6%!

RECOMMENDATIONS

In discussions with JSCOM, we focused on our finding that the reduction in valuation due to extra risk was significantly smaller than the increase in valuation due to the reduced interest cost. We also stressed the need of JSCOM to communicate to its analysts the change in interest rate policy and its expected cost reduction.

CONCLUSION

In this chapter we quantified the impact on the new interest rate risk policy derived in Chapter 7 on the theoretical company valuation. We found that the lower interest cost had a much larger impact on the valuation than the higher risk. This is because JSCOM is an investment-grade company, and therefore interest risk is a relatively small part of the overall risk. For a high-yield company, the effect of the higher interest rate risk would most likely have been much more important.

1 See, for example, Koller *et al* (2010).

2 In this chapter, as in Chapter 7, we assume the historical distribution of interest rates, instead of the risk-neutral distribution.

3 See, for example, Quiry et al (2011).

4 Overlapping 10-year periods are not an ideal statistical sample. However, we had a choice here of reducing the length of observation period, reducing the number of samples or using long overlapping periods.

5 See Quiry *et al* (2011).

6 It is more difficult to compute the equivalent parameter for option (a) (reduced duration), but, due to the approximate nature of this computation, we shall assume the same impact here.

9

Do You Need Inflation-Linked Debt?

Most companies are exposed to inflation in one way or another. At least part of the costs for many companies is positively linked to inflation. Some companies also have revenues that are inflation-indexed; these companies are normally in regulated industries, such as utilities companies or toll-road operators.

On the sovereign side, many countries[1] have issued government debt linked to inflation, and if this debt can be liquidly traded, an inflation market is born, so that banks can offer inflation derivatives to companies and investors, and they hedge the inflation risk through buying and selling the sovereign inflation-linked debt.

In those countries with liquid inflation markets, companies can hedge inflation risk like any other financial risk through inflation-linked derivatives.[2] Another way to manage the inflation risk is to buy or issue inflation-linked bonds. For instance, a company that has inflation-linked revenues is exposed to scenarios of lower inflation. In order to offset or reduce that risk, they can decide to issue an inflation-linked bond. This chapter introduces a framework through which a company can decide how much inflation-linked debt to issue.

Of course, the greatly simplified analysis in this chapter should only form a starting point for a real-life situation. After the company has decided on the required proportion of inflation-linked debt, it has to answer many other questions:

- what are the appropriate currencies and maturities?
- which index[3] best describes our inflation dependence?
- how much investor appetite is there for buying our inflation-linked bonds?
- is it a good moment tactically to issue inflation-linked debt?

Even once inflation-linked debt is in place, a company can still manage its inflation risk by reducing or increasing exposure as a function of market environment and its underlying inflation exposure.

In practice, users of inflation-linked debt and inflation derivatives among European and US non-financial companies have been very limited. It is unclear exactly why this is the case. One reason could be a negative accounting treatment of inflation-linked swaps for those companies that do not have explicit inflation-linked revenues.[4] However, this does not explain why more companies do not issue inflation-linked bonds, which do not present any accounting problems. Another reason is that companies find it difficult to quantify their net inflation exposure. We find this difficult to accept, as many companies issue floating debt, linked to Euribor or Libor, even though they cannot quantify the Euribor exposure of their revenues and costs.

One of the reasons that companies with inflation-linked revenues give for not hedging inflation is that "our shareholders buy our stock because they want to keep the inflation dependence". We find this to be the most legitimate explanation, but it cannot fully explain the dearth of inflation hedging. For example, some metals and mining companies enter into commodity hedges, even though it could be said that their shareholders would want them to keep the commodity dependence.

Perhaps the simplest explanation is that inflation hedges and debt for one reason or another have never achieved critical mass outside of the UK (where they are very popular among utilities due to a favourable regulatory environment). Therefore, non-UK companies are reluctant to enter into new inflation deals, as any potential problem will be met with increased scrutiny, while the much more common choice between fixed and floating debt will be much less scrutinised. We hope that this chapter will convince the reader that, in some cases, inflation hedging and issuance of inflation-linked debt can represent very good risk management techniques.

BACKGROUND

A European utility, Utilco, has revenues that are largely regulated. The tariffs for the services it provides are directly indexed to inflation, thereby exposing Utilco to inflation volatility.

In an effort to improve earnings predictability and the efficacy of its financing programme, the treasury department was tasked with finding a cost-effective solution to managing its financial risks exposure. The issue was to determine the best allocation of its liability between fixed, floating and inflation rates.

Utilco wanted to reduce the inflation risk and improve the overall effectiveness of its financing programme.

COMPANY OBJECTIVES

- To reduce the inflation and interest rate risks.
- To look for the appropriate liability composition between fixed, floating and inflation-linked debt in order to reduce the risks.

ANALYSIS

To determine the optimal liability composition in terms of fixed, floating and inflation rate, we use the efficient frontier analysis, optimising the PBT.

We modelled the distribution of the interest rate and inflation over a five-year time horizon, compared alternative liability composition and found the optimal allocation with the highest expected PBT and its lowest variability.

The approach follows the two steps in Figure 9.1.

Figure 9.1 Risk management approach: step by step

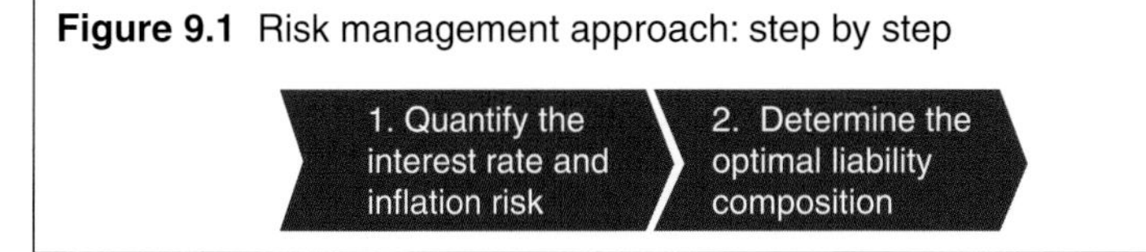

Table 9.1 Split between revenues and costs for Utilco

	Revenues (%)	Costs (%)
Fixed rate	10	30
Inflation	80	50
Floating rate*	10	20

Note: * For instance, linked to three-month Euribor.

STEP 1: QUANTIFY THE INTEREST RATE AND INFLATION RISK

The first step in our analysis is to quantify the PBT risk of Utilco due to interest rate and inflation variability. As Utilco's activity takes place predominantly in the Eurozone, the exchange risk is not relevant here. The sensitivity of revenues and costs to interest and inflation rates is determined based on discussions with the company and on quantitative analysis (Table 9.1). As a matter of fact, the sensitivity of Utilco's activity to inflation risk is particularly high.

- Almost all of Utilco's revenues are regulated and indexed to inflation. Some of Utilco's costs are linked to inflation, so that the overall net revenues of the company are partly linked to inflation.
- Part of Utilco's activity is cyclical and correlated to interest rates. But this linkage is estimated to be poor, and it is assessed that it is the case for no more than 10% of the net revenues.

STEP 2: DETERMINE THE OPTIMAL LIABILITY COMPOSITION

The second step is to assess the optimal liability composition, in order to reduce the sensitivity of Utilco to the previous risks, while minimising the liability cost. So far Utilco has relied entirely on two sources of funding: 50% of its debt is in fixed rates and 50% is in floating rates.

However, Utilco is aware that its liability composition should reflect to some extent its sensitivity to inflation. In the same way, the fixed–floating mix of Utilco's liabilities should match the degree of cyclicality of Utilco's revenues.

We modelled Utilco's PBT sensitivity to inflation and interest rates. The objective of the model was to determine the optimal liability composition in terms of fixed–floating rate and inflation. The model allowed Utilco's treasury to input any debt composition and compare the expected return versus the risk. The return is defined as expected annual PBT over a five-year period, and risk as one standard deviation in PBT over the same period. The treasury could then vary the debt composition between fixed, floating and inflation and find the best risk/return ratio.

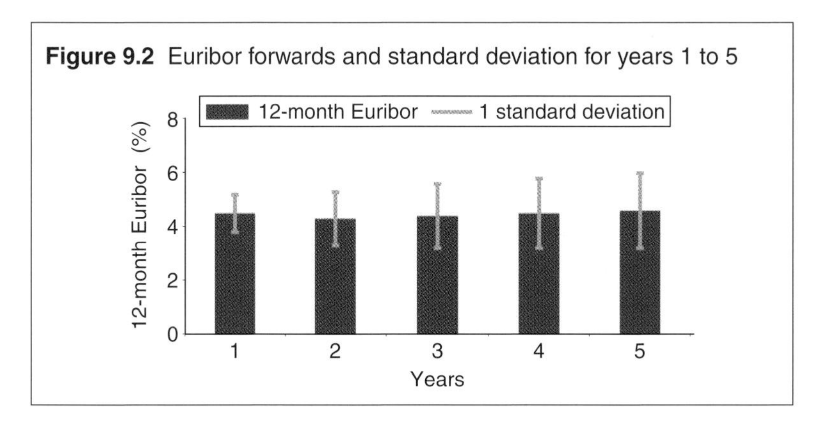

Figure 9.2 Euribor forwards and standard deviation for years 1 to 5

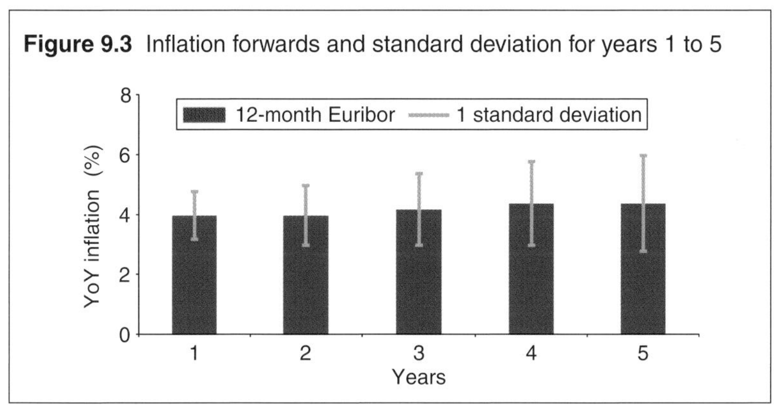

Figure 9.3 Inflation forwards and standard deviation for years 1 to 5

ASSUMPTIONS

The model is based on the simulation of PBT under various economic scenarios of interest rates and inflation:

- to assess the return, we define the baseline scenario for interest rates and inflation as the one derived from the market forward curves;
- to assess the risk, we derive a volatility cone[5] around these forwards that we define as one standard deviation away from the forward Euribor (Figure 9.2) and inflation values (Figure 9.3), based on current market volatilities.

We make the following assumptions:

- PBT is modelled as EBITDA minus the interest cost (the other components of PBT are assumed to be fixed);

- EBITDA is positively correlated with interest rates and inflation based on Tables 9.1 and 9.2;
- the sensitivity of the interest cost is that of the debt composition and therefore depends on the financing strategy chosen.

Based on this central scenario, the continuation of the current financing strategy and a growth assumption for EBITDA and debt provided by Utilco, we derive an expected average PBT over years 1–5 as EUR 1,385 million.

Table 9.2 Utilco financials

	(EUR million)	
	Year 1	**Average for years 1 to 5**
Revenues	8,000	9,000
Costs	6,600	7,490
EBITDA	1,400	1,510
Debt	2,500	2,500
Interest cost	125	125
PBT	1,275	1,385

Based on the volatility cone of interest and inflation rates, we derive a value-at-risk (VaR) of EUR 98 million for PBT at 95% confidence interval over the same period.

The impact of interest rate and inflation changes on the expected PBT and its VaR is as follows

- Increasing the proportion of floating-rate debt (versus fixed rate) increases not only the expected PBT but also its variability. As we saw in the Chapter 7, historically, purely from the perspective of interest cost, it is better to be floating than fixed. The model confirms that, due to the upward slope of the yield curve, increasing the share of floating-rate liability allows for a decrease in the expected interest cost.
- Increasing the proportion of inflation mostly offsets the inflation sensitivity of EBITDA and reduces the VaR up to a certain threshold, above which VaR increases again. The expected PBT is increased, assuming a small inflation risk premium of 10bp.

RESULTS

We derive from the model a set of efficient frontiers (Figure 9.4) parameterised by the fixed-rate debt proportion. For each efficient frontier, the relative proportion of inflation to floating rate ranges from 0% to 100%. For example, the 0% fixed line, which is the right-most line in Figure 9.4 has 11 points. Going from top to bottom, they are 100% inflation plus 0% floating, 90% inflation plus 10% floating, and so on, down to 0% inflation plus 100% floating.

We can see that for certain proportion of fixed debt, increasing the proportion of floating debt reduces the expected PBT, due to the assumed inflation risk premium.

Figure 9.4 Expected PBT versus PBT VaR at 95%, years 1–5 (EUR million)

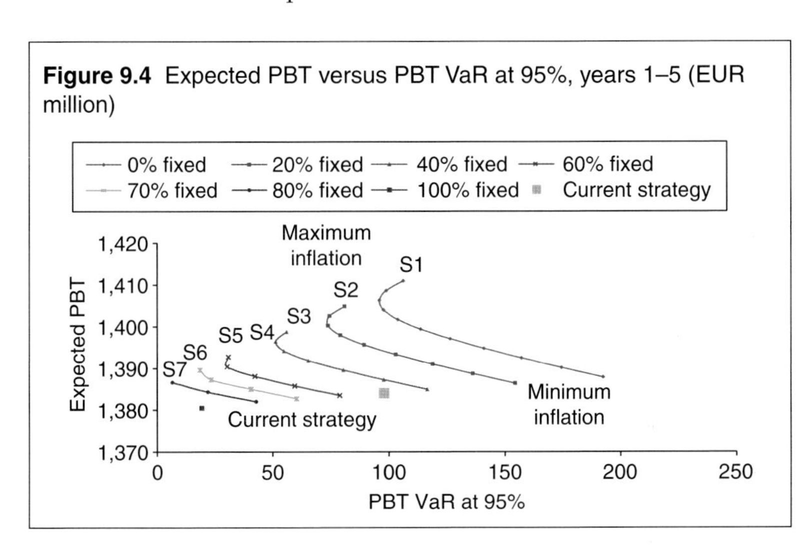

Table 9.3 Scenario analysis for years 1 to 5

Scenario	Fixed rate (%)	Inflation (%)	Floating rate (%)	Expected PBT (EUR m)	PBT VaR (EUR m)
S1	0	100	0	1,412	107
S2	20	80	0	1,405	85
S3	40	60	0	1,399	56
S4	40	50	10	1,397	51
S5	60	40	0	1,393	32
S6	70	30	0	1,390	20
S7	80	20	0	1,387	8

In Figure 9.4 and Table 9.3, we have labelled seven scenarios (S1 to S7), which are at or near the top of each efficient frontier.

For a given fixed-rate proportion, the trade-off between inflation and floating rate depends on

- the sensitivity of net revenues to inflation,
- the correlation between floating rates and inflation,
- the risk appetite of the company.

Table 9.4 Scenario analysis: years 1 to 5

Scenario	Fixed rate (%)	Inflation (%)	Floating rate (%)	Expected PBT (EUR m)	PBT VaR (EUR m)
Current strategy	50	0	50	1,384	98
S3	40	60	0	1,399	56
S4	40	50	10	1,397	51

The treasury of Utilco imposed the constraint that the fixed-rate proportion should be around 40%. Based on such a fixed-rate proportion, the optimal inflation ratio appears to be at least 50%, in line with the high sensitivity of the net revenues to inflation. Switching from the current strategy to strategies S3 or S4 (Table 9.4), where inflation proportion is 60% and 50%, respectively, allows an increase in the expected total PBT over 2008–12 of at least EUR 13 million = EUR 1,397 million − EUR 1,384 million and a significant reduction of the risk, by at least EUR 42 million = EUR 98 million − EUR 56 million.

STRATEGY APPLICATION

In order to reduce its inflation risk, Utilco can opt to issue an inflation-linked bond. The standard market format is that of a multiplicative inflation bond: Utilco pays a fixed coupon on a notional that is inflation linked. An additive inflation bond is an alternative and pays a fixed coupon plus inflation, on a constant notional.

Opting for an inflation swap would be an alternative solution, but, as we mentioned in the introduction to this chapter, the accounting treatment is not as favourable as that of an inflation-linked bond.

Indeed, the use of, for instance, an inflation-linked swap in combination with a fixed-rate nominal bond, synthetically creating inflation-linked debt, does not have the same accounting treatment as the inflation-linked bond. This is due to the current interpretation of IAS 39 prohibiting hedge accounting of nominal bonds swapped to inflation. As a result, such inflation derivatives must be recorded on the balance sheet at fair value with changes in fair value recorded in earnings. However, in certain circumstances, cashflow hedge accounting is allowed when an inflation-linked swap can be demonstrated to be a highly effective hedge of a highly probable future transaction.

RECOMMENDATIONS

We recommended to Utilco the following allocation of liability: 40% fixed rate, 50% inflation and 10% floating. The optimum is based on the following criteria:

- limiting the inflation exposure;
- improving the overall cost of hedging;
- providing a diversification of risks.

Switching to this allocation would allow an increase in the expected total PBT over 2008–12 of EUR 13 million (from EUR 1,384 million to EUR 1,397 million) and a significant reduction of the risk, by EUR 47 million (from EUR 98 million to EUR 51 million).

To apply these strategies, we recommended that Utilco use the following instruments:

- interest rate swaps to realise the fixed–floating-rate mix;
- an inflation-linked bond issued to obtain the inflation exposure.

CONCLUSION

In this chapter, we added another dimension to the fixed–floating dilemma discussed in Chapter 7. Companies that have a proportion of their revenues linked to inflation can opt to reduce their risk by issuing inflation-linked debt or entering into inflation swaps. We described a framework by which this decision can be analysed.

1 For example, France, Italy, Germany and the US.

2 See Benaben (2005) and Benaben and Goldenberg (2008).

3 For instance, a French company can choose between European or French inflation indexes.

4 At the time of writing, under IAS 39, if a company that does not have explicit inflation-linked revenue contracts enters into a swap whereby it pays inflation and receives fixed, it would not get hedge accounting, and this would cause volatility in its P&L. This restriction is likely to disappear in the proposed new accounting standards, IFRS 9, which are most likely set to replace IAS 39 by 2015.

5 For the definition and methodology, see Chapter 10.

10

Prehedging Interest Rate Risk

In this chapter, we discuss the interest rate risk related to future bond issuance. This case deals only with prehedging the interest rate risk. It is also possible to prehedge the credit risk, ie, the bond credit spread at issuance time but this is discussed in Chapter 24.

The topic of prehedging interest rates is commonly discussed between bond issuers and their derivatives dealers.[1] Once a company knows that it will issue a bond within a certain period of time, it can decide whether to fix the interest rate component of its coupon. If the bond is issued in EUR, this normally is done via a forward-starting swap[2] with the starting date given by the expected bond issuance date, and the maturity equal to the expected bond maturity. At the bond issuance date, the forward-starting swap is unwound and its MTM is used to offset the bond coupon until maturity. For example, let us assume that a company wants to issue a five-year bond in three months' time and that initially the three-months-into-five-years forward swap rate is 4%. The company would then enter into a forward-starting swap at a level of 4%. If, at the moment of issuance, the five-year swap rate is 5%, the company will unwind the swap and realise an MTM gain of 1% for the following five years. Under the accounting rules, it can then release this gain to P&L through the duration of the bond, bringing down the actual bond coupon from 5% to 4%, ie, to the original forward-starting swap level. Conversely, if the swap rate goes down to 3% by the time the bond is issued, the company will experience an MTM loss of 1% of the swap notional per year, but at the same time it will benefit from a lower bond coupon by the same amount.

Complexity arises if the bond instrument is not exactly as it was envisaged to be at the moment of prehedging, eg, the bond issued is for six years, while the forward-starting swap has a maturity of five years. We shall discuss the flexibility issues in the case that follows. Another issue is the ideal time to prehedge rates, which will be discussed in detail in Chapter 11.

BACKGROUND

Shuttles is a large EUR-based aerospace company, which, in January 2010, intended to issue a five-year bond between three and nine months later, in order to finance a future expansion project. At that point Shuttles thought that the interest rate environment was very favourable due to low swap rates, and wanted to make sure it would still benefit from favourable rates when it issued the bond. Even though the project was certain, its exact starting date depended on a variety of events. Due to the cost of carry between the funding and deposit rates,[3] Shuttles did not want to issue the bond prematurely. Shuttles approached us for advice on how to hedge the interest rate exposure while taking into account all these aspects.

COMPANY OBJECTIVES

- To create a prehedging strategy for future bond issuance.
- To ensure flexibility in case of a change in the bond issuance date or maturity.
- To ensure good accounting treatment for the prehedge.

ANALYSIS

We show three different solutions and concentrate on the forward-starting swaps for prehedging.

The approach follows the steps in Figure 10.1.

STEP 1: ECONOMIC DECISION TO PREHEDGE OR NOT

We start by analysing the current rates against their history. In our view, it makes most sense to hedge in two cases:

1. **Cost:** if rates are low compared with history (details of this analysis can be seen in Chapter 11).
2. **Risk:** if rates are very volatile, there is a strong probability that rates may worsen before the issuance date. Therefore, it makes sense to prehedge in this case.

Figure 10.1 Prehedging bond issuance: step by step

1. Economic decision to prehedge or not?

- Compare the current rate environment to the history: what does this show us about the time to hedge?
- Look at the risk impact: what is the risk that rates will rise before the issuance of the bond?

2. Design a prehedging solution

- Consider a variety of prehedging solutions
- What is the economic and accounting treatment of such solutions?

3. Test the flexibility of the solution

- What does the issuance date uncertainty mean for the prehedge?
- What would be the effect of changing the bond duration?

Cost

Table 10.1 summarises the position of interest rates in July 2012 compared with historical rates.

Table 10.1 Comparison of swap rates in 2012 with historical data

Swap rate (y)	Current level (%)	Percentile (%)	Historical minimum (%)	Historical average (%)
2	0.43	100.0	0.43	4.47
3	0.53	100.0	0.53	4.65
5	0.87	100.0	0.86	4.95
7	1.24	99.9	1.21	5.18
10	1.63	99.9	1.49	5.42
15	2.01	99.5	1.73	4.43
20	2.08	99.4	1.75	4.54

Note: "current" data from July 16, 2012.

At the time of writing, swap rates, for all tenors, were significantly below their long-term averages. Therefore, it made sense to hedge rather than wait for the rates to eventually return towards their long-term averages.

Therefore, just from cost considerations, there may be benefit in hedging at the current rates because of the limited downside.

Risk

Figure 10.2 EUR five-year swap rate volatility cone: historical and simulation

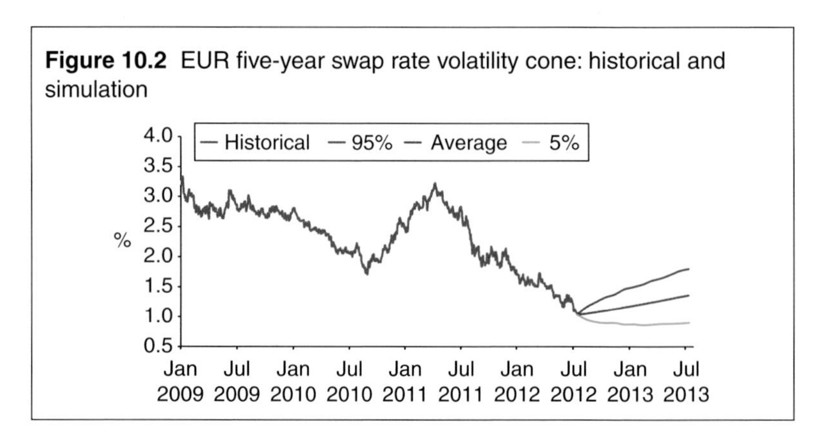

In Figure 10.2 we show the history of the five-year swap rates over the period from January 2009 to July 2012, as well as the volatility cone for these rates for the following year. The volatility cone was calculated using a 1,000-path Monte Carlo simulation,[4] centred on current forward rates and using option market implied volatilities.

Table 10.2 EUR five-year swap rate volatility cone (%)

	Jul 2012	Oct 2012	Jan 2013	Apr 2013	Jul 2013
95%	1.07	1.36	1.53	1.68	1.83
Average	1.07	1.14	1.21	1.30	1.39
5%	1.07	0.93	0.91	0.91	0.93

As can be seen from Figure 10.2 and Table 10.2, according to the interest rate markets, the five-year swap rates can increase by as much as 0.44% over the forward swap rate during the subsequent 12 months, until July 2013 (from 1.39% to 1.83%). This can also be compared with the one-year into five-year forward-starting swap, which is at 1.20%. By locking in the rates, Shuttles may enjoy the forward swap rate and avoid this volatility.

STEP 2: DESIGNING A PREHEDGING SOLUTION

How could Shuttles fix its rate for the future issue?

Shuttles has several options for prehedging this issue.[5]

(i) **Forward-starting swap:** shuttles can enter into a forward-starting pay-fixed swap, which begins in six months and has a tenor of five years. When the company issues the bond, it should do one of the following.

- If the bond was issued before the start date of the swap, Shuttles can unwind the swap at the time of the issuance and can then use the MTM of the swap against the bond coupons (as explained in the accounting treatment below).
- If the bond issuance coincides with the start date of the swap, Shuttles can unwind the forward-starting swap and use MTM against the bond coupons, as in the previous case. In this case, the swap is a perfect hedge to the interest rate part of the bond coupon.
- If the bond is issued after the start date of the swap, at the start date of the swap Shuttles should unwind the forward-starting swap and use the MTM to enter into a new forward-starting swap that will start at the new expected time of issuance.

(ii) **Flexi-swap:** this is a tailor-made solution that allows Shuttles the flexibility to match the start date of the swap with the bond issuance date within a preset window. The fixed rate on the swap is preset in advance, according to a time schedule. The rate is based on the forward swap rate plus the margin, depending on the number of exercise points and the width of the window. Note that this is different from Bermudan swaption, in that Shuttles would have to enter into a swap sometime during the time frame of the flexi-swap, while in the swaption case Shuttles may decide to let the swaption expire without entering into the swap.

(iii) **Bermudan swaption:** this product gives Shuttles not only the flexibility to match the start date of the swap with the bond issuance date within a preset window, but also an option to not enter into a swap. Should Shuttles decide not to issue the bond, the swaption will expire without exercise.

We focus here on the forward-starting swap idea.

Accounting treatment

From the accounting perspective, Shuttles has first to identify a time frame and terms of refinancing needs (in this case a five-year bond issued between three and nine months from the time of writing). However, the precise timing of issuance can remain uncertain.

Under the US GAAP, FAS 133 (DIG Issue G13) provides an example of hedging a forecasted transaction whose timing changes within an originally specified time frame. IAS 39, however, does not provide similarly specific guidance. By analogy to US GAAP, at inception Shuttles would document the hedged item as the variable interest payments resulting from the first five years (or portion thereof) of the bond to be issued within the above-mentioned time frame.

Initially, Shuttles should specify the most likely date of issuance (such as six months from the time of writing), which will be the basis of actual and hypothetical hedging instruments. The actual derivative is the derivative that Shuttles entered into, and the hypothetical derivative is defined as the derivative that would fully hedge Shuttles, given its actual issuance date. As the precise timing of the issuance changes (either moving forwards or being extended), the hypothetical derivative will be modified to match the updated forecast timing. Upon modifying the terms of the hypothetical derivative, the new rate will be based on zero present value in the market that existed at inception of the hedging relationship (ie, if the modified hypothetical derivative had originally been executed at the same time as the actual derivative).

In order to test the effectiveness of the hedge, a regression analysis will usually be performed on the basis of the original actual derivative against the modified hypothetical derivative. As long as effectiveness results are between 80% and 125%, it will be possible to implement cashflow hedge accounting.

As a result of the cashflow hedge accounting, changes in derivative's fair value will be recorded in equity and reclassified to earnings matching earnings impact of hedged transaction. IAS 39 Implementation Issue F.5.5 provides an example of hedging a forecast transaction in a debt instrument. Therefore, there will be no reported earnings impact from the change in MTM of the swap before the bond issuance.

Note that hedge accounting requires documentation of the forecast transaction and that the transaction be highly probable:[6]

> [The] hedged forecast transaction must be identified and documented with sufficient specificity so that when the transaction occurs, it is clear whether the transaction is or is not the hedged transaction.
>
> IAS 39 IG F.3.10

> The forecasted transaction's probability should be supported by observable facts and attendant circumstances.
>
> IAS 39 IG F.3.7

- When the issuance of the underlying debt (giving rise to the hedged interest payments) is earlier than initially forecast (but within the original time frame specified), the actual hedging instrument will be unwound early. The hypothetical derivative will need to be modified to reflect actual timing and used to demonstrate effectiveness for the final retrospective effectiveness assessment. It will be taken as if it was entered at the same time as the actual forward-starting swap but had been planned to start at the actual issuance date. Hedge accounting will stand (subject to a 80% to 125% constraint.[7]) However, some hedge ineffectiveness is likely to result, as the terms of the hypothetical and actual derivatives will not be identical. The MTM impact from the unwound derivative will be kept in equity (not in the earnings) and will remain in equity until hedged interest payments occur.
- When issuance of underlying debt is later than initially forecast (but within the original time frame specified), the actual hedge will mature. Terms of actual derivative modification will be based on the transaction price. On the other hand, the terms of hypothetical derivative will be defined as if it had been entered at the time of the initial hedge and was intended to the new forecast date. The comparison between the two derivatives can take place at the time of the maturity of the actual swap that was entered. Hedge accounting will stand (subject to the 80% to 125% constraint). However, some hedge ineffectiveness is likely to result, as the terms of the hypothetical and actual derivatives will not be identical. The fair value of the hedging instrument will remain in equity until hedged issuance actually occurs within the original time frame specified. Shuttles will then have three options:

1. to execute a new hedging instrument at market and cash-flow hedge the new updated forecast issuance (perfect effectiveness);
2. to execute a new hedging instrument by rolling the PV of the original trade into restructured trade and cash-flow hedge the updated forecast issuance (resulting in ineffectiveness);
3. to leave the updated forecast issuance unhedged.

STEP 3: TEST THE FLEXIBILITY OF THE SOLUTION

Uncertain maturity

Table 10.3 Correlation between different swap rates 2002–12 (%)

	5y	7y	10y	15y	20y
5y	100	98	93	88	83
7y	98	100	98	94	91
10y	93	98	100	98	96
15y	88	94	98	100	99
20y	83	91	96	99	100

In the case that Shuttles decides to change the maturity of the bond, it would be good to know that the forward-starting swap is a good proxy hedge for the swap rate for the actual bond maturity. This can be evaluated be looking at the correlation between the actual maturity swap rate and the forward swap rate. We have calculated this correlation for the 10 years from 2002, and present the results in Table 10.3. As can be seen, the correlations between most long-term rates are above 80% and would allow for a degree of protection in the proxy hedging.

Uncertain starting date

As discussed in the previous paragraph, the debt may be issued earlier or later than forecast. In this case, the hedge may or may not qualify for hedge accounting, and the mismatch between the originally forecast date and the issuance date may cause ineffectiveness of the hedging relationship. The company may then readjust its hedges in one of the three ways listed above (eg, unwind early or roll over into a new instrument).

RECOMMENDATION

Shuttles should consider entering into a forward-starting swap as presented above, ie, a five-year swap starting six months after the hedging time. The analysis above suggests that the hedge should be effective for the entire period that they are considering.

CONCLUSION

In this chapter, we described a procedure for prehedging the interest rate component of future bonds and the kinds of considerations the treasurers go through when deciding on how to prehedge. Next, in Chapter 11, we shall focus on the question of when to prehedge a bond issue.

1 See, for example, Adams and Smith (2011).

2 In USD, the same is normally achieved via a treasury lock, an instrument, which, as its name suggests, allows the user to "lock" the yield on a US Treasury bond.

3 Shuttles issued at Euribor plus 100bp, while their deposits attracted an interest rate of only Euribor plus 10bp.

4 For details of Monte Carlo simulations, see Jäckel (2002) and Glasserman (2003).

5 As mentioned already, this case focuses on prehedging of an EUR bond. In the case of a USD bond, the forward-starting swap would be replaced with a treasury lock, with corresponding analogues of flexi-swaps and Bermudan swaptions.

6 See International Accounting Standards Board (2003).

7 It appears, at the time of writing in 2012, that the 80%–125% constraint from IAS 39 will not be present in the IFRS 9 standards, which are expected to replace IAS 39 in 2015. See International Accounting Standards Board (2003).

11

When to Prehedge

In Chapter 10, on prehedging interest rate risk, we discussed general issues regarding bond prehedging, ie, how to prehedge, while in this chapter we focus on the question of when to prehedge.

Once the company has decided that it wants to go ahead with the future bond issuance, the choice is left of whether the bond should be prehedged for interest rate risk. Like most other hedging situations, this one exposes the company to a choice between higher risk and higher cost. Higher cost comes from the fact that the yield curve is normally upwards-sloping and so therefore the level at which the forward-starting swap is entered into is higher than the equivalent spot level. In this chapter, we subject the forward-starting swap levels to the same kind of statistical analysis as in Chapter 7.

BACKGROUND

LIR offers to its clients hardware solutions, including chip manufacturing, planning and integration for a variety of uses. It operates throughout the globe, but most of its business is located in Europe. LIR is a highly leveraged company with most of its debt maturing in the four years 2012–15.

At the time of writing in July 2012, swap rates were near historical lows, which made LIR consider prehedging future issuance to benefit from this fact. However, financial management was pondering the following questions:

- given the low swap rates, does it make sense to prehedge future bond issuance?
- if yes, what is the optimal prehedging horizon?
- if yes, what is the optimal tenor to prehedge?

LIR asked us to address these issues using a comprehensive quantitative framework. In Figure 11.1, we show the amount of LIR's outstanding debt maturing over the next four years (2012–15).

Figure 11.1 Debt maturing in 2012–15

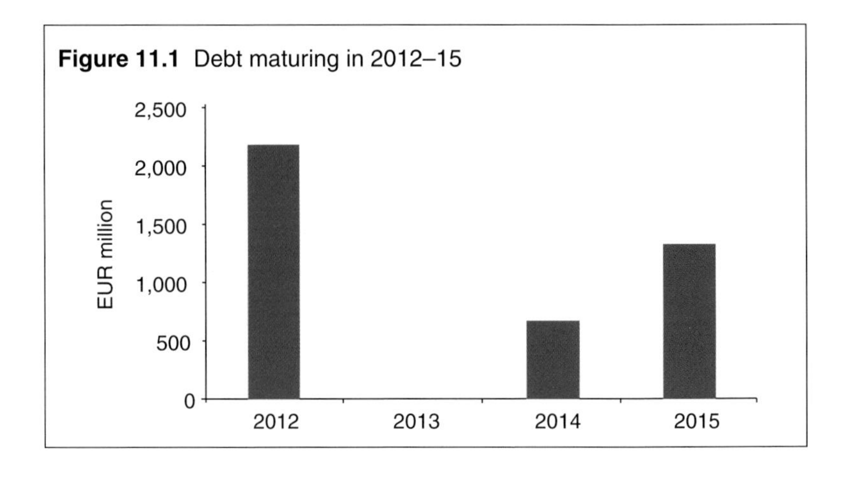

COMPANY OBJECTIVES

- To create a quantitative framework around prehedging.
- To come up with recommendations on the optimal prehedging strategy.

MARKET BACKGROUND

At the time of writing the market environment was highly favourable for a new issue by LIR (Figure 11.2). Although the credit spread was still relatively high, swap rates were near their all-time lows, making the all-in-cost of borrowing very cheap. The common opinion among LIR financial management was that swap rates were eventually going to rise, which would make it prudent to prehedge at the low rate levels available at the time of writing. Moreover, due to the volatility experienced during the financial crisis, LIR financial management learned to appreciate extra stability in its funding cost.

However, the LIR treasurer wondered if there was an associated cost related to prehedging.

Figure 11.2 shows the historical five-year swap rate and LIR's all-in five-year funding cost. As shown by the graph, in July 2012 both these parameters were at lower levels compared with their recent history. The current swap rate was 1.09%, which was the lowest since September 2001 and caused the all-in cost of funding at 2.39% also to be the lowest.

Figure 11.2 Cost of funding 2001–12

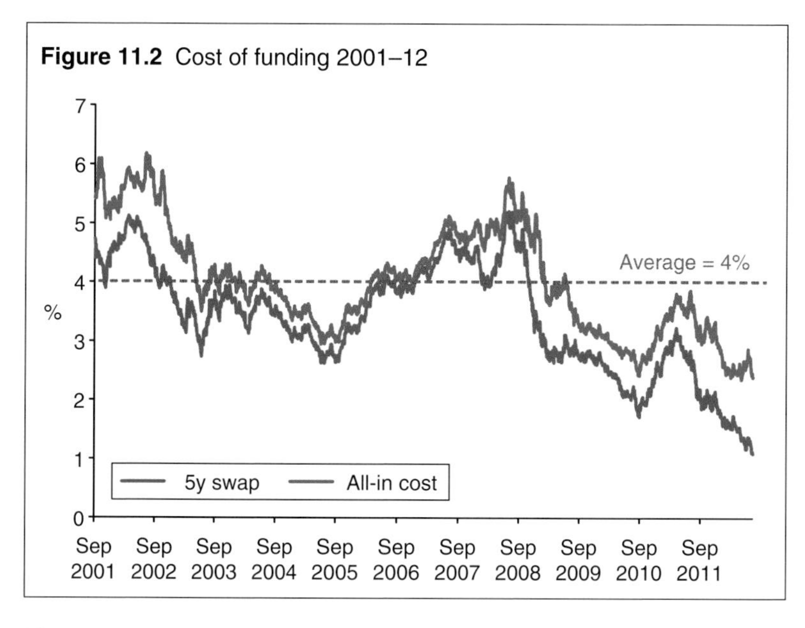

Methodology

We performed a historical analysis of the funding costs, and applied it to the case of LIR. The key assumption was that the future dynamic of the funding cost would not be fundamentally different from the past. We took two different views. One was to treat the current situation as any other point in the past. An alternative approach was to treat the current situation as a special point based on the assumption that we were near the historical lows.

SUMMARY

The analysis consisted in four main steps (Figure 11.3). First, we defined a measure for the prehedging cost. Second, we estimated the historical cost of prehedging. Third, we tried to minimise the prehedging cost by finding when it was lowest. Finally, we examined whether tactically the market conditions justified the need for prehedging.

Figure 11.3 Prehedging cost analysis: step by step

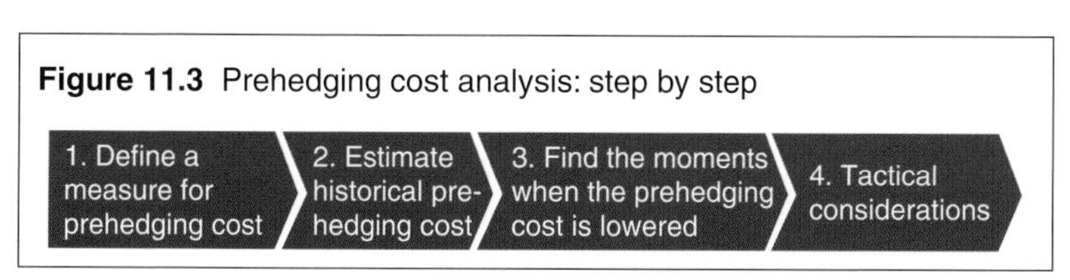

STEP 1: DEFINE A MEASURE FOR PREHEDGING COST

Developing a quantitative framework for analysis of prehedging requires a measure of prehedging cost.

We define the prehedging cost as the difference between the forward swap rate and the actual realised swap rate one year later (if the prehedging period is one year). This is illustrated in Figure 11.4.

Figure 11.4 Definition of the prehedging cost (example)

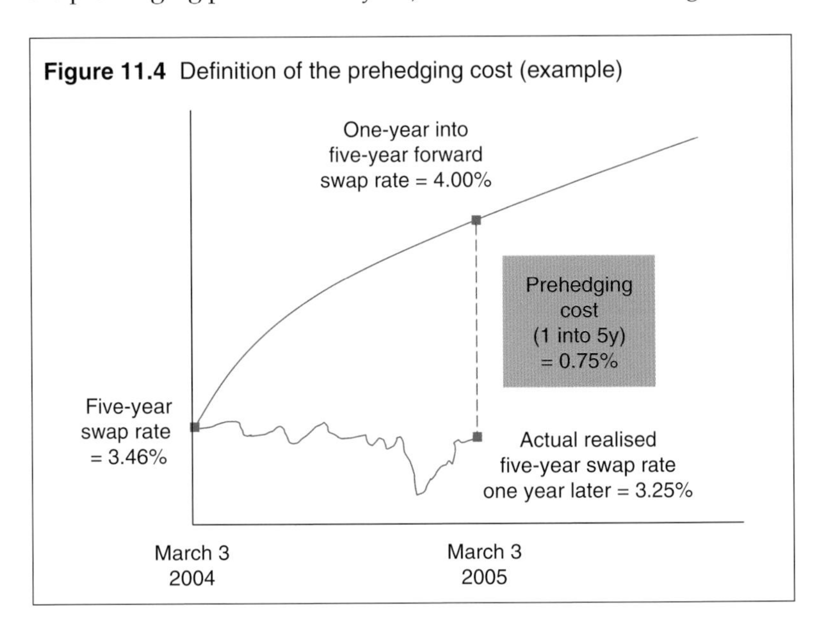

The problem with this definition is that the actual cost of prehedging can only be determined after the bond issuance. However, we can estimate the expected cost based on historical data.

STEP 2: ESTIMATE HISTORICAL PREHEDGING COST

In order to estimate the expected prehedging cost we performed a historical analysis.

We analysed the prehedging cost for a range of prehedging periods and underlying tenors and here we highlight the five-year EUR swap rate one year in advance as an example of such a calculation.

Prehedging cost one into five years

In Figure 11.5, the purple line shows the one-into-five-year forward swap rate and the blue line shows the actual five-year swap rate realised one year later. When the purple line is above the blue line

Figure 11.5 EUR forward swap rates one into five year versus actual

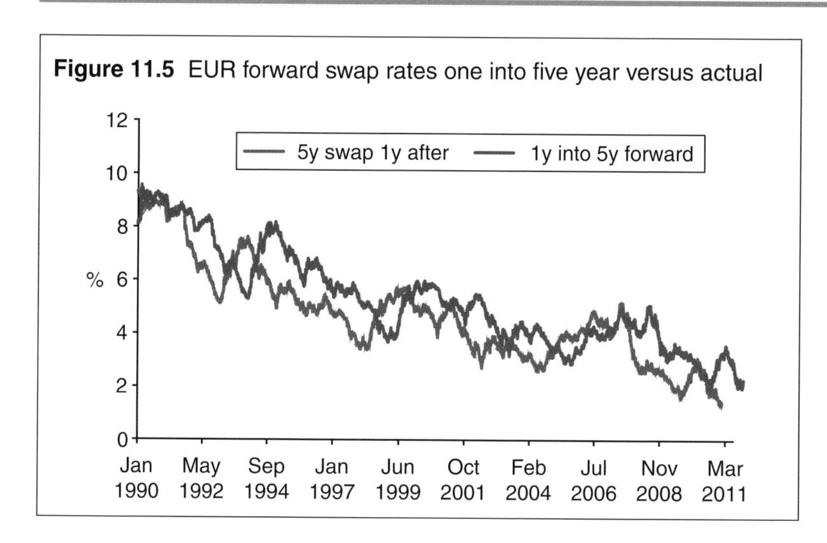

(75% of the cases), the prehedging was more costly than waiting. The difference between the purple and the blue lines is the average prehedging cost, which was 0.63% during this period.

However, as shown in Table 11.1, the average prehedging cost dropped in the late 2000s, as the rates became lower. Since 2005, it has only been 0.48%, which seems low compared with the potential risks of not prehedging, from Chapter 10 on "prehedging interest rate risk" (probability of 5% that five-year swap rates will rise by more than 1.83% in 1 year).

Table 11.1 Prehedging one into five years since 1990

Period	Average prehedging cost (%)	Proportion when cost > 0 (%)
1991–2012	0.63	75
1999–2012	0.50	71
2005–2012	0.48	61

Comparison of the recent prehedging cost

We summarise in Table 11.2 the average prehedging cost for 5-year, 10-year and 15-year swap rates over 3, 6 and 9 months and 1–5 years from 2005 to 2012.

It is clear from the table that a longer prehedging period as well as a shorter underlying tenor implies a higher prehedging cost. An

Table 11.2 Average EUR prehedging cost (%)

	Prehedging period							
Underlying tenor	**3m**	**6m**	**9m**	**1y**	**2y**	**3y**	**4y**	**5y**
5-year swap	0.14	0.26	0.37	0.48	0.96	2.05	2.08	2.23
10-year swap	0.11	0.21	0.30	0.38	0.72	1.44	1.52	1.63
15-year swap	0.03	0.04	0.04	0.05	0.33	1.15	1.23	1.34

immediate conclusion is that in order to hedge risk with a minimum prehedging cost it is better to prehedge for shorter periods and for longer underlying tenors.

In Table 11.3, we show how often the prehedging cost was positive for 5-year, 10-year and 15-year swap rates over 3, 6 and 9 months, and 1–5 years from 2004.

Table 11.3 Percentage of times when EUR prehedging cost exceeds zero

	Prehedging period							
Underlying tenor	**3m**	**6m**	**9m**	**1y**	**2y**	**3y**	**4y**	**5y**
5-year swap	64	61	57	62	67	100	100	100
10-year swap	66	63	62	63	67	100	100	100
15-year swap	65	61	63	62	67	100	100	100

It is clear from Table 11.3 that there is more chance of losing over longer prehedging periods. For instance, for a five-year prehedging period (prehedging over such long horizons is very rarely done among companies in practice, but is mentioned here to stress the effect) the company will lose with certainty, while for a three-month prehedging period there is a slightly above 60% chance of losing, so the prehedging bias (defined as probability of losing minus the probability of gaining) is only about 20%. Since on average probabilities up to two years are slightly biased (60 : 40) against prehedging, the natural question is whether we can predict the best moment for prehedging, when this bias is reduced to zero, and the probabilities are as close as possible to 50%.

STEP 3: FIND THE MOMENTS WHEN THE PREHEDGING COST IS LOWEST

Additional analysis: is the steepness an indicator for the future prehedging cost?

Our first attempt would be to use the steepness of the forward swap curve as an indicator for cost of prehedging. In Figure 11.6 we draw the one-year prehedging cost for five-year swap against the steepness of the curve one into five years (the difference between the one-into five-year forward swap rate and the spot swap rate at the initial moment). It is clear from the graph that there is no correlation between the two. In fact, the correlation squared is only 3%.

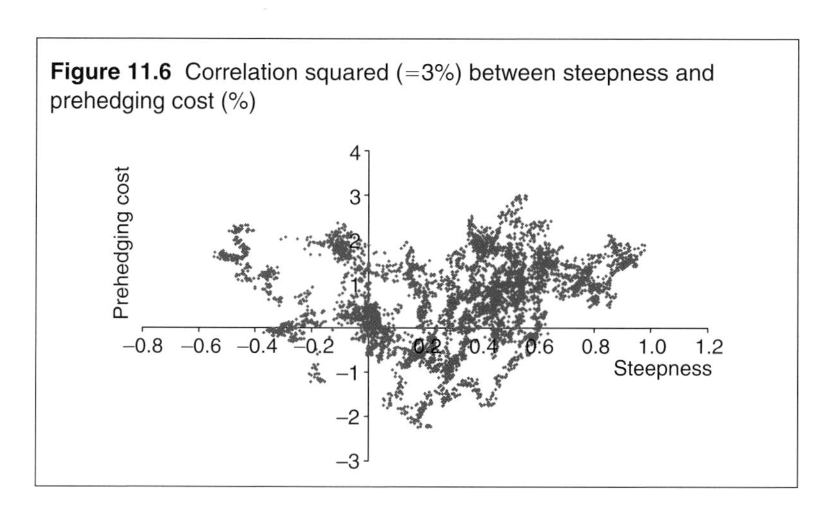

Figure 11.6 Correlation squared (=3%) between steepness and prehedging cost (%)

Instead, let us try to find periods in the past which had a negative prehedging cost. Figure 11.7 indicates such moments with a blue surface.

It is clear from Figure 11.7 that all moments that are good for prehedging are located around a local minimum (except for few isolated spots which cannot be easily seen at this resolution).[1]

Two questions which naturally arise from Figure 11.7 are

- how close do we need to be to the local minimum in order to have a negative prehedging cost?
- how much do we expect to save in the prehedging cost if we are near the local minimum?

Figure 11.7 Optimal prehedging strategy

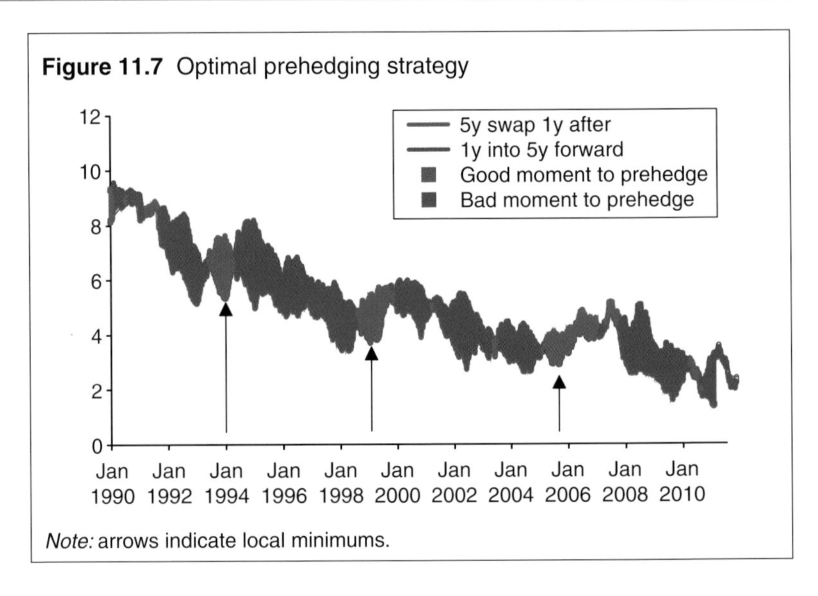

Note: arrows indicate local minimums.

Forecasting the prehedging cost from the distance to local minimum

We attempted to predict the good prehedging moments by using the distance of the swap rate from the local minimum, where the distance from local minimum is defined by the difference between the swap rate at the time and the swap rate at the local minimum. We show in Figure 11.8 the regression between the distance from the local minimum and the one-into-five-year prehedging cost, over the same period as before.

This figure shows a much better correlation, of 73% (squared 53%), between the prehedging cost and the distance from the local minimum than between the steepness and the distance from the local minimum in Figure 11.6. The regression relationship between the prehedging cost and the distance is given by the blue line.

Another thing that we see from Figure 11.8 is that if the distance from the local minimum is less than about 1%, then the prehedging cost is most often negative, ie, it is a best moment to prehedge.

In order to visualise the connection between the distance from the local minimum and the prehedging cost, in Figure 11.9 we plot the graph of the prehedging cost against the predicted prehedging cost from the regression formula from Figure 11.8.

The actual prehedging cost and the forecasted prehedging cost are very similar.

Figure 11.8 Correlation squared (=53%) between the prehedging cost and distance from minimum (%)

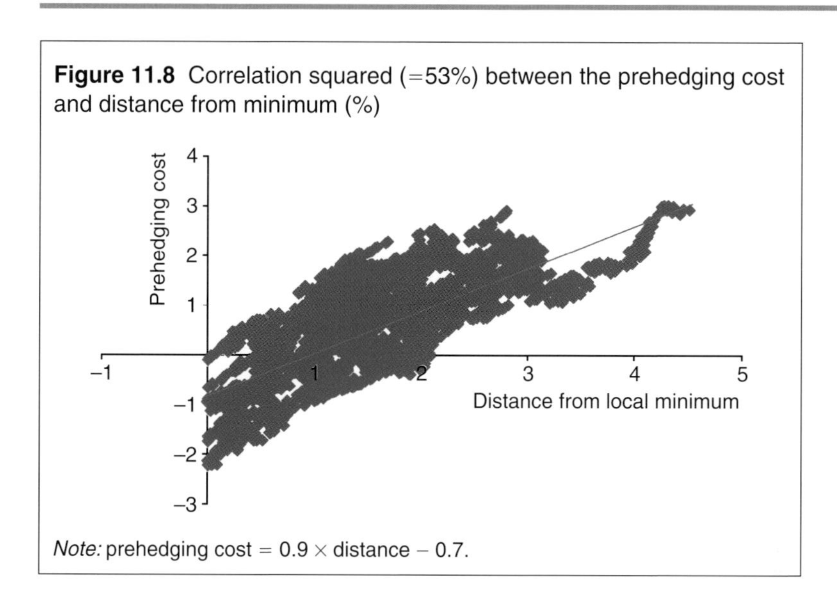

Note: prehedging cost = 0.9 × distance − 0.7.

Figure 11.9 Actual versus forecast prehedging cost

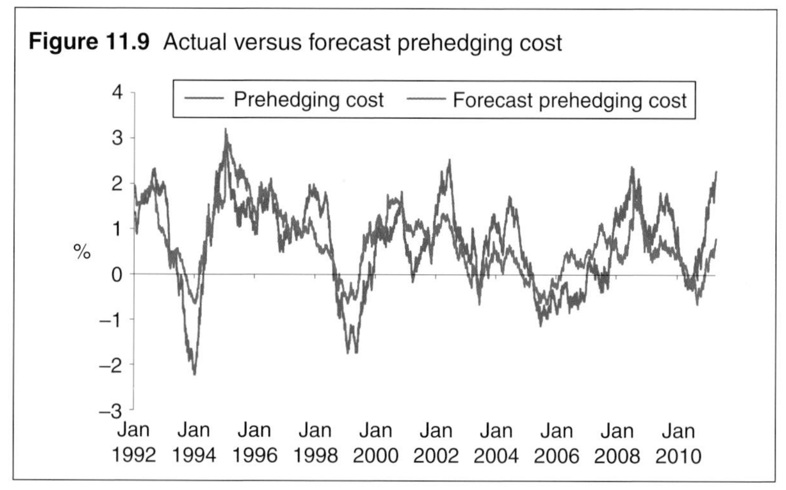

At this point we could safely conclude that the distance from the local minimum is a good indicator for the prehedging cost. The difficult question is how to decide in advance if we are near the local minimum. Of course finding the absolute minimum is impossible in advance of the fact, since, no matter how low the rates, we do not know if they will get any lower. However, for LIR it is not necessary to find the exact minimum. Since, over the whole observed history, the probability of the prehedging cost being positive is only 60 : 40 if LIR avoids the obvious maximums of the swap rates, the company should be able to tilt the probabilities much closer to 50 : 50 or even better. In that case there would be an obvious benefit from risk reduction, without a bias against prehedging.

STEP 4: TACTICAL CONSIDERATIONS

As we have established that when we are close to the local minimum it is a good moment to prehedge, a natural question arises: how close are we today to a local minimum? This question cannot be answered at any point in time with absolute certainty but can only be answered with the benefit of hindsight when the prehedging opportunity has passed. Nevertheless, we can still give it an educated guess.

In Figure 11.10, we show the historical one-year forward into five-year swap rate.

Figure 11.10 One-year into five-year EUR swap rate history

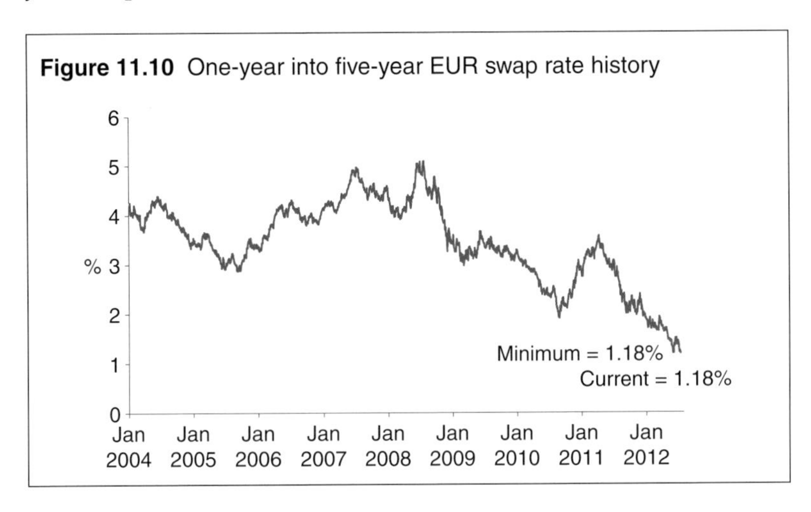

At the time of writing, in July 2012, we are at the historical minimum value. This makes it difficult to decide whether the rates will continue to decrease or start increasing. Since we have no other reference point, we can assume that the distance from the local minimum is zero. When we plug this into the previously derived regression expression, we obtain that the forecast prehedging cost is

$$0.9 \times 0\% - 0.7\% = -0.7\%$$

ie, is negative. Even if we assume that forward swap rates will keep on reducing until they become zero, the distance from the local minimum would only be 1.18%, which would give a low but positive prehedging cost of

$$0.9 \times 1.18\% - 0.7\% = 0.36\%$$

Additional analysis: dynamic of the past swap rate hikes

In the previous steps we analysed the extent to which it is beneficial to prehedge if we are near the minimum and how close we are to the minimum in terms of swap rates. Now we turn to the dynamics of the cycle, or how much time it takes to go from minimum to maximum. In Figure 11.11 we show the recent cycles of the EUR 10-year swap rates. The local minimum points are indicated by a blue dot and the local maximums are indicated by a pink dot. The average increase in a cycle from minimum to maximum is 2.0% and the average time of the increase is 11 months from bottom to top. Similar data is shown in Table 11.5 for 5-, 10- and 15-year swap rates.

Figure 11.11 Previous rise cycles in EUR 10-year swap rates

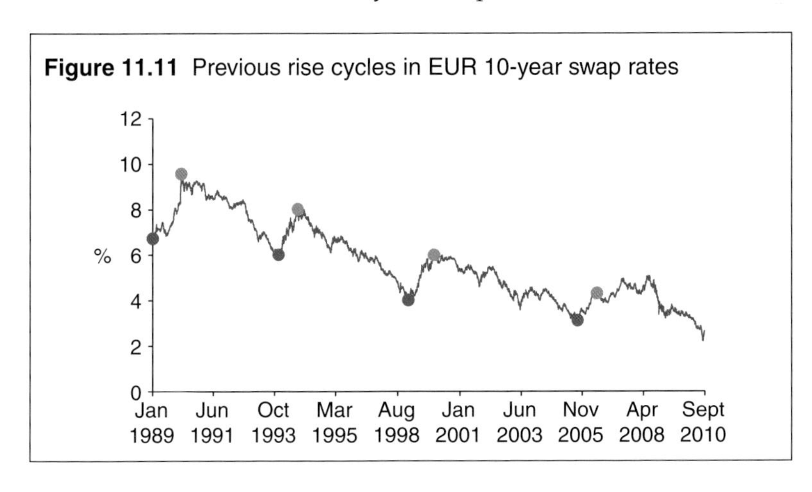

Table 11.4 EUR 10-year rate hikes

Rate hike start	Jan 1989	Dec 1993	Jan 1999	Sep 2005	Avg of maximums
Increase from min. (%)	2.8	2.0	2.0	1.2	2.0
Months from min.	14	9	12	9	11

In Figure 11.12 we show the change in the 10-year EUR swap rate with the previous rate cycles. The horizontal axis shows the time in years from the minimum (for the current cycle, we assume that the minimum is today). On the vertical axis, we show the rise of the 10-year swap rate from the bottom to top of the previous cycle. We can see that, in the past, once the swap rates started increasing, they increased quickly, and nothing suggests that this cycle will be different from previous ones. LIR has to decide whether indeed we are at a local minimum and hence it should hedge, or if not, it should wait for the local minimum to be achieved.

Figure 11.12 Previous rise cycles in EUR 10-year swap rates versus forwards

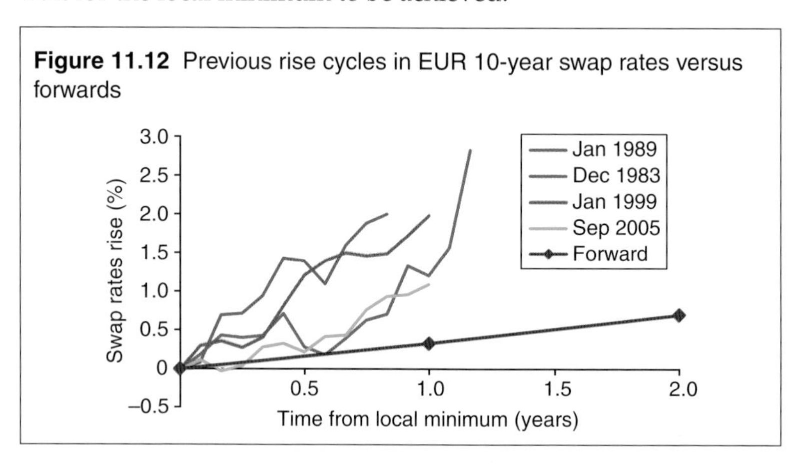

Table 11.5 Potential increase versus forward (in EUR)

	History of hikes		Forward – spot	
	Avg inc. from min. (%)	Time from min. (months)	1y (%)	2y (%)
5-year	2.3	12	0.33	0.70
10-year	2.0	11	0.25	0.50
15-year	1.5	13	0.16	0.30

RECOMMENDATIONS

LIR has strong reasons to prehedge.

- The average cost of prehedging is at the time of writing low compared with risk.
- The best moment to prehedge is when the forward swap rates are close to the minimum, which is still the case at the time of writing.

- The downside from prehedging the swap rates is limited.
- Once the swap rates start going up, they are likely to move fast.

LIR should prehedge longer tenors, ie, 10 years or longer, for periods of up to one year.

CONCLUSION

In this chapter, we discussed the issue of when is the best moment to prehedge future bond issuance, and we came up with a statistical framework which allowed us to answer this question. Of course, as in any other historical analysis, the accuracy of this method depends critically on the extent to which the future development of interest rates is similar to that in the past.

1 We define the local minimum here as the lowest point of forward swap rates between two peaks. The only way that it can be determined accurately is after the rates cycle has ended. So, strictly speaking, it is impossible at any point in time to be absolutely certain how far the point is from the absolute minimum. However, at the time of writing in July 2012, the forward swap rates (1 into 5 years) had reached 1.18%, so by definition the minimum cannot be more than 1.18% away.

12

Constrained Maturity Optimisation

Companies have various objectives and constraints, both internal and publicly communicated. For example, a common objective is that the credit rating should stay at a given level. Another is that the leverage of the company does not exceed a given level. These objectives are chosen by the company management, in order to satisfy them that the financial risks taken are limited. The objectives introduce constraints limiting the allowed amount of company's debt. If the objectives are made public, they should also satisfy shareholders, debt investors and any other stakeholders or observers of the company, eg, employees, politicians, the general public, rating agencies, equity analysts, that the company is safe and prudently managed.

Sometimes a simple constraint introduces significant complexity into the optimisation of the liability structure. In the case that follows, a constraint is imposed on the relative jumps in interest cost from one year to the next. Cases like this lend themselves to Monte Carlo simulations, which allow the sampling of a large range of possible debt allocations and, for each of these, an equally large set of interest rate or currency paths. If the resulting computational complexity is beyond the capabilities of the company, an advisor is selected to assist with the computations.

In this chapter we describe the optimisation of the debt structure between various maturities. The company has imposed an optimisation objective of reducing the variability of interest cost. The constraint is that the interest cost cannot vary too much between two consecutive years. This kind of optimisation problem is more complex than typical corporate problems, but clearly illustrates how problems like this can be tackled using Monte Carlo simulations.

BACKGROUND

Warmwood is a water utility, which has a considerable amount of outstanding debt. Their debt is normally issued in six-month, two-year, five-year and ten-year maturities. Warmwood refinances its debt continuously, so that one-fifth of their five-year debt, one-tenth of their ten-year debt, etc, are refinanced every year. Warmwood also occasionally issues thirty-year debt.

As a relatively leveraged company in a stable business sector, Warmwood wanted to reduce the volatility of its interest cost as its first priority. Since Warmwood takes a very long-term view, encompassing several economic cycles, reducing the absolute amount of interest cost in any given year is a second priority. The first priority of the risk managers at Warmwood was that the rapid changes in rates may cause it to have a substantial jump in interest cost from year to year, and they asked us to advise on an optimal debt maturity, which will accomplish this goal.

COMPANY OBJECTIVES

- To optimise the composition of liabilities by maturity to minimise the variability of interest cost.
- To focus on the Euribor-based interest cost, excluding the credit spread.[1]
- To satisfy the constraint that the interest cost may not, at a 95% confidence level, rise between two consecutive years by more than 5%.
- To decrease the average interest cost over 30 years.

ANALYSIS

We created a Monte Carlo based model (for a simplified algorithm see Figure 12.1) to simulate the future paths for Warmwood's interest cost for a large number of possible portfolios.[2] Each portfolio was defined by a given combination of maturities between floating, two years, five years, ten years and thirty years, with a total equal to 100%.[3] Inputs to the model are historical volatilities[4] (Figure 12.2) and correlations (see Table 12.1) from 1999 to 2012. We use these numbers to simulate the expected interest cost and its volatility for each portfolio.

For each portfolio, we check whether it is compliant with the interest cost increase constraint. From all compliant portfolios, we choose the ones with the lowest interest cost and interest cost volatility.[5]

Figure 12.1 Optimisation model

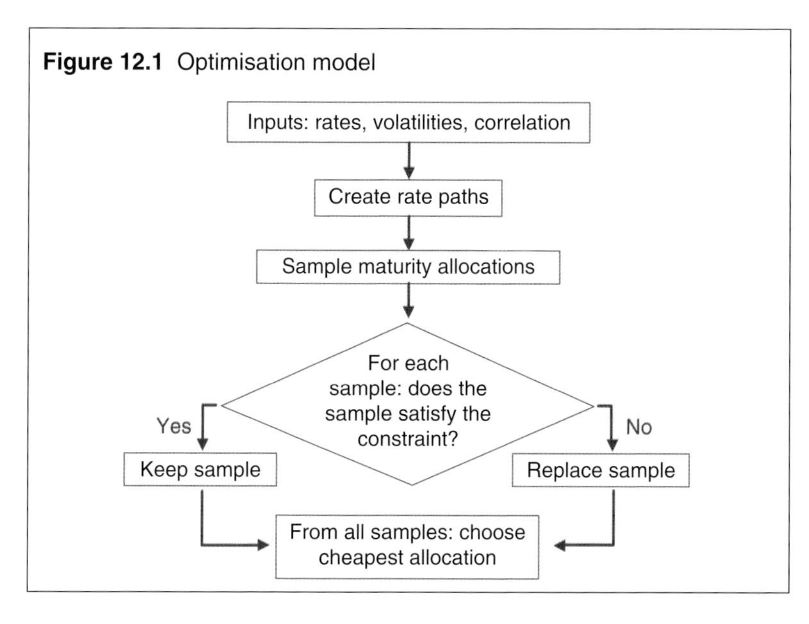

Figure 12.2 Interest rate volatilities 1999–2012

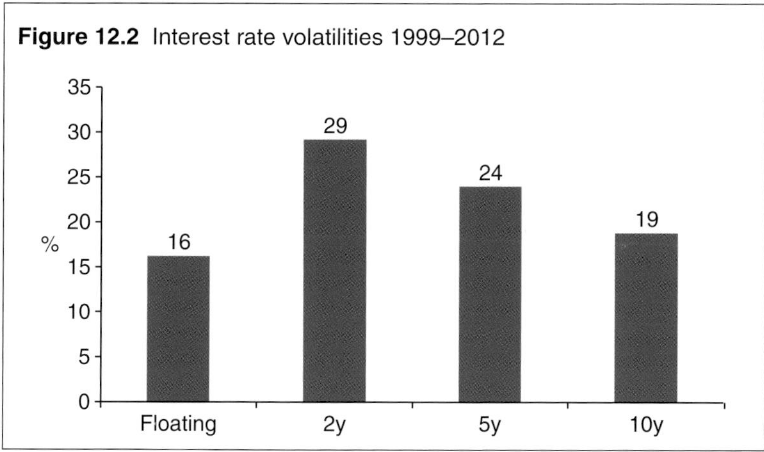

Methodology

As we saw in Chapter 7, historically, floating-rate debt has been cheapest most of the time, but also the most volatile. The 30-year debt, on the other hand, has been more expensive but adds no volatility to the interest cost.[6] The allocation to other intermediate maturities depends on their respective volatilities and current levels.

With this in mind, we would expect a high allocation to the 30-year debt, which has zero volatility over the 30-year observation period, in order to comply with the constraint on the maximum allowed

Table 12.1 Correlation matrix for different maturities 1999–2012 (%)

	Floating	2y	5y	10y
Floating	100	79	68	57
2y	79	100	94	83
5y	68	94	100	95
10y	57	83	95	100

interest cost increase, and the rest in floating, which helps to lower the cost. This creates a characteristic profile of maturities, shown in Figure 12.3.

Figure 12.3 Recommended allocation

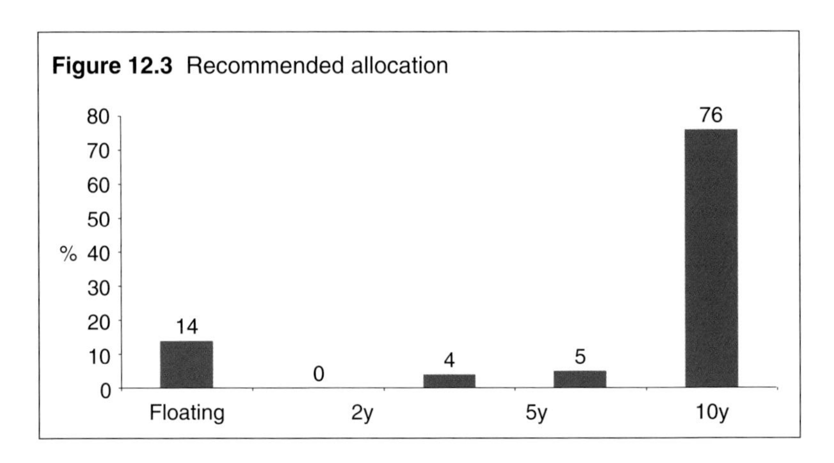

In order to get a quantitative answer, we created a set of Monte Carlo paths for the interest rates, using current forward rates and historical volatilities. We then created a sampling program, which sampled different debt maturity allocations, and used the Monte Carlo paths to calculate the interest cost and the variability arising from the refinancing risk at these maturities. The program sampled the allocation between six-month (floating), two-year, five-year and ten-year debt maturities. All of these maturities were assumed to be partly refinanced every year throughout the life of the bond, as explained above. The remainder of the debt was financed through a long-term 30-year bond, which was not refinanced throughout the period.

Any allocation which was not compliant with Warmwood's constraint was discarded, and replaced by another sample. Eventually, we derived a distribution of possible allocations from which we could choose the lowest interest cost and lowest volatility.

We developed for Warmwood a spreadsheet optimisation model (based on the simplified algorithm from Figure 12.1), which they could use to optimise their maturities allocation. The snapshot of the interface to the model is shown in Figure 12.4.

Figure 12.4 Snapshot of the model

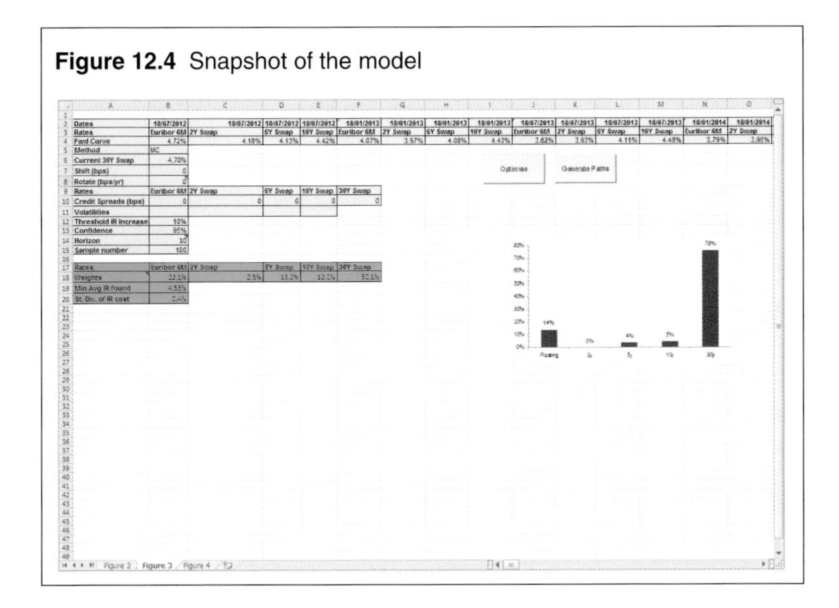

RECOMMENDATIONS

Warmwood should issue 76% of its debt in the 30-year maturity and the rest through the following allocation: 14% floating-rate debt (six months' maturity), 4% in five-year debt and 6% in ten-year debt (Figure 12.3). This allocation is in agreement with the qualitative arguments above, which support a dumb-bell-like debt maturity distribution. In particular, the large 30-year maturity debt would keep the interest cost stable, which would allow the company to satisfy the interest cost increase constraint. The floating rate, on the other hand, would allow for cheaper financing. The choice of the five-year and ten-year maturities over the two-year one was because the two-year maturity has historically had a higher volatility than all other checked maturities, and therefore adding more of this maturity will reduce the ability to comply with the increase constraint.

CONCLUSION

In this chapter we gave an illustrative example of constrained maturity optimisation for a utility company. As an aside we should mention that the subject of constrained optimisation is a large and complex numerical discipline, and well beyond the scope of this book.[7]

1 Warmwood, like many other companies, considers credit spread to be exogenous and has not been managing this risk.

2 For an overview of Monte Carlo simulations, see Jäckel (2002) or Glasserman (2003).

3 For example, one portfolio would be 20% in each of the following buckets: floating, two years, five years, ten years and thirty years.

4 We computed them as annualised volatilities of daily returns, and similarly for correlations.

5 Interest cost is optimised first, and among all the portfolios with lowest interest cost, satisfying the increase constraint, we choose the one with lowest volatility.

6 We observed the volatility of interest cost over a 30-year period. If the period chosen were longer, 30-year swap rates would exhibit volatility.

7 For a detailed introduction to the numerical optimisation techniques, with and without constraints, see Press *et al* (2007).

13 *Asset and Liability Management*

So far in this book, we have focused entirely on the risks arising from company liabilities and disregarded the asset side of the balance sheet. In the past, companies would rarely have kept significant liquid financial assets for a long period of time, as low achievable investment return on those assets was considered to destroy value. However, this view changed after the credit crisis of 2008–9, when many companies found it difficult to refinance their short-term debt.[1] As a consequence of this and other factors,[2] post crisis we have found that many companies tend to have a significant amount of cash and other liquid assets on their balance sheet.[3]

The question of how much liquidity a company requires is an important and complex one, since it affects the company's funding cost and flexibility, but it is outside of the scope of the present volume.[4] The subject of Part II is interest rate risk management, so in this chapter we shall focus on the interaction between company's assets and liabilities and how it impacts the interest rate risk management.

This chapter also illustrates how to integrate currency and interest rate risk in the same analysis, since the company we studied has assets and liabilities in two currencies.

We start with a brief overview of the asset and liability management (ALM) as it applies to any company.

The first question in the mind of many corporate treasurers is how to define their interest rate risk. Let us consider two debt instruments with the same maturity and notional and in the same currency. One of them pays a fixed coupon of 5% per year, while the other pays a floating coupon of six-month Euribor plus 1% credit spread every six months. So, which one of the two has greater risk for the company?

The answer depends on how the company defines the interest rate risk, and there are two possibilities.

1. **Cashflow risk** is a risk to the cashflows due to the volatility of interest rates. Floating-rate debt (loans or floating-rate notes) has cashflow risk. Fixed-rate debt (fixed-rate loans or coupon bonds) does not. This risk is important if debt is kept until maturity, as it affects the interest cost.
2. **Fair-value risk** is a risk to the mark-to-market of instruments due to the volatility of interest rates. Floating-rate debt (loans or floating-rate notes) has no fair-value risk; fixed-rate debt (fixed-rate loans of coupon bonds) has it. This risk is important if the debt is bought back before maturity, as it is affects the unwinding cost.

In summary, which risk (cashflow or fair-value) is more important depends on whether the debt is likely to be unwound or kept until maturity. For instance, if the debt is kept until maturity, the relevant risk is the cashflow risk, and this is minimised by having fixed debt. On the other hand, if the debt is likely to be bought back before maturity, the fair-value risk is minimised by floating debt.

Table 13.1 Risk versus cost on the liability side

	Fixed liability	Floating liability
Cashflow risk (important if debt kept to maturity)	Low	High
Fair-value risk (important if debt likely to be bought back)	High	Low
Cost	High	Low

Before we discuss the asset side of the balance sheet, let us briefly discuss the returns. The equivalent of a high return on the liability side is low expected cost, and from our discussion in Chapter 7 we know that, on the average, lower cost (higher return) is achieved for floating-rate debt.

We summarise the risk/cost choices on the liability side in Table 13.1.

Now, let us turn our attention to the asset side of the balance sheet. Here we have a choice between fixed and floating assets and the risk follows the same pattern as on the liability side. However, the converse applies to returns, since fixed assets tend to pay a higher coupon than the floating ones, for the same reason that the fixed liabilities tend to pay a higher coupon than the floating ones, ie, because the typical shape of the yield curve is upwards sloping.

Therefore, we can summarise the risk–return choices on the asset side through Table 13.2.

Table 13.2 Risk versus return on the asset side

	Fixed asset	Floating asset
Cashflow risk (important if asset kept to maturity)	Low	High
Fair-value risk (Important if asset likely to be sold)	High	Low
Return	High	Low

Now, companies generally tend to keep their liabilities until maturity, while the assets have to be fairly liquid, since the company never knows when it may require extra cash. This means that, for most companies, liability choice is one between high risk/low cost (floating debt) and low risk/high cost (fixed debt). At the same time, assets present a choice between high risk/high returns (fixed assets) and low risk/low returns (floating assets). Therefore, on both sides of the balance sheet, most companies face the decision of whether to go for a more risky but more efficient strategy or for a more conservative but less efficient option.

How does this picture change when a company has both assets and liabilities?

In this case, it turns out that there is an almost perfect solution, which minimises both kinds of risks and maximises the returns at the same time. If a company chooses floating debt (for instance, by issuing fixed bonds and swapping them into floating) and floating assets, it can benefit from minimal risk and maximum return on the liability side:

- floating debt means that the cost is minimised;
- floating debt and assets means that the fair value risk is also minimised, as can be seen from Tables 13.1 and 13.2;

- most importantly, the cashflow risk between floating debt and floating assets will also cancel,[5] assuming the same currency, maturity and size of the debt and assets.

The only thing that is not optimised is the return on the asset side as, in a perfect world, the highest returns would be obtained for fixed assets. Alas, we do not live in a perfect world.

Of course, as in every case in this book, the real-life situation is not so simple. Companies' assets and liabilities tend to vary over time, tenor and currency; therefore, it is not always easy to offset the floating-rate risks. There are also all the operational, tax and other issues, with which the company has to deal before attempting any kind of ALM optimisation. In the example below, we disregard all these issues in order to demonstrate the main ideas of how ALM can be optimised for interest rate and currency risks.

BACKGROUND

This chapter describes a USD-reporting company named Health Care Company (HCC), which develops and manufactures pharmaceuticals and health-care products. Due to a significant proportion of its revenues and operating costs arising from business in Japan, HCC partly finances its activity in JPY.

Following the divestment of a division, HCC has been left with a significant USD cash position, which cannot be returned to shareholders immediately due to tax issues and potential future acquisitions. In order to improve the asset and liability structure, HCC's risk management department has been tasked with finding an optimal fixed–floating and duration mix. The company wants to optimise its portfolio of assets and liabilities, while maintaining sufficient flexibility to unwind them at any time.

COMPANY OBJECTIVES

- To find the appropriate combination of different fixed–floating compositions for both USD assets and JPY liabilities.
- To optimise the duration of USD assets and JPY liabilities.
- To take into account both the CFaR (cashflows-at-risk) and VaR (value-at-risk) measures of risk, with the VaR measure being the principal one, since the company wants to maintain the

flexibility of unwinding the current ALM structure in case of any significant company changes.

ANALYSIS

Methodology

To determine the optimal combination, we use the efficient frontier analysis (Figure 13.1), optimising the interest revenue (IR).

Figure 13.1 Risk management approach

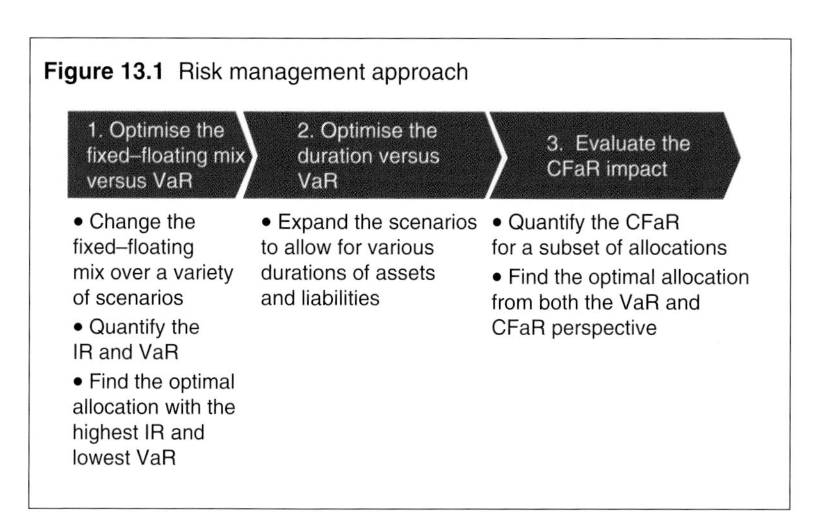

Over a one year time horizon, we modelled the distribution of the USD interest rate, JPY interest rate and the USDJPY foreign exchange rate, compared fixed–floating and duration mixes for both USD assets and JPY liabilities and found the optimal allocation with the highest expected IR and the lowest VaR and CFaR.

Assumptions

HCC has JPY liabilities and USD assets and liabilities. The composition of assets and liabilities is given in Figure 13.2.

We assume that interest expense and revenue are given by USD and JPY interest rates:[6]

- for the floating rate, one-year Libor rate in USD or JPY;
- for the fixed rate, three-year, five-year and seven-year swap rate.

Figure 13.2 Assumptions on assets and liabilities

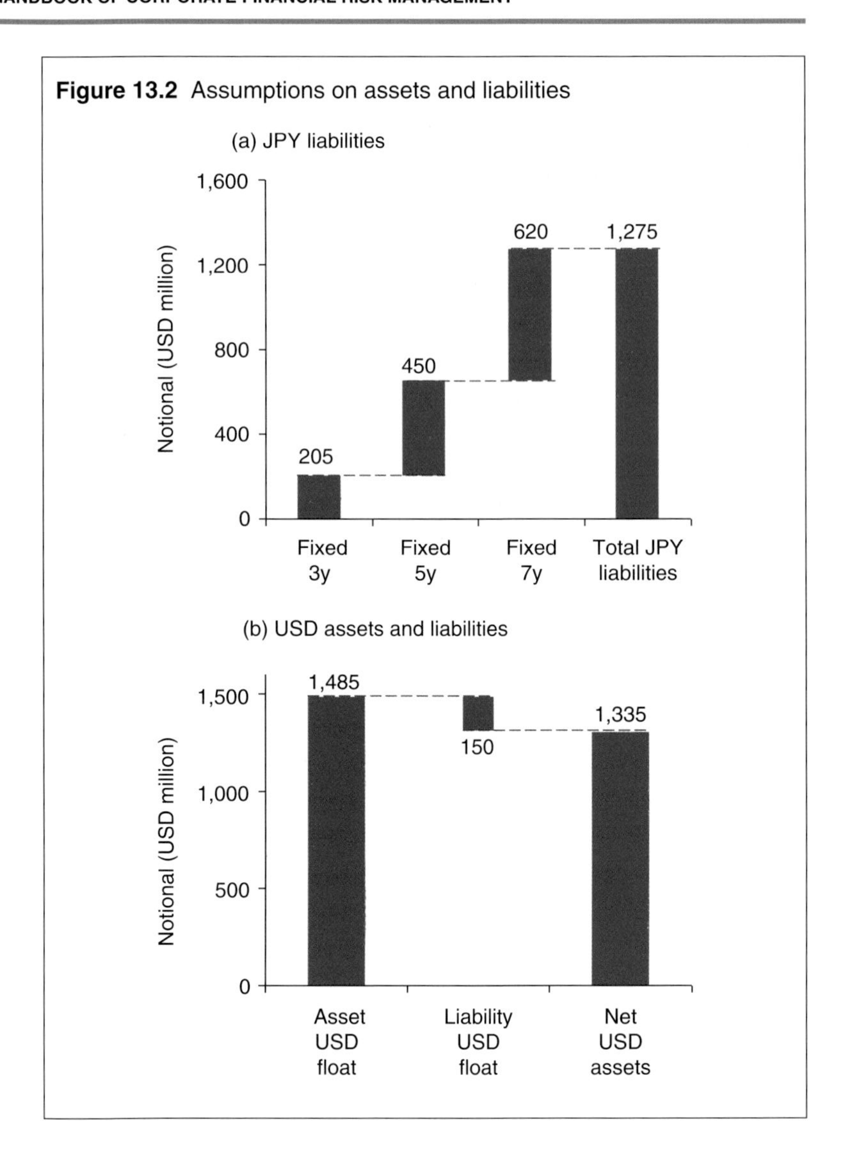

Interest expense comes from JPY and USD liabilities, while interest revenue comes from USD assets. As a result

$$\text{net interest revenue} = \text{interest revenue} - \text{interest expense}$$

We calculate the VaR and CFaR from the foreign exchange and interest rate distribution implied by market data. As before, the mean is given by the forward rates,[7] while the 95th percentile is determined from option markets.

STEP 1: OPTIMISE THE FIXED–FLOATING MIX VERSUS VALUE-AT-RISK

We compared 3,000 scenarios of fixed and floating assets and liabilities in USD and JPY. Each scenario was defined by the proportion of floating versus fixed for three years, five years and seven years in both currencies. For each scenario we computed the one-year interest revenue IR versus the annualised VaR at 95th percentile due to foreign exchange and interest rate changes.

Figure 13.3 Expected interest revenue versus VaR at 95% (USD million)

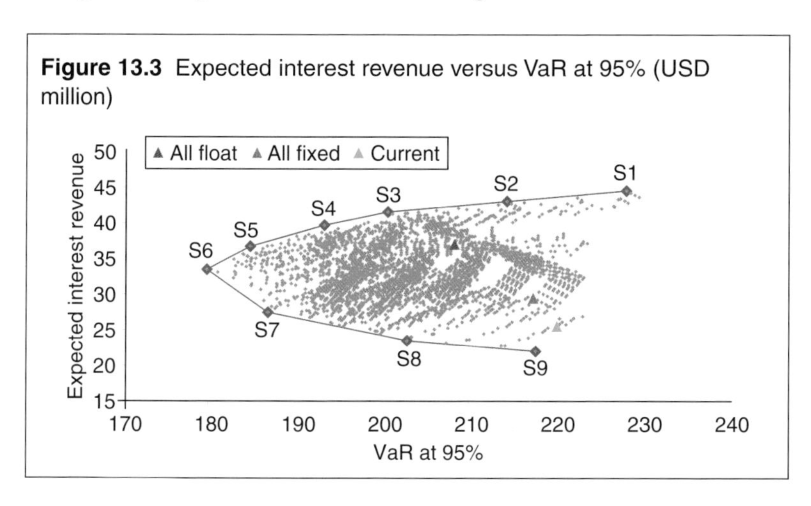

Table 13.3 VaR scenario analysis

Scenario	JPY float liability (%)	USD float asset (%)	Expected IR (USD m)	Annualised VaR at 95% (USD m)
S1	**100**	**0**	**45**	**228**
S2	**100**	**30**	**43**	**214**
S3	**100**	**40**	**42**	**201**
S4	**90**	**60**	**40**	**193**
S5	**30**	**50**	**37**	**185**
S6	**0**	**50**	**33**	**180**
S7	0	50	27	187
S8	0	70	23	203
S9	0	100	22	218
Current	0	100	26	220
All floating	100	100	37	208
All fixed	0	0	29	217

The efficient frontier is defined as the maximum expected IR for minimum VaR. We can see in Figure 13.3 that scenarios S1 to S6 are superior to all the others because they provide the highest IR for a given VaR. These scenarios correspond to having up to 50% floating assets in USD. The optimal floating proportion in JPY depends on the USD proportion (Table 13.3). The choice between these six scenarios can be determined based on the risk appetite of HCC.

The shape of the efficient frontier is explained by the following two competing effects.

1. Due to steep interest rate curves in both USD and JPY, a higher IR is obtained for USD fixed assets and JPY floating liabilities.

2. A higher proportion of fixed assets or liabilities corresponds to a higher VaR (due to higher IR sensitivity), unless there is an offset between fixed assets and fixed liabilities. The offset is highest in portfolio S6, where 100% JPY fixed liabilities partly offset 50% USD fixed assets.[8]

STEP 2: OPTIMISE THE DURATION VERSUS VALUE-AT-RISK

In this step, we expand the scenario definition to include various duration mixes. For each of the nine scenarios S1, S2, ..., S9 from step 1, we tried various combinations of fixed assets and liabilities with maturities split between three, five and seven years. The results are shown in Table 13.4. In order to optimise the IR versus VaR, according to our model, HCC should move from the current position to one of the scenarios S1 to S6 (up to 100% of USD assets fixed for seven years). However, given that the future amount of USD assets is not easy to predict in real life (possible higher dividend payments, acquisitions, etc), fixing such a large proportion for a long period of time may not be feasible.

We thus suggested that HCC consider fixing a smaller amount (no more than 50%) for as long as possible.[9] This should optimise the interest rate risk/reward, while giving HCC sufficient flexibility and liquidity. In Table 13.4 this corresponds to scenarios S5 and S6.

One question that still needs to be answered is whether fixing a significant proportion of USD assets (50%) and JPY liabilities (70–100%), which reduces the VaR, at the same time decreases the CFaR.

Table 13.4 VaR scenario analysis, including duration split

Scenario	JPY float liability	JPY 3y liability	JPY 5y liability	JPY 7y liability
S1	**100**	**0**	**0**	**0**
S2	**100**	**0**	**0**	**0**
S3	**100**	**0**	**0**	**0**
S4	**90**	**10**	**0**	**0**
S5	**30**	**70**	**0**	**0**
S6	**0**	**100**	**0**	**0**
S7	0	0	50	50
S8	0	0	0	100
S9	0	0	0	100
Current	0	20	30	50
All floating	100	0	0	0
All fixed	0	0	0	100

Scenario	USD float asset	USD 3y asset	USD 5y asset	USD 7y asset	Expected IR (USD m)	Annualised VaR at 95% (USD m)
S1	**0**	**0**	**0**	**100**	**45**	**228**
S2	**30**	**0**	**0**	**70**	**43**	**214**
S3	**40**	**0**	**0**	**60**	**42**	**201**
S4	**60**	**0**	**0**	**40**	**40**	**193**
S5	**50**	**0**	**0**	**50**	**37**	**185**
S6	**50**	**20**	**30**	**0**	**33**	**180**
S7	50	0	0	50	27	187
S8	70	0	0	30	23	203
S9	100	0	0	0	22	218
Current	100	0	0	0	26	220
All floating	100	0	0	0	37	208
All fixed	0	0	0	100	29	217

STEP 3: EVALUATE THE CASHFLOW-AT-RISK IMPACT

We compare the 12 scenarios from the previous page to evaluate the impact of fixing a significant proportion from a cashflow perspective, as suggested by the VaR analysis. These are shown in Figure 13.4 and Table 13.5. To analyse this impact, we measure the CFaR, which represents the cashflow variability in the worst case at a 95th percentile confidence level. We note that scenarios S4 and S5 have the lowest CFaR, due to a high fixed proportion.

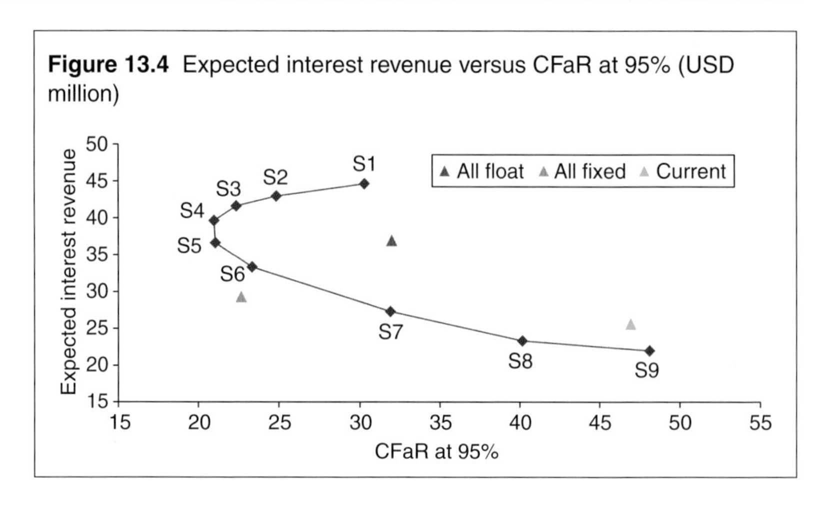

Figure 13.4 Expected interest revenue versus CFaR at 95% (USD million)

Table 13.5 CFaR scenario analysis

Scenario	JPY float liability (%)	USD float asset (%)	Expected IR (USD m)	Annualised CFaR at 95% (USD m)
S1	**100**	**0**	**45**	**30**
S2	**100**	**30**	**43**	**25**
S3	**100**	**40**	**42**	**22**
S4	**90**	**60**	**40**	**20**
S5	**30**	**50**	**37**	**20**
S6	0	50	33	24
S7	0	50	27	32
S8	0	70	23	40
S9	0	100	22	48
Current	0	100	26	47
All floating	100	100	37	32
All fixed	0	0	29	22

Together the VaR and CFaR optimisation leads us to suggest scenario S5 as optimal, subject to flexibility and liquidity constraints mentioned.

RECOMMENDATIONS

HCC could optimise its fixed–floating mix by putting 30% JPY liabilities into floating and 70% fixed for three years, with 50% of USD assets floating and 50% fixed for seven years.

This strategy would allow HCC to increase expected annual IR by about USD 11 million (ie, USD 37 million – USD 26 million), assuming the market rates at the time of writing, and to reduce the annualised VaR by about USD 35 million (ie, USD 220 million – USD 185 million). In addition, one-year CFaR is reduced by almost USD 27 million (ie, USD 47 million – USD 20 million).

At first sight, this strategy seems counter-intuitive, but it is based on a strong offset between MTM of JPY fixed liabilities and USD fixed assets. However, given that the future amount of USD assets may not be easy to predict (due to possible higher dividend payments, acquisitions, etc), fixing a large proportion of assets for a long period of time may not be practical. Therefore, we suggested that HCC consider fixing a smaller amount (approximately 40%) for as long as possible (two to three years). This should optimise the interest rate risk/reward while giving HCC sufficient flexibility and liquidity.

CONCLUSION

In this chapter, we showed how to expand the analysis of optimal fixed–floating mix of liabilities to the situation in which assets are also taken into account and where there is more than one currency. Furthermore, in this chapter, we took into account both VaR and CFaR considerations. The next chapter also deals with the ALM framework, but this time in a corporate pension context.

1 See Chambers (2008).

2 For example, the company keeps significant liquidity in a foreign subsidiary, as transferring it onshore and paying it as a dividend would expose the company to significant tax liabilities.

3 See Moody's (2011).

4 Note that, when we talk about liquidity, we mean the amount of available cash and short-term liquid assets that the company has at its disposal. This is not to be confused with another meaning of liquidity, which is the possibility of trading a company's securities (eg, debt, equity and others) quickly and at a low cost. See, for example, Amihud and Mendelson (2008).

5 For instance, if debt pays Libor plus 1% and assets gain Libor, the volatilities of Libor will cancel.

6 Obviously, in real life, there would be a credit spread on both sides of the balance sheet. We disregard this, as it does not change anything important in our example.

7 We use the same methodology as in Chapter 10.

8 The fact that S6 had the lowest VaR is due to a matrix of correlations between swap rates in USD and JPY that we used in our calculation to compute the VaR of a portfolio. The actual composition of the portfolio S6 by maturity and currency will change as a result of changes in that correlation matrix.

9 In reality this would rarely be longer than 12 months, but here we allow for up to seven years.

14

Pension Fund Asset and Liability Management

This is our second chapter that deals with both the asset and liability sides of the corporate balance sheet. In this case the assets and liabilities come from the corporate pension fund. The subject of ALM for pension funds is quite broad and in this chapter we offer the reader only a peek into this vast area from the perspective of corporate risk. The interested reader should consult Mitra and Schwaiger (2011) or Scherer (2003).

The basic problem in pensions ALM is the mismatch between the pension's assets and its liabilities. Companies that provide to their employees a defined-benefit pension scheme guarantee a certain level of benefits for a period of time after retirement. These benefits form the pension liabilities and are backed by pension assets. Assets can be any financial assets, but most frequently they are equities and government or corporate bonds, held either directly by the pension fund or through third-party asset managers. A certain part of the liabilities is paid every year, but funds must take into account the net present value of future cashflows when computing the pension position. If the present value of all pension liabilities is higher than the present value of pension assets, we say that the pension fund is in deficit. Otherwise, it is in surplus. Pension fund ALM deals with the question of how to reduce the volatility of pension fund deficit or surplus due to various market factors. In this chapter we shall focus on the effect of risk of the pension fund surplus on equity and interest rate volatility only, and disregard other potential sources of risk: actuarial, currency, inflation, etc.

BACKGROUND

CPF is a Canadian pension fund, which owns assets in Canadian, US and European equities, as well as Canadian government bonds.

At the time of writing CPF had a substantial actuarial surplus of CAD 1 billion, but the treasury and the pension fund trustees were worried about the future sustainability of this surplus. They asked us to advise them on the risk management of their assets and liabilities.

COMPANY OBJECTIVES

- To quantify the market risks to CPF's asset and liability portfolio.
- To explore alternative ways to achieve a stable funding surplus.

ANALYSIS

We calculated the value distribution of CPF's assets and liabilities over the five-year period. We could then deduce the projected surplus/deficit and the VaR for it. Finally, we decomposed the risk into its constituents and offered hedging solutions.

The approach follows the steps in Figure 14.1.

Figure 14.1 Risk management approach: step by step

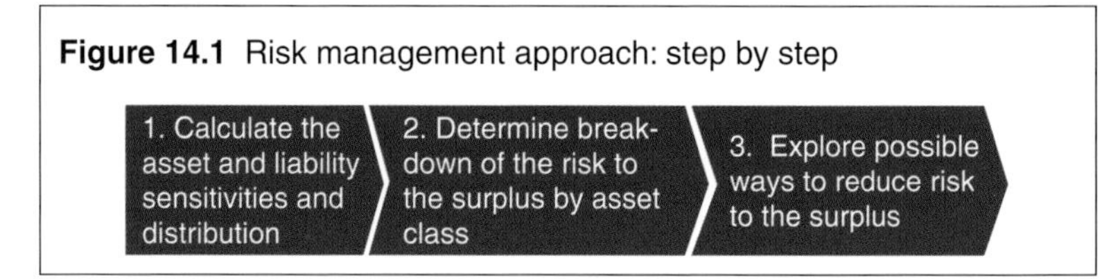

STEP 1: CALCULATE THE ASSET AND LIABILITY SENSITIVITIES AND DISTRIBUTION

Table 14.1 Composition of CPF's assets

Asset class	Proportion (%)	Duration (y)
Canadian equities	27	—
US equities	18	—
EUR equities	15	—
CAD government bonds	40	7.2

CPF has assets valued at CAD 25.7 billion, composed of the asset classes (we assume zero duration for equities) given in Table 14.1. The total weighted duration of the assets is 2.9 years.

CPF has a liability structure based on the projected payments for the next 100 years. The liability has a present value of CAD 24.7 billion and a duration of 13.7 years, which is much longer than the asset duration. The fund surplus can therefore be strongly affected by movements in the Canadian swap rates. In Figure 14.2, we show the sensitivity of assets and liabilities to parallel shifts in CAD swap rates.

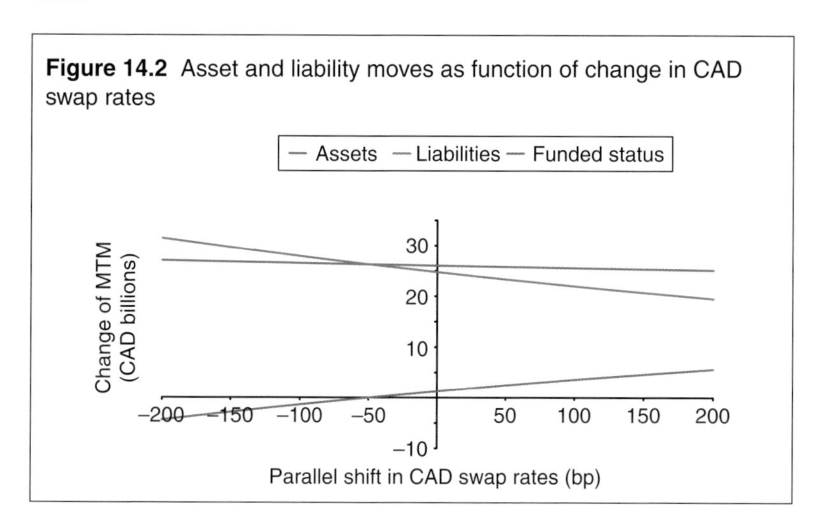

Figure 14.2 Asset and liability moves as function of change in CAD swap rates

There, we can see that the liabilities, due to their long duration, are very sensitive to the reduction in swap rates; as the rates drop, the discounting factor increases, so the liabilities tend to grow. On the asset side we have the opposite situation, but the sensitivity to rates is considerably lower, due to a small proportion of debt instruments among assets and their shorter duration. Therefore, net impact when we take into account both assets (low duration) and liabilities (high duration) is sensitivity to lower interest rates.[1]

Risk from the swap rate volatility is only part of the overall surplus risk. We used a Monte Carlo simulation to calculate the possible future values of the bonds, stocks and liabilities in CPF's portfolio. We then used this data to compute the expected surplus/deficit over the next five years, as well as its VaR and upside potential. The projected surplus and 5% best/worst case intervals are presented in Figure 14.3 and Table 14.2.

As we can see, CPF has a projected rising surplus for the next few years. However, it also has a large risk for this surplus, which may

Figure 14.3 Surplus and 5% best/worst case surplus

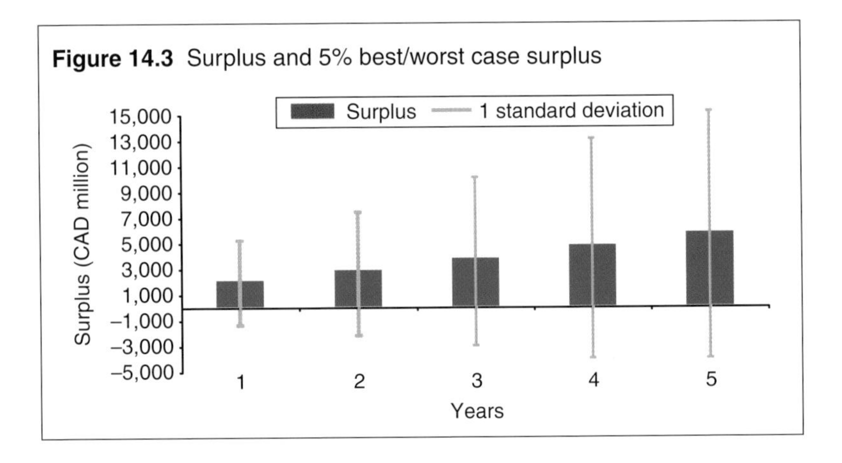

Table 14.2 CPF fund surplus and 5% best/worst case surplus (CAD million)

Surplus (CAD bn)	Year 0	1	2	3	4	5
5% best	1.0	5.2	7.4	10.1	13.1	15.2
Projected	1.0	2.1	2.9	3.8	4.8	5.8
5% worst	1.0	−1.4	−2.2	−3.0	−4.0	−4.0

put CPF into a deficit within one year at a 5% probability. Within five years, the surplus may turn into a substantial deficit (of CAD 4 billion).

STEP 2: DETERMINE BREAKDOWN OF THE RISK TO THE SURPLUS BY ASSET CLASS

We calculate the contribution of each asset class[2] to the VaR of the pension surplus in five years.[3] This breakdown is shown in Figure 14.4. The equity part consists of all stocks owned by the fund, while the fixed-income part consists of both the Canadian government bond assets and the liabilities of the fund. As expected, most of the risk comes from the large equity exposure. This is also the part of the portfolio that may give a higher return. The interest rate risk is smaller, but still substantial. It can be easily hedged with liquid products, such as interest rate swaps, swaptions or caps.

Figure 14.4 Five-year VaR at 95% by asset class

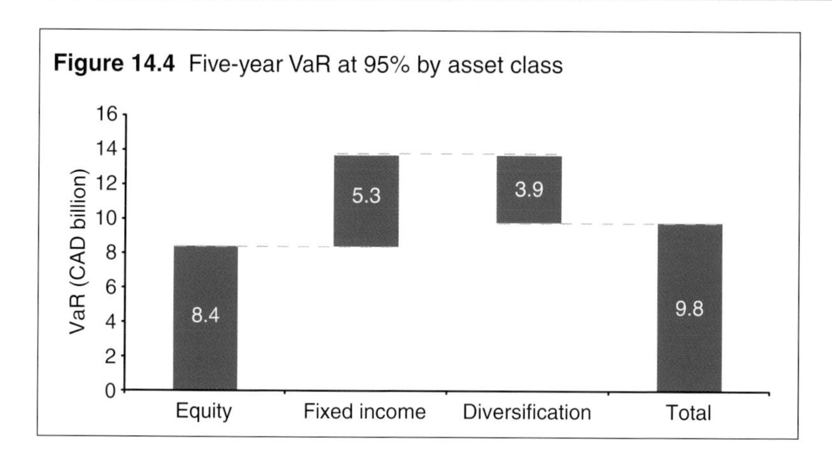

STEP 3: EXPLORE POSSIBLE WAYS TO REDUCE RISK TO THE SURPLUS

CPF can reduce the two different risks independently.

- **Reducing interest rate risk:** CPF could enter into interest rate swaps, which are designed to match the total duration of their assets to that of their liabilities. This procedure reduces the interest rate related risks almost entirely. As an example of this method, assume that interest rates decrease by 1%. The discounted value of CPF's fixed-income assets would then increase by 2.9%, while the liabilities would increase by 13.7%,[4] and therefore the surplus would decrease by 10.8% = 13.7% – 2.9%. In order to counter that risk, CPF should enter into an interest rate swap where it pays floating and receives a fixed coupon. The value of the swap would increase with the decrease in rates, and counter the loss on the liabilities. If interest rates increase instead, the liability value would decrease, but the decrease in the swap value would keep the surplus unchanged.

- **Reducing equity risk:**[5] CPF can enter into equity collars or other equity derivatives[6] to limit its risk. However, this kind of solution limits the upside potential of the investment as much as the downside. Since collars are priced based on the forward value of the equity rather than its expected value, the collars do not incorporate any equity risk premium, which contributes a substantial part of the portfolio return. CPF could also move some of the equity portfolio into structured products, which would allow it more tailor-made solutions matching its required risk and return. The structured products could be capital protected, causing a reduction in CPF's asset risk.

RECOMMENDATIONS

CPF should consider entering into the three swaps in Table 14.3.

Table 14.3 Risk-reducing swaps

Maturity	Notional (CAD bn)	Type
5 years	4.5	Pay fixed
10 years	8.2	Receive fixed
30 years	10.1	Receive fixed

These swaps were chosen to reduce the mismatch between CPF's liability duration and the asset duration, thereby immunising the surplus against interest rate risk, as presented in Figure 14.5. There we can see that the impact of the dollar curve shifts or rotations[7] on swaps (purple line) is opposite from their impact on the CPF surplus (red line), thereby making the net impact flat (blue line).

The inclusion of these swaps can decrease the VaR for the surplus from CAD 9.8 billion to CAD 8.4 billion, which is the equity VaR, as shown in Figure 14.4.

To counter the equity risk, CPF could enter into equity collars. By collaring 15% of the equity portfolio, the portfolio VaR could be further decreased to

$$\text{CAD } 7.0 \text{ billion} = \text{CAD } 5.6 \text{ billion} - (-\text{CAD } 1.4 \text{ billion})$$

over five years, as shown in Figure 14.6 and Table 14.4. This also reduces the possible deficit in year 5 (at 95% confidence interval) from CAD 4.0 billion to CAD 1.4 billion.

CONCLUSION

In this chapter, we illustrated an additional topic for ALM optimisation: optimisation of pension funds and liabilities. We simplified greatly the discussion in order to focus on main ideas and described only the reduction of interest rate and equity risk.

Figure 14.5 Sensitivity to swap curve shifts and swap curve rotation

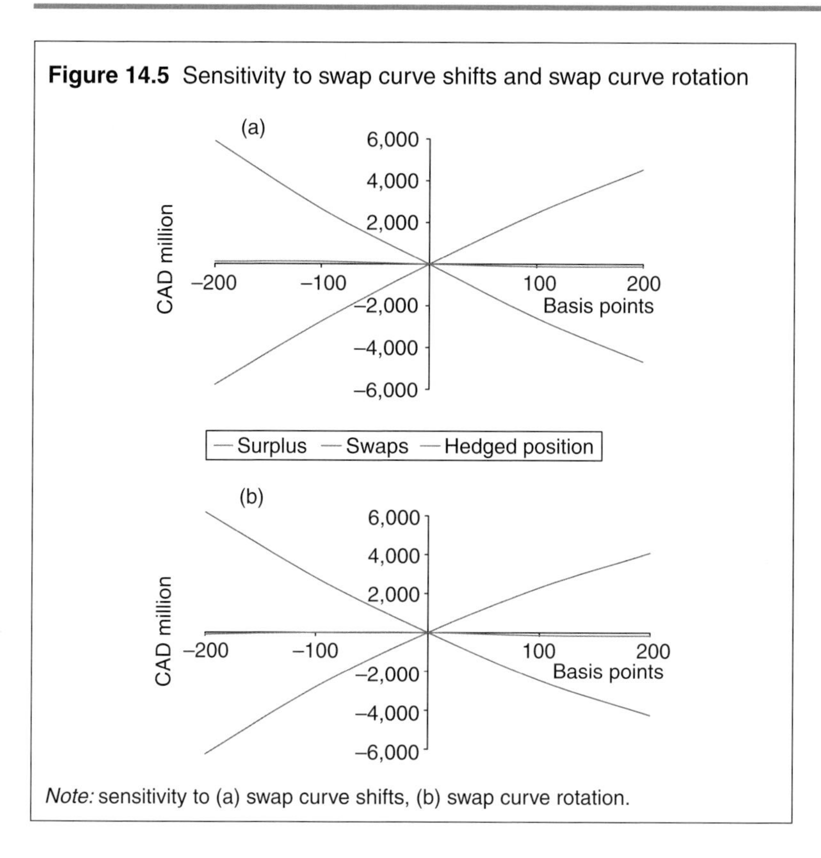

Note: sensitivity to (a) swap curve shifts, (b) swap curve rotation.

Figure 14.6 Surplus and 5% best/worst case surplus including swaps and collars

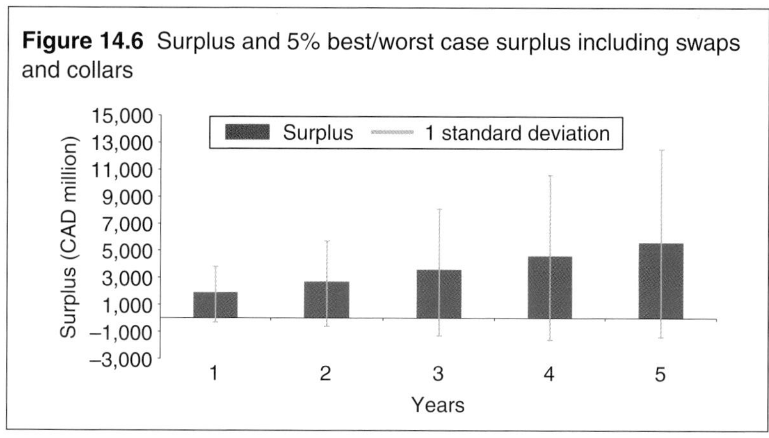

In Part II we have illustrated a variety of issues related to the management of interest rate risk and in Part III we turn our attention to the currency risk.

Table 14.4 Surplus and 5% best/worst case surplus including swaps and collars (CAD million)

Surplus (CAD bn)	Year					
	0	1	2	3	4	5
5% best	1.0	3.8	5.7	8.1	10.6	12.5
Projected	1.0	1.9	2.7	3.6	4.6	5.6
5% worst	1.0	−0.3	−0.6	−1.3	−1.6	−1.4

1 To do this, we subtract liabilities from assets.

2 Since CPF's liabilities are denominated in CAD, while part of their assets are USD and EUR equities, there is also a currency risk between USDCAD rate and EUR–CAD rate. For simplicity of exposure, we shall disregard this risk in the discussion which follows, but in practice pension funds should and do also care about currency risks.

3 A five-year period has been chosen for illustration; in practice, it could be shorter or considerably longer.

4 Remember that the duration of assets (which is equal to the sensitivity of assets to interest rates) is 2.9 years and the duration of liabilities is 13.7 years. So, for a 1% change, assets increase by 2.9% and liabilities by 13.7%.

5 Since CPF's liabilities are denominated in CAD, while part of the assets is in USD and EUR, it would be possible to hedge the currency risk also via currency forwards, options and other instruments.

6 For an overview of equity derivatives as applied to a corporate environment, see Ramirez (2011).

7 Rotation is defined as a steepening of the yield curve at the ten-year maturity by a given number of basis points, keeping the five-year point constant and the proportional shift of all the other points on the curve (negative below five years and positive above).

Part III

Currency Risk

Currency Risk

Among the types of risk with which companies deal, currency, or foreign exchange (FX), risk[1] is the one requiring the most maintenance. Basically, FX affects all aspects of corporate financials: cashflows, earnings, assets and liabilities. Therefore, FX influences all key performance indicators from profitability to leverage. The degree of importance of FX risk management varies across sectors, from tactical for some, to strategic for companies with long production cycles, where the exchange rate is a key component of competitiveness and sometimes even of the company's existence. Whatever the nature or consequence of FX risk, a corporate hedging policy has a unique goal across industries: to reduce the variability of financials in order to ensure sustainable growth and return to stakeholders.

Since FX is a key source of risk for companies, the corporate sector is also a major player in the global FX market. Actually, corporate hedging activity stabilises the currency market for a host of reasons. First, unlike financial institutions who indulge in fast money flows, corporates act as long-term end users. Second, their FX activity is fairly predictable and consistent; treasuries usually buy or sell currencies according to well-defined hedging programmes, regardless of the short-term market noise. Third, corporate flows often mirror the investors' flows, therefore bringing stability to the market.

The FX market has experienced many transformations since 1980. The introduction of options in the 1980s was followed by more complex structures in the 1990s. Since then the fast-growing electronic-trading ("e-trading") has completely changed the practice of corporate treasuries. At the time of writing, almost three quarters of companies trade electronically, allowing both a significant reduction of bid–offer spreads and "straight-through processing" of transactions. At the same time, the market has experienced the rapid growth and development of emerging market currencies,[2] which have come to represent a significant part of the corporate hedging programme. Also, the on-going deleveraging of banks coupled with Basel III regulatory reforms will shape the FX hedging toolbox in the future.

Since the beginning of the financial crisis in 2008, it has seemed that uncertainty is the new standard. Foreseeing cashflows, investment and financing may be challenging for the treasury department in the volatile economic and financial environments in which companies have operated since then. When dealing with currency exposures, whether transaction or translation risk, a new dimension deserves to be integrated: uncertainty, which substantiates the increasing role of options in corporate risk management.

In the future, we expect currency risk innovation to encompass three streams:

1. e-trading will continue to progress, offering corporate treasuries streamlined FX and cash management platforms;
2. emerging markets will continue to mature and converge towards G10 markets in terms of their liquidity and breadth of products;
3. after a slowdown since 2000, FX hedging product innovation will resume. This will be not in order to create complex payouts, but with a view to providing corporate treasuries with Basel III friendly products and solutions permitting growing uncertainty to be managed when predicting foreign exchange exposures.

The risk management literature identifies three classes of FX risk.

1. **Structural risk:** the sensitivity of the long-term profitability of a company to movements in FX rates due to the location of its production and sales and the competitive environment. For instance, the aeronautic sector companies are subject to structural risk, as they all compete in the same USD denominated market with different cost base currencies.
2. **Translation risk:** the sensitivity of the consolidated financial statements (balance sheet and income statement) to changes in FX rates. Utilities produce locally; therefore, they do not have a mismatch between their sales and the cost of sales. However, their financial performance, expressed in their reporting currency, is affected when the currency of affiliates and subsidiaries depreciates. Translation risk affects shareholders' funds, net debt, all income statement lines and all the ratios based on those elements. In Chapter 18, we describe a solution

designed to protect a company from a deterioration of debt covenants due to translation risk.

3. **Transaction risk:** the most common FX risk, and the one that all companies hedge; it relates to the time mismatch between a transaction event (expected, committed or invoiced) and its payment.

For many companies, these three risks are interdependent. Companies reduce their structural risk by relocating their production facilities to where their client bases are. By doing so, they shift their risk from transaction to translation. In fact, we can say that there is only one fundamental type of currency risk, which is manifested in three ways.[3]

It is important to stress that companies sometimes have various ways of managing currency risks that do not involve financial solutions. Besides relocating production to the country of revenues, they can also hedge the currency risk directly through contracts with suppliers or customers. However, non-financial solutions are not always easy or even possible, and for many companies financial solutions are simplest.

An example of supplier contract risk management is Japanese car dealerships. The distributors of Japanese cars in countries pegged to the USD often purchase vehicles at a price linked to the USDJPY exchange rate, in such a way that the strengthening of the JPY against USD is accompanied by a lower underlying JPY car price.

As in the rest of this book, we shall not devote any more attention to non-financial ways of managing currency risk, since they tend to be out of the scope of the financial department.

We begin Part III with an overview of qualitative issues linked to a currency risk management policy. Chapter 15 on how to develop an FX hedging policy is similar to Chapter 6 on interest rate hedging strategy, in that it lists some of the key decisions that currency risk managers must make explicit before implementing the risk management programme.

Chapter 16, on netting FX risks, describes the situation when a company decides to quantify its overall currency exposure on a consolidated basis. In some cases, this process can produce unexpected results, and some of the risks which the company has previously hedged may turn out to cancel upon consolidation. In this case, the company has to find a way to reconcile the proper risk management strategy with accounting rules, which sometimes stand in the way.

Corporate treasuries are often faced with the following dilemma on long-term emerging market currency exposures: to hedge at the expense of significantly affecting the return on the investment, or to bear the risk of possible violent currency devaluations. In Chapter 17, we propose a dynamic risk management methodology for emerging market currencies, called "early warning signals", which deals with this question.

Chapter 18 describes a technical point about a very common covenant in the loan documentation specifying that the leverage has to be less than a certain level. Leverage is defined as debt divided by EBITDA, and, while debt upon consolidation is translated at the spot rate at the end of the period, EBITDA is translated at the average rate for the reporting period. As we shall see in this chapter, this may cause problems in the case of rapid movements of currencies, but it is possible to reduce the risk by using specially designed derivatives products.

In Chapter 19 we devote our attention to managing translation risk. Not all companies manage this risk, as it often is not considered as important as transaction risk. However, when they do, they are generally faced with a choice between risk reduction and the cost of hedging, which is related to the interest rate differential between the currency of the parent company and that of its subsidiary. In this chapter, we introduce a systematic methodology which allows companies to decide on the optimal hedging portfolio by currency. The portfolio can be created either through foreign currency debt or through cross-currency swaps or other derivatives.

We believe that one of the consequences of the Basel III capital rules is that companies will use more options in the future, due to the credit charge applicable to non-collateralised long-dated FX hedges. In Chapter 20, we depict a dynamic risk management methodology aimed at reducing bank capital use and charges linked to FX long-term hedging, with a view to preserving available credit lines and minimising the credit component of the hedging cost. This approach is based on an algorithm that defines, at any point in time, the mix of forwards (capital intensive) and purchased options (capital light) which minimises the expected VaR, while keeping the amount being hedged constant.

1 We shall use the terms "currency risk" and "FX risk" interchangeably throughout this book.

2 For instance, just think how much the ruble FX market has changed since the early 1990s, when the Russian government introduced ruble convertibility.

3 See Pringle and Connolly (1993).

15

How to Develop a Foreign Exchange Hedging Policy

In this chapter, we focus on the qualitative aspects of a currency (ie, FX) risk management policy. This has many themes in common with Chapter 6 (on developing an interest rate hedging policy). In particular:

- company objectives, to determine a proper risk management policy, based on peers but also including the company specificities;
- the choice of risk management approach between conservative, aggressive and dynamic;
- risk management objectives, prioritising reduction of economic variability over the cost and accounting aspects;
- derivatives portfolio composition, which is based on the hedge accounting portfolio wherever possible;
- processes and organisation;
- derivatives risks, introduced by risk management;
- limits on the use of derivatives, which mitigates the derivatives risks;
- performance measures, which allow the company to monitor the success of its risk management programme.
- benchmarking.

We shall not repeat any common themes from Chapter 6, and instead focus on the aspects which are specific to currency risk. However, it is worthwhile repeating that any risk management policy has to strike a balance between being too vague and overly detailed. On the one hand, it has to be specified in sufficient detail to protect the company from an unauthorised use of derivatives and, on the other hand, it should give sufficient flexibility to the financial team to protect the company in a wide variety of situations, instead of paralysing them by forcing them to ask permission for every small decision they make.

BACKGROUND

Media Corporation has now reached a stage where it is expanding internationally and would like to update its interest rate risk management policy to include currency risk. As a result of a recent acquisition, the company has acquired a USD-reporting company and is particularly interested in hedging the EURUSD currency risk. It also has smaller amounts of CHF and NOK exposures.

COMPANY OBJECTIVES

- To perform a peer group analysis.
- To determine a proper currency risk management procedure.

ANALYSIS

The approach chosen again followed the same three steps as in the previous project for the Media Corporation (on interest rate risk management; see Chapter 6 for further details), but this time focused on its currency risk (see Figure 15.1). In the rest of this chapter we focus on step 2: "best practice".

Figure 15.1 Risk management approach: step by step

1. Peer benchmarking	2. Determine risk management "best practice"	3. Develop a bespoke policy
• Determine the relevant peer group • Study their currency risk management policy	• Draw on our previous experience in similar projects and select aspects which work in practice • Synthesise the findings from the peer group in a set of "best practice" recommendations	• Find out what is specific to Media Corporation • Adjust the "best practice" to Media Corporation's specific circumstances

The first question is the scope of currency risk being covered. As we mentioned in the introduction to Part III, we can distinguish three kinds of currency risk:

1. structural risk;
2. translation risk;
3. transaction risk.

Of these three types of risk, structural risk is normally addressed outside of the scope of the company's risk management policy, since it has to do with such issues as the nature of competition in the industry, which is such a strategic issue that it is normally addressed at the board or CEO level. Therefore, in the rest of this chapter, we shall focus on translation and transaction risks only.

Translation risk can be further divided into the impact on consolidation upon the income statement and on the balance sheet. The accounting treatment of hedges depends on which of the two translation risks we are talking about, and the scope of the translation risk management policy should reflect that.

We discuss the accounting treatment of translation risk in more detail in Chapter 16 (on netting the group FX exposure) and we shall return to the subject of translation risk again in Chapter 19 (on how to manage translation risk).

For now let us just say that hedging the translation risk on the balance sheet is easy within International Financial Reporting Standards (IFRS), while hedging the translation risk on the income statement (ie, earnings) is difficult. A company wishing to hedge the translation risk on earnings would normally not be able to obtain hedge accounting treatment; therefore, the changes in the MTM of the hedge would affect the consolidated P&L. This would introduce temporary volatility in the accounts at intermediate periods, but over the full life of the hedge the economic benefit would match the accounting treatment. In other words, the intermediate volatility would eventually cancel out, and the cumulative treatment would be the desired one.

Let us assume that Media Corporation wants to hedge its earnings volatility from a USD subsidiary. The subsidiary is supposed to generate USD 100 million in consolidated earnings over the next 12 months. We assume no seasonality, so earnings are divided into four equal instalments of USD 25 million per quarter. At the end of a year, the USD earnings will be translated at the average rate for the year. In order to hedge this risk, the company can at the start of the year decide to enter into four forwards for USD 25 million, with maturities at the end of every quarter. At the year end, any loss on the average exchange rate will be offset by the gain on the forwards (and vice versa) and therefore the consolidated year-end P&L will be protected against adverse movements. However, at the end of Q1, Q2 and Q3, changes in the MTM of the forwards will be shown in the consolidated P&L with no underlying exposure to match.[1]

Therefore, if a company decides to hedge earnings of its subsidiaries, it has to make a choice between the intermediate accounting volatility and the final economic volatility.

Transactional risk can be also be subdivided according to the kinds of cashflows which are to be hedged:

- current (also known as "contracted") cashflows;
- forecast (also known as "uncertain") cashflows;
- exceptional cashflows (for example, during mergers and acquisitions and other atypical situations).

It is common for the company to cover only the first two categories of cashflows (ie, current and forecast) in their risk policy, while the exceptional cashflows are dealt with on a case-by-case basis, since it is difficult to create a policy which will cover all atypical situations equally well.

HOW MUCH TO HEDGE

Before we focus on the details of hedging policies, it is important to decide whether currency risk management makes sense in the first place. Based on the ratio of the underlying cashflow volatility (ie, unpredictability of future cashflows coming from the business, before any currency risk) to the currency volatility, we can roughly place all currency risks (whether transaction or translation) in one quadrant of Figure 15.2.

For example, if a company had very unpredictable cashflows in Danish NOK and was considering the risk from EURNOK exchange rate (where the volatility is small), it would find itself in the upper left quadrant. The underlying cashflow volatility in NOK is high, but the FX volatility is low. In this case, it does not make sense to hedge the

Figure 15.2 When to hedge the FX risk

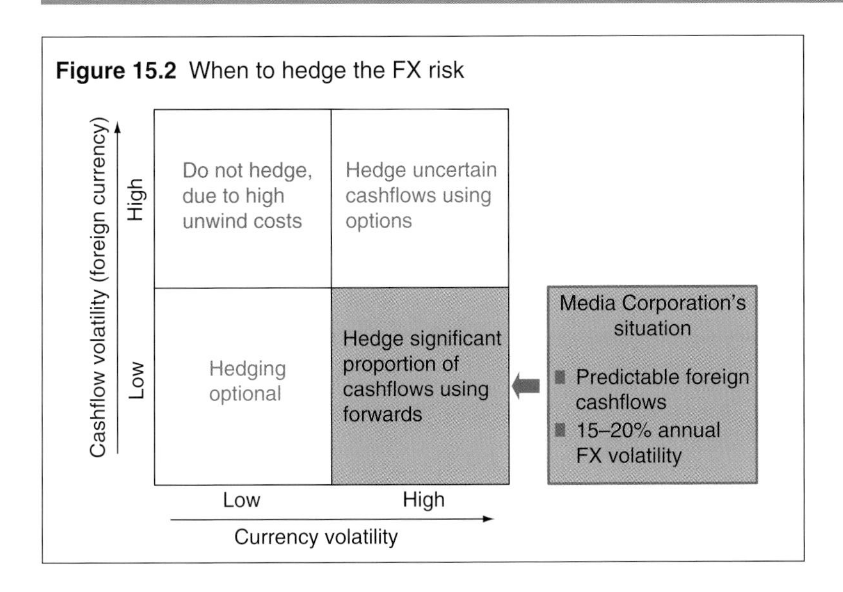

currency risk, as, in the situation of worse company performance in NOK than expected, the company may easily find itself overhedged, in which case it will have to unwind part of the hedges with potential MTM losses.

Media Corporation has found itself in the lower right quadrant, where it makes sense to cover a significant proportion of cashflows using forwards. If it does not do so, it is essentially deciding to run an "uncovered currency position". In practice, we know that such a risk is not usually rewarded.

Table 15.1 Example of the layered hedges

Maturity (months)	Hedging proportion (%)
6	100
12	75
18	50
24	25

Of course, for most companies, business results are easier to predict over shorter time horizons than over longer ones, so the cashflow volatility increases with their maturity. This is a reason why many companies chose "layered hedges", as in Table 15.1.

Sometimes a company finds itself in the upper right quadrant of Figure 15.2, which is the most difficult place to be from the perspective of currency risk. Cashflows are volatile and the currency risk is high, so hedging is essential but it is difficult to forecast the hedged amount.

In this case, the layered hedge approach can be combined with bought options, for the uncertain part of the cashflows, as shown in Table 15.2. In the case of Media Corporation, up to 25% of the cashflows were uncertain, with the uncertainty increasing over time.

Table 15.2 Example of the layered hedge approach with uncertain cashflows (%)

	Maturity (months)			
	6	12	18	24
Option proportion	10	15	20	25
Forward proportion	90	60	30	0

Companies that have more uncertain cashflows should use more options in their risk management strategy.

Figure 15.3 EURUSD history

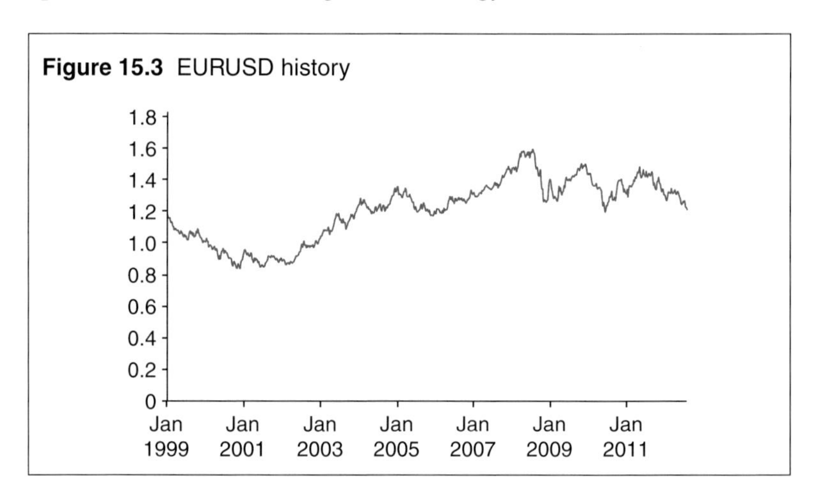

Media Corporation has another possibility to optimise its currency exposure, starting from the "layered hedges" in Table 15.1. If the cashflow exposures are expected to last for a long time and the company estimates that EURUSD exhibits a mean reverting pattern

Table 15.3 Example of the dynamic hedging policy for a USD seller/EUR buyer: hedging proportion (%)

Forward EURUSD level	Maturity (months)			
	6	12	18	24
<1.10	100	100	100	100
1.10–1.30	100	75	50	25
>1.30	100	50	0	0

(Figure 15.3), the company can create a dynamic strategy like the one in Table 15.3.

The idea behind the dynamic hedging policy is that if the company knows that it will have a certain risk exposure over a long period of time, it will increase its hedging proportion at the time when the forward rates are in its favour (Media Corporation would be selling USD and buying EUR, so a weak EUR (below 1.10) is considered favourable). If the EURUSD is in the intermediate range (between 1.10 and 1.30), the company would hedge according to the layered strategy defined in Table 15.1, and if it is in the strong EUR range (above 1.30), it would hedge less.

There are two problems with this strategy: if the EUR strengthens above 1.30, the company will reduce its hedging horizon from 24 months to 12, which may be considered too risky; if the EUR is in the favourable region below 1.10, Media Corporation would be required to hedge 100% of its 12-month, 18-month and 24-month exposures, which could cause it to overhedge, since longer-dated cashflows have increasing uncertainty. Therefore, Media Corporation decided to go ahead with the static, layered approach with uncertain cashflows as described in Table 15.2.[2]

BUDGET RATES

Similarly to benchmarking for interest rates (see Chapter 6), Media Corporation can choose a budget FX rate in a variety of ways: spot rate, forward rate, forecast rate, an external benchmark or any combination of the above. Often, budget rates are set not by the financial department but by business units, and it is the responsibility of the financial department to make sure that the budgeted rate is actually achieved. In periods of high currency volatility, budget rates can sometimes move so far away from the actual market that it is impossible for the financial department to achieve them without taking very high risks. In this case, rather than taking unwarranted risks, the financial department should inform the management that the budget rate is unrealistic.

We advised Media Corporation to keep an eye on the budget rate and to evaluate regularly the probability of achieving it by using the approved hedging products. If the probability were lower than a given threshold (eg, 80%), that should be signalled. This kind of analysis can be performed using a Monte Carlo simulation, of which we have shown many examples so far.

HEDGING PRODUCTS

As we showed in Chapter 6, a large proportion of the hedging portfolio should achieve hedge accounting, which severely limits the kinds of products that are eligible.

In many cases, companies will restrict themselves to using only the simplest currency forwards and options that satisfy hedge accounting. Media Corporation also considered two other kinds of products that do not normally satisfy hedge accounting, ie, average rate or strike options and basket options. The reasons for using average rate products have already been mentioned,[3] and, similarly, basket options allow a company to protect themselves against negative movement in a basket of currencies to which they are exposed. If one currency weakens while the other one strengthens, Media Corporation will not be affected on a consolidated level, and the basket option reflects that risk, while a portfolio of bought options would provide protection on each individual currency basis.

As before, non-hedge accounting products would only be used by Media Corporation when the objectives of risk management cannot be achieved by hedge accounting products.

WHICH CURRENCIES TO HEDGE

Media Corporation had to decide on which currencies to hedge. Table 15.4 shows the geographical composition of exposures.

Media Corporation has its largest foreign exposure (20%) coming from USD, so it is clear that it needs to be hedged. However, it is not clear what to do about the exposures from BRL and CHF. BRL exposure is the most expensive exposure to hedge from the perspective of

Table 15.4 Geographical composition of exposures

Currency	Business proportion (%)	Exchange rate v. EUR	1y Libor (%)	1y interest rate differential currency v. EUR (%)	1y standard deviation of currency v. EUR (%)
EUR	70	1.0	3.40	N/A	N/A
BRL	5	2.0	10.00	6.60	15.0
USD	20	1.4	5.50	2.10	10.9
CHF	5	1.2	1.90	−1.50	2.9

carry (interest rate differential versus EUR), but also the volatility is highest. On the other hand, the CHF has negative carry but a much smaller volatility.

Table 15.5 Carry versus currency volatility

Currency	1y Libor (%)	1y interest rate diff. currency v. EUR (%)	1y SD* of currency v. EUR (%)	Carry/1y SD* of currency v. EUR (%)	Hedging order based on carry/SD of currency
EUR	3.40	N/A	N/A	N/A	
BRL	10.00	6.60	15.0	0.44	Third
USD	5.50	2.10	10.9	0.19	Second
CHF	1.90	−1.50	2.9	−0.52	First

Note: * SD, standard deviation.

We proposed that the company decide on the hedging proportion between CHF and BRL based on the relative carry divided by the volatility (measured by the standard deviation of currency). We show these numbers in Table 15.5.

We can see that the CHF has the best ratio at −0.52, so it should be hedged first, followed by the USD, and the BRL last. The company has to decide whether the relatively high cost of hedging BRL justifies the risk and, in this case, since BRL is a relatively small part of overall cashflows, the company has decided not to hedge BRL.

In this case, the choice was relatively easy, but in some cases companies have a significant amount of foreign currency risk from a country with a high carry compared with currency volatility. In those cases, it is not so easy to decide whether to hedge or not. In practice, companies can choose to hedge the high carry currencies using the "Early Warning Signals" methodology (for details see Chapter 17) or using a proxy hedge. For instance, we have seen an innovative use of Brazilian sovereign CDSs to hedge the BRL currency risk.[4]

The analysis of the exposure to various currencies can be improved by using VaR models to aggregate the overall exposure of Media Corporation to all the risky currencies. We show examples of this in other chapters later in Part III.

RECOMMENDATIONS

After we performed the peer group comparison and analysed the best practices in risk management and how they applied to Media Corporation, we came up with the following recommendations:

- to adopt a static hedging layered approach including options for current and forecast cashflows;
- to focus on hedging the risk from CHF and USD;
- to hedge the balance-sheet translation risk via foreign currency debt and net investment hedges.[5]

CONCLUSION

In this chapter, we reviewed the main qualitative aspects of currency risk management policy. It is important to stress that all companies have a slightly different set of priorities when it comes to managing risk, and that therefore what we have shown in this case is just an example of one such study. Many of the topics are similar to Chapter 6.

1 For instance, at the end of first quarter, the company will show the impact on USD 25 million earnings of the first quarter only, while the contribution from non-hedge accounting forwards will include the changes in the MTM of all four forwards with a total notional of USD 100 million.

2 In practice, we see the dynamic hedging policy only in industries with longer and more predictable cashflows, ie, construction or aerospace. See Chapter 20 for more details.

3 That is, because companies translate foreign earnings at the average rate for the period.

4 See page 356 of the 2009 Annual Report of GDF Suez at http://www.gdfsuez.com/.

5 For more details, see Chapter 19.

16

Netting Foreign Exchange Risks

As we mentioned in Chapter 15, IFRS has many problems. Sometimes, what would in our view be a perfectly reasonable risk management operation does not get the hedge accounting treatment. One of the areas where this becomes most apparent is the treatment of currency risk at the parent company as opposed to a subsidiary level.

For example, let us assume two EUR-reporting companies, "A" and "B", with the following structures. "A" sells a product in USD directly, through one-year USD contracts. "B" has set up a USD-reporting subsidiary, and the subsidiary sells the same product in USD, through the identical USD contracts. "A" can designate the USD exposure as a hedged risk under IFRS and can manage it using a one-year USD hedge. "B" cannot obtain hedge accounting for management of the same risk,[1] because it does not experience it directly in the EUR holding company. It only has exposure to the USD risk through its USD subsidiary, and of course, since the subsidiary is USD reporting, in the subsidiary there is no currency risk from USD contracts. One IFRS-friendly solution for "B" is to hedge dividends from the USD subsidiary, but this can be considered "highly probable" only once they are declared,[2] typically a few months before the payment. Another possibility is to hedge the net USD assets, but in this case, there may not even be any USD assets.

So, the currency risk on the consolidated level is identical between "A" and "B", but "A" can obtain hedge accounting if it decides to hedge it one year in advance, while "B" can get hedge accounting only when the dividends are declared. This is highly inconsistent.

This kind of issue between hedging on a holding company versus subsidiary level forces some companies into inefficient hedging policies and as a result some companies hedge "what is allowed under IFRS" instead of their true exposure. The true exposure of the company should be viewed, on the consolidated level, as the net exposure between all the subsidiaries and the holding company, once all the intercompany flows have been netted off.

In the example that follows, we looked at one company whose structure and currency risks require imaginative thinking in order to find an IFRS-friendly solution, which would offset its "true" net exposure. This required us to cross the line between transaction and translation risk, which we defined in the introduction to Part III.

BACKGROUND

An EUR-reporting global household goods manufacturer, Fridges, has significant currency exposure arising from several sources. Their main foreign subsidiaries have capital expenditure ("capex") and commodity expenses in USD, which they need to buy every year. They also have earnings in the local currency. A significant part of the remaining net profit of the subsidiaries is paid to the EUR holding company as dividends every February. The company would like us to take a look at their currency exposures on a consolidated basis, quantify them and see if there is any inefficiency in their existing currency risk management policy. In particular, Fridges is interested to know if there are any exposures which could be netted on a Group level, but which are not apparent when looking from the perspective of the subsidiaries.

COMPANY OBJECTIVES

- To create a mapping of group FX exposures including all the subsidiaries.
- To review the existing risk management policy for currency exposures.
- To detect whether there are any inefficiencies that appear on the group level.
- To provide a solution with a satisfactory hedge accounting treatment.

ANALYSIS

We shall quantify the economic exposure within the consolidated group based on net earnings-at-risk (EaR). This will allow us to create a single parameter that measures the overall group exposure.

Second, we shall differentiate between the transactional exposures at the regional subsidiaries and the economic risk to group consolidated earnings. Such a distinction will show the economic impact of the current policy to hedge the transaction risk at subsidiary level and will help us to identify the currencies in which the transaction risk is offset at the group level. Finally, we shall propose a hedge accounting-friendly solution to reduce the residual Group risk, after all the independent exposures have been netted.

The approach follows the steps in Figure 16.1.

Figure 16.1 Netting the group FX exposure: step by step

1. Evaluate the net economic risk to the group via an EaR measure	2. Separate between transactional and economic exposures	3. Look for offsets between the two sets of exposures and propose a residual hedge
• Gather data on the individual subsidiary exposures to individual currencies • Integrate them with the perspective of the holding company into a single EaR measure	• Transactional exposures are hedged according to the RM policy • On the other hand, the group policy is not to hedge the group profit, as this is difficult within IFRS	• What would be the impact on EaR if the transaction exposures in certain countries were to be left unhedged? • How could we hedge the residual exposure within the constraints of IFRS?

STEP 1: EVALUATE THE NET ECONOMIC EXPOSURE

We shall start by integrating two sources of economic exposures.

1. **Transaction risk on the subsidiary level:** as mentioned before, each subsidiary of Fridges has clearly defined transaction risks, in particular for acquisition of commodities and capex, and each subsidiary hedges these exposures.
2. **Translation risk to profit on the consolidated level:** on the other hand, the Fridges Group has a translation risk to earnings on the consolidated level, since subsidiaries' earnings are translated into the group reporting currency at the average rate for the period.

Most companies we know treat these two kinds of exposures differently and there are two reasons for this. First, transaction risk is considered to be somehow more fundamental, since it concerns the actual cashflows which the subsidiary has to pay to buy the foreign currency. Second, under IFRS, the translation risk to earnings coming from subsidiaries does not directly affect the consolidated financials of the group, and therefore cannot be considered a hedged item in a hedge accounting relationship.

We believe that the first reason is fundamentally invalid for many companies because, if the foreign subsidiary is profitable, part of the net earnings (in some cases, a significant part) will eventually be transferred to the holding company, through intercompany dividends. In that case, the fundamental separation between the economic (ie, transaction) risk and the accounting (ie, earnings translation) risk disappears. Now consider the case when the company decides to reinvest the earnings in a certain country for a period of time, instead of immediately paying the intercompany dividend. In this case, the company simply pushes the risk later in time, until the moment when the dividends are actually paid. Therefore, if the translation risk (eg, that coming from foreign earnings) is not hedged, the transaction risk will actually be increased from year to year, until the dividend payment is eventually made. This is an example of where the distinction between the transaction and translation risks is blurred, and we give more examples in Chapter 19 ("How to Manage Translation Risk").

To summarise, there are two boundary cases here. Either the dividends are paid from subsidiaries' net profit every year, in which case the transaction risk to dividends is identical to the translation risk on the same amount of net profit, or the dividends are reinvested, in which case the cumulative transaction risk over several years will be equal to the translation risk on that part of net profits. The key point to take from this is that the difference between the transaction and translation risk is actually not a fundamental one, but rather a timing issue.[3]

Unfortunately, that is not the case under the IFRS, where the two kinds of risk are treated differently, for reasons we have already mentioned. Moreover, as we mentioned in the introduction to this chapter, the intercompany dividend can only be hedged once it is declared, which in practice is for too short a period of time to make any significant reduction in risk. The solution then is to designate the foreign earnings hedge as a hedge of net investments, and time its maturity to coincide with the dividend payment. In this way, Fridges can hedge that part of the profit which is paid out as a dividend to the parent company without experiencing the undesirable accounting volatility.[4] On the other hand, hedging the economic risk of that part of subsidiary earnings, which are not paid as dividends by the subsidiary, is more difficult from an accounting perspective. In the rest of this chapter, we shall assume that Fridges pays out most of its net profit to the parent company as dividend, and that therefore the timing problem disappears.

Individual transaction exposures by subsidiary and currency

Table 16.1 summarises the transaction exposure (how much USD each subsidiary needs to buy (positive number) or sell (negative number)) per year.

Table 16.1 Simplified transaction exposure in 2010 (EUR million)

	Currency			
	BRL	**EUR**	**THB**	**USD**
Brazil	−100	0	0	100
Eurozone	0	−100	0	100
Thailand	0	0	−100	100
US	0	0	0	0
Total	−100	−100	−100	300

Table 16.2 Net profit in 2010 (EUR million)

Country	Profit
Brazil	100
Eurozone	100
Thailand	100
US	300
Total	600

In order to simplify the problem, we assumed that each subsidiary except the US needs to buy EUR 100 million worth of USD every year. This exposure stems from the foreign currency needs of subsidiaries, for example, commodities, other operating expenses in

USD or capex, all parameters impacting the net profit. Now let us consider the net profit of each subsidiary (Table 16.2).

Let us consider now a specific territory, eg, Brazil. The net profit of EUR 100 million in 2010 does not reveal the actual underlying exposure. In fact, if (for simplicity) we ignore items like depreciation, amortisation, tax and interest cost, the profit consists of only two elements: BRL revenues and costs and USD costs from the first table. If we assume the exchange rates of EURBRL = 2.20 and EURUSD = 1.30, we can write the net profit of the Brazilian subsidiary as

$$\begin{aligned} \text{profit} &= \text{BRL 440 million} - \text{USD 130 million} \\ &= \text{EUR 200 million} - \text{EUR 100 million} \end{aligned}$$

Note that this gives us the total USD transaction exposure of EUR 100 million (USD 130 million) and a net profit of EUR 100 million equivalent.

We summarise the equivalent exposures for all the territories in Table 16.3.

Table 16.3 Net profit by territory and currency: group economic exposure

Territory	Spot v. EUR	Net profit (EUR m)	Net profit split by currency (m)
Brazil	2.20	100	BRL 440 – USD 130
Eurozone	1.00	100	EUR 200 – USD 130
Thailand	39.50	100	THB 7,900 – USD 130
US	1.30	300	USD 390
Total		600	

Earnings-at-risk calculation

Our next step was to use the information in Table 16.3 to compute the EaR. For this we needed to model the volatility of foreign exchange rates, namely EURBRL, EURTHB and EURUSD. As elsewhere in the book (see, for example, Chapter 10), we did this via a Monte Carlo simulation.

We show in Figure 16.2 and Table 16.4 the volatility cone of the EURBRL. We calculated this using a 5,000-path Monte Carlo simulation, based on the current forward rates and the option market implied volatilities. For comparison, we also show historical data for a few years prior to the time of writing.

Figure 16.2 EURBRL: historical and simulation

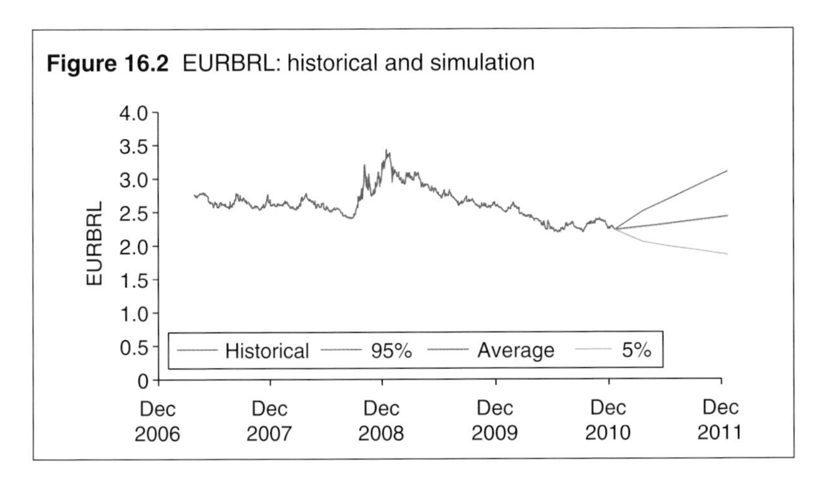

Table 16.4 EURBRL: volatility cone

	Dec 2010	Mar 2011	Jun 2011	Sep 2011	Dec 2011
95%	2.2	2.5	2.7	2.9	3.1
Average	2.2	2.3	2.3	2.4	2.4
5%	2.2	2.0	2.0	1.9	1.8

Similarly, Figures 16.3 and 16.4 and Tables 16.5 and 16.6 show the volatility cones of EURTHB and EURUSD.

Table 16.5 EURTHB: volatility cone

	Dec 2010	Mar 2011	Jun 2011	Sep 2011	Dec 2011
95%	39.5	44.1	46.3	48.2	49.6
Average	39.5	39.5	39.6	39.6	39.6
5%	39.5	35.4	33.6	32.3	31.1

When we apply the FX evolution scenarios from Figures 16.2–16.4 and Tables 16.4–16.6 to the net profit, split by currency from Table 16.3, we obtain the EaR shown in Figure 16.5 in one years' time at the 95th percentile confidence interval.

Figure 16.3 EURTHB: historical and simulation

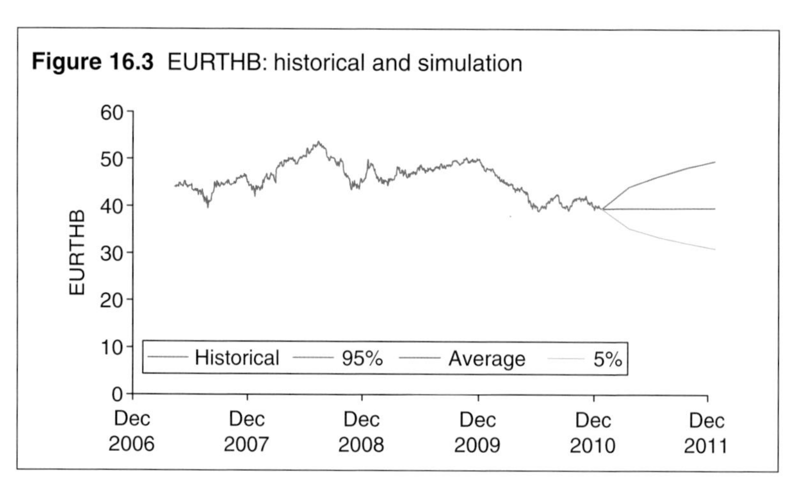

Figure 16.4 EURUSD: historical and simulation

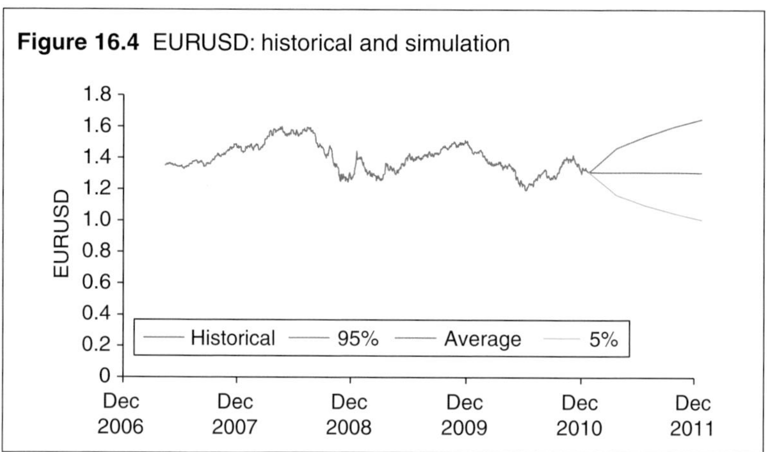

Table 16.6 EURUSD: volatility cone

	Dec 2010	Mar 2011	Jun 2011	Sep 2011	Dec 2011
95%	1.3	1.5	1.5	1.6	1.6
Average	1.3	1.3	1.3	1.3	1.3
5%	1.3	1.2	1.1	1.1	1.0

In Table 16.7 we can see the distribution of earnings due to volatility of FX rates. For example, in BRL, we have the expected earnings of EUR 187 million,[5] with a potential drop to EUR 143 million,[6] due to EURBRL volatility only. We denote this difference "EaR" and it is equal to EUR 44 million. Similarly, we can compute EaR in THB.

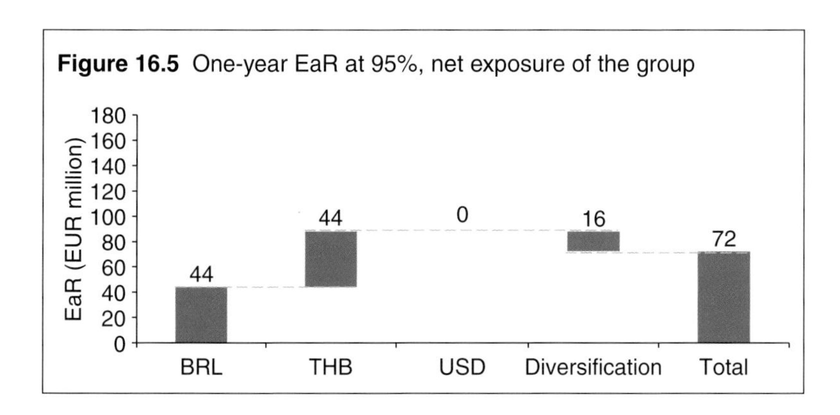

Figure 16.5 One-year EaR at 95%, net exposure of the group

Table 16.7 Earnings-at-risk: one-year net group exposure

	EUR million (equivalent)			
	BRL	**THB**	**USD**	**Total**
95%	238	254	0	671
Average	187	203	0	590
5%	143	159	0	518

Note that in USD there is no volatility, as the group has a net zero USD exposure; Brazilian, Eurozone and Thai subsidiaries need to buy USD 390 million, which is exactly equal to the USD earnings from the US subsidiary. Overall, the total exposure of the group is a potential drop in earnings from EUR 590 million down to EUR 518 million, ie, an EaR of EUR 72 million at 95th percentile.

STEP 2: SEPARATE BETWEEN TRANSACTIONAL AND ECONOMIC EXPOSURES

So far we have integrated the transactional and economic exposure to show the net economic exposure to the group. Due to the different ways that the two kinds of exposure are managed in corporations, we shall now separate the two exposures. Fridges actually has a policy that all the subsidiaries hedge 100% of their transaction exposure but not the dividends or earnings. Therefore, in Table 16.8, we can show the net exposure (starred numbers are where the exposure is hedged).

Note that in Table 16.8 transaction exposure in Brazil, Eurozone and Thailand of USD 130 million short has been hedged, as now

Table 16.8 Net profit by territory and currency: group economic exposure after transactional hedging

Territory	Spot v. EUR	Net profit (EUR m)	Net profit split by currency (m)
Brazil	2.20	100	BRL 440 – USD 130*
Eurozone	1.00	100	EUR 200 – USD 130*
Thailand	39.50	100	THB 7,900 – USD 130*
US	1.30	300	USD 390
Total		600	

Note: * USD exposure has been hedged.

the group is hedging it according to its treasury policy. The group believes that this reduces the risks, but in fact, it is left with a net long USD 390 million position from the US.

We can evaluate the earnings-at-risk using a similar technique to that for Figure 16.5, and the situation we obtain is shown in Figure 16.6.

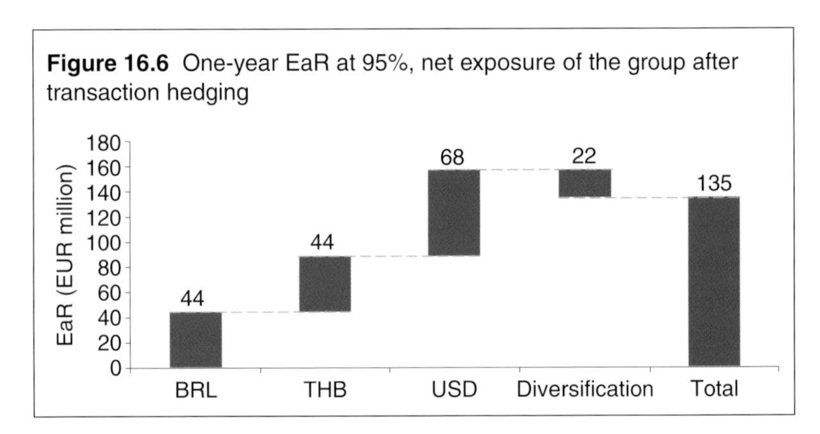

Figure 16.6 One-year EaR at 95%, net exposure of the group after transaction hedging

Note that now we have added the volatility of the USD, which increases the total EaR of the group to EUR 135 million from EUR 72 million (= EUR 595 million – EUR 461 million), ie, the total is almost doubled. And all of this because the group had a policy of hedging the transaction exposure without realising that this actually increases the overall group risk to earnings!

Needless to say, this example is not necessarily typical for all companies. We have seen plenty of opposite examples where hedging

Table 16.9 Earnings-at-risk: one-year net group exposure after transaction hedging

	EUR million (equivalent)			
	BRL	**THB**	**USD**	**Total**
95%	238	254	387	748
Average	187	203	305	595
5%	143	159	237	461

the transaction risk at the subsidiary level actually reduces the net Group exposure, but we have chosen this particular situation as it clearly demonstrates the perils of not having carefully considered the implications of the risk management policy on the net exposure.

STEP 3: LOOK FOR OFFSETS BETWEEN THE TWO SETS OF EXPOSURES AND PROPOSE A RESIDUAL HEDGE

Figure 16.7 Company exposure

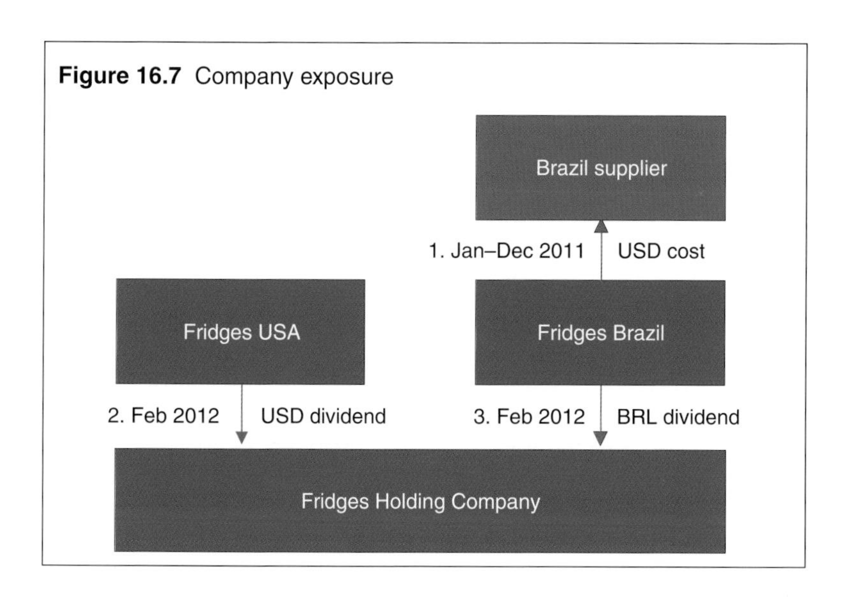

Now that we have highlighted the offset, the remainder of the solution is to find how to reduce it in an accounting-friendly way. Figure 16.7 shows the situation at the time of writing for the US and Brazilian subsidiaries.

These two subsidiaries have three sets of foreign cashflows:

- throughout 2011, Fridges Brazil needs to pay in USD (transaction risk);
- in February 2012, Fridges Holding Company expects a USD dividend from Fridges USA;
- in February 2012, Fridges Holding Company expects a BRL dividend from Fridges Brazil.

Figure 16.8 Company exposure including hedges

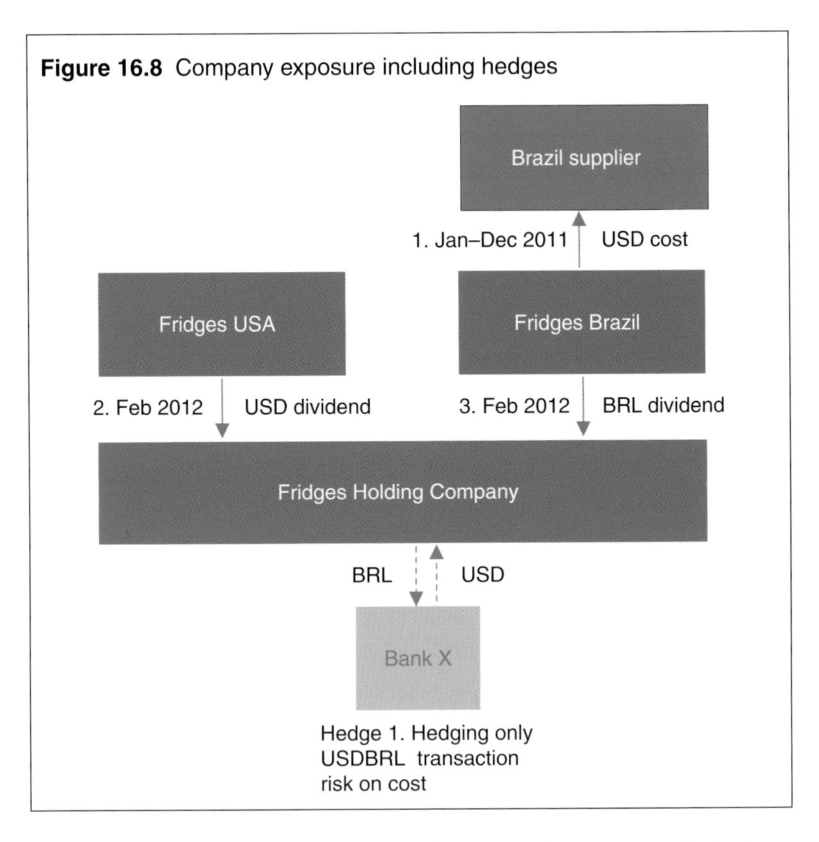

As we saw before, at the time of writing the group only hedges the USDBRL transaction risk on cost.

Ideally, we would want to eliminate these hedges, since, as we saw before, they actually increase the risk. An alternative is to hedge the offsetting USD exposure at the same time.

This could be achieved by entering into two new sets of hedges, for USD and BRL dividends, as shown in red in Figure 16.9. The economic impact of these hedges is to offset the impact of subsidiary

Figure 16.9 Accounting-friendly solution which hedges the net exposure

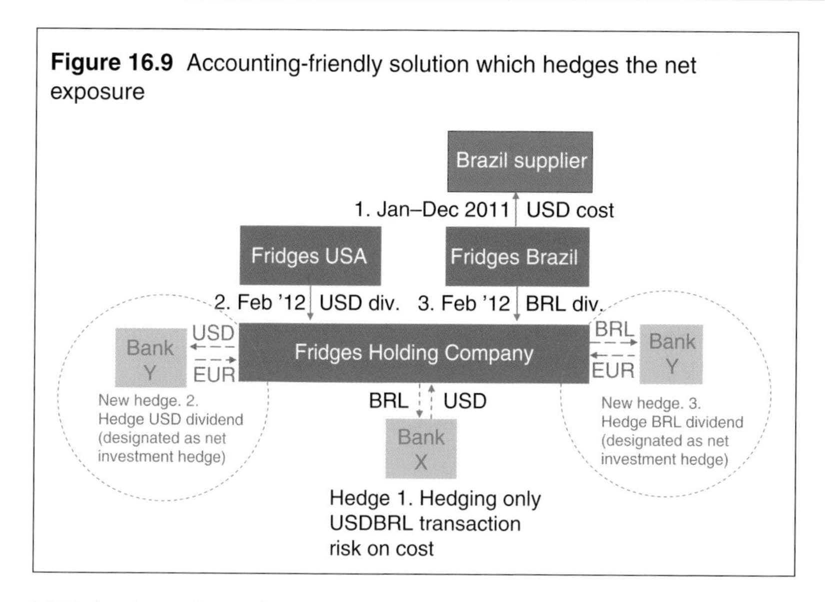

USD hedges. In order to get a good accounting treatment, these hedges are designated as net investment hedges, but the size and timing match the payment of dividends.

Similar hedges have to be put in place for the THB subsidiary, and only then will the net USD exposure be brought back to zero. The only residual risk is the timing between the USD cost payments (throughout 2011) and the USD dividends (February 2012).

RECOMMENDATIONS

Fridges should consider changing its FX hedging transaction policy in one of two ways. The first is to stop hedging the USD transaction exposure on the subsidiary level, in order to benefit from the offsetting position on the Group level. The second is the hedge accounting friendly solution proposed above.

CONCLUSION

In this chapter, we showed how a company should look at the net exposure on a consolidated basis when evaluating its currency risk. Under the existing accounting standards, IAS 39, this is complex, as a company's "real" position necessarily integrates both transaction and translation risks, which are not treated in the same way from an accounting perspective. We proposed a solution that is accounting friendly and helps the company to net the exposure.

1 This is despite the fact that any group entity is allowed to hedge on behalf of another group entity under IFRS.

2 Under IFRS, forecasted cashflows can be designated as a hedged item only once the company can demonstrate that they are "highly probable".

3 See Pringle and Connolly (1993).

4 In case the hedge does not achieve hedge accounting, changes in its MTM will go to P&L and introduce accounting volatility. For more details about the choice between accounting and economic volatility, see Myint (2005).

5 This is equal to BRL 440 million (see Table 16.3) exchanged at the one-year forward rate of 2.4 (see Table 16.4).

6 This is equal to BRL 440 million exchanged at the one-year 95th percentile rate of 3.1 (see Table 16.4).

17

Managing the Risk from Emerging Market Currencies

Emerging markets (EMs) like Brazil, China or Russia are no longer "emerging". It seems that names given to those economies are always outdated. We used to call them "developing countries" in the 1980s, then "emerging markets" thereafter, and now that many emerging markets have emerged perhaps the best term would be "local markets". Faced with a stagnant or low-growing economy in the developed world, many companies are finding that their most significant growth areas are the EMs of Asia, Latin America and Africa. These markets offer high growth due to a rapidly growing population with increasing purchasing power. However, there are many risks, both financial and operational, when exploring new horizons. In this chapter, we focus on the currency risk.

Currency risk in EMs is in many ways different from the developed markets. Key differences are given below.

- Unlike the developed market currencies, EM currencies are often managed or pegged. For example, some Middle Eastern currencies are pegged to the USD, and the Russian Central Bank manages its currency with respect to a basket of USD and EUR. This tends to make the markets more opaque, and therefore the risks of economic and banking crises are higher and often difficult to predict.

- Many countries (eg, India, China) impose restrictions and controls on the exchange and transfer of their currency, so a parallel market often develops in non-deliverable forwards, options and other innovative solutions, which attempt to circumvent these restrictions. In addition, local markets are often not as liquid or as flexible (there is limited maturity, size and types of instruments available, etc).

- Many EM currencies (eg, Brazil, South Africa) are characterised by a high interest rate differential with respect to the developed markets. This is considered a necessary policy tool in order to cool the economic growth, but imposes problems on those companies who have to sell the local currency, as we shall see in this study.
- EM currencies often exhibit cyclical behaviours. Actually, fast-growing economies attract equity and bond investors, but also fast money players such as hedge funds that buy forward the local market currencies to benefit from positive carry. In periods of crisis or risk aversion, foreign capital may "fly out" of the new world causing the currency to depreciate significantly.

Any company's investment in EM is characterised by two stages. In the early stages of investment, significant investment in domestic currency is often required, so the company has to buy the local currency, and is therefore exposed to risks of local currency appreciation. As the local business grows, returns begin to offset the investment needs, and eventually the local company will start paying back the dividends. At this point, the company needs to sell the local currency, and is faced with risks of emerging market currency depreciation. This is the starting point for our study.

BACKGROUND

FRI is a retail company that is based in the US but has strong operations in Brazil and South Africa. The revenues from the latter two countries are received in the local currency and then exchanged into USD. Since revenues in the retail sector are not too cyclical, FRI has highly predictable revenues in the local currencies. However, due to the high volatility of their FX rates, the amount that FRI gets in USD is unstable. On the other hand, if FRI decides to fully hedge its FX exposure via FX forwards, it will have to pay the high interest rate differential (also known as "cost of carry") between the USD and BRL or ZAR.

In order to avoid the high cost of carry and reduce the FX volatility, FRI would like to develop a dynamic hedging policy that would allow it to hedge its currency risk only when the local currency (BRL or ZAR) has a high likelihood of devaluing against the USD and remain unhedged otherwise.

COMPANY OBJECTIVES

- To develop an early warning signal (EWS) method that will provide a warning a short time before the FX crisis occurs.
- To hedge the FX position using forwards when the EWS indicates an imminent crash of the EM currency.
- For the rest of the time, do not hedge the BRL and ZAR exposure, thereby reducing the cost of carry.

ECONOMETRIC SIGNALS OF KAMINSKY AND REINHART

One of the most widely known methods in literature for predicting a currency crisis is that of Kaminsky and Reinhart (KR).[1] The KR method uses a statistical analysis of the major economic indicators to find signs of economic distress. Different emerging markets crises have different mechanisms, and therefore monitoring any individual signal (for example, annual growth of exports) would not capture all the risks. Therefore, the main idea of the KR method is to monitor a variety of econometric indicators and compare them to the historical average. Our implementation of this method involves seven economic indicators for each emerging economy; see Table 17.1.

The value of each indicator is compared to its relative position within the historical distribution. Depending on which percentile the indicator has, compared with its historical distribution, we assign to the indicator a warning signal of 0, 1 or 2. In the case of an extreme event, we assign a signal of 2 to that indicator. In the case of a mild event, we assign a value of 1, and 0 in the case of no event. The extreme event varies for each indicator, eg, for the case of the equity prices an extreme event is when their returns are extremely low compared with their previous history over a long time period (at least 10 years).

Let us illustrate this on an example of the annual growth of equity prices. For the moment, let us assume that we have created a histogram of historical distribution of annual growth of the Brazilian equity index, Bovespa, for every date over the past 10 years. In this example, we shall assume two thresholds, one at the bottom 10th percentile and the other at the bottom 20th percentile of the historical distribution. Let us further assume that the bottom 10th percentile of the distribution corresponds to a −25% annual growth rate of the Bovespa index[2] and the bottom 20th percentile corresponds to

−5% annual growth rate. We compare these thresholds to the growth of the Bovespa index one year before the day of calculation. If the value on the day of calculation is below −25%, the signal is strong and we assign it a value of 2. If the growth is between −25% and −5%, the signal is "mild" and its value becomes 1. Otherwise, the value of the equity signal is 0. We repeat the procedure for the other six indicators.

Once we have assigned a warning signal to all seven indicators, we evaluate their weighted average according to an empirically determined set of weights. This gives us an indicator of economic health, which we call the "early warning signal", which varies between 0 and 2. If this indicator is close to 0 this means that the economy of the country is healthy and it is unlikely that a currency crisis will occur. On the other hand, if we have a signal which is close to 2 this implies that the economy of the country is in distress and there is a high possibility of a currency crisis.

Table 17.1 Economic indicators in the KR method

Index	Risky area
Equity prices (YoY growth)	Low
Real Effective Exchange Rate (REER)[3] (YoY growth)	Low
Current account balance (% of GDP)	Low
M2/reserves (YoY growth)	High
Short-term capital inflows (% of GDP)	High
Exports (YoY growth)	Low
Industrial production (YoY growth)	Low

EWS has some disadvantages. First is the delay at which the indicators are released to the public by the central bank, central statistical bureau or any other relevant government body; this is generally monthly or even quarterly, except for the equity index, which is available intra-daily. Second, the EWS depends on the choice and number of indicators. We have selected a combination of indicators which is easy to obtain and covers all the major types of indicator, but this is by no way the only possible set of indicators. Another problem with the methodological construction of EWS is that it is highly sensitive to the calibration period.

Finally, sometimes an economic crisis in the country does not precede a currency crisis. Let us consider an example of Brazil in 2008.

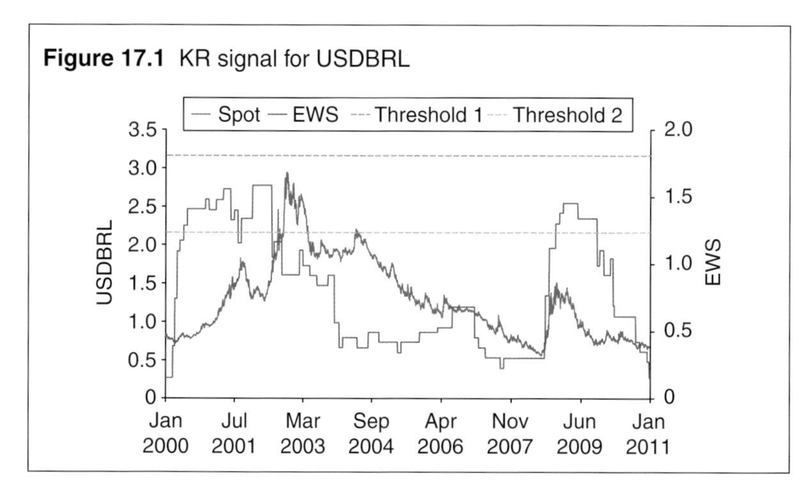

Figure 17.1 KR signal for USDBRL

In Figure 17.1 we show the spot exchange rate against the USD on the left hand axis and the EWS indicator on the right hand axis. We also show two thresholds with dashed lines. We can see that at the beginning of 2008 Brazil had a relatively healthy economy (as indicated by the low value of EWS), but the global credit crisis and the ensuing panic resulted in investors pulling money out of Brazil and a consequent devaluation of the BRL against the USD. In this case, as we can see from Figure 17.1, the EWS gave some indications of distress after the devaluation of the currency because the economic distress was a result of the crisis, rather than its cause. This kind of behaviour is a problem for FRI, as it cannot rely on the EWS to forecast corrections of EM currencies fast enough for the company to be able to do something about it.

MARKET-BASED SIGNALS

In order to address the problems above we proposed several improvements. As we saw above, the 2008 BRL crisis could not have been predicted solely based on the econometric parameters specific to Brazil, as its origins were not in Brazil but elsewhere, in the global investor panic that followed the global credit crunch. In order to monitor the investor sentiment, we decided to add three fast-moving market indicators: country credit default swap (CDS), local equity index[4] and the FX rate itself. All indicators were intra-day so there was no problem with delays.[5] We decided to focus in particular on the CDS market, as it is more sensitive to general investor sentiment than, for instance, the currency market, where, regardless of the situation, a certain amount of commercial flow always takes place.

To evaluate the riskiness of fast-moving indicators, we applied two tests: the non-normality indicator and the relative strength indicator (RSI). The non-normality indicator[6] compares the distribution of the indicator to the normal distribution (Figure 17.2). The RSI test measures the speed of change of the indicator.[7] In this way it is possible to see whether the market expects extremely wide or extremely narrow returns: a sign of uncertainty within the market, which alters the shape of the indicator's distribution.

Figure 17.2 Non-normality signal (illustrative)

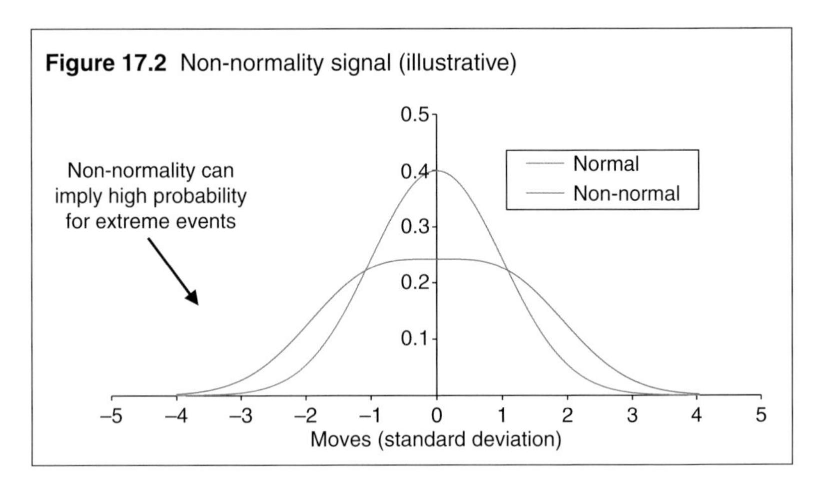

We first computed the non-normality indicator of daily returns of the country CDS over the past 30 days. If the non-normality indicator was less than 15%, we then monitored the level of the RSI indicator for the CDS, equity index and FX rate over the subsequent three months. If at any point during this period all three RSIs were rapidly deteriorating,[8], we considered that the model gave an "on" signal for the crisis; otherwise, it gave an "off" signal.

COMBINING THE TWO METHODS

If we combine the two methods (KR, based on a given threshold, and market-based, as described above), we hope to cover a larger set of causes of underlying risk. The KR method captures the risks from within the economy, while the market-based method should capture all other sources both within and outside the country: global investor appetite, political risk in the country, etc. Therefore, FRI should look at both sets of indicators and decide how much attention to pay to econometric versus market signals.

In Figure 17.3, we introduce a threshold of 0.75 on the KR signal. We consider a signal only if the market based signal defined above turns on, and KR signal exceeds the value of 0.75 at any point within the subsequent eight months. We denote these days with red points.

In Figure 17.3 we point out the "good signals", which are those red points immediately preceding or at the very start of a currency slide. We can see that the method correctly predicts both the 2002 and the 2008 crises. From the perspective of FX hedging, "good signals" turn on early enough to indicate heightened currency in time for FRI to hedge the currency risk before the currency crashes. On the other hand, we notice a lot of "bad signals", which turn on too late, once large part of the devaluation has passed. We found it difficult to eliminate the bad signals, as once the currency experienced a crash there was just too much volatility in both economical and market data, and it was difficult to predict when the currency correction was about to end.

Figure 17.3 Combined signal for USDBRL using a threshold of 0.75 for the KR signal

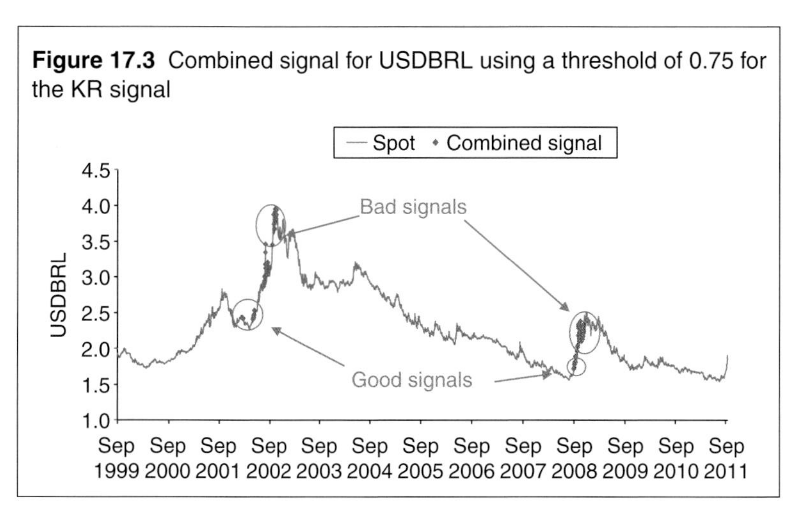

RECOMMENDATIONS

We would provide to FRI on a monthly basis the results of the econometric and market models. FRI would then be able decide how much attention to pay on the EWS versus the market model. By monitoring both sets of signals, FRI could assess whether to take any action to hedge the unwanted currency exposure from their Brazilian and South African operations. Equally importantly, by reducing the hedging proportion when there are no signals indicated, FRI can reduce the average cost of carry it has been paying for hedging the FX risk.

CONCLUSION

In this chapter, we described how companies with currency risk in emerging markets can use early warning signals to forecast times of currency weakness and reduce their hedging cost. This method is not supposed to be used as an automatic hedging algorithm, but more as a warning for the company to focus on a particular currency pair, study its potential sources of weakness and, if it deems it prudent, increase the hedging proportion.

1 See Goldstein *et al* (2000) and Kaminsky (1999).

2 This means that if we compare all the dates over the period observed, the annual growth of the Bovespa index compared with the year before would have been less than −25% in 10% of cases.

3 REER is determined by weighing the real (ie, inflation-adjusted) exchange rates of the country's main trading partners with the proportion of trade, as determined by the Bank for International Settlements.

4 Even though local equity index is already part of the KR method, we use it in a different way, not related to its historical distribution.

5 In fact, our algorithm only uses end-of-day data in order to eliminate the noise of intra-day moves.

6 We used the Kolmogorov–Smirnov method, which is well established in statistics, and we looked at the maximum difference between the cumulative probabilities of two distributions: the normalised distribution of CDS returns over the last 30 days versus the standard normal distribution. If this parameter is higher than 15%, the distribution is considered non-normal.

7 We define this as

$$\text{RSI} = 100\% \times \frac{\sum \text{positive returns}}{\sum \text{positive returns} - \sum \text{negative returns}}$$

8 Defined as RSI over 30 days less than 45% for Equity Index and larger than 55% for FX spot and CDS.

18

Currency Risk on Covenants

In this chapter, we come back to the subject of financial constraints. One of the most important is the financial leverage, commonly defined as total debt/EBITDA.[1] Leverage is important as it affects the company's credit rating and cost of funding, and sometimes it is also explicitly restricted by loan covenants to not exceed a certain level.

There are three ways that leverage constraints can be endangered. The first is if the denominator, EBITDA, unexpectedly drops, as a result of weaker business than originally envisaged. The second is if the debt rises, since the company has to borrow more than expected. The third is the most interesting for us, since it has to do with currency risk. If a significant part of EBITDA is in a foreign currency, EBITDA may fall, even though the underlying business is fine, purely as a result of depreciation of the foreign currency against the reporting currency of the company. Similarly, if a part of the debt is in a foreign currency, strengthening of that currency will increase the total debt.

This kind of risk can be hedged against by matching the debt and assets by currency. For example, if an EUR-based company has one-third of its EBITDA coming from EUR, USD and GBP, a natural thing would be to match it with a similar composition of debt by currency. That way, if, for example, the USD weakens against EUR, consolidated EBITDA would suffer, but this would be matched by the lower contribution of USD debt to consolidated debt. Therefore, the leverage ratio would be stabilised.

But this is not all. First, in practice, companies have multiple ratios that they try to optimise. For instance, many companies match their debt to the free cashflows by currency[2] rather than to EBITDA by currency. The two compositions are rarely the same, since generally more cash is generated in one currency than in the other. So if the company matches the cashflows, leverage may not be matched.

Other companies may decide to match their assets or even their equity with the debt by currency.

Another reason is due to the way that the leverage is computed. Debt is normally computed at the spot exchange rate at the end of the period, while EBITDA is computed at the average rate during the period. This discrepancy can cause problems with the leverage covenants, as the following example will show.

BACKGROUND

Staples Inc is a GBP-reporting company, created as a result of a merger of equals of an EUR-based company and their UK counterpart. Both EBITDA and debt are half in EUR and half in GBP, as shown in Figure 18.1.

Figure 18.1 Composition of debt and EBITDA (GBP million)

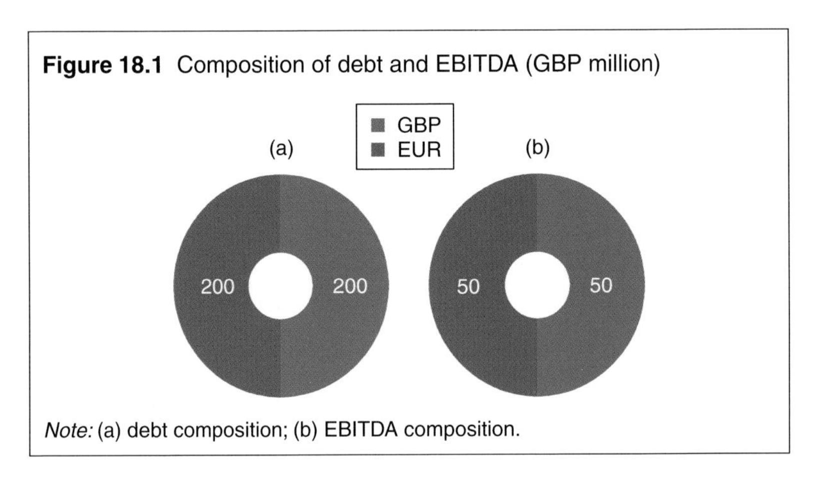

Note: (a) debt composition; (b) EBITDA composition.

The main funding has been a three-year bank loan of GBP 400 million, half of which has been swapped into EUR. This loan included a covenant that the leverage of the company, measured by net debt divided by EBITDA, should not exceed a limit of four. At the beginning of 2012, the company was concerned that the rapid moves of EURGBP exchange rates experienced in 2008 would happen again, and that this would jeopardise the covenants. Even though the split of debt follows the split of EBITDA (both are split 50 : 50 between GBP and EUR), the covenants were still at risk due to a technical problem. In calculation of leverage, net debt is converted at the spot FX rate, while EBITDA is converted at the average FX rate for the period. So, if the spot moves rapidly against Staples (the EUR strengthens against GBP), as it did in 2008, the average FX rate move will lag the move of the spot FX and EBITDA will increase less than the net debt, thereby endangering the leverage covenant.

COMPANY OBJECTIVES

- To provide a solution that protects Staples Inc leverage against rapid moves of GBPEUR.
- To ensure that the timing of payment and reference rate are as close as possible to the end of the reporting period, since the covenants are evaluated at that time.
- To ensure that the accounting treatment is advantageous to Staples Inc.

ANALYSIS

Since the origin of the problem is in the discrepancy between the spot and average rate during the period, we shall structure a derivative solution, which pays to Staples Inc the difference between those two rates, if positive. In order for the solution to be zero cost, Staples must pay to its counterparty bank the difference between spot and average rates, if negative.

In Figure 18.2, we show the impact on the Staples Inc leverage during 2008.

During 2008, the EURGBP exchange rate strengthened very rapidly from 0.7342 on January 1 to 0.9575 on December 31, with the average rate for 2008 at 0.8026. We show this in the top table in Figure 18.2.

In the bottom left table of Figure 18.2 we show the situation at the beginning of 2008. Staples had GBP 400 million of debt, as well as GBP 100 million of EBITDA, both equally split between GBP and EUR. The EUR component of debt at that time was EUR 272 million (= GBP 200 million/0.7342) and the EUR component of EBITDA was EUR 68 million (= GBP 50 million/0.7342). So the leverage was

$$\frac{\text{debt}}{\text{EBITDA}} = 4\left(= \frac{\text{GBP 400 million}}{\text{GBP 100 million}}\right)$$

We shall assume that debt and EBITDA remained constant in their own currencies throughout 2008.

Now let us see how this situation changed at the end of 2008.

The EUR part of the debt now became GBP 261 million (obtained by converting the EUR 272 at the year-end rate of 0.9575). Together with the GBP 200 million debt in GBP, this gave a total debt of GBP 461 million. However, the EUR component of the EBITDA of EUR 68 million was converted at the average rate of 0.8026, which is GBP 55 million, thereby giving a total EBITDA of GBP 105 million. So the year-end leverage was 4.4 (= GBP 461 million/GBP 105 million).

Figure 18.2 Accounting mismatch in 2008

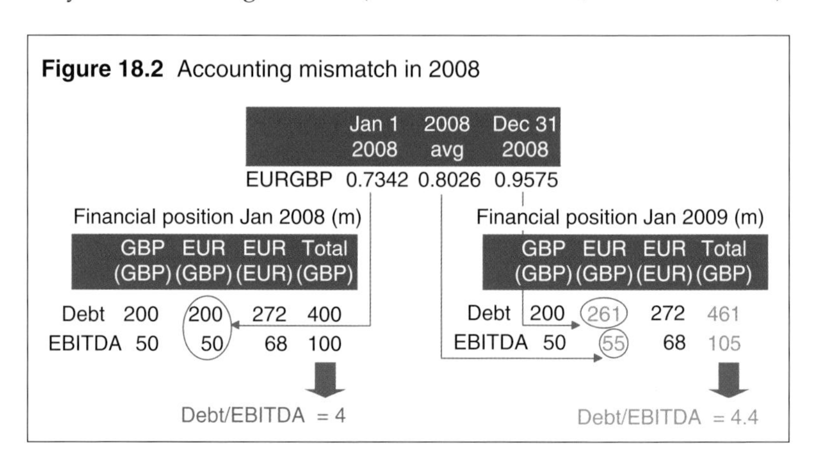

Figure 18.3 How the accounting mismatch is removed if the final exchange rate is set to the average

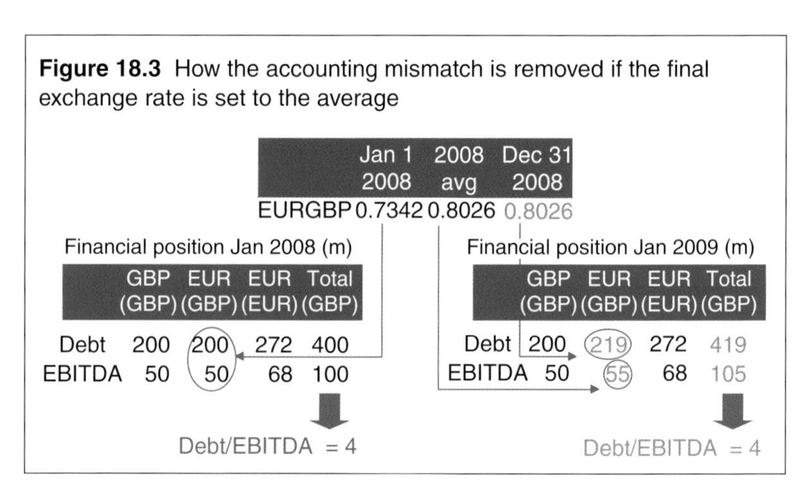

As can be seen, the impact follows from the fact that the spot moved more rapidly than the average. In Figure 18.3 we show the impact on the leverage, assuming that the spot moved in tandem with the average.

Obviously, in this case the covenant is protected.

We propose three structures (ie, the "solutions" below), which satisfy the requirements of Staples Inc.

Solution 1: average strike call

This simple solution enables Staples Inc to receive cash compensation at expiry, providing that the average EURGBP rate for the first half of 2012 is less than the rate at the end of June 2012, hence protecting the covenants. This solution has a cost (premium), which is payable usually two business days after the trading date (spot date).

- **Mechanics:** Staples Inc buys an EUR call/GBP put for the required amount of the EUR debt.
- **Start date:** any point in January 2012.
- **End date:** June 30, 2012.
- **At expiry:**
  - if the end of June (H1) rate is greater than average rate (AR) for the first half of the year, then Staples Inc exercises the option and receives a cash compensation crystallising this difference

$$\text{payout} = \text{notional} \times (\text{H1 rate} - \text{AR})$$

  - if H1 is less than AR for the first half of the year, then Staples Inc does not exercise the option and benefits from the favourable effect of the decrease in rates on the covenant ratio.

Solution 2: average strike collar

This solution has reduced or no cost. The idea is for Staples Inc to sell an EUR put/GBP call in order to mitigate part of the premium attached to the EUR call.

- **Mechanics:** Staples Inc buys an EUR call/GBP put for the required amount of the EUR debt and Staples Inc sells an EUR put/GBP call for the required amount of the EUR debt.
- **Start date:** any point in January 2012.
- **End date:** June 30, 2012.

- **At expiry:**
  - if H1 > AR for the first half of the year, increased by 10%, then Staples Inc exercises the option and receives a cash compensation crystallising this difference

$$\text{payout} = \text{notional} \times (\text{H1 rate} - \text{AR} \times 1.10)$$

  - if AR < H1 < (AR × 1.10), then Staples Inc does not exercise the option and benefits from the favourable effect of the decrease in rates on the covenant ratio down to the level of the sold EUR put;
  - if H1 < AR, then Staples Inc has to pay the difference

$$\text{payout} = \text{notional} \times (\text{AR} - \text{H1 rate})$$

Solution 3: average strike forward

Staples Inc is able to buy EUR against GBP at the monthly average rate (plus an amount of points to be defined depending on the swap point curve, implied volatility and potential slippage on the fixing days).

- **Mechanics:** Staples Inc enters into EUR forward against GBP for the required amount of the EUR debt.
- **Start date:** any point in January 2012.
- **End date:** June 30, 2012.
- **At expiry:**
  - if H1 > AR for the first half of the year, then Staples Inc will close the hedge out by selling EUR at a better rate and will receive a positive cashflow

$$\text{payout} = \text{notional} \times (\text{H1 rate} - \text{AR})$$

  - if H1 < AR for the first half of the year, then Staples Inc will close the hedge out by selling EUR at a worse rate, and will therefore have a negative cashflow:

$$\text{payout} = \text{notional} \times (\text{AR} - \text{H1 rate})$$

ACCOUNTING TREATMENT

Assuming that the proposed solution is entered into during the first half of 2012 and the payout is on June 30, 2012, the impact on the net debt/EBITDA covenant is twofold.

1. Net debt is reduced by the option payout and increased by the premium (if any). This would be booked as any cash received/ paid on the hedges.
2. EBITDA is increased by the option payout and reduced by the premium (if any). This would probably be booked as "other income".

This double-counting, which depends on the accounting treatment of the option payout, allows reducing the notional size by half, as the positive payout has impact both on the net debt and EBITDA.

We presented three solutions that allow Staples Inc to reduce the mismatch between the final and average FX rates. They are all based on the EURGBP exposure, but we can adjust the solution to all currency pairs either individually or through a basket.

COMPARISON OF SOLUTIONS

All of these solutions would help in hedging the risk of breaching the covenants, but use a different approach.

- The average strike option will give full protection and will enable Staples Inc to improve the ratio with no limit on the downside if GBP appreciates against the EUR. Nevertheless, this requires a premium payment.
- The average strike collar reduces part of the premium. In order to achieve such a result, the average strike would be incremented by a certain factor (in this case 20%), and any favourable market move (end of June rate below the average rate for H1) would be capped to a certain limit.
- The average strike forward gives full protection at zero cost but potentially involves negative cashflows.

RECOMMENDATIONS

Given the sensitivity of Staples Inc to the leverage covenant, and the unfeasibility of redefining the covenant, Staples Inc should compare the three solutions depending on their risk reward preferences.

CONCLUSION

In this chapter, we have shown how compliance with a leverage covenant can be endangered by the rapid devaluation of one currency. We propose three solutions which reduce this risk and compare their advantages and disadvantages. Note that the solutions have slightly structured payouts (based on the average foreign exchange rate achieved during the period), which may make hedge accounting difficult. The payout is a consequence of the accounting treatment of the covenants. There is an important lesson here. As we noted in Chapter 15, there is no reason for a company to opt for a non-hedge accounting solution if a hedge accounting solution can do the job. In this case, there is no hedge accounting solution so we are forced to consider alternatives.

1 Less often, it is defined as net debt/EBITDA.

2 In order to be able to pay back the local currency debt from the free cashflows in that currency.

19

How to Manage Translation Risk

As we saw in the introduction to Part III, translation risk is defined as the impact of currency volatility on the consolidated balance sheet and P&L of a company. Balance-sheet risk is easy to hedge from the accounting perspective, but the income statement risk is not.

Before we describe how to hedge translation risk, our first question should be: why hedge translation risk? Who cares about the volatility of the balance sheet? The income statement risk would be easier to understand, as the company's earnings are heavily scrutinised by investors, analysts and other company observers. But who scrutinises the book value of the company?

First, let us see how the consolidated balance sheet is affected by currency risk. Let us consider an EUR-reporting company with a USD subsidiary. The subsidiary has a very simple balance sheet, consisting of USD 200 million in assets, USD 100 million in debt and USD 100 million in equity.

Let us say that, at the first reporting date, the exchange rate is EURUSD = 1. At that point the assets and debt of the subsidiary get translated in the consolidated accounts to EUR 200 million in assets and EUR 100 million in debt and therefore a contribution to consolidated equity of EUR 100 million from the subsidiary.

If, however, at the next reporting date, the exchange rate weakens to EURUSD = 2, then both the assets and debt get translated at a weaker USD rate to EUR 100 million in assets and EUR 50 million in debt, and therefore the contribution to consolidated equity now falls to EUR 50 million.

So, in this example, consolidated assets, debt and equity all experience variability due to currency fluctuation.

When does a company care about its consolidated equity? We summarise the conditions in Table 19.1.

If a company decides to hedge the balance sheet translation risk in principle, it still has to decide which currencies merit hedging. An

Table 19.1 When is balance-sheet translation risk important?

	Situation	Description
1	Regulated equity	Banks and insurance companies often hedge their equity for regulatory purposes
2	Immediate disposals	Companies hedge translation risk when they decide to dispose or acquire foreign assets, as the translation risk will have a direct cashflow impact
3	Private ownership	Many private companies hedge equity as it is directly related to family wealth
4	Covenants	Stabilising loan covenants based on financial ratios (net debt/EBITDA, EBITDA/interest cost) or tangible net worth are often used as the objective when deciding on the translation risk policy
5	Rating agency ratios	In a similar way, rating agency ratios, which determine the financial flexibility (FFO)/adjusted net debt (S&P) and RCF/adjusted net debt (Moody's) can be used to optimise the translation risk
6	When translation risk matches the cashflow risk	For many companies, hedging translation risk allows a good accounting treatment for hedging dividends; forward is designated as a net investment hedge, but in fact allows reduction of the cashflow risk related to dividends
7	Opportunistic	When the interest rate differential is low, the benefit of hedging translation risk outweighs the cost

important consideration when deciding whether to hedge the translation risk of a given subsidiary is the relative size of risk versus the cost of hedging it. Normally, the most often used translation risk hedges are foreign currency debt, cross-currency swaps or currency forwards. In all three cases, the key driver of the cost is the interest rate differential between the currency of the parent company and the currency of the subsidiary. This parameter should be compared with the potential risk to equity if that currency is left unhedged. Often companies decide to hedge the translation risk in all the currencies where the interest rate differential is not prohibitive. This makes sense to us, as it gives a company the option to systematically decide on which translation risks to hedge and which ones to leave unhedged.

In the example that follows, we use this argument in a more complicated analysis, based on the "efficient frontier" methodology.[1]

BACKGROUND

Information Technology Company (ITC) offers multimedia solutions, software and services integration. It operates in 40 countries worldwide but most of its business is based in Europe (EUR, GBP, NOK and CHF) and the US.

The ever-changing international scope poses unique financing and risk management challenges, requiring the continuous evolution of financial practices. To illustrate the scope of change of the international exposure, foreign assets as a percentage of total assets increased from 20% to 60% between 2002 and 2012.

Given this situation, the ITC's risk manager is concerned about the increase in the translation risk exposure which affects equity upon consolidation to EUR, ITC's reporting currency.

ITC asked us how to improve the effectiveness of its translation risk management programme from a cost and risk perspective.

COMPANY OBJECTIVES

- To find the optimal currency mix of assets and liabilities that reduces the translation risk at minimal interest cost.
- To satisfy accounting constraints for net investment hedges.

ANALYSIS

We shall analyse the composition of assets and liabilities of ITC. Our objective is to reduce the translation risk while minimising the interest cost. We also impose the constraint that liabilities per currency are no larger than the assets (in order to allow designation as net investment hedges).

Figure 19.1 demonstrates the following four-step approach.

Figure 19.1 Risk management approach: step by step

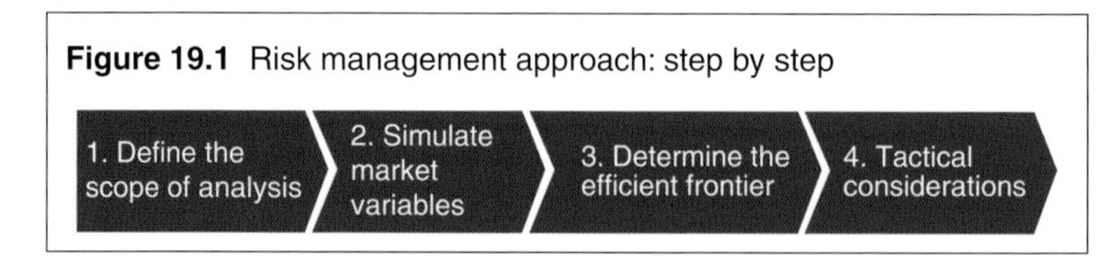

1. The first step in our analysis is to determine the key parameters we want to optimise. To perform this we look at the net IC and the VaR of the asset–liability position. The objective is to find the optimal liability currency mix for maximum reward IC versus minimum VaR.
2. Next, based on this objective, we evaluate the foreign exchange rates that affect the value of the firm by converting the value of foreign assets into EUR, and determine their distribution over the time horizon of the analysis. To simulate the foreign exchange rates in five major currencies, we use a correlated-variables model using one-year interest rates and one year of historical volatilities and correlations.
3. We then determine the efficient frontier by comparing the risk (measured by VaR) versus return (measured by IC) for 1,000 scenarios that differ in terms of currency composition in five major currencies (EUR, GBP, USD, NOK and CHF). The optimal currency mix is therefore obtained by introducing the accounting constraint that the total liability can be no greater than the total assets.
4. To restructure the debt according to our recommendation, tactical options should be considered through bank borrowing, issuance and bond buy-backs or cross-currency hedges, taking into account the pricing and timing implications.

STEP 1: DEFINE THE SCOPE OF ANALYSIS

The aim of the analysis is to evaluate the asset–liability mismatch in foreign currencies that introduces translation risk in equity upon

Figure 19.2 Composition of ITC assets and liabilities by currency

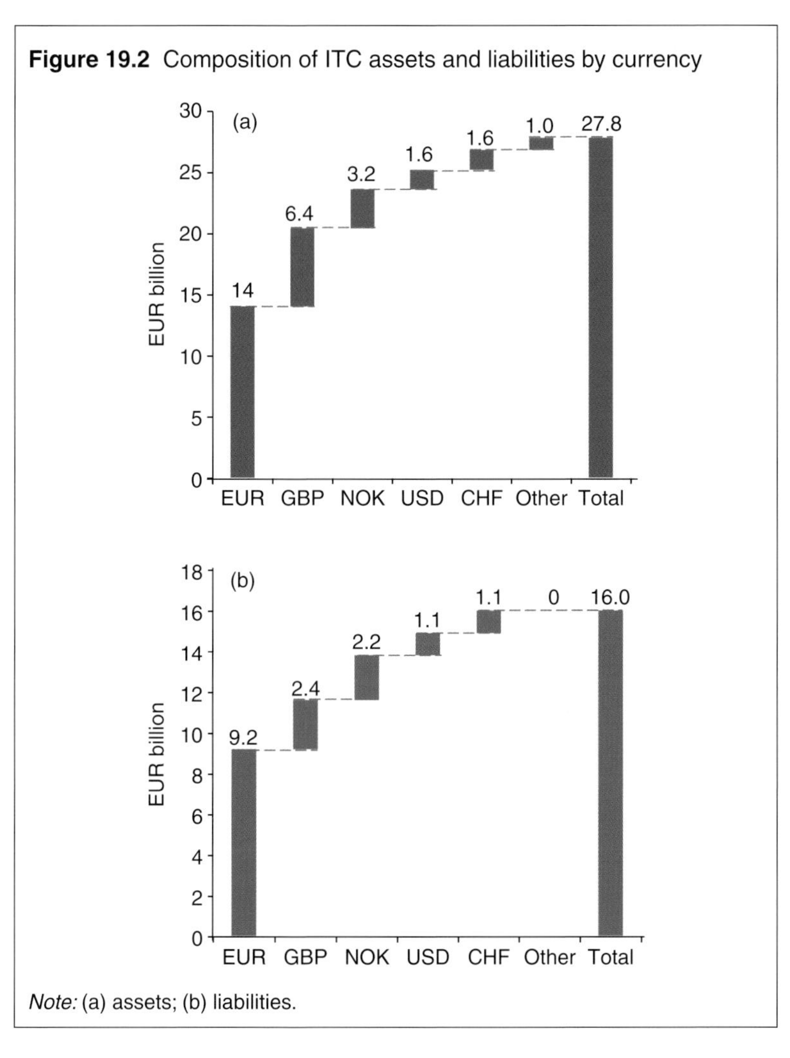

Note: (a) assets; (b) liabilities.

conversion to EUR. In Figure 19.2 we show the assets and liabilities of ITC.

In Table 19.2 we show the key market parameters for the five main currencies.[2]

As a rough approximation (excluding the correlation effect), currency risk is proportional to the size of the mismatch between assets and liabilities and currency volatility versus EUR. We notice that the most significant mismatch is in GBP (EUR 4 billion) and NOK (EUR 1 billion). The highest volatility versus EUR is observed in NOK and USD.

Table 19.2 Market data

Main currency	Exchange rate v. EUR (%)	1y Libor (%)	1y interest rate differential currency v. EUR (%)	1y SD of currency v. EUR (%)
EUR	1.00	3.4	N/A	N/A
GBP	1.10	4.9	1.5	7.2
NOK	1.33	4.3	0.9	11.8
USD	1.40	5.5	2.1	10.9
CHF	1.20	1.9	−1.5	2.9

STEP 2: SIMULATE MARKET VARIABLES

We show the annualised VaR of translation risk at a 95% confidence interval by simulating the foreign exchange rates over the next year and show the contribution to VaR by currency in Figure 19.3. We show separately the contributions from the four main currencies and the correlation component, which in this case decreases the risk, due to the diversification between currencies.

Figure 19.3 Annualised VaR of translation risk at 95%

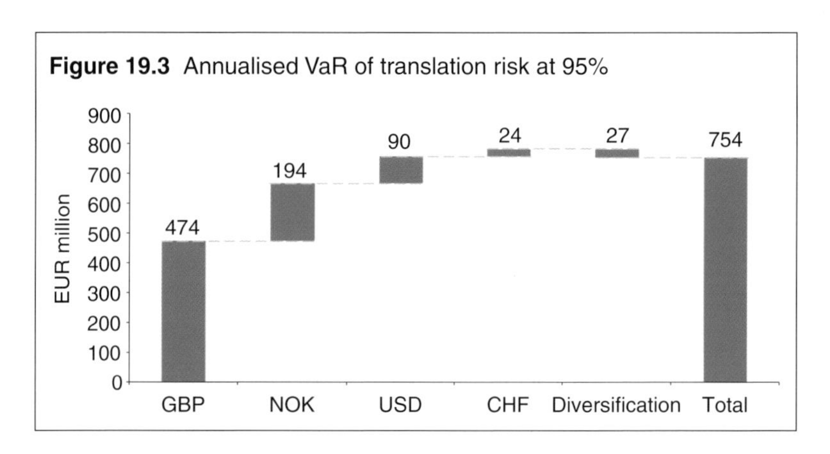

Under normal market conditions, in one year's time, the VaR of the translation risk equals ±EUR 754 million at a 95% confidence interval. The most significant contribution arises from GBP (±EUR 474 million) and NOK (±EUR 194 million) due to high net assets and high standard deviation of EURGBP (7.2%) and EURNOK (11.8%).

Therefore, any attempt to minimise translation risk should focus on GBP and NOK.

STEP 3: DETERMINE THE EFFICIENT FRONTIER

Optimal currency split without accounting constraints

In Figure 19.4 we compare 1,000 portfolios of currency composition in five major currencies (EUR, GBP, NOK, USD and CHF): 100% in EUR, 90% in EUR plus 10% in GBP, and so on up to 100% in CHF. Each portfolio is shown by a purple dot.

We shall define the efficient frontier as the minimum expected IC for minimum VaR.

Figure 19.4 One-year expected interest cost versus VaR at 95% (EUR million)

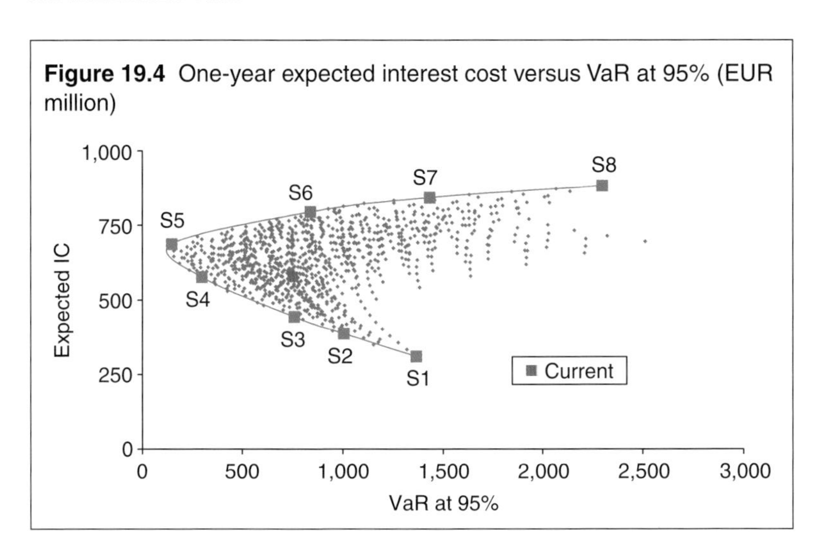

Table 19.3 Scenario analysis

	Proportion of debt (%)					Expected IC	VaR at 95%
Scenario	**EUR**	**GBP**	**NOK**	**USD**	**CHF**	**(EUR m)**	**(EUR m)**
S1	**0**	**0**	**0**	**0**	**100**	**311**	**1,369**
S2	**0**	**10**	**10**	**0**	**80**	**388**	**1,008**
S3	**0**	**20**	**10**	**0**	**70**	**444**	**760**
S4	**0**	**40**	**20**	**0**	**40**	**577**	**301**
S5	**20**	**40**	**20**	**10**	**10**	**678**	**150**
S6	0	70	10	20	0	795	844
S7	0	40	0	60	0	843	1,437
S8	0	0	0	100	0	882	2,302
Current	58	15	14	7	7	606	754

One can see in Figure 19.4 and Table 19.3 that the highlighted scenarios S1 to S5 are superior to all others as they have the lowest IC for a given VaR. The choice between these five scenarios can be determined based on the risk appetite of ITC.

The lowest interest cost corresponds to scenario S1 with 100% of liabilities in francs and the lowest risk corresponds to the scenario S5 with 20% of liabilities in EUR, 40% in GBP, 20% in NOK and 10% in USD and CHF. This is quite intuitive. CHF have the lowest one-year interest cost, so S1 consists entirely of franc liabilities. On the other hand, the composition of S5 exactly offsets the assets in GBP, NOK, USD and CHF.

This is primarily due to

- a significant mismatch between assets and liabilities in GBP and NOK (Figure 19.2),
- negative interest rate differential with CHF which compensates the positive differential due to GBP and NOK (Table 19.2),
- low EUR–CHF annualised volatility (2.9%), reducing CHF risk (Table 19.2).

The conclusion is that, based on the VaR analysis, the present debt composition (current scenario) is not efficient. ITC could improve its risk/reward profile if the EUR proportion is significantly reduced:

- moving from the current scenario to S3 would decrease the IC by EUR 162 million (from EUR 606 million to EUR 444 million) while keeping approximately the same VaR at 95%;
- moving from the current scenario to S4 will decrease the VaR by EUR 453 million (from EUR 754 million to EUR 301 million) while keeping approximately the same IC.

However, scenarios S1–S4 would involve having 40–100% of debt in CHF (EUR 6.4 billion–EUR 16.0 billion), which is significantly higher than the assets (Figure 19.2). At this point we need to introduce accounting constraints.

Optimal currency split including accounting constraints

If we introduce the constraint that the liabilities per currency can be no higher than the assets,[3] the number of available scenarios is greatly reduced. In Figure 19.5, constrained scenarios are labelled in red. Results including the constraints are shown in Table 19.4.

Figure 19.5 One-year expected interest cost versus VaR at 95%, with accounting constraints (EUR million)

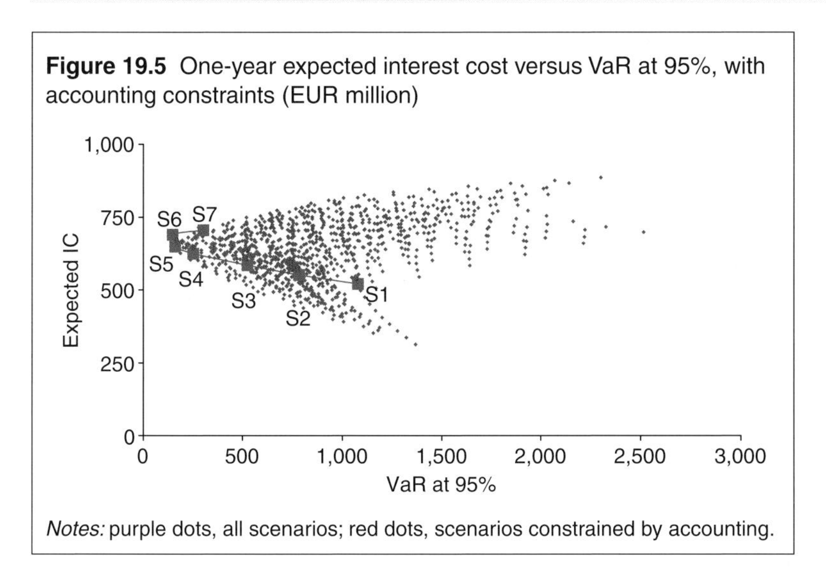

Notes: purple dots, all scenarios; red dots, scenarios constrained by accounting.

Due to accounting constraints, ITC should have no more than 10% in CHF, 10% in USD, 20% in NOK and 40% in GBP.

Table 19.4 Scenario analysis

	Proportion of debt (%)					Expected IC	VaR at 95%
Scenario	**EUR**	**GBP**	**NOK**	**USD**	**CHF**	**(EUR m)**	**(EUR m)**
S1	**90**	**0**	**0**	**0**	**10**	**518**	**1,079**
S2	**70**	**0**	**20**	**0**	**10**	**549**	**783**
S3	**60**	**20**	**10**	**0**	**10**	**582**	**525**
S4	**40**	**30**	**20**	**0**	**10**	**622**	**252**
S5	**30**	**40**	**20**	**0**	**10**	**646**	**162**
S6	**20**	**40**	**20**	**10**	**10**	**678**	**150**
S7	30	40	20	10	0	703	303
Current	58	15	14	7	7	606	754

We can see that the highlighted scenarios S1–S6 are superior to all others,[4] since they have a lower expected interest cost for a given VaR among all the constrained scenarios. Having 10% of the total debt in CHF will reduce the interest cost. Increasing the proportion of GBP and NOK debt will also reduce the translation risk.

The conclusion is that, based on the VaR analysis, from an economic and accounting perspective the present debt composition is not efficient. ITC could improve its risk/reward profile if the EUR proportion is significantly reduced:

- moving from the current scenario to S3 will decrease the VaR by EUR 229 million (from EUR 754 million to EUR 525 million) while lowering the IC by EUR 24 million (from EUR 606 million to EUR 582 million);
- moving from the current scenario to S2 will decrease the IC by EUR 57 million (from EUR 606 million to EUR 549 million) while only modestly increasing the VaR.

STEP 4: TACTICAL CONSIDERATIONS

ITC decided to accept the conclusions of the previous analysis, but decided to modify it in view of the current market conditions. In general, it is good practice to do so, rather than follow the model results automatically. ITC was expecting weaker GBPEUR and so decided to wait before implementing the increase in GBP debt until the market volatility was reduced.

RECOMMENDATIONS

Even though ITC is, at the time of writing, already close to the optimal point (including accounting constraints), it could still improve its position and reduce its annualised foreign exchange VaR at the 95th percentile confidence interval from EUR 754 million to EUR 525 million, while lowering the IC by EUR 24 million (from EUR 606 million to EUR 582 million). This can be achieved by moving from the current portfolio to S3.

An alternative is to reduce the interest cost from EUR 606 million to EUR 549 million by moving the liabilities from GBP to NOK and benefiting from the lower interest rate differential.

In order to implement this, tactical options should be considered through bank borrowing, bond issuance and buy-backs or cross-currency hedges.

CONCLUSION

This chapter described hedging translation risk on the balance sheet. We focused on the interplay between costs of hedging measured by the interest rate differential and the risk of not hedging, measured by the VaR at the 95th percentile. We compared costs and risks using the "efficient frontier" methodology, but even companies who do not use such sophisticated quantitative tools can create a translation risk hedging strategy based on the relative size of risk and cost.

1 The "efficient frontier" is a concept in portfolio optimisation theory (see, for example, Copeland *et al* 2003), where various combinations of assets are compared on their risk and expected return. Those portfolios with the highest expected return for a given amount of risk define a curve which is called the "efficient frontier".

2 Numbers have been chosen randomly and do not correspond to any particular point in time.

3 Under IFRS, net investment hedges are constrained in size by the amount of assets.

4 Note that scenarios S1–S6 are different from the original scenarios before we took the accounting considerations into constraint, despite the same labelling.

20

Managing Foreign Exchange Risk with a Dynamic Option Strategy

We have already referred to a difference between static and dynamic risk management in Chapter 15. In this chapter, we shall see another application of the dynamic policy.

Some companies have long-dated exposures due to the nature of their contracts. These are often found in construction and aerospace sectors. Normally contracts are signed in USD and a significant part of operating costs is in EUR, GBP or another currency. For these companies, currency (or FX) risk management is a strategic issue, since often they participate in tenders where their pricing is compared against companies with a large part of USD costs.

When their currency appreciates against the USD, European contractors are uncompetitive since they have to pass on their costs to the buyer. At the same time, USD-based contractors are more competitive. Strangely, USD-based contractors are also exposed to strategic currency risk, even though their revenues and expenses are all in USD. This is because, in the opposite case when the USD is strong against EUR or pound, European contractors' costs become lower and they become more competitive against their USD peers.

For European contractors, it may be possible to manage the resulting currency risk in three ways:

1. move part of production to USD, in order to reduce the non-USD costs;
2. invoice their client in the currency of their main costs (most often EUR or GBP), in order to reduce the USD revenues;
3. enter into currency derivatives whereby the company sells USD and buys the domestic currency, thereby fixing the costs in advance.

The first two solutions are not always possible, and so we focus our attention on the third one: currency risk management of long-term risks.

As we mentioned in the introduction to the book, the new capital rules for banks will affect corporate funding and risk management.[1] We only briefly summarise the impact here, as it is a main motivation for this chapter.

Generic effects of Basel III are:

- a tighter definition of capital;
- higher required levels of capital;
- taxes on risk weighted assets (RWAs);
- new liquidity ratio constraints.

The impact on corporate hedging is likely to be that long-dated non-collateralised derivatives are affected by the combination of VaR on credit valuation adjustment (CVA) (additional capital charge after January 2013) and increased funding costs.

Banks will either factor the cost of hedging their counterparty risk with CDSs into the CVA in order to avoid the capital charge, or reflect the additional capital charge in their required return on equity.

New constraints on liquidity ratios, especially a net stable funding ratio (NSFR) greater than 100%, are expected to increase the cost of term funding for the industry from 2018, with many banks already preparing for it at the time of writing.

The consequence for corporates is that long-dated hedging using non-collateralised derivatives will become more expensive under new capital rules.

Contrary to the VaR profile of interest rate swaps, which have a bell-curve shape, FX forwards and cross-currency swaps exhibit a growing VaR profile with a peak at maturity, which makes them particularly capital intensive.[2] As a result, we expect that long-term FX hedgers will see a significant increase in the cost of hedging, and eventually less capacity available from a credit line standpoint.

In contrast, options purchased by companies attract no capital charge, as the seller bears no counterparty risk once the premium has been received. The growing component of credit charge in long-term FX hedging now makes purchased options cheaper than before in relative terms. The option premium is significant for long-term hedges and greater than the credit charge for a forward. However, since the premium is the present value of the expected future payout, a regular hedger will, over the long run, recoup the premium paid by taking advantage of favourable market moves. Therefore, leaving aside the bid–ask spread of the option premium, over the long term purchased options become more attractive than before, because they are exempt of capital charge.

In this chapter, we follow a construction company that is already hedging its long-term USD currency risk, and is now looking for ways to optimise its risk management in view of the upcoming changes.

BACKGROUND

Bridges is a GBP-based construction company, which has long-term contracts in USD. At present, Bridges hedges its long USD exposure mostly via long dated (more than one year) FX forwards. When the GBP weakens, the MTM of the existing sell USD forwards becomes negative, which increases the credit utilisation and might even result in Bridges reaching the credit limits with its banks. In this case, paradoxically, Bridges' capacity to lock favourable FX levels drops exactly when Bridges would most want it, ie, when the GBP is weak against the USD. This anomaly is likely to be exacerbated with the more stringent capital requirements under Basel III, which we mentioned earlier. Therefore, there is an urgent need to consider alternative approaches to FX hedging that optimise the credit utilisation.

One alternative is for Bridges to sign a credit support annex (CSA), but this would introduce cashflow volatilities and operational burden, since the company would be required to post more collateral when the existing hedges move against it.

Another solution is to create a dynamic hedging strategy that increases the relative proportion of USD puts purchased as USD weakens against the GBP. We back test such a strategy over a 12-year period and notice that it significantly reduces the credit utilisation.

COMPANY OBJECTIVES

- To create a dynamic hedging strategy, using only forwards and options.
- To take into account the long-term nature of Bridges' USD cashflows.

- The strategy should be very simple and based on where forwards are with respect to their historical distribution.
- To perform back-testing of the strategy and compare the credit utilisation against static strategies using forwards, options or collars.

ANALYSIS

The approach follows the four steps in Figure 20.1.

STEP 1: EVALUATE CREDIT USE OF STATIC STRATEGIES

We shall limit ourselves to a three-year hedging horizon and will first consider two static hedging strategies:

- **Strategy 1: forwards.** Every quarter, Bridges enters into a three-year USD forward, whereby it sells USD and buys GBP.
- **Strategy 2: options.** Every quarter, Bridges buys a three-year USD put/GBP call with an ATM forward strike.[3]

We define the credit utilisation as the future MTM of the hedging portfolio at the 90th percentile confidence interval in one year (Figure 20.1). Only the negative market values (from Bridges' perspective) are taken into account. Since the option premium is paid up front, bought options do not contribute to Bridges' credit utilisation but they require cash.

In Figure 20.2, we show the credit utilisation on a one-year time horizon for the two static strategies. Credit utilisation is expressed as a percentage of the annual notional hedged.

We can see that forwards have a high exposure when the GBP is weakening (eg, at the end of 2008). This is to be expected, since in that situation the contracts which have been entered into at higher GBP values become out-of-the-money.

At the same time, we can see that a static option strategy has no credit utilisation, as expected, since Bridges pays an upfront premium and then its counterparty pays the payout value if positive, at maturity.

STEP 2: EVALUATE CREDIT USE OF DYNAMIC STRATEGIES

In Figure 20.3 and Table 20.1, we define a dynamic strategy, whereby every quarter Bridges enters into the same constant amount of USD

Figure 20.1 Dynamic FX hedging approach: step by step

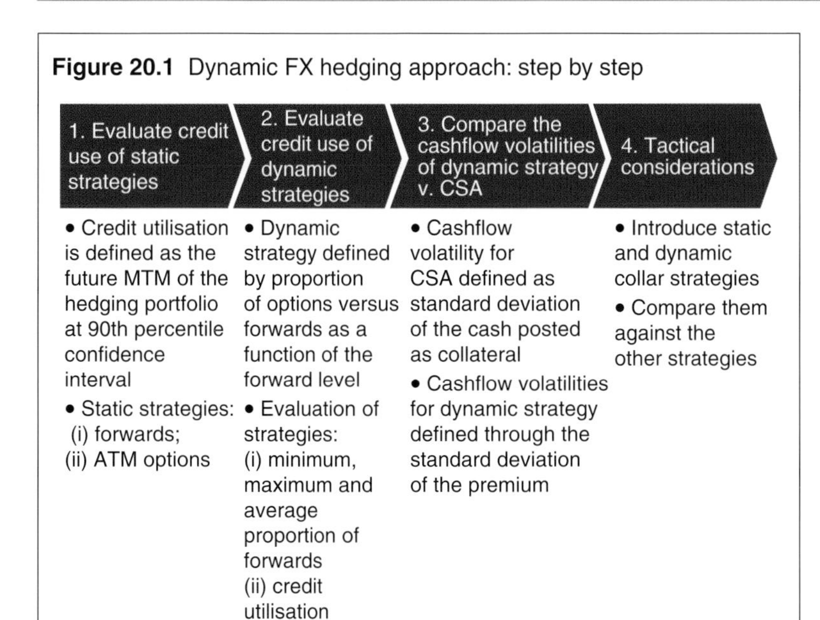

Figure 20.2 One-year credit utilisation at 90% (as a percentage of GBP notional hedged per year)

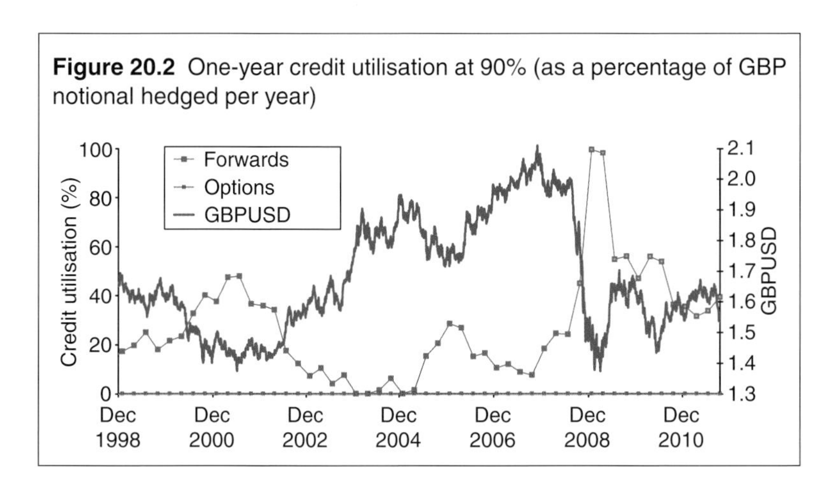

hedges, which is split between forwards and options according to a simple formula. The blue line represents the percentage of new forwards versus options Bridges should enter into as a function of GBPUSD forward levels. For comparison, the purple bars show the historical distribution of GBPUSD from 1988 to 2011.

Our strategy assumes no unwinding of previous positions, ie, the existing positions from previous quarters are maintained until maturity.

Figure 20.3 Allocation of forwards as a function of GBPUSD forward

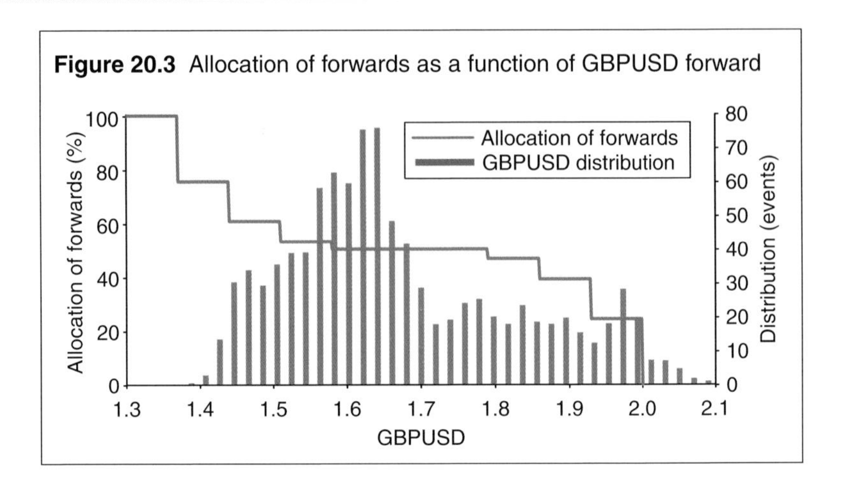

Table 20.1 Allocation of forwards as a function of GBPUSD forward

GBPUSD forward	Forwards (%)
<1.37	100
1.37–1.44	76
1.44–1.51	61
1.51–1.58	53
1.58–1.79	50
1.79–1.86	47
1.86–1.93	39
1.93–2.00	24
>2.00	0

For example, at a forward level of 1.45, Bridges would enter into 61% forwards/39% options for that quarter. If the GBP were to strengthen to 1.80 by next quarter, the new allocation would be only 47% of forwards and 53% options. This also helps Bridges not to lock in a "bad level" of high GBP rates via forwards while still maintaining some protection via options.

In Figure 20.4, we back-test the dynamic options strategy and show the cumulative proportion of forwards since 1998.

The minimum proportion of forwards was 30% in 2008, as a result of GBPUSD strengthening to 2.0 two years previously.[4] The maximum proportion of forwards was 61% in 2002, as a result of the GBPUSD weakening to 1.40 two years previously. The average proportion of forwards over the whole period was 48%.

Figure 20.4 Cumulative proportion of forwards in the dynamic options strategy

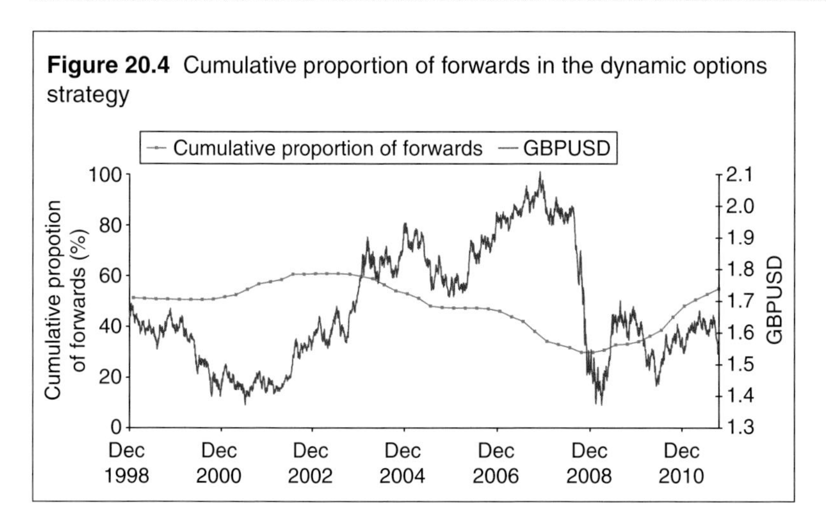

Figure 20.5 One-year credit utilisation at 90% (% of GBP total notional): comparison of the three strategies

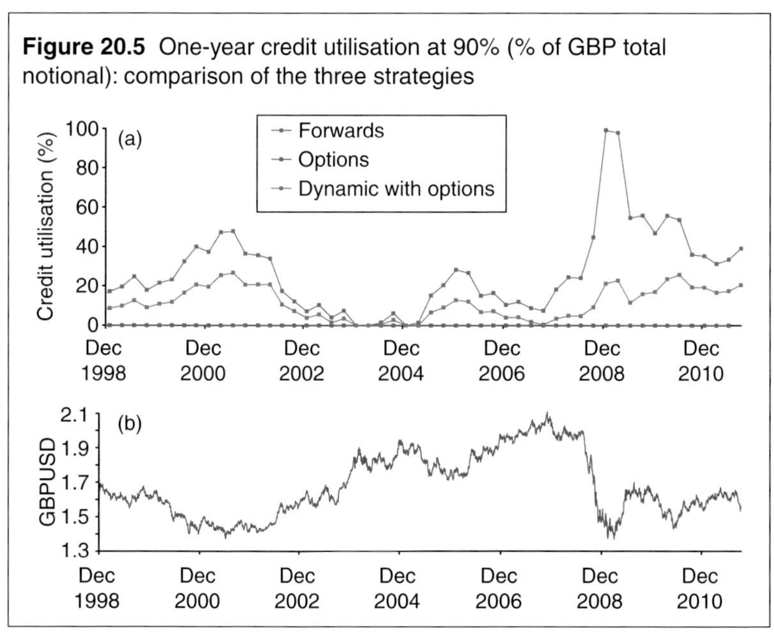

In Figure 20.5, we show the credit utilisation with the following three strategies:

- **Strategy 1:** forwards;
- **Strategy 2:** options;
- **Strategy 3:** dynamic options.

We can see that by opting for the dynamic strategy in the past, Bridges would have significantly reduced its credit utilisation in comparison with a forward strategy. Since the average proportion of forwards is approximately halved (actually, it is 48%), the average credit utilisation is roughly halved as well.

Moreover, the impact is particularly pronounced when the GBP is weak (for instance, in 2008) and when it is particularly worthwhile to lock the favourable rates.

STEP 3: COMPARE THE CASHFLOW VOLATILITY OF DYNAMIC STRATEGY VERSUS CSA

In Figure 20.6 we compute the cashflow volatility of the dynamic strategy in terms of the annual premium required.

Figure 20.6 Annual premium with the dynamic options strategy

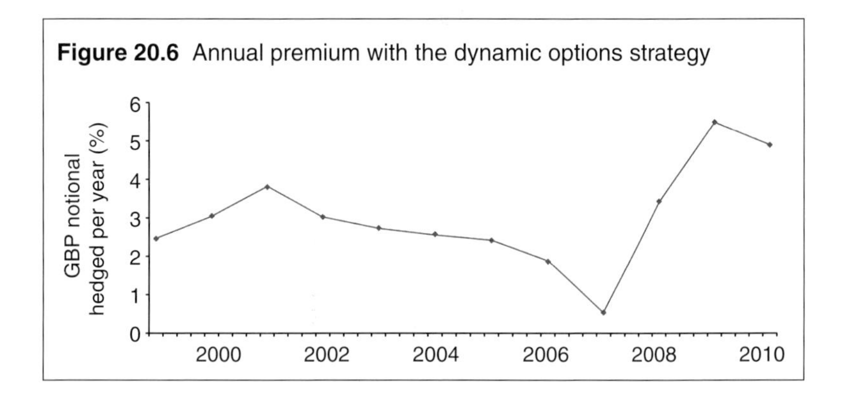

The average annual premium is 3.0% of the GBP notional, while the maximum annual premium was 5.5% in 2009. The standard deviation is 1.3%.

For comparison purposes, we compute also what would have been the quarterly cashflow volatilities assuming that Bridges signed a CSA, but based on the forwards strategy.

We make the following assumptions concerning the CSA:[5]

- **Reset:** quarterly;
- **Threshold:** zero;
- **Minimum transfer amount:** zero.

In Figure 20.7 and Table 20.2 we compare the two solutions.

Figure 20.7 Quarterly cashflow volatilities (GBP million): forwards plus CSA versus dynamic strategy

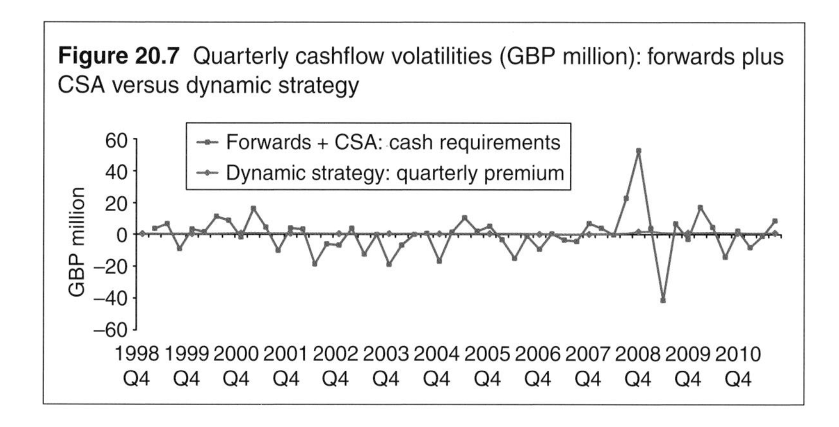

Table 20.2 Comparison of the cashflow volatilities

	Quarterly CF volatility (% of GBP notional)			
	Average (%)	SD (%)	Max. (%)	2011 Q3 (%)
Dynamic strategy: option premium	0.8	0.4	2.1	1.2
Forwards + CSA: cash requirements	0.3	13.1	53.1	9.0

We can see that forwards plus CSA strategy introduces a much higher cashflow volatilities than the option premiums with the dynamic strategy.

STEP 4: TACTICAL CONSIDERATIONS

Another possibility is to use the zero-cost collars. In Figure 20.8, we show the exposure when the strategy is balanced between forwards and zero-cost collars using 35 delta USD puts.[6]

We can see that because the written USD call options can also have a negative MTM, the exposure is higher than with options. Nevertheless, without paying any premium, the credit utilisation is still diminished compared with the dynamic option strategy.

RECOMMENDATIONS

In Table 20.3 we compare six strategies: unhedged, forwards, options, dynamic options, collars and dynamic collars.[7]

Figure 20.8 One-year credit utilisation at 90% (% of GBP notional hedged per year): comparison of three strategies

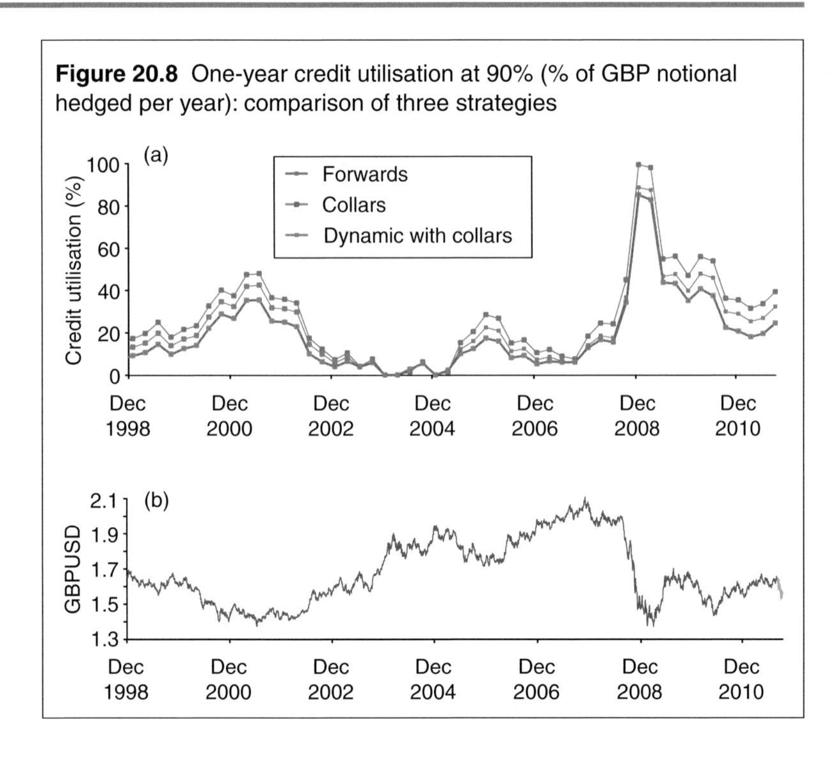

Table 20.3 Comparison of strategies (quarterly data from 1998 Q4 to 2011 Q3)

	0	1	2	3	4	5
Average exchange rate	1.68	1.65	1.65	1.64	1.67	1.65
Volatility (%)	10.70	0.00	3.10	1.50	5.40	2.50
Average credit utilisation (% of notional per year)	0.00	27.00	0.00	11.20	13.60	19.70

Note: 0, unhedged; 1, forwards; 2, options; 3, dynamic options; 4, collars; 5, dynamic collars.

We show, as previously, the average credit exposure (in percentage of notional hedged per year), the volatility and the average exchange rate. The average exchange rate is virtually identical across the strategies. In any case, this parameter would vary depending on the back testing period, but we would expect it to be independent of the strategy in over a sufficiently long period.

We can see that the dynamic collars strategy reduces the average credit exposure to 19.7%. However, the static collar strategy has an even lower credit utilisation, at 13.6%. This should be compared with the dynamic options strategy, which has a different risk profile and requires cash payment.

CONCLUSION

In this chapter, we proposed a dynamic hedging strategy based on forwards and options. The strategy allows Bridges to adjust the proportion of forwards versus options in order not to lock in a disadvantageous forward level. We show that the dynamic strategy reduces the average credit exposure.

1 At the time of writing, the jury is still out on the possible carve-out for corporate hedgers regarding the so-called VaR on CVA, nevertheless, Basel III will impose higher capital requirements for banks, which are the hedge providers.

2 We assume that capital usage is proportional to VaR. For IRS, the VaR is increased until half of the life and then falls, while for FX forwards and CCS it grows all the way until maturity. So the VaR is larger and the capital is higher.

3 ATM stands for "at-the-money".

4 Since we enter into a three-year strategy every quarter, we are concerned about the average level over the three-year period preceding the observation point. This is why the maximum or minimum two years previously defines the extreme points of cumulative proportion of forwards.

5 For the calculation of the CSA, we do not take into account the interest earned/spent and the CVA charges.

6 We assume no volatility smile or skew.

7 For options and dynamic options, we include the upfront premium when computing the average exchange rate.

Part IV

Credit Risk

Credit Risk

Credit risk is the risk that one counterparty defaults on its payments to the other. The payments can be any kind of payable including coupons and principal on debt, derivative payments or payments not linked to financial transactions, for example, payments for a delivery of a commodity or equipment.

Credit risk is generally a key risk for financial corporations due to their role as credit providers to the economy. However, as in the rest of this book, in this part we shall focus on non-financial companies ("companies" for short).

Companies are normally affected by credit risk in one of three ways:[1]

1. a counterparty risk on derivatives positions, ie, the risk that the bank with whom the company has entered into a derivative position will default, which would expose the company to the risk of unwinding or replacing the derivative;
2. a counterparty risk on deposits, ie, the risk of default of the bank with whom the company has deposited money;
3. the company's own cost of credit, which affects the refinancing cost of the company (this has a direct impact not on the company's own credit risk, but on the risk of its creditors).

We shall cover each kind of risk in turn in the four chapters that follow, but first let us talk briefly about the management of counterparty risk in non-financial companies.

In the list of financial risks managed by non-financial companies, counterparty risk is often the last to be analysed and managed. Why is this so? Non-financial companies have traditionally paid much more attention to the management of currency and interest rate risks, while the issue of counterparty risk was rarely addressed at all, and when it was addressed in the risk management policy it barely merited a few bullet points, such as the example below, taken from a risk management policy of a European media company:

- instruments up to five years must be executed only with banks with a minimum credit rating of A3/A−;

- instruments beyond five years must be executed only with banks with a minimum credit rating of Aa3/AA−;
- the maximum concentration of exposure is EUR 1 billion notional per single counterparty.

This simple policy, based on the minimum credit rating requirement and maximum concentration limit, was standard up until about 2007, and then everything changed as a result of the credit crisis of 2008–9. Companies first realised how slow credit ratings are to change during the crisis, as evidenced by the response of rating agencies to the deterioration of Lehman Brothers.

So a static risk management policy based on counterparty ratings will no longer do, and should be replaced by a more dynamic policy based on CDS levels,[2] volatilities and correlations. Just consider the following excerpt from the Telefónica 20-F report for 2011:[3]

> In addition, since Lehman went bankrupt, the credit ratings of rating agencies have proved to be less effective as a credit risk management tool. Therefore, the 5-year CDS (Credit Default Swap) of credit institutions has been added. This way, the CDS of all the counterparties with which Telefónica, S.A. operates is monitored at all times in order to assess the maximum allowable CDS for operating at any given time. Transactions are generally only carried out with counterparties whose CDS is below the threshold.

At the same time, individual positions would need to be aggregated into portfolios of exposure with different counterparties, and in doing so the counterparty risk management of corporates starts to resemble more the practices of financial companies.

Chapter 21, on counterparty risk methodology, explains counterparty risk in general and how the methodology used by banks can be implemented in a corporate setting. We show how most of the weaknesses implicit in an "old-style" counterparty risk policy can be cured without imposing excessive burden on a corporate treasury.

Chapter 22, on counterparty risk protection, applies this methodology to the concrete situation of a company with a significant derivatives portfolio with a risky counterparty. The company has several ways of reducing the risk, which we compare.

Chapter 23, on optimal deposit composition, tackles counterparty risk from the perspective of deposits. The company described in this chapter has to decide how to allocate deposits between various banks. Again, we start from the banks' CDS and develop two approaches to this problem, between which the company can choose depending on the level of its risk aversion.

Finally, Chapter 24, on prehedging credit risk, expands the discussion in previous chapters on prehedging (see Chapters 10 and 11) to the topic of managing credit risk, ie, the variability of the credit spread of the issuer at the time of bond issuance. Motivation for this kind of risk management is the same as for interest rate risk management, ie, reducing the risk on the coupons of the future bonds. The main difference is the fact that, unlike the interest rates, which are the same for all issuers, credit spread is company specific. This makes it tricky to hedge, due to several issues, including self-referencing and market liquidity.

In summary, we have gathered here a series of case studies, which we hope will stimulate the reader to seriously consider credit risk; in particular, what kinds of implications it has for the company and what the company can do about it.

1 Here we are focusing on financial credit risks, which can be managed using financial tools, and not the credit risks on the receivables, nor indirect risks from the creditworthiness of their suppliers and customers.

2 For those companies where CDSs are not liquid, an alternative is to consider the credit spread of liquid bonds.

3 See page F-75 of the Telefónica 20-F report for 2011 at http://www.telefonica.com/.

21

Counterparty Risk Methodology

As we mentioned in the introduction to this part of the book, counterparty risk is the risk that one counterparty may default on their obligation to another. Companies experience it in many ways (for example, through the risk on their suppliers, competitors or clients), but here we focus on the risks from their banking counterparties, through company deposits and corporate derivatives.

In this chapter we discuss how to develop a counterparty risk management policy. Through it, a company could optimise its existing portfolio in several ways:

- by reducing the potential exposure to selected banks according to predetermined criteria;
- freeing up credit lines by combining potential offsetting derivatives;
- reducing the transaction cost (eg, credit and funding charges) on new trades.

In this chapter we focus on the management of counterparty risk on a simplified derivatives portfolio. The main focus will be to show how the methodology that banks and other financial institutions use to manage counterparty risk can be adapted to a corporate situation.

BACKGROUND

Gas and Water Power Utility (GAWPU) has significant counterparty exposure to two banks, SaferBank and RiskyBank. With the reduction in the creditworthiness of both of these banks as a result of the credit crisis, GAWPU is concerned about its exposure to them. The CFO of GAWPU would like to find a systematic approach to optimising the hedging with each of their counterparties in order to minimise its credit risk.

COMPANY OBJECTIVES

- To create a framework for handling the credit risk from several counterparties.
- To optimise the credit exposure to GAWPU's counterparties.

ANALYSIS

We define a methodology for the measurement of credit risk from all counterparties, and use it to calculate an efficient credit portfolio for the credit risk and cost of hedging for any combination of the two banks. We then discuss possible implementations of the strategy.

The approach follows the four steps in Figure 21.1.

Figure 21.1 Risk management approach: step by step

1. Identify risky positions and possible actions to limit risk	2. Calculate the credit risk from each counterparty	3. Suggest the optimal allocation under a portfolio approach	4. Reduce and manage portfolio risk
• Risk factors: potential future exposure, the default probability and the expected recovery rate • Determine the exposure by counterparty after netting and collateral agreements • Potential future exposure is linked to the evolution of the MTM. Positive MTM generates counterparty exposure, while negative MTM does not	• Simulate evolution of MTM using Monte Carlo and historical data • Map exposures to counterparties in terms of CDSs • Consider the correlation and volatility of CDSs • Determine the loss distribution due to MTM evolution and counterparty evolution	• Perform a portfolio analysis including simulations of MTM and default of counterparties • Consider the portfolio impact of alternative possible solutions Find the lowest cost protection within risk limits • Replace the riskiest counterparties, close the riskiest positions, include collateral agreements if possible	• Implement the solutions • Manage the ongoing counterparty risk on a portfolio basis • Update the risk management policy • Communicate internally

STEP 1: IDENTIFY RISKY POSITIONS AND POSSIBLE ACTIONS TO LIMIT RISK

GAWPU has the open positions shown in Table 21.1, both of them over a five-year horizon.

Table 21.1 GAWPU open derivative contracts

Type	Counterparty	Notional (EUR bn)	Current MTM (EUR m)
Buy EUR/sell USD FX forward	RiskyBank	5	13
EUR pay fixed interest rate swap	SaferBank	1	12

The CDS values for the counterparties are given in Table 21.2.

Table 21.2 CDS values for counterparty banks

Bank	Five-year CDS (bp)
RiskyBank	350
SaferBank	200

Note: we shall assume everywhere a flat credit curve, ie, one-year CDS = two-year CDS = · · · = *n*-year CDS.

We use a recovery rate of 40% to compute the probabilities of default, which is the standard assumption.[1] The default probability can be approximated[2] from a CDS spread using the formula

$$\text{probability} \times \text{time} = \frac{\text{CDS}}{1 - \text{recovery rate}}$$

As an example, a CDS of 2% per year and a recovery of 40% imply a 3.33% of default within one year, and 15.58% over five years.[3]

STEP 2: CALCULATE THE CREDIT RISK FROM EACH COUNTERPARTY

We use a Monte Carlo engine to derive the possible paths of the future value of the derivative contracts[4] and use the counterparty's CDS spread to estimate their default probability. From these we can deduce the probability distribution of losses from the default of the current portfolio over the next year, which is shown in Figure 21.2.

In Figure 21.2, we can see that the highest probability is for a zero loss (almost 83%). The reason for such a small probability is that a non-zero loss only occurs when two conditions are met: the counterparty defaults and the MTM of the derivative portfolio is

Figure 21.2 Loss distribution from current portfolio

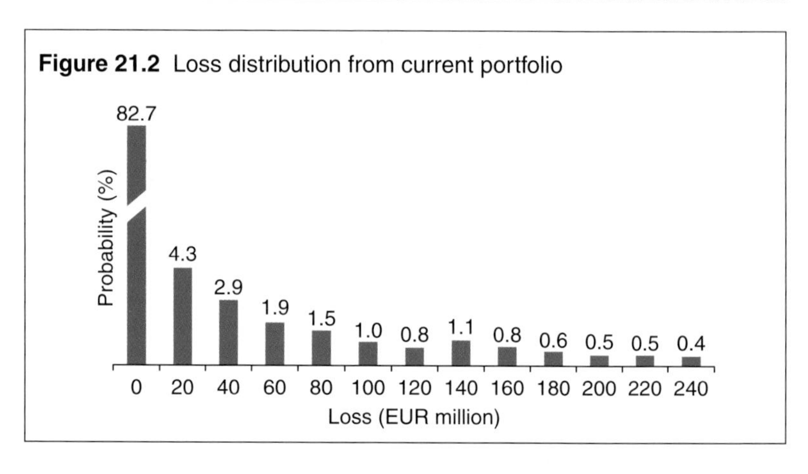

positive from GAWPU's point of view (ie, when GAWPU is owed the money by the counterparty).

STEP 3: SUGGEST THE OPTIMAL ALLOCATION UNDER A PORTFOLIO APPROACH

We first outline below the options faced by GAWPU to reduce the risk from any one of its counterparties, as well as their accounting implications. We then try to build a more wholesome portfolio approach. The options faced by GAWPU with relation to either counterparty are (for accounting treatment see Table 21.3) as follows.

- If GAWPU believes that the counterparty will not default, it may prefer to do nothing. This is an easy solution, but is also risky. Moreover, it may affect the accounting treatment of the derivatives and reduce its effectiveness. GAWPU has ruled this option out as too passive.
- If GAWPU believes that the counterparty may default, it may want to replace its current counterparty with a safer one. This strategy obviously lowers risk. However, GAWPU will now be exposed to the risk on the new counterparty. Furthermore, an assignment is a tri-party negotiation,[5] and the required approval of the current counterparty may be difficult to obtain at a time when liquidity is scarce.[6] The new counterparty will apply a new credit charge on the assigned transaction, affecting the economics of the hedge. From the accounting perspective, assignment to a more creditworthy counterparty should be a continuation of the existing hedging relationship. However,

execution of the new swap with a more creditworthy counterparty will require the restart of hedge accounting (IAS 39.91(a) and 101(a)). If the new hedge has an initial MTM of zero, the hedge should be perfectly effective, but if the new hedge has the same initial MTM as the old swap, it will not be perfectly effective.

- If GAWPU believes that the counterparty may default but cannot replace it, it can hedge itself by buying a CDS on this counterparty. In principle, this strategy is able to reduce risk significantly. However, it may be costly to implement, and causes GAWPU to have a credit exposure to the seller of the CDS. Furthermore, the MTM of the derivatives changes constantly, which would force GAWPU to dynamically rebalance its CDS position. Since GAWPU, like many other corporations, has no previous experience in the CDS markets, it is facing a steep learning curve and as a result of this will incur some administrative effort and transaction costs. The accounting treatment for this case depends on the type of hedge accounting employed. For fair value hedges, if the corporation is including counterparty creditworthiness in the hedge MTM, the purchase of the CDS should reduce the impact of creditworthiness on derivative valuation (IAS 39.9). In the case of fair value hedges, therefore, the hedge will be more effective. However, the CDS is likely to cause some earning volatility in the case when GAWPU is using a cashflow hedge (IAS 39 IG F.4.3).
- If GAWPU thinks that the current counterparty may default, but for whatever reason cannot replace it and does not want to dynamically hedge the exposure, it could buy a contingent credit default swap (CCDS) on the particular trades. The CCDS is a contract that pays (1 – recovery) × MTM of the reference derivative portfolio if this MTM is positive in the case of default of the counterparty. If the MTM is negative when the counterparty defaults, the CCDS expires worthless (see Chapter 22 for details). This instrument almost exactly covers the risk from default that GAWPU faces. This option reduces risk, and could be a very good solution for GAWPU, assuming that it is satisfied with the accounting treatment. However, it leaves GAWPU with the residual risk on the counterparty that sold them the CCDS.

Summary of single counterparty options

In Table 21.3, we summarise the accounting treatment of the single counterparty options.

Table 21.3 Summary of single counterparty options

Option	Accounting
Ignoring credit risk	The creditworthiness of the counterparty should affect the fair value of the hedge through the discounting. Fair value is defined as an exit price (IFRS 13.2): • Derivative's counterparty creditworthiness should be included in its valuation (IFRS 13.42, 48, 82(c)(iii)). • There is diversity in practice when hedgers "credit-adjust" derivative valuations (eg, no adjustment to mid-market swap curve, valuation at mid-market swap curve then revaluation with hedger's or bank's credit spread depending on whether derivative has positive or negative value, credit adjustment based on simulation of potential future exposure, etc). Counterparty creditworthiness and hedge accounting (IAS 39 IG F.4.3). Change in creditworthiness is a source of hedge ineffectiveness; however, it is often ignored in practice: • Fair value hedge – hedging instrument valuation is affected, while hedged item valuation is not affected. • Cashflow hedge – hedging instrument valuation is affected, while hedged risk valuation is not; additionally, hedging instrument ceases to be highly effective if it becomes probable that the counterparty will default.

Alternatively, GAWPU could attempt to reduce the risk by using a portfolio-based approach, ie, by distributing the positions between the counterparties in an efficient manner.

The redistribution could be achieved by assigning portions of transactions or synthetically using CCDS, if possible. This would require either a new credit charge or a CCDS net premium to be paid.

Table 21.3 Continued

Option	Accounting
Replacing counterparty	Novation of hedging instrument to more creditworthy counterparty should be a continuation of the existing hedging relationship. • It will affect derivative valuation and hedge effectiveness as per above. • Execution of new hedging instrument to more creditworthy counterparty is likely to require restarting of hedge accounting (IAS 39.91(a) and 101(a)).
Vanilla CDS	For fair value hedges, if the corporation is including counterparty creditworthiness in the MTM of the hedge, valuation of CDS will reduce impact of creditworthiness on derivative valuation (IAS 39.9). For cashflow hedges, CDS is likely to cause earnings volatility.
CCDS	The accounting treatment is unclear.

Figure 21.3 Five-year expected loss versus loss at 95% (EUR million)

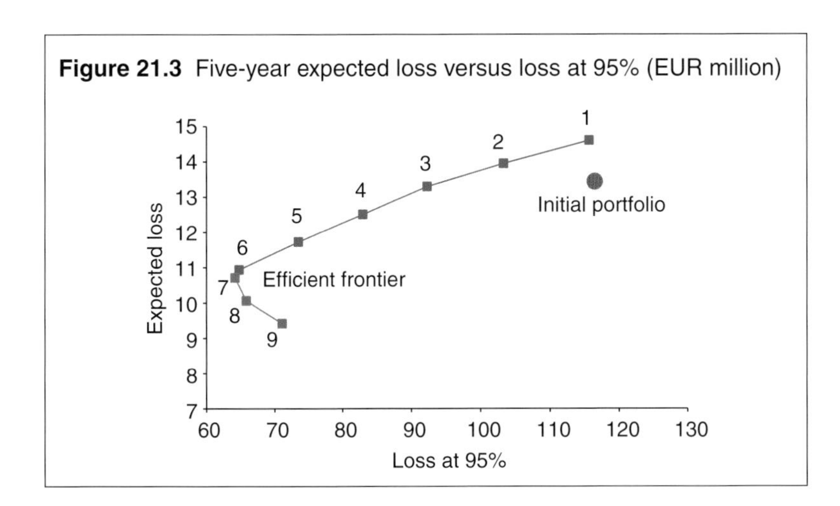

This approach can be optimised through the efficient frontier technique as illustrated in Figure 21.3 and Table 21.4.

In Figure 21.3 and Table 21.4, the expected loss is the expected value of loss due to counterparty default over the next five years. The loss at 95% represents the 95% worst loss that could occur due to default of one or both counterparties. Both of these parameters can be changed by modifying the allocation among the derivatives counterparties. The graph shows the efficient frontier of possible allocations for both the foreign exchange and interest rate derivatives. The red dot corresponds to the current allocation of GAWPU, which is clearly not efficient, since it has roughly the same expected loss as point 3 but a higher loss at 95%. A more efficient distribution is to put 78% of either derivative with SaferBank and 22% with RiskyBank (point 7). This allocation relies on the diversification of credit risk to reduce the expected loss and the loss at 95% on the whole portfolio.

Table 21.4 Efficient frontier

Point no.	RiskyBank IR swap (%)	SaferBank IR swap (%)	RiskyBank FX fwd (%)	SaferBank FX fwd (%)	Loss at 95% (EUR m)	EL*
1	98	2	88	12	115.7	14.6
2	100	0	74	26	103.4	13.9
3	71	29	66	34	92.4	13.3
4	64	36	51	49	83.0	12.5
5	56	44	37	63	73.5	11.7
6	49	51	23	77	64.9	10.9
7	**22**	**78**	**22**	**78**	**64.2**	**10.7**
8	**5**	**95**	**12**	**88**	**65.9**	**10.0**
9	**0**	**100**	**0**	**100**	**71.1**	**9.4**
Initial	0	100	100	0	117.0	13.4

Note: * EL, expected loss (EUR million).

STEP 4: REDUCE AND MANAGE PORTFOLIO RISK

At this point, GAWPU should implement the solution and update the risk management policy. We shall not dwell on the implementation issues here, but we come back to this topic in the next chapter.

RECOMMENDATIONS

GAWPU should move 22% of its derivatives to RiskyBank and 78% to SaferBank (point 7). This way, the company can diversify its risk and move towards the efficient frontier. As shown in Table 21.4, this would reduce its loss at a 95% confidence interval from EUR 117 million to EUR 64 million and its expected loss from EUR 13.4 million to EUR 10.7 million.

The process as described above should from now on form part of the regular risk management practices, and the portfolio of counterparty exposures should be periodically updated and optimised to reflect changes to the exposures and credit worthiness of counterparties. GAWPU should also update its risk management policy to reflect the new procedures.

CONCLUSION

In this chapter, we have illustrated several issues related to the Risk management of counterparty risk. We continue our discussion in the next chapter, where we enter into a more detailed discussion of protection against the risk of counterparty default.

1 This assumption can be misleading. For example, the settlement on CDS of Lehman Brothers was based on a recovery rate of 8.625 cents on the USD.

2 This follows from the formula

$$\text{risky discount factor} = \text{discount factor} \times [\text{default probability} \times \text{recovery rate} + (1 - \text{default probability})]$$

where discount factor $= \exp(-r \times T)$ and risky discount factor $= \exp[-(r + \text{CDS}) \times T]$ and where r is the risk-free interest rate, in the limit CDS $\ll 1$. For more details, see Arvanitis and Gregory (2001).

3 If one-year probability of default is 3.33%, that means that the probability that the company will not default in any one year is 96.67%. Therefore, the probability that the company will not default in five years is $96.67\%^5 = 84.42\%$, so the five-year probability of default is 15.58% (= 100% − 84.42%).

4 For example, in the case of the two derivatives positions of GAWPU, we would need to simulate EURUSD FX rate and EUR interest rates in a wide variety of scenarios in order to determine future paths of the MTM of GAWPU positions. These paths would then be used in a valuation model that would give us, for each path and time, the portfolio MTM with each counterparty.

5 Between GAWPU, the old counterparty and the new counterparty.

6 If the existing counterparty owes money to GAWPU and has a collateral agreement with the new counterparty, they would have to post money, which may be difficult if the old counterparty has credit problems already.

22

Counterparty Risk Protection

In this chapter, we explore further the subject of counterparty risk and show how it can be reduced using credit derivatives. We use the methodology developed in the previous chapter in order to quantify counterparty risk before and after the protection (ie, hedge) is put in place. The goal of this chapter is to move from the abstract to the concrete and show how a company dealt with their counterparty risk, which it considered excessive.

BACKGROUND

Shakers & Co is a European manufacturer that has a portfolio of interest rate swaps with an investment bank (ABC Bank). The derivatives portfolio is significantly in the money for Shakers, with a current positive MTM of EUR 41 million.[1]

Given the financial market turmoil since 2008, and the vulnerable position of many investment banks, Shakers is concerned about the significant exposure it has to its derivatives counterparty and would like to reduce it through products available in the market.

COMPANY OBJECTIVES

- To quantify Shakers' counterparty risk.
- To explore ways to reduce that risk to an acceptable level.

ANALYSIS

In order to quantify the counterparty risk that Shakers & Co is facing, we first calculate the probability distribution for the future MTM over the life of the swap portfolio.

We then use the probabilities of default[2] implied from ABC Bank's credit default swaps to determine the implied counterparty risk over the same horizon. Finally, we explore alternative ways of reducing the risk.

The approach follows the steps in Figure 22.1.

Figure 22.1 Risk management approach: step by step

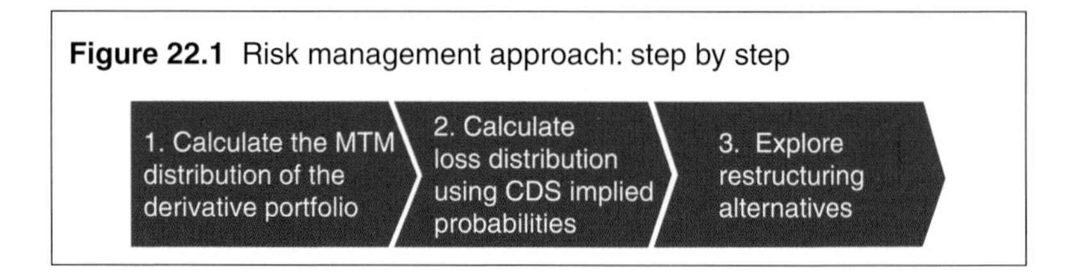

STEP 1: CALCULATE THE MTM DISTRIBUTION OF THE DERIVATIVE PORTFOLIO

Shakers' portfolio consists of five interest rate swaps, which are shown in Table 22.1.

Table 22.1 Swap contracts for Shakers & Co

Type	Notional (EUR m)	Fixed rate (%)	Maturity	Frequency
Receive fixed	200	3.35	01/01/2020	Semi-annually
Receive fixed	500	2.22	01/07/2019	Semi-annually
Pay fixed	300	1.55	01/01/2019	Semi-annually
Pay fixed	400	1.35	01/01/2018	Semi-annually
Pay fixed	200	2.00	01/01/2017	Semi-annually

The total MTM for all swaps is currently EUR 41 million.

Figure 22.2 Mark-to-market distribution of interest rate swap portfolio

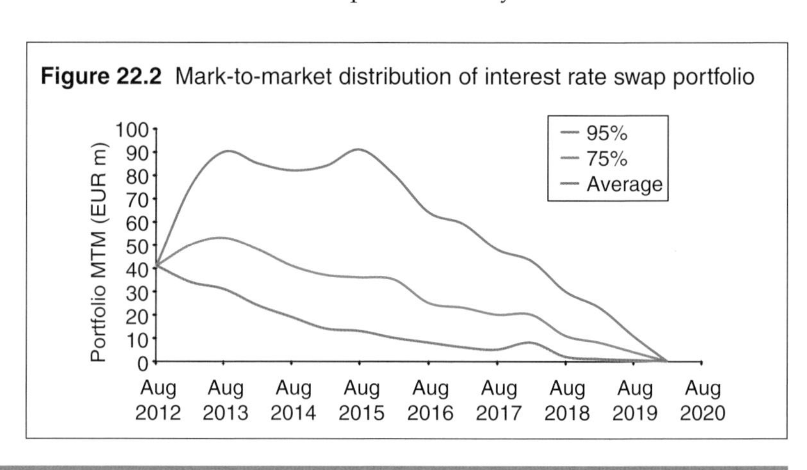

We used a Monte Carlo engine to calculate the future MTM of the portfolio quarterly over an eight-year horizon. The MTM distribution is presented in Figure 22.2.

The red line shows that the MTM of the swap portfolio is not expected to become negative, but rather that it will decrease gradually towards zero during the lifetime of the swaps. At a 95% confidence interval (purple line), the swaps may reach an MTM of EUR 91 million during 2015, and a default at that time would cause Shakers a significant loss.

STEP 2: CALCULATE LOSS DISTRIBUTION USING CDS IMPLIED PROBABILITIES

We calculate the probability of default for ABC Bank from its traded CDS, and assuming the recovery of 40%. The current CDS spreads for ABC are given in Table 22.2.

Table 22.2 CDS spreads for ABC Bank

Tenor	Spread (bp)
1 year	210
2 year	230
3 year	240
4 year	245
5 year	240
7 year	220
10 year	200

In parallel with interest rates, we simulate the default probability for ABC Bank. Today's default probabilities are implied from the CDS levels in Table 22.2.[3] For every path, we calculate the probability of default at any time step. We then check the MTM of the derivative portfolio in case of default. If the MTM is negative (Shakers owes ABC Bank money), the debt would be repaid and Shakers does not incur any further loss from the default. If, on the other hand, the mark-to-market is positive, Shakers only receives (1 – recovery) × MTM, possibly generating a large loss.

From these calculations, we can derive a probability distribution for the loss arising from ABC Bank default. This distribution is presented in Figure 22.3 and Table 22.3.

Figure 22.3 Distribution of loss resulting from current counterparty default

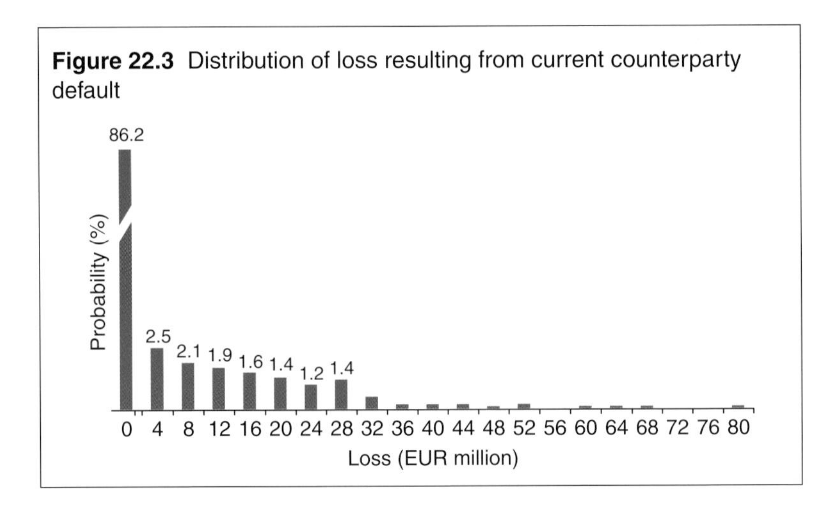

Table 22.3 Loss probabilities

Maximum loss (EUR m)	Probability (%)
0	86.2
4	2.5
8	2.1
12	1.9
16	1.6
20	1.4
24	1.2
28	1.4

The probability of no loss is 86.2%, which includes the possibility of no default by ABC Bank or of its default when the MTM is negative from Shakers' point of view.

The probability of loss between 0 and EUR 4 million is 2.5%, which Shakers would like to reduce.

The probability decreases mildly as the possible losses increase. Overall, the expected loss from the portfolio is EUR 2.5 million.

STEP 3: EXPLORE RESTRUCTURING ALTERNATIVES

We offered Shakers the following three solutions.

1. Shakers can protect itself from all possible losses by buying a CCDS (defined in the previous chapter) from another bank,

Bank DEF. This instrument reimburses Shakers for the expected losses on the portfolio in case of default of Bank ABC. Under the unilateral CCDS Bank DEF would pay Shakers (1 – recovery)[4] of the MTM of their portfolio at the time of default of Bank ABC if this MTM is positive, and zero if it is negative. This exactly matches the possible losses by Shakers. The price of this instrument is equivalent to the expected loss from default of Bank ABC after the hedging cost, ie, about EUR 2.5 million.

2. Shakers may choose to protect itself only from extreme losses, allowing for possible small losses to be absorbed. For example, the CCDS can be structured so that the first EUR 4 million of loss will not be reimbursed by the Bank DEF, but only the losses in excess of EUR 4 million. This would decrease the cost of the CCDS to EUR 2.0 million.

3. Shakers could enter into an amortising CDS, where Shakers specifies the expected MTM of the portfolio at each time interval. If ABC Bank defaults, Shakers will receive from Bank DEF the expected[5] MTM multiplied by (1-recovery). The price of this solution depends on the expected MTM profile.

The last solution is less suitable for Shakers than the first one, since it does not exactly fit their actual loss. For example (see Figure 22.2), Shakers may lose EUR 90.4 million if the default happens in 2015 and rates move in its favour (assuming zero recovery). If Shakers decides to go for the third solution, it would not receive the full compensation for this loss if it occurs, but would receive only EUR 13.0 million, which is the "expected" MTM for this period.

In case the cost of protection is too high, Shakers can also choose a so-called "Lazarus swap". This instrument is in effect a set of replacement swaps, struck at today's ATM rates. These swaps knock-in if and when ABC Bank defaults. If Shakers chooses this solution, its hedge will remain in place whether or not ABC Bank defaults, but in case of default of ABC Bank, the counterparty would change to a new bank, DEF Bank. Note that the swap will knock-in regardless of whether the MTM to Shakers is positive. For example, assume that the MTM of the original swap portfolio increases by EUR 5.0 million on the day after the Lazarus swaps are traded, and that ABC Bank defaults.

The loss to Shakers from the default itself would be, assuming zero recovery, EUR 41.2 million + EUR 5.0 million = EUR 46.2 million.

Furthermore, the Lazarus swaps would knock in with a positive MTM of EUR 5.0 million, limiting the loss to the MTM at EUR 41.2 million. If however, the swaps' MTM decreases by EUR 5.0 million, Shakers would lose EUR 36.2 million from the default, but the Lazarus swaps would knock-in with an MTM of EUR (−5.0 million), again making the total loss EUR 41.2 million.

RECOMMENDATIONS

We offered Shakers a unilateral CCDS, which would exactly match its possible losses. The CCDS pays to Shakers (1 − recovery) of the MTM of its portfolio at the time of default if this MTM is positive, and zero if it is negative.

Figure 22.4 Probability distribution of loss with and without CCDS

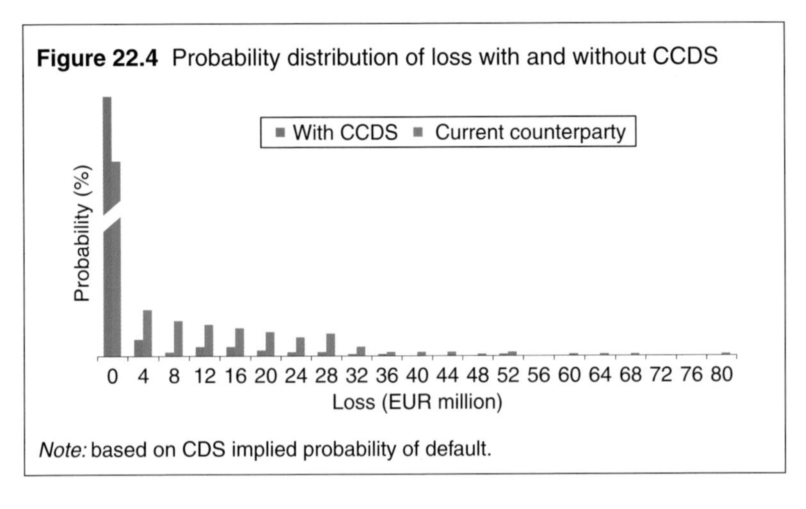

Note: based on CDS implied probability of default.

Once this solution is implemented, Shakers is no longer directly exposed to the credit risk of ABC Bank. Instead, it is only exposed to the more remote possibility of both the protection bank DEF Bank and ABC Bank defaulting, as shown in Figure 22.4 and Table 22.4.

CONCLUSION

In this chapter, we have shown how CCDS can be used to manage the counterparty risk on a portfolio of derivatives products with a risky banking counterparty. In the next chapter, we turn our attention to counterparty risk on deposits.

Table 22.4 Comparison of ABC Bank possible losses with and without protection bank CCDS

Maximum loss (EUR m)	Probability (%)	
	Without CCDS	With CCDS
0	86.2	96.8
4	2.5	0.8
8	2.1	0.2
12	1.9	0.4
16	1.6	0.4
20	1.4	0.3
24	1.2	0.2
28	1.4	0.2

1 To clarify, a positive MTM means that ABC Bank owes Shakers EUR 41 million.

2 We gave an example of this calculation in the previous chapter. For more details see Arvanitis and Gregory (2001).

3 We assume zero correlation between interest rates and default probabilities.

4 The recovery is determined during the credit event auction. For more details see http://www.isda.org/credit.

5 The expected is defined at the beginning of the deal and does not follow the "actual" development of the portfolio MTM. In Figure 22.2, it is shown by the red line.

23

Optimal Deposit Composition

In this chapter we turn our attention to the issue of counterparty risk on bank deposits. Given the low deposit rates we see at the time of writing, cash deposits cannot achieve a return which is in excess of the companies' funding cost.[1] Therefore, most companies consider cash as a liquidity buffer in case capital markets funding becomes difficult and at the same time the company finds it difficult to generate cash through operations. Cash is therefore normally kept on short-term deposits only with maturities ranging from overnight to a maximum of twelve months. However, an example of how to use cash efficiently when the liquidity constraints are removed is given in Chapters 3 and 13.

The company described in this chapter is looking for a systematic way to split cash deposits between its various banking counterparties, while not locking it for too long.

BACKGROUND

Sigma is a highly profitable consumer good company, with a significant and constantly increasing amount of cash on its balance sheet. The amount of cash at the time of writing is EUR 1,800 million, and Sigma wants to split this amount among its 12 relationship banks for deposits less than 12 months in maturity. There is no netting possible between the deposits and derivatives.

At the same time, Sigma is undergoing a review of its counterparty risk management policy and as part of this process would like to optimise its deposit allocation among banks based on CDS levels. Financial department would like to approve two alternative policies ("risk on" and "risk off") between which it can switch at will. The "risk off" or "conservative" policy would be applied in moments of perceived high counterparty risk and would consist in constant monitoring of its banking counterparties CDS at the time of observation and allocating deposits in order to minimise the risk without taking returns into account. The "risk on" or "strategic" policy would be applied in moments of lower counterparty risk and would allow Sigma to allocate deposits based on the average CDS levels and their volatilities over a period of time, while taking into account the deposit rates, ie, returns it hopes to achieve on its cash.

COMPANY OBJECTIVES

- To develop a counterparty risk management policy for deposits.
- To find the best way to incorporate CDS levels into such a policy.
- To develop two policies:
  - conservative, whose goal is risk minimisation over short-term;
  - strategic, whose goal is to optimise the returns versus risk.

ANALYSIS

We shall introduce the required models in order of increasing complexity; first starting from a simple conservative model with a smaller set of banking counterparties. It is a good idea to do so in order to illustrate the methodology, since a full conservative model with 12 banks is more difficult to describe.

The approach follows the steps in Figure 23.1.

STEP 1: SIMPLIFIED CONSERVATIVE MODEL

We start from the matrix (Table 23.1) of one-year CDS levels and correlations.[2] Correlations are based on one year of daily changes in CDS levels. In this step we shall focus on the five banks only, in order to simplify the exposition, while we expand our analysis to all 12 banks in step 2.

It is important to note that the correlation matrix changes all the time, and the absolute levels are very volatile; therefore, this is only a snapshot of the situation as it was on a given date. Moreover, correlations change depending on the length of the observation period, frequency and whether you consider absolute levels or returns. Nevertheless, the picture shown is that at the time of writing all the banks

Figure 23.1 Optimal debt composition: step by step

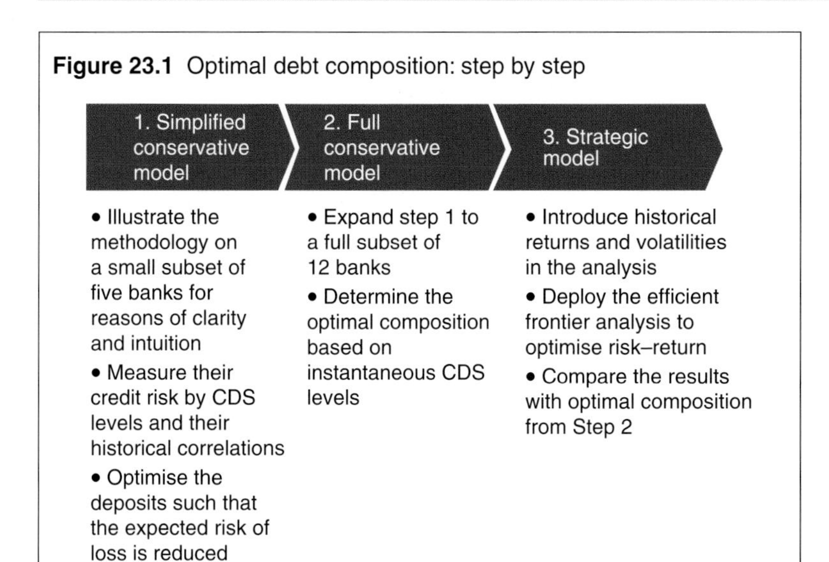

Table 23.1 Correlation matrix and absolute levels of banks' one-year CDS, as of June 2012

	One-year correlation (%)				
	Bank A	Bank B	Bank C	Bank D	Bank E
Bank A	100	60	54	78	77
Bank B	60	100	92	89	92
Bank C	54	92	100	86	88
Bank D	78	89	86	100	98
Bank E	77	92	88	98	100
1y CDS (bp)	133	332	232	267	336

exhibit a high correlation of CDS (between 54% and 98%), due to the presumed common sources of risk between various European banks.

Deposits

We assume that the objective of the policy is to satisfy the following three goals, in decreasing order of importance:

1. to reduce the expected risk of loss due to counterparty default;
2. to reduce the concentration of risk between correlated banks;

3. to reduce the necessary frequency of rebalancing, ie, operational burden on the treasury.

In order to satisfy the first constraint, a maximum expected loss threshold is imposed upon deposits with a given counterparty, computed as

$$\text{expected loss} = \text{deposit} \times \text{CDS}$$

For instance, if Sigma deposits EUR 100 million with Bank E, with a CDS of 336bp (Table 23.1), the expected annual loss is

$$\text{EUR 100 million} \times 3.36\% = \text{EUR 3.36 million}$$

The expected loss threshold will be defined by Sigma, but here, for instance, we set it at EUR 5 million. Instead of setting the threshold in absolute terms, it could be defined as a proportion of the total expected loss over all the banks, ie, a single bank expected loss is less than 40% of the total expected loss. An alternative would be to impose a separate threshold on the notional and CDS, ie, the threshold is exceeded when both the notional is more than 100 million and the CDS is more than 5%.[3]

Once the threshold with a given bank is exceeded, deposits must be reduced radically, otherwise, Sigma risks having to continually reduce the exposure if the counterparty CDS keeps rising. Let us assume that the mandatory reduction factor is 50%. So, in our example, if Bank E's CDS rises above 5% (expected loss on EUR 100 million rises above EUR 5 million), the notional has to be reduced from EUR 100 million to EUR 50 million (that way, the expected loss from Bank E is also halved).

Now the question is what to do with the EUR 50 million of cash which has to be transferred from Bank E. This has to be distributed among the other four banks, in such a way that the expected loss with any of these banks is not exceeded, and the concentration of risk is minimised. We shall deal with the former objective first.

The idea is to increase the deposits in order of the bank with the lowest CDS first up to the expected loss threshold minus the buffer, then the second lowest CDS bank, etc. The buffer can be defined to be, for instance, 20% of the expected loss threshold, ie, EUR 1 million in our example.

If we assume that the lowest CDS is from Bank A (CDS of 133bp in Table 23.1), and we assume that Sigma has EUR 100 million of deposits with them already, then, by transferring EUR 50 million from Bank E to Bank A, the amount of deposits at Bank A becomes EUR 150 million and the expected loss becomes

$$\text{EUR 150 million} \times 133\text{bp} = \text{EUR 1.995 million}$$

which is below the

$$\begin{aligned}\text{expected loss threshold} - \text{buffer} &= \text{EUR 5 million} - \text{EUR 1 million} \\ &= \text{EUR 4 million}\end{aligned}$$

So there is no problem. If the amount had exceeded EUR 4 million, the excess would have to be transferred to the bank with the next lowest CDS (Bank C in our matrix), etc.

This process minimises the expected loss, and avoids getting close to the expected loss threshold on the bank to which the new deposits are transferred, but it does not fully diversify the risks, since the correlations are never explicitly accounted for.[4] If Sigma wants to explicitly include the correlations in its policy, it could require that, when transferring money from Bank E to the new, safer bank, there is a certain maximum threshold of correlations, eg, 80%. Based on Table 23.1, this would allow Sigma to transfer deposits from Bank E to Bank A but not, for example, to Bank D, whose correlation with Bank E is 98%. In our opinion, given that Sigma's banks are all highly correlated, a reasonable correlation threshold would be quite high, ie, around 80% or 90%. If Sigma were to set the correlation threshold much lower, it may be impossible to satisfy the rules with its set of banks and the correlations we see in the market at the time of writing.

To summarise, we suggested the following parameters, which can be adjusted according to Sigma's preference:

- expected loss threshold of EUR 5 million;
- buffer of EUR 1 million;
- mandatory reduction factor of 50%;
- correlation threshold of 80%.

Obviously, Sigma could review these parameters on a regular basis.

Now that the principle of the model is clear, we shall apply it to all 12 banks.

STEP 2: FULL CONSERVATIVE MODEL

In this section we illustrate the above methodology based on the full sample of 12 banks.

Table 23.2 Assumptions in the full conservative model

Cash (EUR million)	1,800
Relationship banks	12
Average notional (EUR million)	150
Average CDS (bp)	306
Total exp. loss pa (EUR million)	55.2
Average exp. loss pa (EUR million)	4.6

All the assumptions are listed in Table 23.2 and we also assume that initially the deposit is distributed equally, ie, EUR 150 million with each bank.

Table 23.3 Banks' one-year CDS and exposure

Bank	1y CDS (bp)	Exposure (EUR million)
A	133	2.0
B	332	5.0
C	232	3.5
D	267	4.0
E	336	5.0
F	**452**	**6.8**
G	**528**	**7.9**
H	**468**	**7.0**
I	260	3.9
J	289	4.3
K	189	2.8
L	191	2.9

Based on the current CDS levels, there are three banks, Bank F, G and H whose exposure is over the threshold of EUR 5 million, highlighted in Table 23.3.

According to the policy above, the exposures with these banks should be cut in half, ie, we would need to transfer EUR 75 million of deposits from each of the three banks.

We have two limits on the resulting exposures. The first constraint is that the resulting exposure with any new bank cannot exceed threshold – buffer = EUR 4 million. This eliminates Banks B, D, E, I and J, since there the exposures are close to or over the limit.

The second limit is that the correlations of old and new banks have to be less than 80%. Table 23.4 shows the correlation matrix, and we highlight those banks whose correlation is above 80% with Banks F, G and H.

Table 23.4 Correlation matrix of one-year banks' CDSs (%)

	Bank											
Bank	**A**	**B**	**C**	**D**	**E**	**F**	**G**	**H**	**I**	**J**	**K**	**L**
A	100	60	54	78	77	**83**	72	79	75	49	75	78
B	60	100	92	89	92	61	**83**	**84**	86	89	86	89
C	54	92	100	86	88	61	74	74	74	78	91	86
D	78	89	86	100	98	77	**94**	**96**	89	83	89	93
E	77	92	88	98	100	71	**90**	**93**	89	84	90	94
F	83	61	61	77	71	100	79	79	63	41	73	66
G	72	83	74	94	90	79	100	**99**	84	80	76	82
H	79	84	74	96	93	79	**99**	100	89	81	80	87
I	75	86	74	89	89	63	**84**	**89**	100	88	80	91
J	49	89	78	83	84	41	**80**	**81**	88	100	70	83
K	75	86	91	89	90	73	76	**80**	80	70	100	94
L	78	89	86	93	94	66	**82**	**87**	91	83	94	100

This eliminates the following banks:

- Bank A from Bank F;[5]
- Banks B, D, E, H, I, J and L from Bank G;
- Banks B, D, E, G, I, J, K and L from Bank H.

Starting from Bank H, which is the most restricted one, we would need to transfer EUR 75 million and distribute it in order of increasing CDS with Banks A, C and F. In fact, Bank A has so much headroom that transferring to it the whole amount of EUR 75 million will only increase the notional from EUR 150 million to EUR 225 million, and therefore the overall exposure with Bank A to EUR 225 million × 133bp = EUR 2.993 million.

Next, we shall transfer EUR 75 million from Bank G to Bank A, thereby increasing the overall exposure with Bank A to

$$\text{EUR 300 million} \times 133\text{bp} = \text{EUR 3.99 million}$$

ie, just below the threshold – buffer.

Finally, we can transfer EUR 75 million from Bank F to the banks with lowest CDS left after Bank A, ie, EUR 60 million to Bank K and EUR 15 million to Bank L.

Table 23.5 Full conservative model: step by step

	Notional			
Bank	**Initial**	**Step 1**	**Step 2**	**Final**
A	150	**225**	**300**	**300**
B	150	150	150	150
C	150	150	150	150
D	150	150	150	150
E	150	150	150	150
F	150	150	150	**75**
G	150	150	**75**	**75**
H	150	**75**	**75**	**75**
I	150	150	150	150
J	150	150	150	150
K	150	150	150	**210**
L	150	150	150	**165**

We summarise the steps in Table 23.5 (changing numbers are highlighted).

We can now compute the expected annual loss by multiplying the exposures in the final column of Table 23.5 by the relevant banks' CDS and we arrive at an expected loss of EUR 47.7 million, which is lower than the initial exposure of EUR 55.1 million.

So, by moving the deposits around using our simple rules, we managed to reduce the overall counterparty risk by EUR 7.4 million (= EUR 55.1 million – EUR 47.7 million).

A downside of this procedure is that there is a concentration of risk with Banks A and K in proportion to their creditworthiness. This is a result of our optimisation algorithm. If the situation with several counterparties worsens, it may be necessary to place deposits outside of the banking group or, if this is not possible or preferable, increase the thresholds.

STEP 3: STRATEGIC MODEL

If the company assesses that the counterparty risk has decreased, it can adopt the strategic approach, described in this step.

We now introduce three changes with respect to the conservative model:

1. Sigma will take into account historical volatility of CDS, and not just correlations;
2. instead of the CDS at a given moment in time, Sigma will take into account average CDS level over a year;
3. Sigma will take into account the deposit rates offered by the banks.

We shall use the efficient frontier methodology in order to maximise the return on deposits while minimising the risk. The main assumption we make here, for the purpose of illustration, is that the returns are equal (or proportional) to the CDS levels.[6] This assumption will be refined by Sigma with the actual returns on various deposits. In this step, we shall use the one-year historical averages and volatilities of one-year CDS, which are shown in Table 23.6.

Table 23.6 Banks' one-year average CDSs and volatilities over the period from June 2011 to June 2012

Bank	1y CDS (bp)	Volatility (%)
A	114	0.24
B	304	0.49
C	197	0.38
D	228	0.55
E	298	0.74
F	338	0.65
G	412	1.11
H	375	1.06
I	227	0.46
J	300	0.83
K	153	0.29
L	172	0.35

We shall compare several scenarios of different allocations of deposits between the various counterparties (see Table 23.7). Risk is defined here as the volatility of the CDS portfolio weighted by deposits, including correlations.[7] We define the efficient frontier as the maximum return for minimum risk. The efficient frontier is shown in blue in Figure 23.2. S1–S5 provide the highest return for a given risk. The purple line represents the worst allocation possible; it gives the lowest return for a given risk. All the other allocations are between the purple and blue lines.

Figure 23.2 One-year efficient return versus volatility

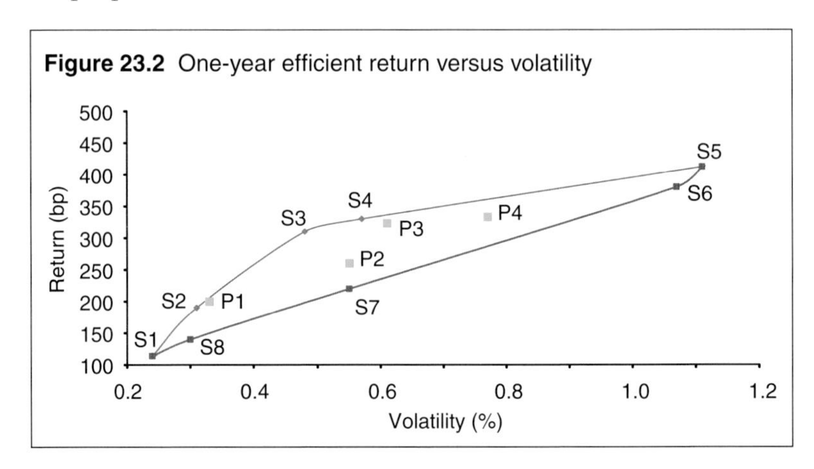

We also show four different combinations below the efficient frontier (green points).

1. P2 includes all 12 banks equally; this point is not optimal. For a return of 260bp, we could have a risk of 0.40% if the repartition were optimal. In this case, the risk is 0.55%. However, P2 is the most diversified portfolio, excluding correlation.
2. P3 is a combination of Banks F and J. These two banks have the lowest correlation, so we are really close to the efficient frontier.
3. P1 and P4 are built with the constraint that the weight for any bank should not be above 25%. P4 is much more aggressive than P1, as the return of P4 is 333bp, while the return of P1 is 200bp.

We show in Table 23.8 the split of the optimal portfolio of EUR 1,800 million for P1 and P4, which should be compared with the example from step 2.

Table 23.7 Composition of portfolios (%)

	S1	S2	S3	S4	S5	S6	S7	S8
Risk	0.24	0.31	0.48	0.57	1.11	1.07	0.55	0.30
Return	114	190	310	330	412	380	220	140
Bank A	100	60	1	0	0	0	60	90
Bank B	0	40	73	42	0	0	0	0
Bank C	0	0	0	0	0	0	0	0
Bank D	0	0	0	0	0	0	0	0
Bank E	0	0	0	0	0	0	0	0
Bank F	0	0	25	50	0	0	0	0
Bank G	0	0	0	9	100	13	0	0
Bank H	0	0	0	0	0	87	40	10
Bank I	0	0	0	0	0	0	0	0
Bank J	0	0	0	0	0	0	0	0
Bank K	0	0	0	0	0	0	0	0
Bank L	0	0	0	0	0	0	0	0

	P1	P2	P3	P4
Risk	0.33	0.55	0.61	0.77
Return	200	260	323	333
Bank A	25	8	0	0
Bank B	25	8	0	0
Bank C	19	8	0	0
Bank D	0	8	0	25
Bank E	0	8	0	0
Bank F	6	8	60	25
Bank G	0	8	0	25
Bank H	0	8	0	15
Bank I	0	8	0	0
Bank J	0	8	40	10
Bank K	25	8	0	0
Bank L	0	8	0	0

Note: risk, CDS standard deviation in percent. Return, CDS in basis points.

In order to compare these two portfolios with the final portfolio from step 2, we compute the expected loss, using the CDS numbers from that section. The expected loss for P1 is EUR 42.1 million, and that for P4 is EUR 74.1 million, which are comparatively smaller and

Table 23.8 Optimal portfolios

Bank	No return	P1	P4
A	300	450	—
B	150	450	—
C	150	350	—
D	150	—	450
E	150	—	—
F	75	100	450
G	75	—	450
H	75	—	280
I	150	—	—
J	150	—	170
K	210	450	—
L	165	—	—

larger, respectively, than the expected loss for the final portfolio in step 2, which was EUR 47.7 million.

RECOMMENDATIONS

We recommended that Sigma implement the two policies, conservative and strategic, depending on its risk appetite and its assessment of its counterparties creditworthiness. The resulting portfolios are shown in Table 23.9.

CONCLUSION

In this chapter, we have shown how a company can use the banks' CDS levels to optimise its deposits with banks. The main idea is to measure risk and return via CDS or its volatility, and to use this information to systematically allocate the deposits. We derived two alternative policies depending on the risk appetite of the company.

APPENDIX: APPLYING OPTIMAL DEPOSIT COMPOSITION METHODOLOGY TO A DERIVATIVES EXPOSURE

In this chapter, we discussed the counterparty exposure on banking deposits. Can this methodology be used for the derivatives exposures, which we discussed in Chapter 22?

The difference between deposits and derivatives exposure is that derivatives are generally longer dated[8] and less liquid, so the derivatives policy has to take into account a certain amount of break-up

Table 23.9 Alternative proposed portfolios

	Notional			
Bank	**Initial**	**Conservative**	**Strategic P1**	**Strategic P4**
A	150	300	450	—
B	150	150	450	—
C	150	150	350	—
D	150	150	—	450
E	150	150	—	—
F	150	75	100	450
G	150	75	—	450
H	150	75	—	280
I	150	150	—	—
J	150	150	—	170
K	150	210	450	—
L	150	165	—	—

cost. Moreover, the future derivatives' exposure is not clear at the outset, as their MTM will change over time. The best way to deal with this is to measure the derivatives exposure via expected loss and probability of loss at a certain confidence interval, but for this a company would need a VaR model, which not all companies have.

If a company does not have a VaR model, it has to base its counterparty risk policy on the static MTM only. It could then apply the methodology we expound in this chapter, but this would severely restrict the quality of the model results. Therefore, the discussion that follows is to be considered only as an intermediate step, before the full dynamic methodology is developed.

Similarly to the deposits, we start by computing the expected loss as

$$\text{expected loss} = \begin{cases} \text{MTM} \times \text{CDS} & \text{if MTM is positive to Sigma} \\ 0 & \text{otherwise} \end{cases}$$

Then we impose the expected loss threshold, which should be lower than for deposits because of illiquidity and the volatility of MTM. On the other hand, it should not be much lower, as Sigma does not want to keep on breaking derivatives with their counterparties too regularly.

For example, Sigma could consider a derivatives expected threshold of EUR 2.5 million. This would correspond to a portfolio with an

EUR 500 million notional with an MTM of 10% with a counterparty whose CDS is 5% (EUR 500 million × 10% × 5% = EUR 2.5 million). Assuming that Sigma can net the overall derivatives exposure, the threshold should be computed on a portfolio basis with each individual counterparty.

If the derivatives expected threshold on a given counterparty is exceeded, steps should be taken to reduce the exposure. This is not as mechanical as moving deposits from one bank to another, and will involve negotiations with the original bank and alternative counterparties. Therefore, it is difficult to create a very precise procedure, but it is similar in principle to the case of deposits, while including various solutions discussed in Chapter 21: cancellation of the original position and putting it back on with another counterparty, novation, CDS, amortising CDS, contingent CDS, etc.

1 This does not mean that having cash is necessarily "value destroying", since higher liquidity improves the creditworthiness of the company and therefore implicitly reduces the funding cost. Each company should determine its optimal liquidity requirement as that amount of cash beyond which the marginal cost outweighs the benefit. For more details on cash management see Brealey *et al* (2010) and the references therein.

2 The most liquid maturity of CDS is almost always five years, but this is inconsistent with the deposit maturity, which has to be below one year, as stipulated by Sigma. In practice, we would have to use one-year CDS levels, but these may not be accurate due to the illiquidity of the CDS. We shall disregard this issue in the discussion that follows. A possible solution would be to base the policy on the five-year CDS levels prevailing in the market and to adjust the estimate of expected loss in some way to account for the difference between one- and five-year CDS levels.

3 A threshold on both notional and CDSs is not recommended, as one parameter could be just under the threshold and their product still be unacceptably large.

4 However, diversification is partly taken care of via the expected loss thresholds.

5 That is, when moving EUR 75 million from Bank F, we cannot transfer it to Bank A, since their correlation is above the threshold of 80% (Table 23.4).

6 Of course, the corporate deposit rate depends on a variety of factors, including the interest rates and competition for attracting deposits.

7 For example, if we have two banks, A and B, with deposits split according to weights x and $(1-x)$,

$$\text{volatility}^2 = \text{vol}(A)^2 x^2 + \text{vol}(B)^2 (1-x)^2 + 2x(1-x)\rho \times \text{vol}(A) \times \text{vol}(B)$$

where ρ is the correlation between the two CDS levels.

8 Most companies can only lock in their deposits for a short period of time, ranging from overnight to less than 12 months, whereas derivatives can have a maturity of up to 30 years or, exceptionally, even longer.

24

Prehedging Credit Risk

We now turn to the issue of prehedging the credit spread component of bond issuance. In practice, companies do this much more rarely than prehedging the interest rate component, which we described in Part II. One of the reasons is that the credit hedge cannot be perfect, since hedging your own credit spread is not really possible in practice. Therefore, companies have to decide whether to enter into a proxy hedge on a liquid credit index or not hedge at all.

During the period 2008–12, we have seen huge volatility in the credit spread of companies and, at the same time, interest rates have become a relatively small part of the credit spread. Maybe the increased volatility and increased relative importance of credit spread is going to make this kind of hedging more common in the future.

The basic dilemma is conceptually similar to the prehedging of interest rate risk. A company has decided to issue a bond at some point in the future and it would like to lock in the credit spread available. The difference is that the credit spread is specific to a company unlike the swap rates which apply to all companies. We shall focus on this difference in the rest of this chapter.

BACKGROUND

Company XYZ intended to issue a bond in the first half of 2010 in order to refinance upcoming loan and bond maturities. The bond was expected to be of benchmark size (minimum of EUR 500 million) and have a 5–7 year maturity. Timing would be subject to publication of the company's forthcoming annual results and satisfactory conditions in the debt capital market.

Against the backdrop of the global credit crisis of 2008–9 and the associated market volatility, and given the importance of the forthcoming issue to its 2010 financing plan, the company was keen to manage its potential risks ahead of this bond issue. It viewed the pricing indications at that time as attractive and, having opted to undertake interest rate prehedges, it was open to ideas of hedging the credit element of its forthcoming bond issuance.

COMPANY OBJECTIVES

- To obtain 5-7 year financing and diversify its financing via the public bond market.
- To minimise potential risks to the bond execution process.
- To take advantage of current pricing levels which it considers attractive.
- To protect itself against a deterioration in the credit markets.

ANALYSIS

As shown in Figure 24.1, before the 2008–9 financial crisis, the credit spread (iTraxx and basis spread) only represented 9% of the all-in coupon of a bond issue, while 91% of the coupon was the swap rate. In January 2010, the credit spread element was estimated at 33%, though at the height of the crisis in December 2008 it was up to 59%. Therefore, based on 2010 levels, a prehedge on swap rates only protected 67% of the coupon level.

XYZ's credit spread is driven by both idiosyncratic issues and systemic market factors.

Hedging the idiosyncratic risk would rely on buying CDSs on XYZ's own name. However, no CDS trades on XYZ and even if it did, this would raise several issues such as self-referencing and market abuse etc. In addition, often CDS liquidity can be insufficient for the size of the benchmark bond issue which XYZ envisages.

It could be argued that only the systemic risk is beyond the control of XYZ. If we take the purpose of risk management to be to eliminate risks beyond the control of the corporation, it makes sense to hedge the systemic risk.

Systemic risk is also easier to manage as XYZ could buy the iTraxx Europe index as a market proxy. This index, known as the "main", comprises the most liquid 125 CDS-referencing European investment grade credits and is itself the most liquid of the credit indexes.

Figure 24.1 All-in coupon split of XYZ's funding cost

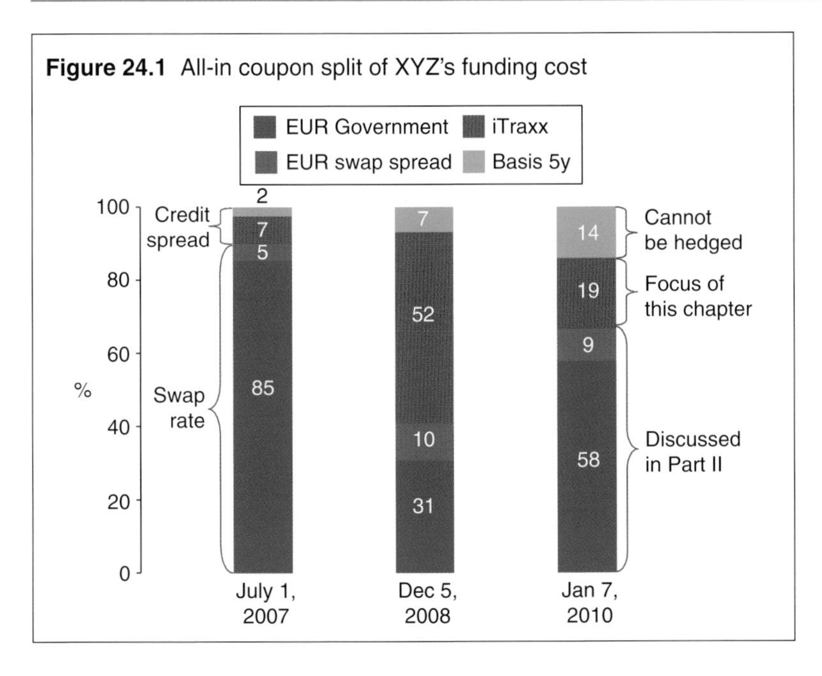

However, this strategy has one major downside: in the unlikely scenario whereby the index tightens while XYZ's credit spread widens, XYZ would lose on both sides.

Options on iTraxx would, however, enable XYZ to benefit from the upside while simultaneously limiting the downside. There are several advantages of this strategy.

- The systemic risk is hedged.
- XYZ knows the downside from the outset and it is limited to the option premium.
- Options on iTraxx are very liquid and the full size of a future bond issue can be hedged. Indeed, a size of EUR 500 million to EUR 1.0 billion is considered entirely feasible when hedging using on-the-run series of the iTraxx Main Index.
- The structure is very flexible, and XYZ can layer options and strikes to create a tailored strategy.
- A credit spread hedge can be combined with an interest rate prehedge, in order to allow XYZ to hedge an all-in level.

From an accounting perspective iTraxx options are treated as marked-to-market. Nevertheless, as the options are short term, it can be possible to avoid crossing reporting dates.[1] It may also be possible to obtain hedge accounting whereby the mark-to-market is posted to equity using cashflow hedging rules by designating the option as a hedge of a portion of XYZ's credit spread (subject to auditor validation).

The timing for XYZ to consider the use of iTraxx options was also opportune. As iTraxx had reduced significantly, the options were significantly cheaper and consequently the break-even was reached at a much lower level. Additionally, going into 2010, many economists remained concerned by the prospect of 'W'-shaped global recovery, ie, a double-dip recession which would increase credit spreads again. They were proven right.

HEDGING STRATEGY

XYZ could undertake a number of different option strategies in order to hedge its systemic credit risk. We outline below two such approaches: the straight call and call spread.

iTraxx indexes have standardised maturity dates. In 2010, the standard maturity dates were: March 17, June 16, September 15 and December 15. As XYZ intended to issue its bond within a six month time frame, it should buy options at maturity on June 16.

STRAIGHT CALL

The rationale for this is unlimited protection on widening of credit spreads.

Long call on iTraxx at 90bp (see Figure 24.2):

- underlying = iTraxx Main Series 12;
- underlying maturity = December 20, 2014;
- option maturity = June 16, 2010;
- strike $K = 90$bp
- duration = 4.5 years;
- premium = 45bp;

In the event that iTraxx widens,

$$\text{gain} = (\text{iTraxx} - \text{Strike}) \times \text{duration} - \text{premium}$$

For example, if iTraxx were to widen to 150bp, this would generate a gain of 225bp, which would be offset against the wider

Figure 24.2 Straight call: iTraxx option payout profile

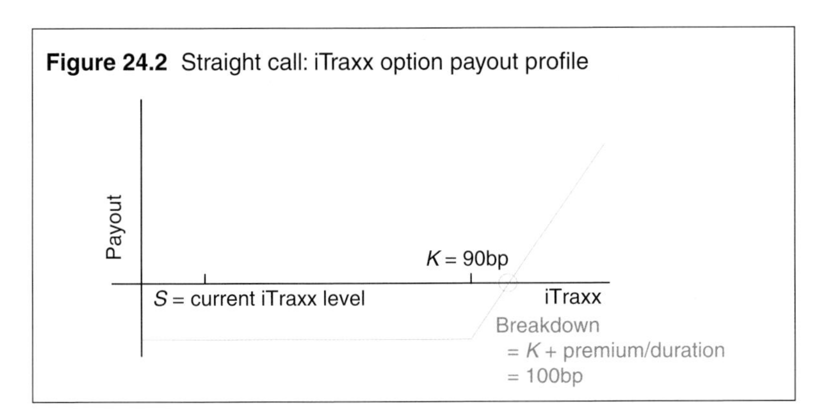

credit spread achieved upon XYZ's actual bond issuance. Though the correlation with cash credit spread is not perfect, by entering into the trade, XYZ would effectively be able to take advantage of favourable credit spreads and protect itself against significant widening in credit.

If, however, iTraxx tightens, XYZ's downside is both limited and known at the outset. The maximum loss is the 45bp option premium; however, XYZ will most probably gain from its credit spread also tightening.

The rates and credit prehedge can be easily combined into an all-in hedge with the premium spread over the life of the rates swap. In the above example, this equates to an additional 10bp per year over the life of the 4.5-year swap.

If spreads widen in excess of the 90 strike, rationally, XYZ should exercise its option and its counterparty will deliver protection at a price of 90bp running. This protection can be monetised by terminating the contract with the counterparty or by transacting an equal and opposite option at the then market level.

CALL SPREAD

The rationale for this is protection against widening of credit spreads at a reduced upfront cost but limitation of protection above a certain level.

Long call on iTraxx at 90bp plus short call at 130bp (see Figure 24.3):

- underlying = iTraxx Main Series 12;
- underlying maturity = December 20, 2014;

- option maturity = June 16, 2010;
- strike $K1$ = 90bp;
- strike $K2$ = 30bp;
- duration = 4.5 years;
- net premium = 0.31%.

Figure 24.3 Call spread: iTraxx option payout profile

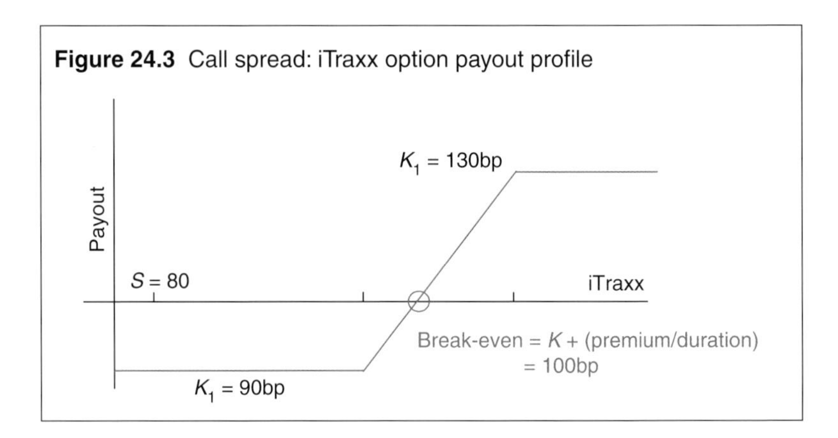

Compared with the previous call strategy example, XYZ's downside is limited to the option premium. However, in order to cheapen the option cost, the upside is limited by selling a call at 130bp. For a reduction in premium to 0.31%, the potential payout (excluding option premium) is now limited to 130bp (no limit previously).

If combined with an interest rates prehedge, this strategy has a reduced cost of 7bp per year over the 5.5-year swap.

If the long call were exercised on June 16, 2010, the counterparty would deliver protection at a price of 90bp running. If the short call were also exercised, the counterparty would deliver protection at price of 130bp running. As with the previous example, this protection can be monetised at the time of bond issuance or option expiry.

RECOMMENDATIONS

iTraxx options are a viable and flexible approach which allow XYZ Corp to manage the systematic risk in the context of a forthcoming bond issuance. iTraxx Options are especially pertinent for issuers who

- believe there is a significant risk of a double-dip with the consequent rise in credit spreads, or

- wish to lock-in current interest rates but wish to protect themselves against a scenario whereby rates subsequently decrease but credit spreads increase.

The key benefits for XYZ to consider with respect to iTraxx options are the following:

- the options are highly liquid, enabling significant size (EUR 500 million to EUR 1.0 billion);
- a three- to nine-month option life ties in well with bond visibility horizons;
- there is a known and limited downside in the event the bond is not issued or there is a correlation breakdown between the bond coupon and iTraxx;
- the credit spread protection can be combined with rates hedge to provide all-in hedge.

CONCLUSION

In this chapter, we have expanded the analysis of Chapter 10 (on how to prehedge interest rate risk) to the credit spread element of bond issuance. There are issues with hedging your own credit spread, so a company would normally enter into a proxy hedge, in this case on a well-known and liquid credit index.

1 For example, if XYZ enters into a hedge on January 2, 2012, with expiry March 29, 2012, the hedge will expire before the first reporting date on March 30, 2012, and its MTM will therefore not affect the P&L.

Part V

M&A-Related Risks

M&A-Related Risks

Mergers and acquisitions (M&A) are an important part of corporate development strategy and key moments in the CFO's and group treasurer's professional lives. Banks mandated by acquisitive companies coordinate numerous teams on M&A projects: corporate finance, legal, loan and capital market financing, as well as hedging specialists. On the corporate side, financial decision-making concentrates on a few individuals, often led by the CFO and treasurer, who must take a host of strategic and far-reaching decisions very quickly. Therefore, we think that the reader will be interested in examples of best practices in acquisition-driven financial risk management, as well as M&A-specific solutions, ranging from the impact on credit ratings to the hedging of uncertain FX risks.

The financial crisis we have experienced since 2008 has greatly transformed the parameters of M&A financial risk management. Bank deleveraging and on-going regulation reforms[1] negatively affect both the availability and the cost of acquisition financing, reinforcing the need for companies to quickly refinance deals in the capital markets. Also, the company's need to maintain the adequate credit rating and the importance of understanding its rating drivers have increased. Furthermore, political and economic uncertainty and market volatility, illustrated by the frequent switch between risk-on and risk-off modes, have pushed companies to increase the degree of risk awareness under which they implement acquisitions. This risk-conscious approach has been reflected in the way financial managers handle their ALM choices and hedging decisions.

M&A-related financial risk management is particular in many ways: it is strategic by nature; it is often transforming for the company; it is event-specific and must normally be handled outside of existing policies; there is a high degree of uncertainty about the underlying risk position.[2] We shall describe each of these aspects in turn.

Strategic

Acquisitions are a key component of corporate strategy, and, given their magnitude, they entail significant execution risks. The main objective for the finance department is to limit these risks without compromising the benefits of the planned transaction. The one-off feature and the scale of operations mean that their implementation will be scrutinised by the board and the stakeholders of the company.

Transforming

Not all the M&A transactions are transforming, but the most important ones are. In those transactions, assets and liabilities are significantly changed, and there is a high impact on the debt amount and, potentially, credit ratings, which sometimes requires a capital injection. M&A transactions may also affect debt covenants or even trigger technical events of default, which necessitates a thorough analysis of the debt structure and remedial actions. Finally, in the case of cross-border transactions, the change in currency composition of assets, debt and cashflows may substantiate a profound review of the ALM policy of the company.

Event specific

Given their strategic and often transforming nature, risk management in M&A transactions cannot be handled within the usual day-to-day framework.

- The high sensitivity of material non-public information, obliges companies to restrict the deal team on a need-to-know basis; therefore, they cannot rely on the full financial department resources.
- The interdependence between capital structure, financing options, ALM considerations, and hedging needs makes the decision-making complex. The size of the financing and hedging needs may be abnormally high and above market capacity. This is especially topical for M&A in emerging markets. So it is important to choose adequate tactical options in order not to create market disturbance, which would be detrimental for the economics of the M&A transaction.

Uncertainty

The uncertainty of the outcome is closely linked to M&A and it complicates significantly the hedging choices. Between intention and closing, many events can threaten the transaction, among which are

Figure V.1 M&A risk management: step by step

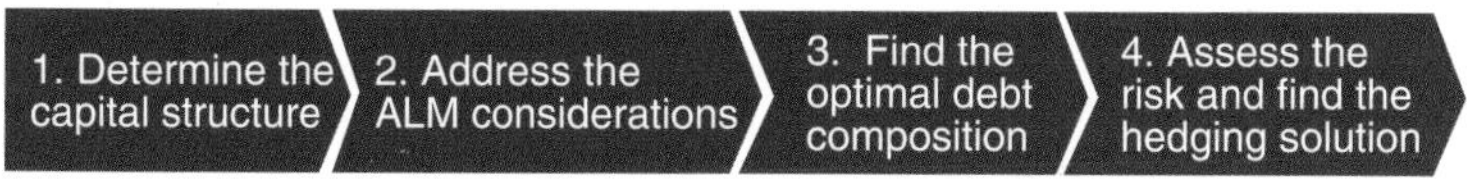

1. Determine the capital structure	2. Address the ALM considerations	3. Find the optimal debt composition	4. Assess the risk and find the hedging solution

the appearance of an interloper and a negative verdict of antitrust bodies.

The best practice in risk management consists in hedging an exposure when it becomes highly probable. Following this logic, currency risk (for cross border M&A) should be hedged once the share and purchase agreement (SPA) has been signed. However, the prospect, however remote, of a failure of the transaction makes a firm hedge difficult to consider, as the breakage cost could be significant. This combination of low probability but high impact events are what makes hedging so tricky. Companies are often left with a dilemma: to keep the exposure unhedged or spend a significant premium to buy an option.

SUMMARY

The approach follows four steps. As stated above, the different building blocks of an M&A transaction are interdependent, but, while they are all important, some are strategic and others are tactical. Therefore, our approach to risk management is organised according to the four steps in Figure V.1.

Step 1: determine the capital structure

As we mentioned in the introduction to Part I, trade-off theory[3] states that the optimal capital structure is the one which minimises the weighted average cost of capital (WACC). The practice shows that, for M&A, the exercise consists in determining the amount of debt, which is sustainable for a minimum target rating set by the company's senior management, rather than locating the optimal spot in the so-called WACC curve.

The rating advisory exercise, described in Chapter 25, has to do with assisting the acquirer in anticipating the rating agencies' considerations and determining the capital structure compatible with the company's rating objective.

Step 2: address the ALM considerations

Once the debt composition has been addressed, it is crucial to consider ALM options as, for instance, the currency in which the debt will be issued may differ from the one needed to match assets or cashflows.

The ALM analysis answers two questions:

1. what is the optimal currency mix of liabilities?
2. for each of the currencies, what is the appropriate proportion of fixed versus floating versus inflation-linked debt?

There is no single answer to either of these questions and the result depends on a host of factors including the cashflows out of which the debt will be repaid, the sensitivity of cashflows to currency movements, translation risk policy, cyclicality of the business, leverage, etc.

We have already addressed the second question in Chapters 7 and 9.

Chapter 26 illustrates an ALM analysis which uses quantitative techniques to determine the appropriate currency mix of debt, in order to satisfy the major objective to maintain an investment grade rating.

Step 3: find the optimal debt composition

For big acquisitions, banks usually provide an acquisition-financing package, which will eventually be partly or totally refinanced in the capital markets through a combination of bonds and, potentially, rights issues. As in the rest of the book, we focus our attention on the debt. In addition to seniority and secured versus unsecured features, corporates will choose the desired maturity and the currency in which they will issue debt. This could be different from the currency they need from an ALM standpoint as described in the preceding paragraph.

Let us not forget the sale side of M&A. In this part of the book we give two examples of innovative solutions related to debt capital markets. The first one, "amendments to bond documentation" (Chapter 27), shows how a divestment may create a technical default event, via the cessation of business clause, and how the technical default can be cured, thereby avoiding the need for the company to refinance debt while keeping the bond investors satisfied. The second one is "monetising deferred consideration" (Chapter 28). In this situation, the transaction occurs in two steps: an upfront cash payment and a deferred payment through a put agreement. The benefit of the monetisation is to obtain financing from capital markets at favourable conditions and de-risk the seller from a buyer default.

Step 4: assess the risk and find the hedging solution

Once the capital structure and the debt composition after swaps have been decided, it is essential to ensure that market risk will not affect the economics, or even endanger the contemplated transaction until closing or refinancing. Often, the most important factor to consider is currency risk. In a cross-border transaction, if there is a currency mismatch between sources and uses of funds, the buyer faces the risk that the debt will increase if the currency of the target appreciates and that, in some cases, the additional leverage could affect the rating. Similarly, in periods of high volatility of interest rates or credit spreads, there is a risk until refinancing on the cost of debt, which could affect the return on investment.

So the resulting market risks need to be carefully assessed, but, as we saw earlier, the major hurdle in M&A hedging is uncertainty. Treasurers are often left with a dilemma: to keep the exposure unhedged, or spend a significant premium to buy an option.

In Chapter 29, on hedging of uncertain exposures, we describe a decision-making model that allows a company to resolve this dilemma in a rational way. The approach consists in measuring company's unique risk appetite or aversion, applying a market distribution to different hedging strategies and finding, according to the estimated degree of certainty of the M&A transaction, the solution which best suits the company's cost/benefit preference.

1 We refer here primarily to Basel III, but also the Dodd–Frank Act, European Market Infrastructure Regulation (EMIR) and Markets in Financial Instruments Directive (MiFID) Review.

2 For example, a buyer may not know the size of their FX risk position until their offer has been accepted by the shareholders and the relevant competition authorities.

3 See, for example, Brealey *et al* (2010).

25

Rating Impact of an Acquisition

In Chapter 1 we described the process of obtaining a credit rating. Of course, the ratings change with time and the company's situation, and one of the main events which can affect a rating is an acquisition, which is the subject of this chapter. As we said before, credit rating assessment encompasses two main areas: business profile and financial profile, and both of these could change as a result of an acquisition.

The business profile, which we define as the stability of operating cashflows, will be affected if the business combination resulting from the acquisition has a significantly different business risk from the original company. On the other hand, the financial profile of the company will be affected by the details of the transaction, the amount of new debt and other financial parameters.

In this short chapter, we take a company through the process of reassessment of its credit rating post acquisition, which changes both the business and financial profiles.

BACKGROUND

The subject of this chapter is the Diversified International Company (DIC). The company's growth over recent years has been a combination of above-sector-average organic growth and selective medium-sized acquisitions across mature and developing markets.

In line with its strategy to access faster growing segments, DIC identified a large strategic acquisition opportunity. DIC plans to finance the acquisition with a combination of cash, proceeds from an asset disposal and incremental debt but is unsure how this financing scheme and the implied execution risk would be viewed by the rating agencies and how this would affect its investment grade ratings.

COMPANY OBJECTIVES

- To assist DIC in understanding the likely considerations of the rating agency ("agency" for short) relating to the financing plan.
- To estimate the impact on the company's ratings.

ANALYSIS

The approach follows the steps in Figure 25.1.

Figure 25.1 Risk management approach: step by step

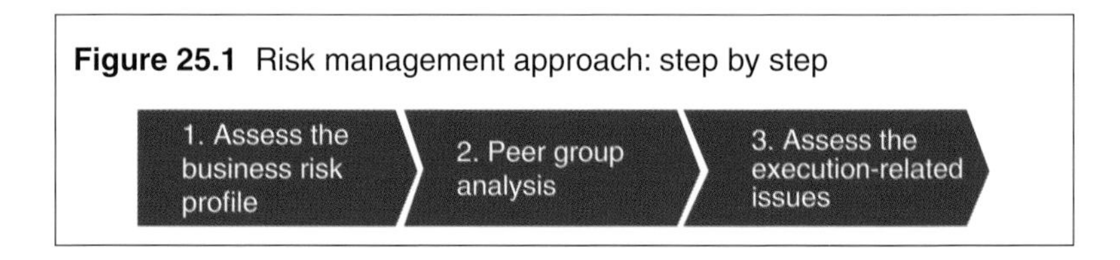

STEP 1: ASSESS THE BUSINESS RISK PROFILE

The first step for us is to analyse the target and to establish the strength of the business risk profile and the extent to which the target's business would enhance DIC's existing solid business risk profile. The business risk profile is an assessment of the stability of operating cashflow generation, so any material enhancement in this as a result of the acquisition should help to partially mitigate rating agency concerns related to expected higher leverage following the transaction.

To assess the business risk profile of the target, we considered the following factors:

- the quality of the brands;
- market share/market leadership;
- number of business segments;
- geographical diversity;
- track record of sales growth;
- cost efficiency and profitability;
- scale.

Table 25.1 DIC: illustrative peer group

Business profile	**DIC + target (estimate)**	**ABC**	**DEF**	**GHI**
Rating range	—	BBB	BBB	BBB
Business profile	**Very strong**	Strong	Strong	Satisfact.
Financial profile	**Intermed.**	Intermed.	Intermed.	Intermed.
No. of main business segments	**4**	6	4	3
Geographical diversity	**High**	Very high	Medium	Very high
Organic sales growth (5y avg)	>**5%**	>5%	3–5%	>5%
EBITDA margin	**21%**	25%	22%	15%
Shareholders v. debt providers	**Balanced**	Balanced	Balanced	Balanced
Key credit metrics	**DIC + target (estimate)**	**ABC**	**DEF**	**GHI**
FFO/net debt	**23%**	25%	27%	26%
FFO/net debt S&P stated min for rating	**25%**	25%	25%	30%
Net debt/EBITDA	**2.7**×	2.8×	3.0×	2.25×
Net debt/EBITDA S&P stated max for rating	**3.0**×	3.0×	3.0×	2.5×
RCF/adjusted net debt	**17%**	22%	20%	25%
FCF/adjusted debt	**5%**	7%	5%	4%

We then considered the existing business risk profile of DIC and the extent to which its business risk profile would be augmented by the strengths of and the challenges facing the target. With DIC already enjoying a solid business risk profile,[1] we concluded that the acquisition of the target would lead to a moderate improvement but, over the short-term, integration risks would partially limit the benefits afforded to the business risk profile.

STEP 2: PEER GROUP ANALYSIS

Once we are comfortable with the business risk profile of DIC post acquisition,[2] the second step is to consider the impact of the more leveraged final financial structure on DIC's ratings. To make this assessment, we

- undertook a peer analysis of other companies in the same industry,
- looked carefully at free cashflow generation of the enlarged DIC, since this illustrates the capacity of the company to reduce debt and improve its financial profile,
- assessed the financial risk profile factoring in forecast credit metrics, an assessment of management's appetite for leverage and its policies regarding returns to debt providers and shareholders,
- considered the guidelines incorporated within published rating agency methodologies and the extent to which these apply to this situation.

We then assess DIC factoring in the acquisition and the revised business and financial risk profiles compared with peers as shown in Table 25.1.

The combination of a strong business profile and solid financial profile compared with peers supports a rating in the high BBB range.

Based on an analysis of the peer group above, we provided DIC with an estimate of how the agencies would rate the enlarged DIC group. Our rating analysis also factored in

- the funding structure of the acquisition factoring in the cash contribution, the proceeds from the disposals, the amount of debt financing and assumed debt,
- an assessment of the capacity for deleveraging post acquisition,[3]
- the strength of the liquidity profile,
- an assessment of the time the rating agencies may allow the company's financial profile to recover following the acquisition,
- the impact of possible additional claims on cash on the evolution of the company's credit metrics,

- DIC's track record in integrating previous acquisitions and the challenges and opportunities associated with integrating the target's business operations.

STEP 3: ASSESS THE EXECUTION-RELATED ISSUES

The final step was to consider each of the execution-related issues associated with the proposed transaction and how these factors would likely affect the timing and the nature of the rating actions made by the agencies on DIC.

After having estimated the impact on the rating, assuming the transaction closed as planned, we examine how the agencies would likely respond should the timing of the transaction not proceed as anticipated.

We considered the following scenarios:

- the offer for the target company could be rejected and/or there could be other bidders;
- the asset disposal could be delayed beyond the closing date of the acquisition;
- the asset disposal could fall through, leaving the DIC needing to find a new buyer.

RECOMMENDATIONS

We provided rating advisory input to DIC as one element of the overall acquisition financing package. Through identifying the likely business and financial risk issues flowing from the transaction DIC was able to

- anticipate expected rating agency concerns,
- have a good understanding of subsequent rating agency actions and their significance,
- have reasonable expectations and supporting rationale for the final rating following completion of the disposal and acquisition.

CONCLUSION

We described the qualitative aspects of an M&A transaction and how it would affect the credit rating of the acquirer. In doing so, we reviewed both the business and the financial profile of the company after the acquisition. In the next chapter, we shall focus on the quantitative aspects and the risk management side.

1 If the business risk profile of DIC were not solid to start with, it is unlikely that it would be improved upon the acquisition.

2 By this we mean making sure that the business risk profile after the acquisition will not be significantly worse than before. For details see later in the text.

3 In other words, how quickly the company generated cashflows would allow it to reduce its leverage.

26

Risk Management for M&A

This chapter talks about risk management within the context of M&A. In such situations companies often focus on the deal execution first, and funding, second, while the risk management is sometimes the last priority. Our goal is to show how risk management can be an important part of the overall M&A process and how to implement it.

What are the typical sources of risk related to risk management?

There are several sources of financial risk we have seen in M&A transactions.

- **FX translation risk:** when the acquisition changes the currency composition of assets, net investments in foreign companies will, upon conversion to the reporting currency, affect the equity of the consolidated company due to currency variability. Similarly for earnings. This can affect the leverage, which is often under pressure in M&A situations.
- **FX transaction risk:** when the uses and sources of funds are not in the same currency, the company is exposed to currency transaction risk until the moment of payment or refinancing.
- **Interest rate risk:** when the transaction is financed by a large amount of debt, the overall cost will depend on the interest rates paid.

In these situations, risk management is intricately linked to the M&A process and needs to be addressed at an early stage. In this chapter we shall illustrate the first two points, since we have already extensively covered the interest rate risk in Part II.

BACKGROUND

The Sporting Club Company (SCC) is an EUR-based company which manufactures luxury sporting goods and equipment. Its business split[1] is 60% EUR and 40% GBP. As the industry in Europe offers little potential for organic growth, SCC has decided to acquire a US firm, USLux, which is purely USD-based.

Due to the transformational nature of the transaction, the CFO and treasurer need to analyse the market risks of this cross-border acquisition carefully. More importantly, SCC's treasury team wants to make sure that market risks will not endanger the key strategic objectives of the company.

SCC asked us to identify key risks due to foreign exchange and interest rates and their economic and accounting impact.

COMPANY OBJECTIVES

SCC would like to determine the optimal liability composition in terms of capital structure (debt versus equity) and debt structure (currency composition) of the combined entity after the merger, in order to achieve the following strategic objectives:

- to ensure investment grade rating after the acquisition;
- to maintain the investment grade rating in the medium term.

If the resulting risk is deemed to be unacceptable, SCC would like to understand how the risk can be managed via the appropriate hedging strategies.

ANALYSIS

Understanding the transaction

At time T (see Figure 26.1) SCC announced its intent to purchase all the shares of USLux approved by shareholders of both firms for a consideration of USD 1.6 billion, a 15% premium over its market capitalisation. This friendly acquisition would enable the new entity to maintain profit margins during the consolidation phase, as well as to expand into new markets while gaining control of the key new distribution channel.

At the time of acquisition, the exchange rates were EURUSD = 1.32, GBPEUR = 1.23. We shall use these rates throughout.

Deal parameters and timeline

The deal is structured as an all-cash offer[2] with a bridge loan facility for the equity value of USLux of around USD 1.6 billion, with a refinancing exercise[3] as soon as possible but no later than 15 months. The timing of the acquisition is shown in Figure 26.1.

Figure 26.1 Timing of the acquisition

T	$T+1m$	$T+3m$	Before $T+15m$
	SPA	Closing	Refinancing

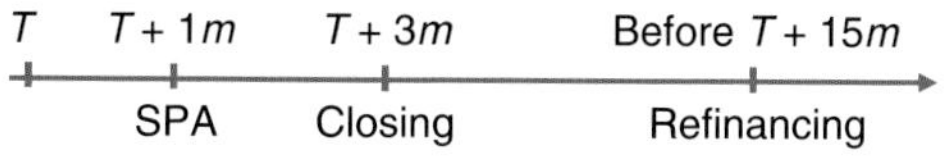

Note: SPA, sale and purchase agreement.

Table 26.1 Key financial variables (EUR million)

Full year *n*	SCC	USLux	Combined entity
Rating	Baa1/BBB+	Baa2/BBB	Baa3/BBB−
Rating outlook	Pos/pos	Stable/stable	Watch downgrade
M&A premium (%)			15
Sales	2,839	457	3,296
EBITDA	568	95	663
% margin	20	21	20
FFO	387	63	403
Interest expense	64	13	77
Interest on new debt			73
Total asset	4,376	725	5,891
Cash and securities	473	71	544
Goodwill			790
Shareholders' funds	2,376	425	2,376
Other liabilities	660	79	739
Total debt	1,340	221	2,776
New debt			1,215
Net debt	867	150	2,232
EV	6,041	1,206	7,406
EV/sales	2.1×	2.6×	2.2×
EV/EBITDA	10.6×	12.8×	11.2×
Market cap	5,173	1,057	—

Without getting into all the details of the M&A process, which is beyond the scope of this book, we note three key dates in the transaction:

- within one month of T, a sale and purchase agreement[4] (SPA) will be produced by SCC, in which all the details of the proposed acquisition will be specified, including the acquisition price;
- the deal is expected to close around three months from T, subject to necessary approvals;
- the bridge loan must be refinanced up to 15 months from T.

The key financials of SCC, USLux and the combined entity are summarised in Table 26.1.

SCC reports under IFRS and USLux accounts have been restated under IFRS. Potential synergies are not included, and the interest expense, for simplicity's sake, is a blended estimate of the two entities' costs of borrowing.

With a more aggressively leveraged company, and with operations around the world in multiple currencies, the new combined entity will need to look carefully at a sound refinancing plan and an intelligent derivatives overlay. We shall next address the financing structure of the entity assuming that the acquisition is financed entirely with debt.

Figure 26.2 Capital structure: year *n*

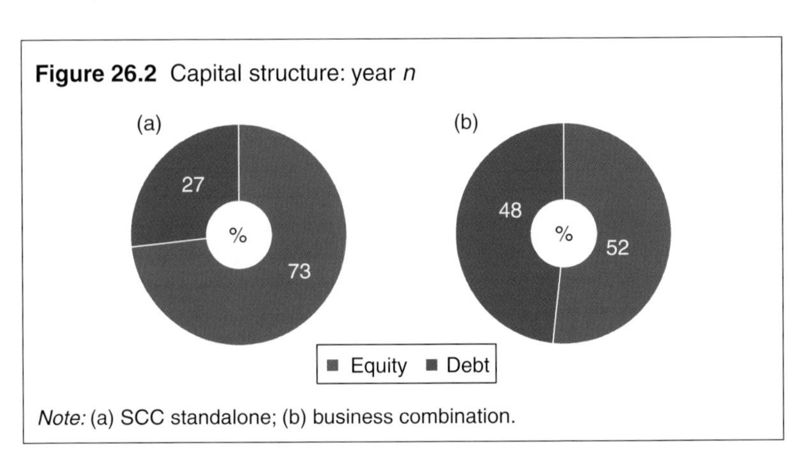

Note: (a) SCC standalone; (b) business combination.

FINANCIALS: ASSUMING ALL-DEBT FINANCED

The original capital structure (Figure 26.2(a)) is less leveraged than the combined entity (Figure 26.2(b)) in the case where the acquisition, is all-debt financed. Indeed, after the acquisition the debt will represent 48% of the total liability compared to 27% in the original capital structure.

CURRENCY CASHFLOW MIX

The combined entity (Figure 26.3(b)) will have a significant part of its revenues in USD, ie, about 14% of the total cashflows.

Figure 26.3 Currency composition of revenues: year *n*

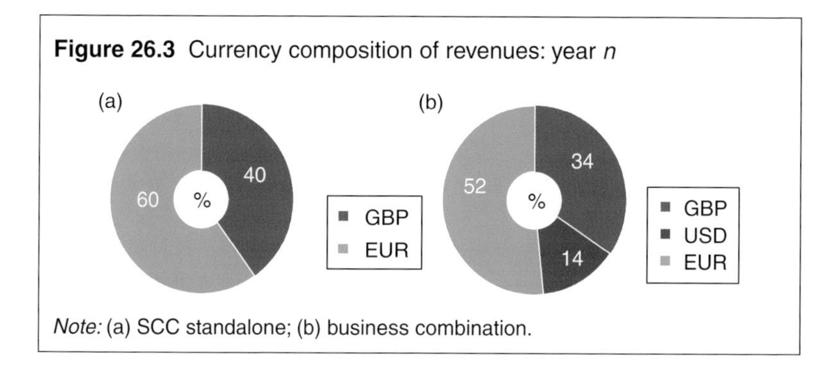

Note: (a) SCC standalone; (b) business combination.

The debt composition of SCC and USLux follows their currency split of revenues. Therefore, the debt of SCC standalone is 60% in EUR and 40% in GBP, while the debt of USLux is 100% in USD.

In Table 26.2, we show the financial projections of the combined entity, assuming that the acquisition is entirely debt financed.

CAPITAL STRUCTURE

SCC's standalone credit outlook is very strong. The BBB+ rating from Standard & Poor's reflects the group's conservative financial policy and strong organic free cashflow generation ability. The rating is also supported by its leading position in the European market and the growth opportunity offered by the group's strong, international name franchise.

From a financial risk profile perspective, if the acquisition is 100% debt funded, the combined entity will display ratios that are outside the adjusted FFO/adjusted net debt[5] level of 20–30% that is required for an investment grade rating (BBB−). For a BBB− rating, Standard

Table 26.2 Financial projections (EUR million): assuming all-debt financed

	SCC standalone	Combined pro forma Year			
	Year n	n	$n+1$	$n+2$	$n+3$
Income statement					
Revenues	2,839	3,296	3,395	3,497	3,602
EBIT	398	464	478	492	507
Interest	−64	−150	−150	−150	−150
Profit before tax	334	314	328	342	357
Tax (at 35%)	−117	−110	−115	−120	−125
Net income	217	204	213	223	232
Cashflow statement					
EBITDA	568	663	683	703	724
Tax and interest	−181	−260	−265	−270	−275
Other non-cash items	0	0	0	0	0
FFO	387	403	418	434	450
Changes in working capital	−14	−16	−17	−17	−18
Gross Cashflow	373	387	401	416	432
Dividends	−65	−61	−64	−67	−70
Retained cashflow	308	325	337	349	362
Capital expenditure	−256	−298	−418	−270	−278
Net increase (decrease) in cash	52	27	−81	79	84
Balance sheet					
Assets					
Fixed assets	2,011	2,381	2,594	2,653	2,714
Intangibles	0	790	790	790	790
Current assets	2,365	2,720	2,704	2,851	3,004
Cash	473	544	463	543	626
Other assets	1,892	2,176	2,241	2,309	2,378
Total assets	4,376	5,891	6,089	6,294	6,508
Liabilities					
Gross debt	1,340	2,776	2,776	2,776	2,776
Other liabilities	660	739	794	850	908

& Poor's expects this ratio to reach a level of 25–30% within the next years on a normalised and sustainable basis. As shown in Table 26.3, it is impossible to satisfy this if 100% debt finance is used, because the ratio falls to 17% in years n and $n + 1$ and only reaches the required 20% three years after the acquisition.

Table 26.3 100% debt financed: inconsistent with investment grade

S&P credit metrics	SCC standalone Year *n*	Combined pro forma Year *n*	*n*+1	*n*+2	*n*+3
FFO/adjusted net debt	45%	**17%**	**17%**	**19%**	**20%**
Debt/capital	36%	54%	52%	51%	50%
EBITDA/interest coverage	8×	5×	5×	5×	5×
Adjusted net debt/EBITDA	2×	3×	4×	3×	3×

So if the combined entity requires an investment grade rating, it needs to reduce the debt composition. In Table 26.4 we show the same credit metrics, but this time assuming only 60% debt financing (the rest will have to be refinanced by equity[6]).

Table 26.4 60% debt financed: consistent with investment grade

S&P credit metrics	SCC standalone Year *n*	Combined pro forma Year *n*	*n*+1	*n*+2	*n*+3
FFO/adjusted net debt	45%	**23%**	**23%**	**25%**	**27%**
Debt/capital	36%	44%	43%	42%	41%
EBITDA/interest coverage	8×	6×	6×	6×	6×
Adjusted net debt/EBITDA	2×	3×	3×	3×	2×

As we can see in Table 26.4, the ratios are now within the required range of above 20%. We estimate that the transaction would require an EUR 0.5 billion capital increase, which is approximately 40% of the needed financing, to support a BBB– rating from S&P. We base this estimate on the following assumptions:

- the business risk-profile of the enlarged business would be materially stronger post acquisition;
- significant cost saving synergies are expected starting from year 2 post acquisition;

- no material improvement in the financial profile of enlarged entity expected over the intermediate term due to a planned progressive dividend policy.

Table 26.5 Financial projections: assuming 60% debt financed

S&P credit metrics	SCC standalone Year *n*	Combined pro forma Year *n*	*n*+1	*n*+2	*n*+3
Income statement					
Revenues	2,839	3,296	3,395	3,497	3,602
EBIT	398	464	478	492	507
Interest	−64	−124	−124	−124	−124
Profit before tax	334	340	354	369	383
Tax (at 35%)	−117	−119	−124	−129	−134
Net income	217	221	230	240	249
Cashflow statement					
EBITDA	568	663	683	703	724
Tax and interest	−181	−243	−248	−253	−258
Other non-cash items	0	0	0	0	0
FFO	387	420	435	451	467
Changes in working capital	−14	−16	−17	−17	−18
Gross cashflow	373	404	418	433	449
Dividends	−65	−66	−69	−72	−75
Retained cashflow	308	337	349	361	374
Capital expenditure	−256	−298	−418	−270	−278
Net increase/ (decrease) in cash	52	39	−69	91	96
Balance sheet					
Assets					
Fixed assets	2,011	2,381	2,594	2,653	2,714
Intangibles	0	790	790	790	790
Current assets	2,365	2,720	2,716	2,875	3,040
Cash	473	544	475	566	662
Other assets	1,892	2,176	2,241	2,309	2,378
Total assets	4,376	5,891	6,101	6,318	6,544
Liabilities					
Gross debt	1,340	2,290	2,290	2,290	2,290
Other liabilities	660	739	794	850	908

In Table 26.5 we restate the financial projections, based on the assumption of 60% debt financing.

These projections will be used by SCC for internal planning.

OPTIMAL DEBT STRUCTURE

Moving from our optimal capital structure composition (acquisition funded by 60% debt and 40% equity), to ensure an investment grade rating immediately after the acquisition, we now focus on the remaining objective to maintain an investment grade rating in the medium term horizon – by optimising the currency mix of the total debt.

OPTIMAL CURRENCY SPLIT OF THE TOTAL DEBT

Since maintaining an investment grade rating is key for the company, we illustrate the impact on one of the main ratios used by the rating agencies "FFO/adjusted net debt" by changing the currency composition of the debt. Although this ratio is important in rating considerations, conclusions based on it have to be taken into account together with other quantitative and qualitative factors.

We simulate the ratio FFO/adjusted net debt at the end of year *n* and its distribution due to foreign exchange risk by changing the currency composition in EUR, USD and GBP from 100% in EUR, 90% in EUR plus 10% in USD, ..., 100% in GBP. For each scenario, we simulate the currency evolution over a one-year time horizon. We apply this to FFO and adjusted net debt and compute the expected value and 95th percentile of the ratio. We call the 95th percentile the "worst-case scenario" and the difference between the worst and average the "ratio-at-risk". We indicate the worst case for the 11 selected scenarios (S1 to S11 in Figure 26.4 and Table 26.6), as well as the comfortable level of 23–26% (grey shaded area), which we consider sufficient for an investment grade rating.

The expected ratio in year *n* follows from the interest rates by currency; they are lowest in EUR and highest in USD.

The ratio-at-risk is affected by the composition of FFO and adjusted net debt by currency. It is lowest when adjusted net debt follows roughly the same composition as the FFO, which is the case in scenario S4 (the optimal scenario). In that case, changes of EURUSD and GBPEUR FX rates on the numerator of the ratio (FFO) have the

Figure 26.4 FFO/adjusted net debt: worst case scenario, year *n*

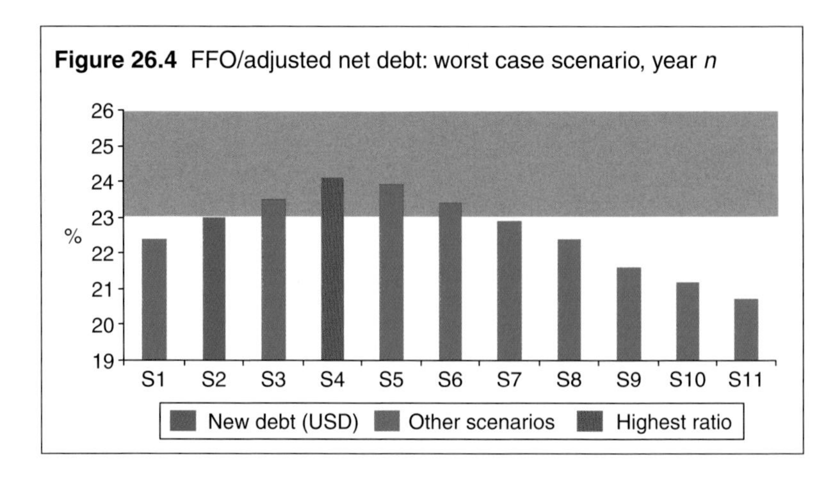

Table 26.6 Scenario analysis: total debt (existing and new debt, %)

Scenario	EUR	USD	GBP	Expected ratio	Ratio-at-risk at 95%	Worst-case scenario
S1	30	50	20	24.6	2.2	22.4
S2	40	40	20	24.6	1.6	23.0
S3	50	30	20	24.6	1.1	23.5
S4	**50**	**20**	**30**	**24.7**	**0.6**	**24.1**
S5	50	10	40	24.7	0.8	23.9
S6	50	0	50	24.7	1.3	23.4
S7	40	0	60	24.6	1.7	22.9
S8	30	0	70	24.6	2.2	22.4
S9	20	0	80	24.5	2.9	21.6
S10	10	0	90	24.4	3.2	21.2
S11	0	0	100	24.2	3.5	20.7

same impact as on the denominator (adjusted net debt) and the risk is minimised.

It can be seen that changing the debt composition from S2 (the situation that corresponds to keeping all the new debt in USD) to the optimal scenario S4 will have a significant impact on the expected FFO/net debt and its variability during year *n* (the worst case improves from 23.0% to 24.1%, in line with an investment grade rating[7]).

This contains an important and slightly unexpected message; even though the target is entirely USD-based,[8] financing its acquisition with USD debt only is not the safest strategy! The lowest risk is obtained when the overall debt structure matches the overall currency composition of combined assets.

We summarise the debt compositions by currency:

- SCC standalone = EUR 1,340 million (60% in EUR and 40% in GBP);
- USLux standalone = EUR 221 million, all in USD;
- after acquisition, optimal scenario S4 = EUR 2,290 million, (50% in EUR, 20% in USD and 30% in GBP).

Since the difference between the debt after acquisition and standalone is the new debt (= EUR 727 million), we can derive that the optimal composition of new debt is 47% in EUR (= EUR 340 million), 33% in USD (= EUR 237 million equivalent) and 21% in GBP (= EUR 150 million equivalent).

SCC has decided to finance the acquisition via EUR and USD bond issues only, so the desired composition can be achieved for example via the following three transactions:

- an EUR 500 million bond;[9]
- a USD 300 million bond;
- the EUR bond is partly swapped into GBP for EUR 150 million (= GBP 122 million equivalent).

SOURCE OF RISKS

Market risks will arise from a mismatch between the following.

- The source of funds from the bridge loan of USD 1.6 billion and the optimal target liability structure after refinancing:
  - equity issue of EUR 490 million;
  - a new bond for EUR 500 million;
  - a new bond for USD 300 million.
- A cross-currency swap from EUR 150 million to GBP 122 million.

RECOMMENDATIONS

Due to the mismatch between the original and the target liability structure, we notice three kinds of market risks and potential solutions below.

- **FX translation risk:**[10] as USLux is USD functional, net investment in USLux will, upon conversion to EUR, affect the equity of SCC due to USDEUR variability. This will affect only the book value and not cashflows. As shareholders and rating agencies do not focus on book value of SCC, we do not propose solutions to hedge this specific risk.
- **FX transaction risk:** at $T + 3$ months, SCC would reach the optimal debt structure using cross-currency swaps and will therefore create a foreign exchange risk from the mismatch between source of funds, optimal liability structure and use of funds. This will affect the EUR amount of debt to be refinanced. Solutions to hedge this risk can be achieved via
  - a USDEUR forward cross-currency swap to convert the USD bridge loan into EUR synthetic debt to have the optimal currency structure,
  - a USDEUR foreign exchange transaction to hedge the cross-currency swap initial exchange versus USD payment,
  - similar transactions or swaps for EURGBP.
- **Interest rate risk:** the risk arising from the exposure to EUR and USD interest rates from the debt between time T and bond refinancing in $T + 15$ months. This risk can be hedged via interest rate derivatives. For details see Chapters 10, 11 and 24.

CONCLUSION

In this chapter, we described risk management issues in the context of a cross-border acquisition and illustrate a variety of issues which are specific to M&A. Formalising the risk management process lays the groundwork for evaluating various liability scenarios to determine the potential impact of changes in interest and exchange rates on the key strategic objectives.

This strategic perspective is particularly useful in identifying the materiality of various exposures in the context of the competitive environment and therefore the optimal liability structure.

Once we have reached a general understanding of the company's exposures and its target liability structure, an extensive risk assessment exercise can be performed to implement the appropriate solutions.

1 For simplicity, we assume the same split for revenues, costs, EBITDA, assets and cashflows.

2 For details of the M&A process see Quiry *et al* (2011).

3 The bridge loan is supposed to provide only short-term funding, since it is an expensive way to fund an acquisition and banks do not want to be over-exposed to the credit of the resulting entity for long. Therefore, the conditions of the bridge loan stipulate that a large part of it will be refinanced within 15 months in equity, bond and syndicated loan markets.

4 Also known as a "share purchase agreement".

5 Rating agencies normally adjust the reported Net debt by various other liabilities, eg, pension liabilities, leases, etc. For simplicity, we shall disregard this in the discussion that follows. For details see Moody's (2010) and Standard & Poor's (2008).

6 Most companies are reluctant to issue equity due to shareholder dilution, and would prefer to avoid this unless doing so would jeopardise another more important objective, which in this case is to preserve the desired credit rating.

7 The difference between 23.0% and 24.1% may not seem significant, but in some cases even a small incremental headroom on the FFO may be important, and in any case the point of this chapter is to illustrate a debt optimisation methodology, without focusing on the actual numbers.

8 And despite the fact that before the acquisition, both SCC and USLux had a perfect match between their assets and debt by currency.

9 We have rounded these numbers from the exact values above (EUR 490 million and USD 312 million).

10 For more details on translation risk and when to hedge it, see Chapter 19.

27

Amendments to Bond Documentation

This succinct chapter introduces an innovative solution that allows the avoidance of a technical event of default as a result of divestment. In some cases bond documentation includes a default clause that can be triggered as a result of the so-called "cessation of business" clause (defined in the "analysis" section of this chapter).

It is clearly undesirable for a company to have a technical default event, since this would have important repercussions on many aspects of its financing, so the company would be looking for an innovative solution. One way to avoid a technical default would be to refinance the debt, but in the example shown here this is not deemed to be an optimal solution since the bonds are trading above par. Instead, we propose another solution, using a procedure called "consent solicitation".

BACKGROUND

Atlas Fabrics is a textile manufacturer. Due to competitive pressures from low-cost producers in emerging markets, its profit margin has been shrinking. Atlas Fabrics has announced a substantial corporate restructuring that involves divesting a number of business lines via a spin-off or a trade sale.

The company's financial structure (and resultant risk profile) was expected to remain broadly unchanged and no impact was expected on its credit rating. However, the documentation of Atlas Fabrics' bonds included an "event of default" that could potentially be triggered by a material "cessation of business".

COMPANY OBJECTIVES

- To avoid any risk of a technical event of default under the "cessation of business" clause.
- Not to redeem the bonds early.

- To minimise the cost.
- To maintain good investor relations.

ANALYSIS

According to Atlas Fabrics' bond documentation, an "event of default" could be deemed to have occurred under any of the following three conditions.

1. **Cessation of business clause:** "If the issuer or any of its principal subsidiaries ceases to carry on the whole or a substantial part of its business".
2. **Cross default:** "If any indebtedness for money becomes due and repayable prematurely by reason of an event of default amount to at least EUR 25,000".
3. **Winding up:** "If any resolution is passed for the winding up of any of its principal subsidiaries".

As a consequence "any holder of a note may, by written notice to the issuer at the specified office of the agent declare any notes held by the holder to be forthwith due and payable at its nominal amount."

Although the bond is trading substantially over par, which removes the investor incentive to call an event of default (at par), the risk that the Atlas Fabrics notes would fall victim to a technical default is considered unacceptable.

The company therefore needs to obtain a one-time waiver from noteholders of the relevant event of default clause via a "consent solicitation".

CONSENT SOLICITATION OVERVIEW

Atlas Fabrics needs the consent of its noteholders to waive their rights under the current events of default.

This is done by convening a meeting of noteholders (something Atlas Fabrics may do at any time) and asking them to agree to a waiver of the terms and conditions.

Atlas Fabrics' bond documentation specifies in the noteholder meeting and voting procedures the conditions under which a noteholder meeting can be convened, as well as the particular number (quorum) of noteholders that must be either present or otherwise represented, in order to constitute a valid meeting (Table 27.1).

Table 27.1 Voter thresholds provided by the bond documentation

		Required quorum	**Minimal % of votes**
First meeting	Held after an official notice period of at least 21 clear days	One or more persons holding greater than or equal to half of the outstanding amount of the notes	75% of the persons in attendance
If not quorate: Second meeting	An adjourned meeting is held between 14 and 42 clear days after the first meeting	One or more persons holding greater than or equal to one third of the outstanding amount of the notes	75% of the persons in attendance

The key risks are

- the lack of quorum at the first meeting might be viewed negatively,
- participation in consent solicitation is generally low because of investor inertia.

To solve the problem, an incentive payment (a "consent fee") has to be made to the investors to encourage early participation (ie, to participate in the first meeting) and to vote to pass an amendment. The level of the consent fee is dependent on the degree to which the bondholders are negatively affected by changing the terms of the bond.

RECOMMENDATIONS

A standalone consent solicitation document was launched to seek existing noteholders' response to an extraordinary resolution to

- approve the terms of Atlas Fabrics' proposed divestment,
- waive their rights to call an event of default in respect of this de-merger.

A consent fee of 0.15% on the nominal amount was offered to investors submitting instructions in favour of the proposal and within 20 days after the announcement.

This fee was at the lower end of the typical range, reflecting the fact that the changes were broadly neutral to investors. By setting an early consent fee deadline before the meeting, Atlas Fabrics had an early indication of the expected participation levels and the flexibility to extend the deadline if the quorum was likely to be missed.

RESULTS AND OUTCOME

More than 83% of all existing noteholders voted in favour of the proposals by the consent deadline, with a further 2% submitting positive responses by the final deadline, 48 hours before the meeting.

The high hit rate put Atlas Fabrics in the comfortable position of knowing the outcome of the meeting more than a week in advance.

The noteholders' meeting was held as scheduled, and the resolution to waive the events of default in respect of the de-merger was passed with immediate effect.

CONCLUSION

We found a solution to meet Atlas Fabrics' objectives:

- Atlas Fabrics was able to keep their bond outstanding;
- the cost was minimal (the consent fee was well judged to be low by market standards but high enough to provide a successful outcome);
- in case of a negative reaction, Atlas Fabrics would have had the flexibility to extend the deadline or to go to the second meeting, taking advantage of a lower quorum.

28

Monetising Deferred Consideration

This is the second chapter (together with Chapter 27) dealing with risks arising from divestment situations.

In divestments, sometimes part of the consideration is deferred. In such a case a variety of risks can arise, including the credit risk on the buyer. The objective of the seller is to offset this risk, and in some cases it can do this via the set of tools[1] that we discussed in Part IV. In other situations, it may not be possible to offset the buyer credit risk because there is no liquid CDS traded on the buyer.

In this example, we look at one of the ways that the risk introduced by the deferred consideration can be mitigated via an innovative capital market strategy.

BACKGROUND

A US corporation (the seller) wanted to sell an Australian company (Sidney) to an Italian listed company (the buyer). Sidney was to be acquired by the buyer in two steps, with a payment for 60% of the shares upfront and a deferred payment for 40% of the remaining shares in two years' time through a put agreement, owned by the seller.

The put agreement is a two-year equity put[2] on Sidney at a fixed price, which is defined as 40% of the price of Sidney at the time of writing, capitalised at an annual rate of 7%,[3] adjusted with the dividends received by the seller during the put period. The value of the put at the time of writing was USD 200 million.

The seller (from whose perspective this chapter is written) was interested in financing itself using the deferred consideration as collateral.

COMPANY OBJECTIVES

- To receive USD 200 million upfront.

- To remove its exposure from the buyer default.
- To receive cash upfront on no-recourse basis[4] to improve its net debt position.

ANALYSIS

Methodology

The seller sells 60% of the shares to the buyer. It receives cash proceeds upfront from the buyer as for any normal disposal. The seller retains a 40% minority interest in Sidney but obtains a put option on these shares from the buyer. Importantly, the put option is irrevocable and for a fixed monetary amount of USD 200 million at the time of writing.

Figure 28.1 Deferred consideration monetisation structure

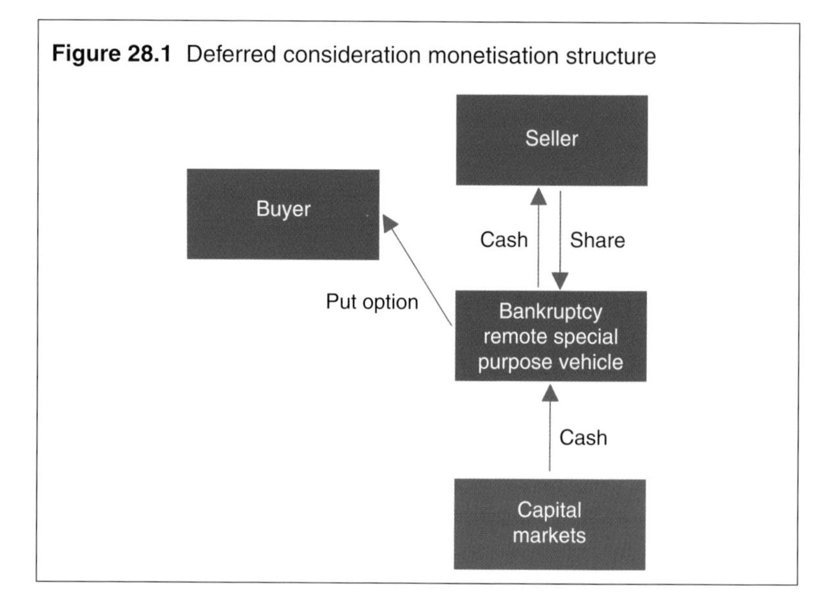

We combined the shares plus the put option into a package to create a fixed-income obligation that could be distributed to the capital markets, as illustrated by Figure 28.1.

RESULTS

Optimal structure

In order to facilitate the monetisation, the following steps were taken.

- Forty percent of shares were transferred to an issuing SPV (voting rights were retained by the seller).[5]

- The rights and obligations under the put option were transferred to the SPV.
- The SPV issued notes of a size, currency and maturity that matched the put obligation. (It would be possible to bridge a currency mismatch[6] through the use of a cross-currency swap but this would have increased complexity.)
- The documentation stated that the put exercise would be mandatory rather than optional. This ensured that the note investor could see that there was a clear and unconditional obligation by the buyer to acquire the shares.

Financing the SPV in the capital markets

In addition to attractive pricing, a successful monetisation requires that certain key criteria are met. Most importantly, the put agreement has to be considered as a *pari passu* obligation versus other buyer's debt. This means that in a bankruptcy scenario it needs to have the same rights as other senior unsecured debt. Additionally, the notes need to have covenants that are commensurate with those found in the debt of the buyer. Finally, the notes need to obtain credit rating from one of the main agencies.

A number of contracts had to be drawn, and in particular it was necessary to obtain the buyer's consent to create the whole deferred consideration structure.

PRICING

As summarised in Figure 28.2, the key pricing inputs are as follows.

- **Rate component:** two-year USD swap rate.
- **Buyer credit risk:** benchmark two-year CDS for the buyer.
- **Basis premium:** the premium required by investors for the fact that this is a cash bond.
- **Structural premium:** while the structure is designed to be as close to plain vanilla debt as possible, there is a premium for low liquidity and residual legal and operational risk.
- **Structuring and placement fees:** to compensate the bank for its services.

Figure 28.2 Pricing breakdown

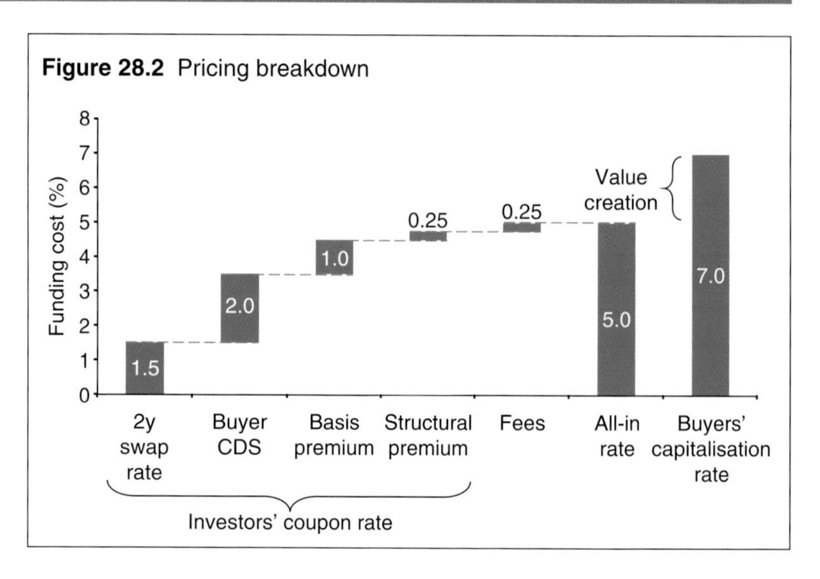

Value was created because the all-in financing cost was cheaper than the 7% capitalisation rate negotiated between the buyer and the seller.

RECOMMENDATIONS

The sale and purchase agreement required some important adjustments to allow for the structure described here, following which the monetisation would be executed to meet all of the seller's objectives. Importantly, the difference between the all-in cost and the capitalisation rate meant that significant additional benefit could be generated.

CONCLUSION

In this chapter, we have shown how the credit risk arising from a deferred consideration upon a disposal can be reduced.

This is the penultimate chapter in this part of the book, on risk management in the context of M&A. So far, we have always assumed that the underlying exposure is known and that the only decisions for the risk manager are whether, when and how to hedge it. But, M&A situations are rarely so simple. In many cases, there is a significant uncertainty about whether the transaction will go ahead and if it does, in what form. Our next chapter deals with hedging under this kind of uncertainty.

1 For example, the seller can buy a CDS on the buyer.

2 As in the rest of the book, the focus here is not on the equity risk, but on the financing side. For more details of equity derivatives, see Ramirez (2011).

3 In other words, the sale price on 40% would be expected to accrue at a 7% rate annually until maturity in two years' time.

4 The notes investors would have no recourse to the seller.

5 SPV denotes "special purpose vehicle".

6 For example, to issue notes in EUR and then swap them into USD to match the put obligation.

29

Hedging Uncertain Exposures

So far in this book we have dealt with risk management due to the volatility of the market parameters, such as interest rates, currencies or inflation. But there is another source of uncertainty (Chapter 15): the underlying cashflow volatility, ie, the unpredictability of the underlying exposure which does not come from the market volatility, but from the riskiness of the business itself.

For instance, an EUR-based company selling in USD is exposed primarily to the market volatility of the EURUSD exchange rates. However, it is also exposed to the uncertainty about its sales and costs in USD due to business cycles, competition in the industry and other factors beyond the control of the company that are not directly linked to the financial markets. We call all of these sources of uncertainty the "business risk".

Business risk is outside the scope of this book, since it is generally not dealt with by the financial departments and is rarely hedged using financial instruments. Nevertheless, business risk affects the management of financial risks. In Chapter 15, we described a decision matrix (Figure 15.2) that can be used to decide when to hedge the FX risk. We divided all the possible situations into four groups according to the underlying cashflow volatility and the currency volatility. The most difficult situation in this matrix is the case of high cashflow volatility and high currency volatility,[1] since the exposure is difficult to predict but the currency risk is high. If such a situation is exacerbated by the high amount of exposure at stake, things become particularly tricky. This is the case in many M&A transactions:

- the underlying exposure can be large compared with the size of the company, in transformational cross-border acquisitions or disposals;

- the uncertainty about the deal can be high, and depends on many factors including the competitors' actions, acceptance by the target company and decisions by competition authorities;
- the underlying FX volatility can be high.

In this chapter, we describe a methodology that can help companies deal with the situation when the underlying exposures are uncertain. It is the most "experimental" technique described in this book, as we only applied it to one actual company situation. Nevertheless we want to share it with the reader, as "food for thought", and in hope that it stimulates further work and applications in real cases. The idea is to integrate the management of financial risk with ideas from the so-called "real options" methodology,[2] which is based on the estimation of real-life probabilities of success of various projects, including the choices that the company can make at various stages.

BACKGROUND

Redview, an EUR-based health-care company would like to sell a non-core USD asset for USD 700 million to a USD company. The deal is subject to approvals by the US competition commission and obtaining their approval will take at least nine months. The company wants to make sure that the value creation for the shareholders of Redview is not affected by EURUSD volatility over the uncertain period until closing.

The problem here is that over the nine-month period Redview is exposed to the EURUSD volatility. If the transaction goes through, it will have USD 700 million to sell for EUR and it will be exposed to a weakening USD. However, if the deal does not get approved at all, or if it does but is reduced in size due to required disposals, the size of the USD exposure will be reduced, potentially down to zero. This uncertainty about the size of the underlying exposure is what makes hedging the currency risk so difficult.

COMPANY OBJECTIVES

- To preserve the value creation for shareholders from the volatility of EURUSD.
- To minimise the cost of unwinding the FX hedges, should the transaction fail to occur.

- To use simple and liquid products for hedging, due to a large deal size.
- To limit the P&L volatility until the closing date, due to accounting constraints.

ANALYSIS

We developed a methodology which would allow Redview to determine the right combination of hedging instruments as a function of its assessment of the deal probability and its risk aversion appetite.

The approach follows the five steps in Figure 29.1.

Figure 29.1 Duration optimisation approach: step by step

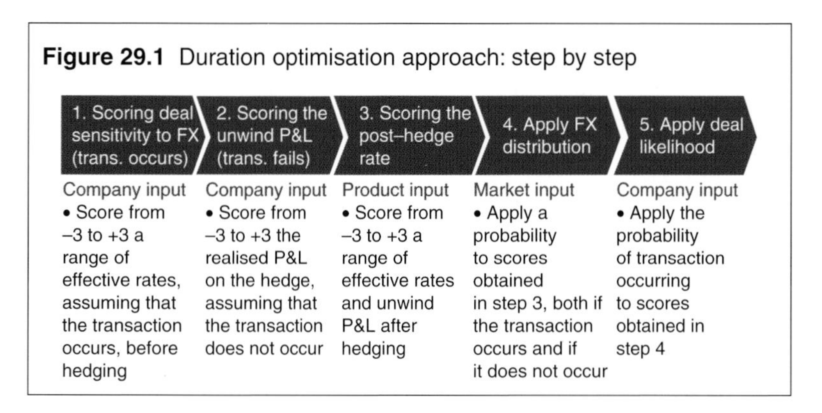

STEP 1: SCORING DEAL SENSITIVITY TO FX (TRANSACTION OCCURS)

Throughout this chapter, we shall use the scoring system described in Figure 29.2, by which we subjectively label various outcomes on a scale from −3 (unacceptable) to +3 (excellent).

Figure 29.2 Scoring scale

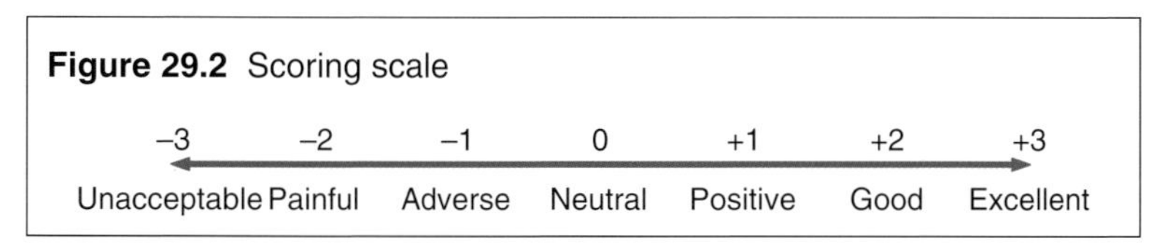

In this step, we shall illustrate this method by scoring the sensitivity to the EURUSD FX rate.

In this analysis we consider the FX risk on USD 700 million. We make the following assumptions, which depend on the risk preference of Redview.[3]

Figure 29.3 Deal scoring for EURUSD

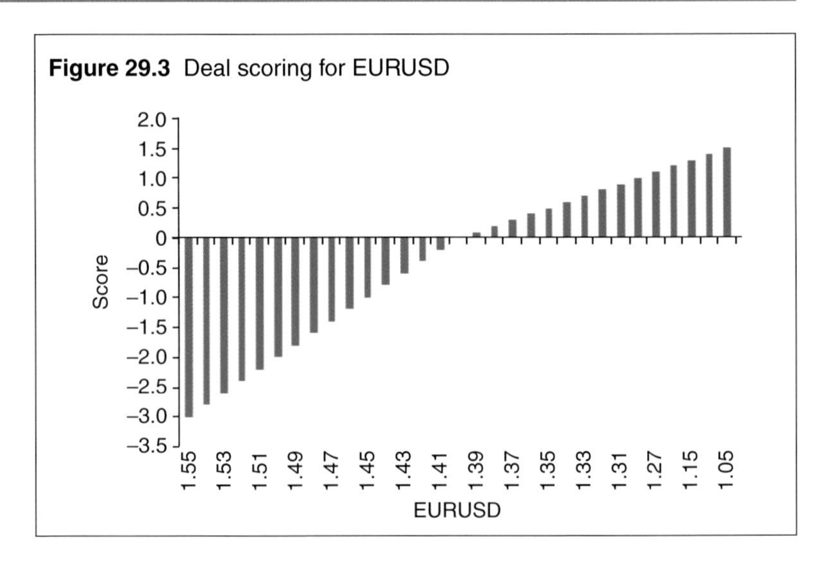

Table 29.1 Deal scoring for EURUSD

Effective rate	Score	Effective rate	Score
>1.555	−3.0	1.405–1.415	0.0
1.545–1.555	−2.8	1.395–1.405	0.1
1.535–1.545	−2.6	1.385–1.395	0.2
1.525–1.535	−2.4	1.375–1.385	0.3
1.515–1.525	−2.2	1.365–1.375	0.4
1.505–1.515	−2.0	1.355–1.365	0.5
1.495–1.505	−1.8	1.345–1.355	0.6
1.485–1.495	−1.6	1.335–1.345	0.7
1.475–1.485	−1.4	1.325–1.335	0.8
1.465–1.475	−1.2	1.315–1.325	0.9
1.455–1.465	−1.0	1.305–1.315	1.0
1.445–1.455	−0.8	1.275–1.305	1.1
1.435–1.445	−0.6	1.225–1.275	1.2
1.425–1.435	−0.4	1.150–1.225	1.3
1.415–1.425	−0.2	1.050–1.150	1.4
		<1.050	1.5

- Neutral case: around 1.41; score = 0.
- Stronger EUR: higher than 1.555 is unacceptable, as it would reduce the EUR amount by EUR 46 million

$$(= \text{USD 700 million}/1.555 - \text{USD 700 million}/1.41)$$

score = −3.

- Weaker EUR: lower than 1.050 is between positive and good, as it would increase the EUR amount by EUR 170 million

$$(= \text{USD 700 million}/1.050 - \text{USD 700 million}/1.41)$$

score = 1.5.

We show these in Figure 29.3 and Table 29.1.

We can see that Redview has an asymmetric view of the EURUSD. EURUSD strengthening to 1.555, which is the downside for Redview, is penalised with a score of −3 (unacceptable), while the weakening to 1.050 is rewarded only with a score of 1.5 (between positive and good). This reflects the conservative view that is common in many companies: a strong aversion to risk, and only partial appetite for reward.

STEP 2: SCORING THE UNWIND P&L (TRANSACTION FAILS)

In this step, we shall score the P&L of the currency hedge, assuming that the transaction does not occur. We show the scores in Table 29.2 and Figure 29.4.

Table 29.2 Scoring the unwind P&L (transaction fails)

P&L (EUR million)	Score
< −30	−3.0
−30 to −20	−2.5
−20 to −10	−2.0
−10 to 0	−1.0
0 to 15	0.0
15 to 30	0.0
30 to 45	0.0
45 to 60	0.5
60 to 70	0.5
>70	0.5

Again, we have assumed risk aversion, in the sense that any amount beyond EUR 30 million cancellation cost is considered unacceptable,[4] while again, positive MTM on unwind can at best be between "positive" and "good". This makes sense, as Redview is not trying to make money from this transaction, but is very much focused on not losing any money either.

Figure 29.4 Scoring the unwind P&L

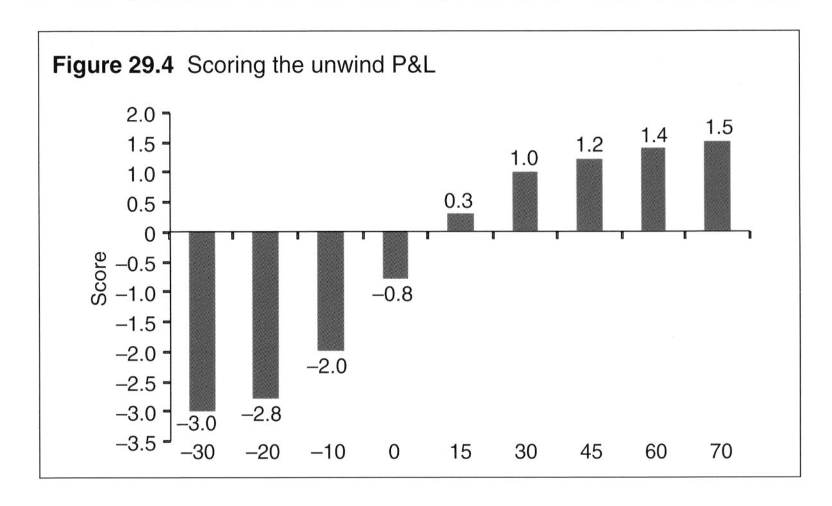

Table 29.3 Hedging strategies

Product	Rationale	Description
1. ATM option	• Hedged at 1.4070 and benefits if USD appreciates • Upfront premium is 4.99% in USD • Strike $K = 1.4070$	Buy option to buy EUR/sell USD at 1.4070 at maturity
2. OTM option	• Hedged at 1.5200 and benefits if USD appreciates • Premium is lower than an ATM option • Upfront premium is 1.97% in USD • Strike $K = 1.5200$	Buy option to buy EUR/sell USD at 1.5200 at maturity
3. Cancellable forward	• Hedged at 1.4500 without any upfront payment • Cancellation fee is 7.56% at maturity • $K = 1.4500$	Enter into a forward to buy EUR/sell USD at 1.4500 with the right to cancel the trade by paying a cancellation fee at maturity

STEP 3: SCORING THE POST-HEDGE RATE

Redview has been considering the five hedging strategies in Table 29.3, all with a maturity of nine months.

Table 29.3 Continued

Product	Rationale	Description
4. Contingent forward	• Hedged at 1.4784, if the transaction goes through • If the transaction does not go through, the forward disappears and no side has any more obligations • No upfront premium • $K = 1.4784$	Enter into a forward to buy EUR/sell USD at 1.4784, if and only if the acquisition is closed
5. Compound option	• Hedged at 1.4070 • If, on decision date, Redview decides the hedge is not needed, no more payments are due and no deal occurs • If, on decision date, Redview decides the hedge is needed, an additional premium of 3.00% in USD is to be paid • Upfront premium is 2.96% in USD • $K = 1.4070$	Buys the right to purchase an EUR call/USD put at 1.4070 in six months, for a further premium of 3%

We shall not describe any of the hedging strategies in more detail because they are fairly well known (see, for example, Hull (2011)), with the exception of contingent forward. Contingent forward has the same features as a normal forward, with the important difference that it only exists if the transaction is closed. If the transaction does not go through, the forward disappears and no side has any more obligations. This is very convenient for Redview, but has an impact on pricing, which is reflected in a strike of 1.4784, compared with the vanilla forward struck at 1.4070.

From now on, we shall focus on the first four strategies. It is not easy to introduce the compound option or other dynamic strategies into the scoring methodology because of another time horizon (intermediate decision time). However, it is easy to see that dynamic strategies such as compound options are an extension of the static strategies, which is particularly attractive as the information flows gradually before closing.

Now we shall apply the payouts of the first four strategies to the sample rates corresponding to the ranges in Table 29.1, and apply the score to resulting rates. This is shown in Table 29.4.

Table 29.4 Apply the hedge payout, assuming that the deal occurs

	(a) ATM option		(b) OTM option		(c) Cancellable forward		(d) Contingent forward	
Pre-hedge rate	Post-hedge rate	Score	Post-hedge rate	Score	Post-hedge rate	Score	Post-hedge rate	Score
1.747	**1.4809**	**−1.4**	1.5531	−2.8	1.4500	−0.8	1.4784	−1.4
1.647	1.4809	−1.4	1.5531	−2.8	1.4500	−0.8	1.4784	−1.4
1.567	1.4809	−1.4	1.5531	−2.8	1.4500	−0.8	1.4784	−1.4
1.487	1.4809	−1.4	1.5186	−2.2	1.4500	−0.8	1.4784	−1.4
1.407	1.4809	−1.4	1.4353	−0.6	1.4500	−0.8	1.4784	−1.4
1.327	1.3925	0.2	1.3521	0.6	1.4289	−0.4	1.4784	−1.4
1.247	1.3047	1.1	1.2692	1.2	1.3366	0.7	1.4784	−1.4
1.167	1.2174	1.3	1.1864	1.3	1.2451	1.2	1.4784	−1.4
1.087	1.1306	1.4	1.1038	1.4	1.1544	1.3	1.4784	−1.4

We shall clarify the calculation on one example. Let us consider the highlighted top left corner of Table 29.4. If the prehedge rate at maturity is EURUSD = 1.747, and the strategy chosen is (a) ATM option, the payout on (a randomly chosen amount of) USD 100, net of option premium of 4.99% is (USD 100 – USD 4.99)/1.4070 = EUR 67.5267. This means that the post hedge rate is USD 100/EUR 67.5267 = 1.4809. Note that the definition of the post-hedge rate includes option premium. When we look up the score corresponding to the rate of 1.4809 in Table 29.1, we obtain the score of −1.4.

In conclusion, for every strategy and each EURUSD at maturity, we can obtain a score that reflects Redview's perception of the desirability of the hedging outcome.

If the deal does not go through, Redview has to unwind the hedge position. Using Table 29.2, and the estimated payouts of the four different strategies, we can obtain the scores for every situation. These are shown in Table 29.5.

Table 29.5 Scoring of hedge P&L, assuming that the transaction does not occur

Prehedge rate	(a) ATM option		(b) OTM option		(c) Cancellable forward		(d) Contingent forward	
	P&L	Score	P&L	Score	P&L	Score	P&L	Score
1.747	**72**	**0.5**	50	0.5	82	0.5	0	0
1.647	48	0.5	26	0	58	0.5	0	0
1.567	26	0	4	0	36	0.5	0	0
1.487	2	0	−10	−1	12	0	0	0
1.407	−25	−2.5	−10	−1	−15	−2	0	0
1.327	−25	−2.5	−10	−1	−38	−3	0	0
1.247	−25	−2.5	−10	−1	−38	−3	0	0
1.167	−25	−2.5	−10	−1	−38	−3	0	0
1.087	−25	−2.5	−10	−1	−38	−3	0	0

Again, we give an example of the highlighted part of the table. The unwind cost is

$$\text{USD 700 million} \times \left[\frac{(1-0.0499)}{1.4070} - \frac{1}{1.747}\right] = \text{EUR 72 million}$$

which corresponds to a score of 0.5 based on Table 29.2.

STEP 4: APPLY FX DISTRIBUTION

Now we shall apply the probability distribution to the EURUSD rates (Table 29.6). We shall do this using a Monte Carlo simulation[5] around the forward rates and the implied volatility from EURUSD options.

When we apply these probabilities to the scores in Table 29.4, we get a probability weighted score for every hedging strategy in the case where the transaction occurs.

Table 29.6 Distribution of EURUSD at maturity (nine months)

Prehedge rate	Probability (%)	Prehedge rate	Probability (%)
1.747	5.3	1.327	17.4
1.647	6.0	1.247	15.3
1.567	8.8	1.167	12.1
1.487	12.6	1.087	7.1
1.407	15.3		

Table 29.7 Probability weighted scores, assuming that the transaction occurs

	(a) ATM option		(b) OTM option		(c) Cancellable forward		(d) Contingent forward	
Pre-hedge rate	**Post-hedge rate**	**Prob. wtd score**	**Post hedge rate**	**Prob. wtd score**	**Post-hedge rate**	**Prob. wtd score**	**Post-hedge rate**	**Prob. wtd score**
1.747	**1.4809**	**−0.07**	1.5531	−0.15	1.4500	−0.04	1.4784	−0.07
1.647	1.4809	−0.08	1.5531	−0.17	1.4500	−0.05	1.4784	−0.08
1.567	1.4809	−0.12	1.5531	−0.25	1.4500	−0.07	1.4784	−0.12
1.487	1.4809	−0.18	1.5186	−0.28	1.4500	−0.10	1.4784	−0.18
1.407	1.4809	−0.21	1.4353	−0.09	1.4500	−0.12	1.4784	−0.21
1.327	1.3925	0.03	1.3521	0.10	1.4289	−0.07	1.4784	−0.24
1.247	1.3047	0.17	1.2692	0.18	1.3366	0.11	1.4784	−0.21
1.167	1.2174	0.16	1.1864	0.16	1.2451	0.14	1.4784	−0.17
1.087	1.1306	0.10	1.1038	1.40	1.1544	1.30	1.4784	−1.40
	Wtd avg	**−0.21**	**Wtd avg**	**−0.39**	**Wtd avg**	**−0.11**	**Wtd avg**	**−1.40**

To illustrate this step, we shall focus again on the highlighted upper left corner of the table. In step 3 we showed that in the case when the EURUSD at maturity is 1.747, the score in strategy (a) is −1.4. When we multiply this with the probability to reach a rate of 1.747,[6] which according to Table 29.6 is 5.3%, we obtain −0.07. Adding the scores for each hedge solution across all the prehedge rates, we obtain their weighted averages in the last row of Table 29.7. For strategy (a) this is −0.21.

Similarly, we can apply probabilities of outcomes from Table 29.6 together with the scoring of hedge P&L assuming that the transaction does not occur from Table 29.5. This is shown in Table 29.8. For strategy (a) this is −1.62.

Table 29.8 Probability weighted scores, assuming that the transaction does not occur

	(a) ATM option		(b) OTM option		(c) Cancellable forward		(d) Contingent forward	
Pre-hedge rate	**P&L**	**Prob. wt score**	**P&L**	**Prob. wtd score**	**P&L**	**Prob. wtd score**	**P&L**	**Prob. wtd score**
1.747	72	0.03	50	0.03	82	0.03	0	0
1.647	48	0.03	26	0	58	0.03	0	0
1.567	26	0	4	0	36	0.04	0	0
1.487	2	0	−10	−0.13	12	0	0	0
1.407	−25	−0.38	−10	−0.15	−15	−0.31	0	0
1.327	−25	−0.43	−10	−0.17	−38	−0.52	0	0
1.247	−25	−0.38	−10	−0.15	−38	−0.46	0	0
1.167	−25	−0.30	−10	−0.12	−38	−0.36	0	0
1.087	−25	−0.18	−10	−0.07	−38	−0.21	0	0
	Wtd avg	**−1.62**	**Wtd avg**	**−0.77**	**Wtd avg**	**−1.76**	**Wtd avg**	**0**

Table 29.9 Final weighted score

Deal probability (%)	(a) ATM option	(b) OTM option	(c) Cancellable forward	(d) Contingent forward
100	−0.21	−0.39	**−0.11**	−1.40
90	−0.35	−0.43	**−0.28**	−1.26
80	−0.50	−0.47	**−0.44**	−1.12
70	−0.64	**−0.50**	−0.61	−0.98
60	−0.78	**−0.54**	−0.77	−0.84
50	−0.92	**−0.58**	−0.94	−0.70
40	−1.06	−0.62	−1.10	**−0.56**
30	−1.20	−0.66	−1.27	**−0.42**
20	−1.34	−0.70	−1.43	**−0.28**
10	−1.48	−0.73	−1.60	**−0.14**
0	−1.62	−0.77	−1.76	**0.00**

STEP 5: APPLY DEAL LIKELIHOOD

The final step is to apply the estimated likelihood of transaction to the two cases of the transaction occurring or not occurring. Redview estimates that the probability is 90% for the deal to go forward. In that case, the expected value of Strategy (a) ATM option is $90\% \times -0.21 + 10\% \times -1.62 = -0.35$.

Since in practice it is not easy to estimate the probability of a transaction occurring, we show in Table 29.9 the final weighted score for each of the four hedging strategies, for a variety of probabilities of deals occurring from 0% to 100%.

We have highlighted the strategy which has the highest score for every level of deal probability. We can see that for high deal probabilities (80% or higher), the optimal solution is (c) cancellable forward. For medium deal probabilities (50–70%), the optimal solution is (b) OTM option, and for low deal probabilities (below 50%) the optimal solution is (d) contingent forward.

It is interesting to see that the solution (a) ATM option is not optimal under any probability scenario, even though if we had not gone through this analysis, it would intuitively seem well suited for an uncertain situation, like the one we have here.

RECOMMENDATIONS

We have recommended to Redview to update the scoring methodology as they see fit, and use this as a basis for their hedging strategy.

CONCLUSION

In this chapter, we have shown an experimental methodology to deal with hedging of currency risk, when the size of exposure is not known and depends on external situation. We quantify the outcomes by probability of happening and score them based on the subjective preferences of the company.

1 In this chapter we continue to refer to the "currency volatility", but the discussion could equally apply to any other market risk, including interest rates, inflation, etc.

2 For an introduction to real options, see Amram and Kulatilaka (1998), Copeland and Antikarov (2003), or Quiry *et al* (2011).

3 For example, if Redview were more risk averse, it could assign a score of −3 to a much closer EURUSD value, ie, 1.45 and higher. If it were less risk averse, it could assign a score of −2 to an EURUSD value of 1.555, etc.

4 The attentive reader will notice that the same score ("unacceptable") corresponds to EUR 46 million loss in Step 1 (transaction occurs) and to EUR 30 million loss in Step 2 (transaction

does not occur). This reflects that, in our experience, it is more difficult to explain a hedging loss if the transaction does not occur.

5 See Chapter 16 for an illustration of the method.

6 We simplify things a little here. Of course, the possibility to reach 1.747 exactly is much lower than 5.3%. We are actually dividing the EURUSD distribution into ranges. For instance, 1.747 falls into a range of "larger than (1.647 + 1.747) / 2", and this has a probability of 5.3% according to the distribution we have chosen.

Part VI

Commodity Risk

Commodity Risk

As we mentioned in the introduction to this book, in some sectors (eg, transportation, metals and mining, food industry) commodity risk can be a very important component of the overall risk. However, we shall discuss it last, for three reasons.

First, unlike currencies or interest rates, commodities come in a variety of specifications.[1] For instance, a company that needs to hedge fuel risk has to specify a variety of parameters, eg, a specific grade of crude oil (Urals, Brent, WTI, etc). Crude oil comes in many varieties and each one has a slightly different composition and price. Compare this to the currency world, where, for example, we have only one definition of the USDRUB currency rate, which is fully specified by the Reuters page (or an equivalent) on which it is shown. So any discussion of commodity risk management necessarily requires a lot of detailed specifications of the exact commodity being hedged. We find that if those details are stripped away, managing commodity risks follows similar principles as managing the currency risks.

Second, this book is devoted mostly to financial risk managers, treasurers, CFOs and other parties involved in the management of financial risk. We noticed that in many companies this role tends to be separated from the hedging of commodity risk, which is often performed by another department, eg, the procurement department, of the company, because commodity risk management is more linked to the normal business than other financial risks.

Third, while managing the interest rate and currency risks is most often done via a prudent choice of the funding structure and use of financial derivatives, commodity price risk is commonly hedged directly through contracts with suppliers or customers. For example, energy companies in the UK often provide gas to customers with a variable price, linked to the wholesale gas prices. So the end-user provides risk protection to the energy company, instead of the company having to enter into a commodity derivative.

Among the four major types of financial risk discussed in this book (interest rates, currency, credit and commodities), commodity risk is arguably the least common, followed by credit risk. Most companies have exposure to currency risk; those who have debt have also the interest rate risk, but not all the companies have a direct and significant exposure to commodity risk. For example, a media company may have exposure to commodity risk through the price of fuel for trucks delivering its products, but many companies do not hedge that level of risk.

Despite all of this, it is important to stress that there are many companies for whom commodities are one of the main sources of risk. Their cost base is often linked to the price of energy, metals or soft commodities (eg, food producers or clothes manufacturers). We can identify two categories of commodity risk.

1. **Cost risk:** the risk of higher costs that a company experiences due to a volatility of commodity prices. An example would be a clothes manufacturer, whose operating costs are linked to cotton prices.
2. **Revenue risk:** the risk of lower revenues due to a volatility of commodity prices. An example would be an aluminium producer, whose revenues are clearly linked to the price of aluminium.

We devote a chapter to each of these kinds of risk, but in each case we consider the commodity risk together with another source of risk, namely the currency risk.[2] We want to show how the correlations between the currency and commodity risks affect the risk management options of a company.

It is important to stress that those companies who have revenue risk on commodities often also have some kind of commodity risk on the cost side, so that they should manage the net exposure. The opposite does not hold true; since there are many companies with purely cost exposures.

On the revenue side, hedging activities come in two varieties. If the sales contracts are variable in price, the company may decide to fix the price via financial derivatives. On the other hand, if the contracts are fixed in price, the company may decide to float it[3] via financial derivatives. Take as an example the following excerpt from the BHP Billiton Form 20-F 2011:[4]

> Where group commodity production is sold to customers on pricing terms that deviate from the relevant index target, and where a relevant derivatives market exists, financial instruments may be executed as an economic hedge to align the revenue price exposure with the index target.

This raises an interesting dilemma: is the commodity revenue exposure something that needs to be fixed or should it remain floating? Many metals and mining companies argue that their shareholders want to participate in the principal revenue-side commodity exposures because that is the main reason why they are buying the stock in the first place. Also, at least in theory, if investors in an oil company are not happy with the risk of the oil price going down, they can either sell the oil stock or hedge the oil exposure via commodity derivatives.[5] Then, also, there is the issue of the asymmetry of information. A commodity company can have better information about the market than its investors, and so it may make sense for it to use this advantage to protect itself against the falling commodity prices. See the same BHP Billiton report:

> The active presence in the commodity markets provides us with physical market insight and commercial knowledge. From time to time, we actively engage in these markets in order to take commercial advantage of business opportunities. These trading activities provide not only a source of revenue, but also a further insight into planning, and can, in some cases, give rise to business development opportunities.

Even though we said at the outset that the management of commodity risk is not fundamentally different from that of the currency risk, there is one important difference between the two,[6] which is the mean reversion due to the very nature of the supply and demand in the commodity sector. When the prices of commodities are high, more producers enter the market and the resulting increase in supply lowers the cost of commodities. Conversely, when the prices are low, high cost producers reduce the production and the reduced supply pushes prices back up. This causes mean reversion in the commodities markets which is not observed in the currency markets.

If the cyclicality follows the cycles in the business environment, which in turn follow the cycles in interest rates, then a commodity producer can use this to reduce the net risk by increasing the proportion of the floating rates. See the Anglo-American Annual Report 2011:[7]

> The Group policy is to borrow funds at floating rates of interest as, over the longer term, this is considered by management to give somewhat of a natural hedge against commodity price movements, given the correlation with economic growth (and industrial

Figure VI.1 Breakdown of cyclicality (metals price index versus Fed funds)

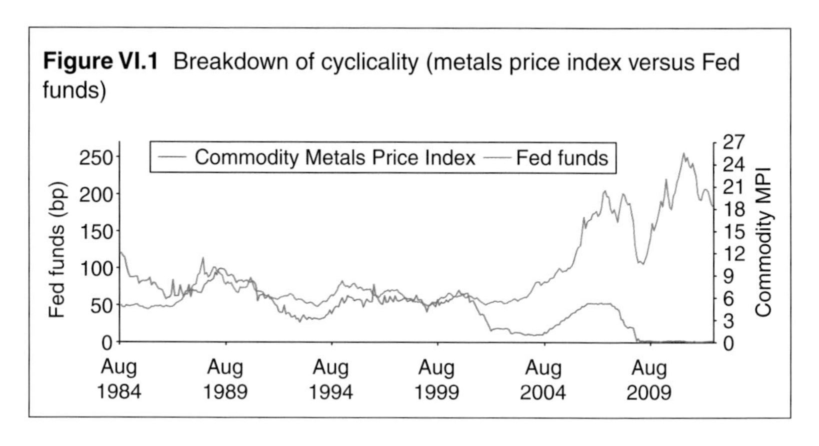

activity) which in turn shows a high correlation with commodity price.

In practice, we do not notice that the resulting risk reduction is significant enough to be relied on as a risk management tool. In Figure VI.1, we show the IMF metals price index versus Federal Reserve funds. It is easy to see that, even if there was a certain amount of correlation before 1999 (for instance, both curves dip in 1992 and increase in 1999), it almost totally disappears subsequently. This is presumably due to increased speculation and the impact of China as both producer and user of metals as well as other factors. Of course, the picture is different for every company, and for some commodities correlation with interest rates will be stronger than for others.

Another, less common way that companies experience commodity price risk is through their working capital. When commodity prices rose in early 2008, many companies who used commodities for production noticed an increase in working capital.[8] This increases the need for debt, and therefore the interest cost rises.

Chapter 30 discusses the case of an oil producer which has exposure to commodity risk through its revenues and to currency risk through its RUB-based costs. Since the company has commodity risk on the revenue side, it has decided not to hedge it. This complicates its hedging options, as we shall see.

Our second example is devoted to the cost risk. In Chapter 31 we describe the project by a USD-based food company to quantify and manage its risks to corn and EURUSD exchange rate. An important part of this process is the estimation of the correlation between the two sources of risk. Even though the quantification procedure and the correlation between risks are similar, the actual options which the company has are simpler, because it can choose whether to hedge commodity risk.

In summary, we hope that these two examples will give the reader a taste of the kinds of issues linked to hedging the commodity and currency risks together.

1 For an overview of commodities and commodity derivatives, see Geman (2005).

2 It would be equally easy to consider interest rate and commodity risk together.

3 That is, to link it to a market index of aluminium prices.

4 See page F-66 of the BHP Billiton 20-F report for 2011 at http://www.bhpbilliton.com/.

5 In practice, the second option is not so easy, since many institutional investors do not have the means or the mandate to hedge the commodity exposure.

6 Another important difference is that the volatility of spot commodities tends to be very high due to issues linked to the limited storage capability and the fact that at spot, the information flow tends to be maximised, with producers and consumers competing with speculators to determine the fair value. For an overview of modelling issues linked to commodities see Schwartz (1997). For similar reasons, the forward curve often tends to be backwardated.

7 See page 156 of the Anglo-American annual report for 2011 at http://www.angloamerican.com/.

8 See Urry *et al* (2008).

30

Managing Commodity-Linked Revenues and Currency Risk

This chapter is the first in which we investigate commodity and currency risk management. In the example discussed here, commodity risk is inextricably linked to the currency risk and the risk manager has to consider them both at the same time. The commodity risk affects the company's revenues and the company has decided not to hedge it.

BACKGROUND

Oilco is based in Russia. The company has a broad international client base and sells oil and related products across the world. As is common in this industry, the oil is paid for in USD, and Oilco, which reports in USD, therefore faces a double risk.

- **Oil price risk:** if the oil price decreases, Oilco profits decrease.
- **Currency risk:** as a large part of the operating costs is denominated in RUB, a strengthening of RUB against USD reduces Oilco's profits.

COMPANY OBJECTIVES

- To analyse the commodity risks.
- To provide potential solutions.
- Obtaining hedge accounting is not a constraint.
- Oilco does not want to hedge its oil risk.

ANALYSIS

For a comprehensive assessment we follow the four-step approach in Figure 30.1.

Figure 30.1 Risk management approach: step by step

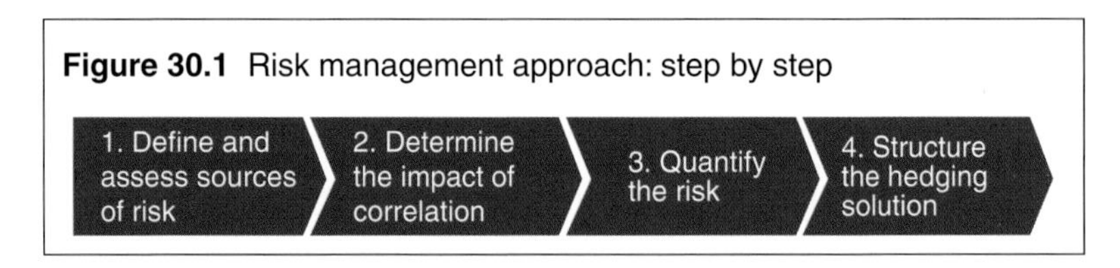

1. We determine the main risk drivers, including historical evolution and the simulation of future scenarios, based upon historically observed and market-implied parameters.
2. We introduce the correlation among sources of risk.
3. Next, we quantify the risk and evaluate the impact of the risk factors on P&L.
4. Finally, we structure the hedging solutions to reduce the profit variability.

STEP 1: DEFINE AND ASSESS SOURCES OF RISK

In the following we discuss two main sources of risk for Oilco: oil price risk and the currency risk.

Figure 30.2 and Table 30.1 show the historical evolution of USDRUB, together with a simulation of the future evolution of USDRUB over the next year. The percentage numbers in the graph give respective confidence levels for the simulated highest (95%) and lowest (5%) values. The simulation is based upon the current forward curve (as the average in the graph) and implied market volatility.

Figure 30.2 USDRUB: historical and simulation

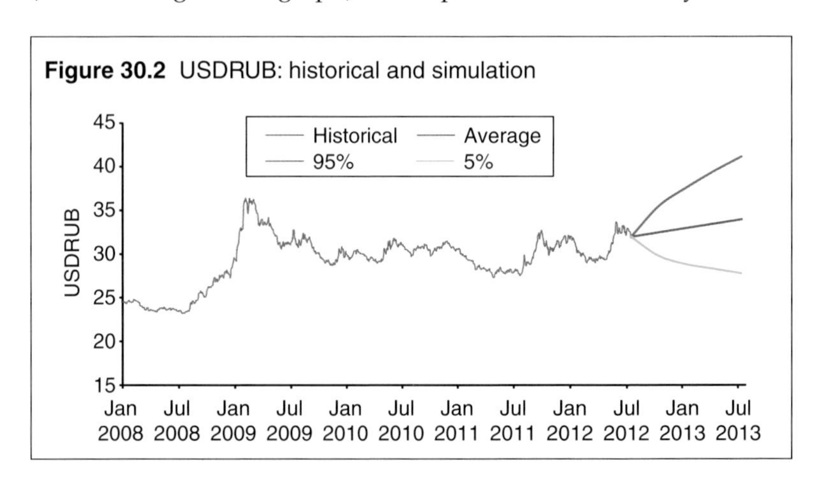

Table 30.1 USDRUB volatility cone

	Jul 2012	Oct 2012	Jan 2013	Apr 2013	Jul 2013
95%	32.0	35.4	37.6	39.5	41.1
Average	32.0	32.5	33.0	33.5	33.9
5%	32.0	29.8	28.8	28.3	27.8

Similarly, Figure 30.3 and Table 30.2 show the historical evolution of the oil and a simulation of the future evolution over the next year.

Figure 30.3 Oil price per barrel: historical and simulation

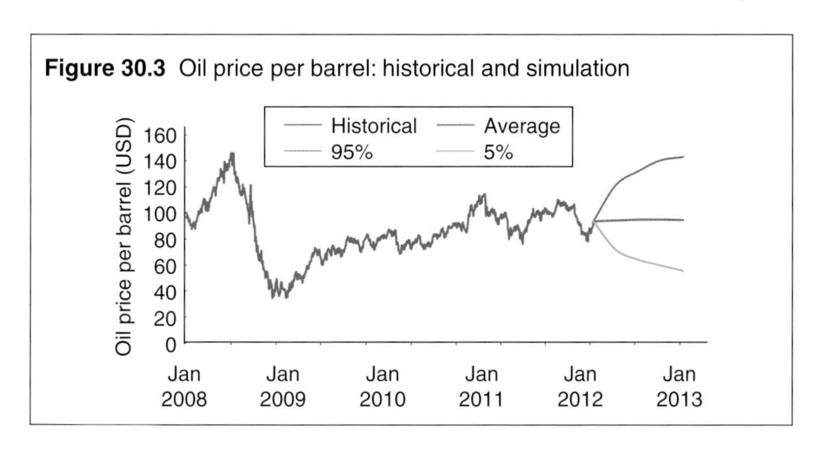

Table 30.2 Oil price volatility cone

	Jul 2012	Oct 2012	Jan 2013	Apr 2013	Jul 2013
95%	93.1	120.9	131.6	139.8	142.4
Average	93.1	93.8	94.4	94.5	94.2
5%	93.1	71.3	63.6	59.3	55.1

We can see that in July 2013, the oil price has a 5% chance of reaching the value of USD 55.1 per barrel, while USDRUB has a 5% chance to reach 27.8. These are the two main sources of risk for Oilco as they would both weaken the P&L.

STEP 2: DETERMINE THE IMPACT OF CORRELATION

So far we have looked at two risk factors in isolation, foreign exchange and oil. Increase of oil price and USD appreciation against

RUB are both beneficial for Oilco, since revenues would increase and costs would decrease.

To assess the total risk, however, it is necessary to quantify the joint impact of both risk factors. Therefore, we look at the correlation between USDRUB and the oil price.

There are two distinct situations depending on the sign of correlation

1. **Positive correlation:** high oil prices tend to coincide with high values of USDRUB and vice versa. This means that revenues tend to be high whenever costs are low and the two risk factors reinforce each other.
2. **Negative correlation:** high oil prices tend to coincide with low values of USDRUB and vice versa. This means that revenues tend to be high whenever costs are high and the two risk factors partially offset each other

We can see in Figure 30.4 the historical co-evolution of oil price and USDRUB. The correlation measured on the daily returns over the past year is slightly negative at around −22%, which corresponds to the second case. This is a better situation for Oilco, as the natural correlation reduces the overall risk to P&L. However, what is the residual risk?

Figure 30.4 Oil price and USDRUB

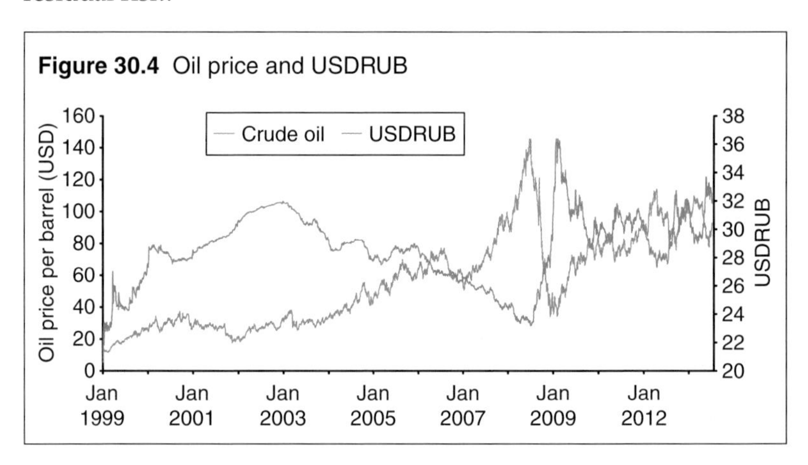

Before discussing the impact of risk on P&L, we want to illustrate the slight negative correlation between oil price and USDRUB in another way. In Figure 30.5, we show a scatter plot of the scenarios of oil price and USDRUB achieved over one year starting from July

2012. We generated this using 1,000 path Monte Carlo simulation based on the volatility cones above and a correlation between daily returns of −22%. This historical correlation translates into a correlation at maturity of −20%. We have also divided the plot into four quadrants based on the current spot levels of oil price and USDRUB. Very negative correlation would be represented by most points being in off-diagonal quadrants 2 and 3. Therefore, any solution which makes the correlation more negative[1] would remove points from the diagonal quadrants 1 and 4.

Figure 30.5 Oil price versus USDRUB at one year

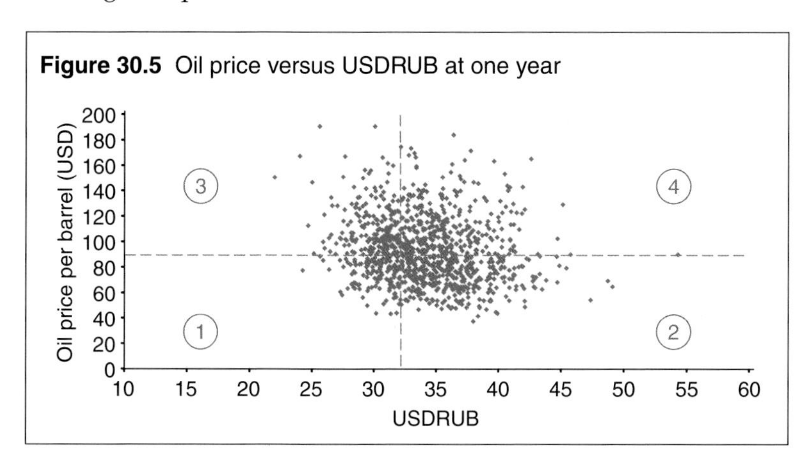

STEP 3: QUANTIFY THE RISK

To quantify the risk from the foreign exchange and oil price exposure, we simulate both risk factors on a quarterly basis over a time horizon of one year. We use a Monte Carlo simulation which takes into account current forward rates and implied volatilities as well as the historical correlation between USDRUB and oil price. We then apply the simulated rates on a quarterly basis to the revenues and operating costs of Oilco and compute the 95th percentile of the distribution.

The operating costs of Oilco are entirely in RUB and represent USD 4.2 billion per year, whereas the revenues are USD 5.0 billion per year. Operating profit is therefore expected to be USD 0.8 billion. Out of the USD 4.2 billion of expenses, USD 1.8 billion come from taxes related to oil extraction and exportation which are dependent on the oil price and fixed in USD (while payable in RUB). Hence, the net RUB exposure is USD 2.4 billion.

The results of the Monte Carlo simulation on net earnings are shown in Figure 30.6.

Figure 30.6 One-year EaR at 95%

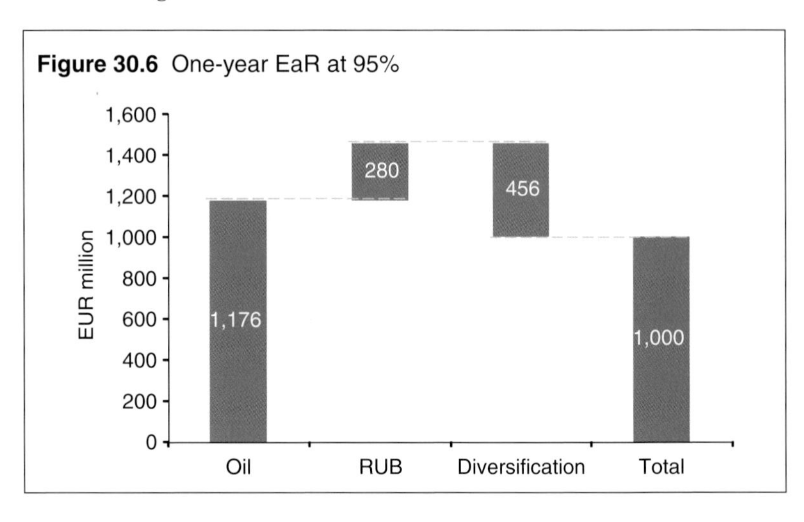

The impact of the foreign exchange and oil risk is USD 1,000 million. We define this as earnings-at-risk. EaR is derived from the difference between the expected earnings and the worst-case earnings at a confidence level of 95% over one year.

STEP 4: STRUCTURE THE HEDGING SOLUTION

As we mentioned, a negative correlation between USDRUB and oil reduces the volatility of profits. However, the historically observed correlation is low in absolute number (−22%) and therefore the natural protection is low. This causes the risk to earnings at 95th percentile to be as high as USD 1,000 million. We need to introduce an artificial negative correlation through a hedging product.

The instrument we discuss below provides an example of how to modify the correlation to provide better protection if revenues are low and costs are high.

During one year, on a quarterly basis:

- if USDRUB is less than 32.1 and oil is less than 93.0, then Oilco sells USD 600 million against RUB at 37.2 (bad FX and oil scenario, so improved FX rate);
- if USDRUB is more than 32.1 and oil is more than 93.0, then Oilco sells USD 600 million against RUB at 28.2 (good FX and oil scenario, so worse FX rate);

- otherwise, Oilco sells USD 600 million against spot RUB.

Figure 30.7 shows the impact of our product on the joint distribution of oil price in one year's time. The pink bars indicate the strike rates of the hedging contract as specified in the instrument description in the text above. The arrows show how the contract alters the joint distribution of USDRUB and oil. The dashed lines show the thresholds as set out in the specifications. When we compute the correlation of the oil price with the actual USDRUB FX rate including the hedge solution, we obtain a value of −70%, so the product actually makes the correlation more negative as required.

Figure 30.7 Oil price versus USDRUB: impact of hedging

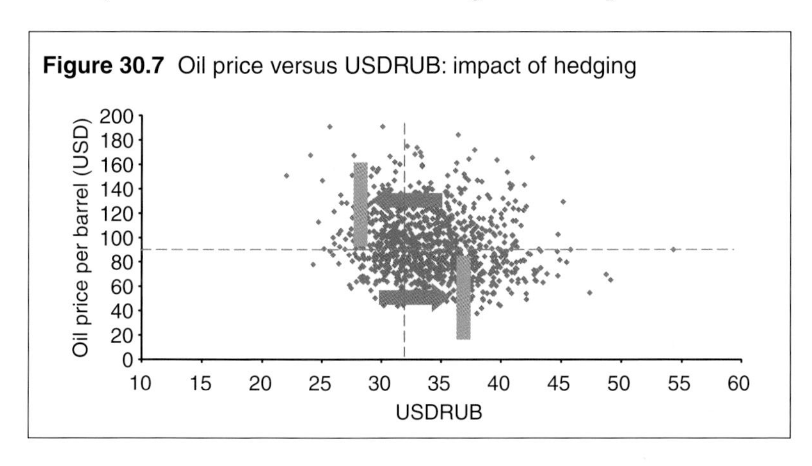

RESULTS

When we evaluate the impact of the hedging solution we notice a significant reduction of earnings-at-risk from USD 1,000 million to USD 790 million, ie, by about 21%.[2] This is a result of the hedging solution which artificially increases the negative correlation from −20% to −70%, as can be seen in Table 30.3.

Table 30.3 Impact of hedge solution on correlation and earnings-at-risk

Scenario	Original	Hedging solution
Correlation (oil versus USDRUB) at one year	−20%	−70%
Earnings-at-risk (USD)	1,000 million	790 million

RECOMMENDATIONS

In order to strengthen the negative correlation between oil price and USDRUB, the Oilco should introduce artificial correlation through its currency hedging programme. One possible solution is shown here. The only downside is that the instrument as it stands does not obtain a hedge accounting treatment and quarterly changes in its MTM will affect the company accounts in intermediate reporting periods. Oilco now has to decide whether the risk reduction shown justifies this undesirable behaviour.

CONCLUSION

In this chapter, we analysed the correlation between the risk factors Oilco is exposed to, and this allowed us to quantify the impact of correlation in terms of earnings-at-risk. In a second step, we provided a hybrid commodity/currency solution which artificially increases the negative correlation and therefore reduces the earnings-at-risk, but does not achieve hedge accounting.

1 We say "makes the correlation more negative" in a loose way. Correlation between oil price and USDRUB is given by actual historical data points and cannot be made more negative. What we mean is to include the impact of the hedging solution on the USDRUB effective exchange rate, and compute the resulting correlation between the oil price and the effective exchange rate.

2 We cannot improve the EaR much more than this, due to the residual high volatility due to the oil price.

31

Managing Commodity-Linked Costs and Currency Risk

This chapter has many similarities to the preceding one. Therefore, we shall try to avoid repetition wherever possible and focus on the different nature of hedging costs from revenues.

Again, we are in the domain of hedging commodity and currency risk. The difference from hedging the commodity risk on the cost side turns out to have significant repercussions for the final solution which reduces the hybrid risk from the two risk factors.

BACKGROUND

Gateau is a USD-reporting food manufacturer. Most of the sales are in USD, while the costs are USD 6,000 million and EUR 1,200 million. The company's primary raw material is corn, of which it needs 100 million bushels every year. The company therefore faces a double risk.

- **Corn price risk:** if the corn price increases, Gateau profits decrease.
- **Currency risk:** as a large part of the operating costs is denominated in EUR, a strengthening of EUR against USD reduces Gateau's profits.

COMPANY OBJECTIVES

- To analyse the commodity risks.
- To provide potential solutions.
- To obtain hedge accounting.
- To hedge its corn risk, due to high volatility, if necessary.

There are two main differences in the objectives of Gateau and Oilco. First, hedge accounting is an absolute requirement at Gateau (as it is with many other companies). Second, unlike Oilco, Gateau is willing and able to hedge its commodity risk, since it affects the cost and not the revenues.

ANALYSIS

For a comprehensive assessment we follow the same four-step approach as in the previous chapter (see Figure 31.1).

Figure 31.1 Risk management approach: step by step

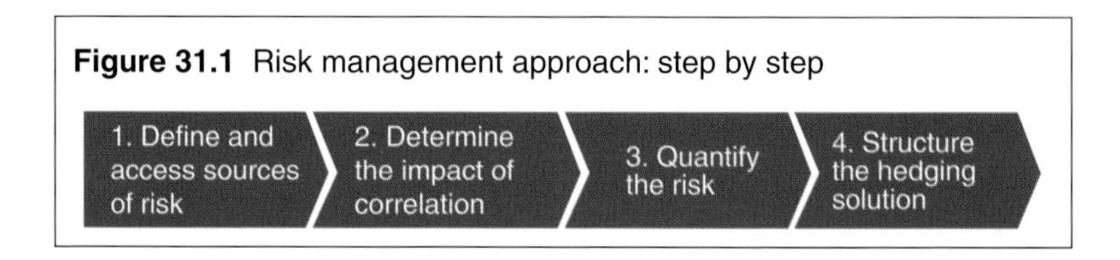

1. We determine the main risk drivers, including historical evolution and the simulation of future scenarios, based upon historically observed and market-implied parameters.
2. We introduce the correlation among sources of risk.
3. We quantify the risk and evaluate the impact of the risk factors on P&L.
4. We structure the hedging solutions to reduce the profit variability.

STEP 1: DEFINE AND ASSESS SOURCES OF RISK

In the following we discuss two main sources of risk for Gateau: corn price risk and the currency risk.

Figure 31.2 and Table 31.1 show the historical evolution of the EURUSD, together with a simulation of the future evolution of EURUSD over the next year. The percentage numbers in the graph give respective confidence levels for the simulated highest (95%) and lowest (5%) values. The simulation is based upon the current forward curve (as the average in the graph) and implied market volatility.

Similarly, Figure 31.3 and Table 31.2 show the historical evolution of the corn price and a simulation of the future evolution over the next year.

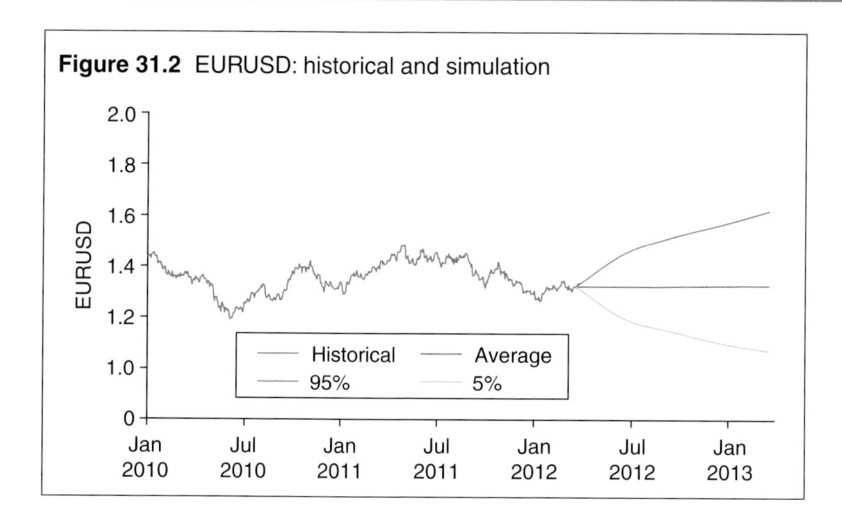

Figure 31.2 EURUSD: historical and simulation

Table 31.1 EURUSD volatility cone

	Mar 2012	Jun 2012	Sep 2012	Dec 2012	Mar 2013	Avg
95%	1.32	1.45	1.52	1.57	1.62	1.50
Average	1.32	1.32	1.32	1.33	1.33	1.32
5%	1.32	1.20	1.15	1.10	1.07	1.17

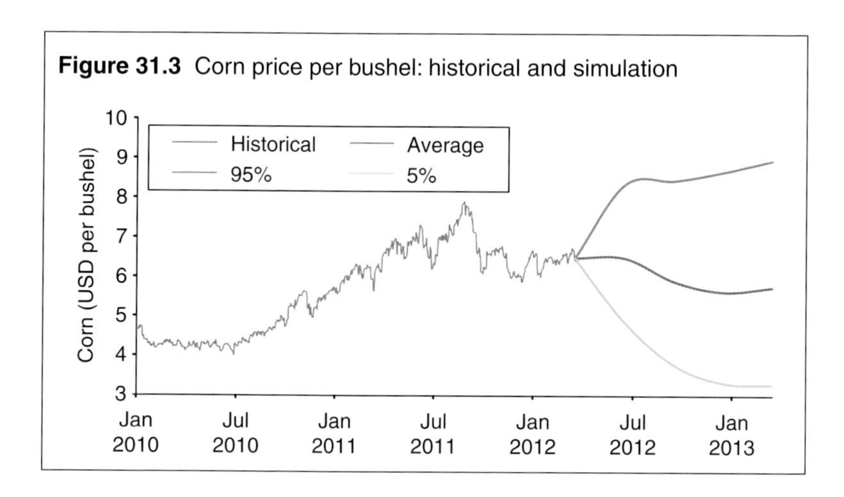

Figure 31.3 Corn price per bushel: historical and simulation

We can see that in March 2013 the corn price has a 5% chance of reaching the value of 8.94 USD per bushel, while the EURUSD has a 5% chance of strengthening to 1.62. These are the two main sources of risk for Gateau, as they would both weaken the P&L.

Table 31.2 Corn price volatility cone

	Mar 2012	Jun 2012	Sep 2012	Dec 2012	Mar 2013	Avg
95%	6.49	8.34	8.43	8.66	8.94	8.17
Average	6.49	6.48	5.88	5.63	5.74	6.04
5%	6.49	4.86	3.76	3.31	3.26	4.34

STEP 2: DETERMINE THE IMPACT OF CORRELATION

So far we have looked at two risk factors in isolation: foreign exchange and corn. An increase of corn price and EUR appreciation against USD are both bad for Gateau, since the costs would increase.

To assess the total risk, however, it is necessary to quantify the joint impact of both risk factors. Therefore, we look at the correlation between EURUSD and the corn price.

We can see in Figure 31.4 the historical coevolution of corn price and EURUSD. The correlation measured on the daily returns over the past year is around 18%, which is similar to the average historical correlation of 17% since 2000.

Figure 31.4 One-year correlation between the corn price and EURUSD

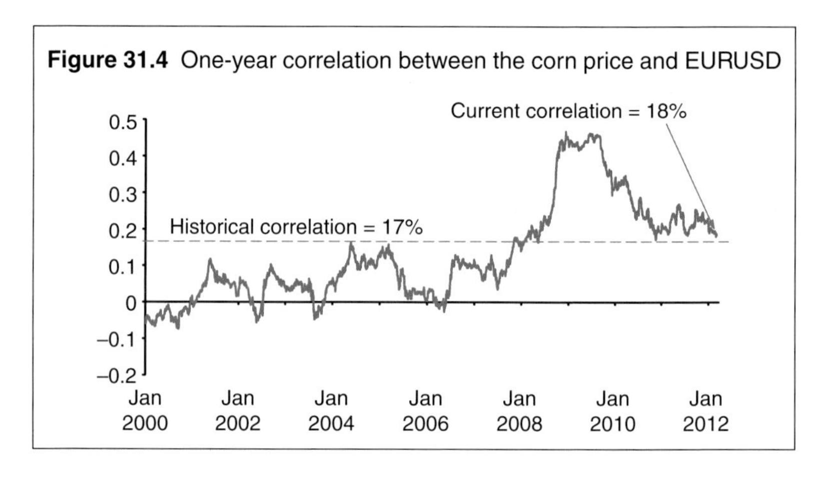

STEP 3: QUANTIFY THE RISK

To quantify the risk from the foreign exchange and corn price exposure, we simulate both risk factors on a quarterly basis over a time horizon of one year. We use a Monte Carlo simulation that takes into account current forward rates and implied volatilities as well as the historical correlation between EURUSD and corn price. We then apply the simulated rates on a quarterly basis to the operating costs of Gateau and compute the 95th percentile of the distribution.

Foreign operating costs of Gateau are EUR 1,200 million per year, whereas the annual Corn requirements are 100 million bushels.

The results of the Monte Carlo simulation on net earnings are shown in Figure 31.5.

Figure 31.5 One-year EaR at 95%

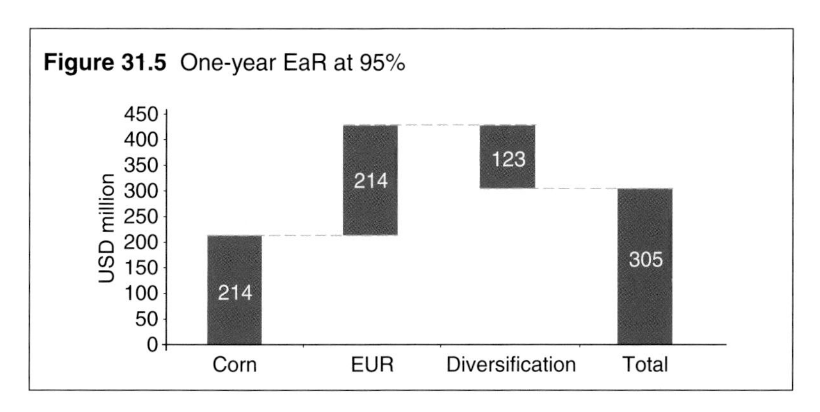

The impact of the foreign exchange and Corn risk is ±USD 305 million. We define this as earnings-at-risk. EaR is derived from the difference between the expected earnings and the worst-case earnings at a confidence level of 95% over one year.

STEP 4: STRUCTURE THE HEDGING SOLUTION

If Gateau decides to hedge the corn and/or EUR exposures, in order to protect the net income, there are several potential hedging solutions:

- currency hedges, which protect Gateau against the rise of EUR costs;
- corn hedges, which protect Gateau against the rise in the price of corn;
- hybrid currency and corn solutions, eg, solutions that protect it against the rise in a basket of EURUSD and corn price.

The third option would not get Gateau the required hedge accounting treatment, so the set of solutions is limited to individual forwards, options or zero-cost collars on EURUSD or corn price.

Premium payment:

- purchase of a call on corn;
- purchase of an EUR call USD put.

No premium to be paid:

- zero cost collar or forward on corn;
- zero cost collar or forward on EURUSD.

RESULTS

In Figure 31.6, we compare three hedging strategies:

1. hedging only the EUR exposure (reduces EaR by 30%);
2. hedging only Corn exposure (reduces EaR by 30%);
3. hedging both EUR and Corn exposure (reduces EaR by 100%).

The reason why Gateau gets a bigger impact from hedging both than the sum of the two (100% > 30% + 30%) is the diversification; if it hedges only EUR or only corn, it loses the diversification (USD 123 million, see Figure 31.5) between the two sources of risk.

Figure 31.6 One-year EaR: impact of hedging

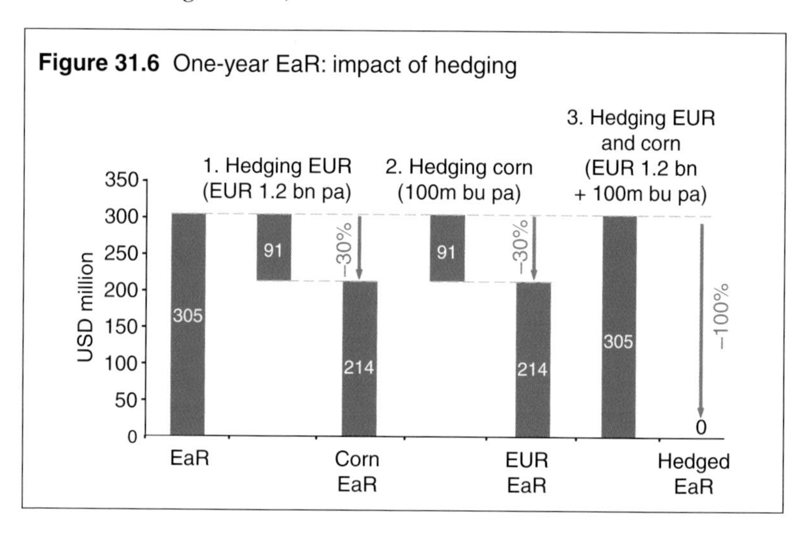

RECOMMENDATIONS

We proposed to Gateau to either hedge both the corn and EURUSD exposures or not hedge any, depending on whether the resulting risk to earnings is acceptable. The alternative solution to hedge only the corn or EURUSD exposure is not efficient, since it has downside of removing the diversification benefit[1] between the two kinds of risk.

CONCLUSION

In this chapter, we showed a different situation from the one facing Oilco in the previous chapter, even though both cases dealt with hedging the commodity and currency risk. The main difference is that Gateau can decide which of the two risks to hedge and this allows it to reduce the overall risk significantly using a hedge accounting solution.

1 The diversification benefit will depend on the actual correlation, and is high when the correlation is low.

REFERENCES

Books on Corporate Risk Management

Brown, G. W., and D. H. Chew (eds), 1999, *Corporate Risk: Strategies and Management* (London: Risk Books).

Culp, C. L., and M. H. Miller (eds), 1999, *Corporate Hedging in Theory and Practice: Lessons from Metallgesellschaft* (London: Risk Books).

Jameson, R. (ed), 1997, *Financial Risk and the Corporate Treasury* (London: Risk Books).

Leautier, T. O., 2007, *Corporate Risk Management for Value Creation: A Guide to Real Life Applications* (London: Risk Books).

Triana, P., 2006, *Corporate Derivatives* (London: Risk Books).

Capital Structure Papers

Amihud, Y., and H. Mendelson, 2008, "Liquidity, the Value of the Firm, and Corporate Finance", *Journal of Applied Corporate Finance* 20(2), pp. 32–45.

Cenci, M., and A. Gheno, 2005, "Equity and Debt Valuation with Default Risk: A Discrete Structural Model", *Applied Financial Economics* 15(12), pp. 875–81.

Graham, J., and C. Harvey, 2002, "How Do CFOs Make Capital Budgeting and Capital Structure Decisions", *Journal of Applied Corporate Finance* 15(1), pp. 8–23.

General Books, Papers and Articles

Adams, J., and D. J. Smith, 2011, "Pre-Issuance Hedging of Fixed-Rate Debt", *Journal of Applied Corporate Finance* 23(4), pp. 102–12.

Amram, M., and N. Kulatilaka, 1998, *Real Options: Managing Strategic Investment in an Uncertain World* (Oxford University Press).

Arvanitis, A., and J. Gregory, 2001, *Credit: The Complete Guide to Pricing, Hedging and Risk Management* (London: Risk Books).

Baker, H. K., and G. S. Martin (eds), 2011, *Capital Structure and Corporate Financing Decisions: Theory, Evidence And Practice* (Chichester: John Wiley & Sons).

Benaben, B. (ed), 2005, *Inflation-linked Products: A Guide for Investors and Asset and Liability Managers* (London: Risk Books).

Benaben, B., and S. Goldenberg (eds), 2008, *Inflation Risks and Products: The Complete Guide* (London: Risk Books).

Brealey, R. A., S. C. Myers and F. Allen, 2010, *Principles of Corporate Finance: Global Edition*, Tenth Edition (McGraw-Hill).

Chambers, A., 2008, "Why Corporate Refinancing Is Next Up in the Cycle of Despair", *Euromoney*, December 1.

Copeland, T. E., and V. Antikarov, 2003, *Real Options: A Practitioner'S Guide* (London: Texere Publishing).

Copeland, T. E., J. F. Weston and K. Shastri, 2003, *Financial Theory and Corporate Policy* (London: Pearson).

Deloitte, 2011, *Deloitte iGAAP 2012: Financial Instruments – IAS 39 and Related Standards* (London: Tolley).

Dowd, K., 1998, *Beyond Value at Risk: New Science of Risk Management* (Chichester: John Wiley & Sons).

Geman, H., 2005, *Commodities and Commodity Derivatives* (Chichester: John Wiley & Sons).

Glasserman, P., 2003, *Monte Carlo Methods in Financial Engineering* (Springer).

Goldstein, M., G. L. Kaminsky and C. M. Reinhart, 2000, "Assessing Financial Vulnerability: An Early Warning System for Emerging Markets", Institute for International Economics.

Hull, J., 2011, *Options, Futures and Other Derivatives*, Eighth Edition (London: Pearson Education).

International Accounting Standards Board, 2003, *IAS 39 Financial Instruments: Recognition and Measurement*, IAS 39.

Jäckel, P., 2002, *Monte Carlo Methods In Finance* (Chichester: John Wiley & Sons).

Jorion, P., 2006, *Value at Risk*, Third Edition (McGraw-Hill).

Kaminsky, G. L., 1999, "Currency and Banking Crises: The Early Warning of Distress", International Monetary Fund Working Paper.

Koller, T., M. Goedhart and D. Wessels, 2010, *Valuation: Measuring and Managing the Value of Companies: University Edition*, Fifth Edition (Chichester: John Wiley & Sons).

Merton, R., 1974, "On the Pricing of Corporate Debt: The Risk Structure of Interest Rates", *The Journal of Finance* 29, pp. 449–70.

Merton, R., and A. Perold, 1993, "Theory of Risk Capital in Financial Firms", *Journal of Applied Corporate Finance* 6(3), pp. 16–32.

Mitra, G., and K. Schwaiger, 2011, *Asset and Liability Management Handbook* (Basingstoke: Palgrave Macmillan).

Moody's, 2010, "Moody's Approach to Global Standard Adjustments in the Analysis of Financial Statements for Non-Financial Corporations", December 21, URL: http://ssrn.cim/abstract=959001.

Moody's, 2011, "European Corporates Likely to Conserve Cash in 2012", December 15, URL: http://www.moodys.com.

Myint, S., 2005, "The Value of IAS 39", *Risk Magazine*, February, pp. 49–50.

Press, W. H., S. A. Teukolsky, W. T. Vetterling and B. P. Flannery, 2007, *Numerical Recipes: The Art of Scientific Computing*, Third Edition (Cambridge University Press).

Pringle, J., and R. A. Connolly, 1993, "The Nature and Causes of Foreign Currency Exposures", *Journal of Applied Corporate Finance* 3(6), pp. 61–72.

Quiry, P., Y. Le Fur, A. Salvi, M. Dallochio and P. Vernimmen, 2011, *Corporate Finance: Theory and Practice*, Third Edition (Chichester: John Wiley & Sons).

Ramirez, J., 2007, *Accounting for Derivatives: Advanced Hedging under IFRS* (Chichester: John Wiley & Sons).

Ramirez, J., 2011, *Handbook of Corporate Equity Derivatives and Equity Capital Markets* (Chichester: John Wiley & Sons).

Scherer, B. (ed), 2003, *Asset and Liability Management Tools: A Handbook for Best Practice* (London: Risk Books).

Schwartz, E. S., 1997, "The Stochastic Behaviour of Commodity Prices: Implications for Valuation and Hedging", *The Journal of Finance* 52, pp. 923–73.

Smithson, C. W., and D. H. Chew, 1992, "The Uses of Hybrid Debt in Managing Corporate Risk", *Journal of Applied Corporate Finance* 4(4), pp. 79–89.

Standard & Poor's, 2008, "Corporate Ratings Criteria 2008", April 15.

Urry, M., J. Blas and J. Wiggins, 2008, "Rising Costs Hit Food Producers", *Financial Times*, February 26.

Van Binsbergen, J. H., J. R. Graham and J. Yang, 2011, "An Empirical Model of Optimal Capital Structure", *Journal of Applied Corporate Finance* 23(4), pp. 34–59.

Woodson, H., 2002, *Global Convertible Investing: The Gabelli Way* (Chichester: John Wiley & Sons).

Index

(page numbers in italic type relate to tables or figures)

A

acquisitions:
  rating impact of, 293–8, *295*; *see also* M&A risk
    analysis, 294
    background, 293
    company objectives, 294
    overview, 293
    recommendations, 297
agency meetings, 13–16
asset and liability management, 147–57, *148*, *149*, *151*, *152*, *153*, *155*, *156*
  analysis, 151–2
    assumptions, 151–2, *152*
    methodology, 151
  background, 150
  overview, 147–50
  recommendations, 156–7
  risk management approach, step by step, 151–6, *151*
    Step 1: optimising fixed–floating mix versus VaR, 153–4
    Step 2: optimising duration versus VaR, 154–5
    Step 3: evaluating cashflow-at-risk impact, 155–6
asset and liability management, pension funds, 159–66, *160*, *161*, *162*, *163*, *164*, *165*, *166*
  analysis, 160
  asset and liability management for, and equity risk, reducing, 163–4
  background, 159–60
  company objectives, 160
  and equity risk, reducing, 163–4
  and interest rate risk, reducing, 163
  overview, 159
  recommendations, 164
  risk management approach, step by step, 160–4, *160*
    Step 1: calculating asset and liability sensitivities and distribution, 160–2
    Step 2: determining breakdown of risk to surplus by asset class, 162
    Step 3: exploring ways to reduce risk to the surplus, 163–4

B

back-testing, 80–2, 100
Basel III:
  focus of, on financial institutions, xxvii
  and increase in credit valuation adjustment charge, xxvii
benchmarking risk management performance, xxiv–xxv
bond documentation, amendments to, 313–16, *315*
  analysis, 314
  background, 313
  company objectives, 313–14
  consent solicitation overview, 314–15
  overview, 313
  recommendations, 315–16
  results and outcome, 316
bond issues, and credit rating, 9

C

cash tender offer, 27–32
  background, 27
  company objectives, 28
  market background, 29
  results, 31
  solution, 29–30
  structure summary, 30–1
cashflow-at-risk:
  evaluation of, 155–6
  expected interest revenue versus, *156*
  scenario analysis, *156*
cashflow risk, 148
commodity-linked costs and currency risk, 353–9, *354*, *355*, *356*, *357*, *358*
  analysis, 354
  background, 353
  company objectives, 353–4
  overview, 353
  recommendations, 358
  results, 358
  risk management approach, step by step, 354–8, *354*
    Step 1: defining and accessing risk sources 354–5
    Step 2: determining impact of correlation 356
    Step 3: quantifying risk, 356–7
    Step 4: structuring hedging solution, 357–8
commodity-linked revenues and currency risk, 345–52
  analysis, 345–6, *346*, *347*, *348*, *349*, *350*, *351*
  background, 345
  company objectives, 345
  overview, 345
  recommendations, 352
  results, 351
  risk management approach, step by step, 346–51, *346*
    Step 1: defining and assess risk sources 346–7
    Step 2: determining impact of correlation 347–9
    Step 3: quantifying risk, 349–50
    Step 4: structuring hedging solution, 350–1
commodity risk, 339–59
  and commodity-linked revenues and currency risk 345–52; *see also* commodity-linked revenues
    and currency risk
    analysis, 345–6, *346*, *347*, *348*, *349*, *350*, *351*
    background, 345
    company objectives, 345
    overview, 345
    recommendations, 352
    results, 351
    risk management approach, step by step, 346–51
  and currency risks and commodity-linked costs 353–9, *354*, *355*, *356*, *357*, *358*
    analysis, 354
    background, 353
    company objectives, 353–4
    overview, 353
    recommendations, 358
    results, 358
    risk management approach, step by step, 354–8, *354*
  section overview, 339–43
company valuation, impact of fixed–floating policy on, 93–105, *95*, *96*, *98*, *99*, *100*, *101*, *103*, *104*
  analysis, 94
  and back-testing, 100
  background, 94
  company objectives, 94
  and consensus forecasts, 98
  discounted cashflow methodology, 96–7
  and equity, higher cost of, 102–4

overview, 93–4
recommendations, 104
and share price, step by step, 95–104, *95*
Step 1: determining duration mix and interest cost saving, 95–6
Step 2: computing increase in valuation, 96–101
Step 3: monitoring risk impact, 101–4
and valuation, 98–100
and WACC calculation, 98
constrained maturity optimisation, 141–6
analysis, 142–5
methodology, 143–5
background, 141–2
company objectives, 142
recommendations, 145
corporate financial risk management (CFRM):
and asset and liability management, 147–57, *148*, *149*, *151*, *152*, *153*, *155*, *156*
analysis, 151–2
background, 150
overview, 147–50
recommendations, 156–7
risk management approach, step by step, 151–6
and commodity-linked costs, 353–9; *see also* commodity-linked costs and currency risk
and commodity-linked revenues, 169–273; *see also* commodity-linked revenues and currency risk
and commodity-linked revenues and currency risk 345–52
and commodity risk, 339–59
section overview, 339–43
and company valuation, impact of fixed–floating policy on, 93–105, *95*, *96*, *98*, *99*, *100*, *101*, *103*, *104*
analysis, 94
and back-testing, 100
background, 94
company objectives, 94
and consensus forecasts, 98
discounted cashflow methodology, 96–7
and equity, higher cost of, 102–4
overview, 93–4
recommendations, 104
and share price, step by step, 95–104, *95*
and valuation, 98–100
and WACC calculation, 98
and constrained maturity optimisation, 141–6
analysis, 142–5
background, 141–2
company objectives, 142
recommendations, 145
and credit risk, 241–83, 255, *256*, *257*, *258*, *260*
analysis, 255
background, 255
company objectives, 255
and counterparty risk methodology, 245–53
and counterparty risk protection, 255–61
overview, 255
recommendations, 260
section overview, 241–3
and currency risk, 169–237; *see also* commodity-linked costs and currency risk; commodity-linked revenues and currency risk
on covenants, 207–14; *see also* covenants; currency risk
and FX hedging policy, how to develop, 175–84
section overview, 169–72
and funding, 3–50, *see also main entry*

and funding cost drivers, 41–50, *43*, *44*, *45*, *46*, *48*
analysis, 42–3
background, 42
company objectives, 42
recommendations, 48–9
Step 1: historical analysis and peer benchmarking 43–6
Step 2: selecting main drivers, 46–7
Step 3: creating single- or multi-factor model of cost, 47
Step 4: analysing implications for company 47–8
and hedging policy, 57–68; *see also* hedging policy, developing
and hedging uncertain exposures, 323–35, *325*, *326*, *327*, *328*, *329*, *330*, *331*, *332*, *333*
analysis, 325
background, 324
company objectives, 324–5
and duration optimisation approach, step by step, *325*
overview, 323–4
recommendations, 334
and inflation-linked debt, 107–16, *109*, *111*, *112*, *113*, *114*
analysis, 109
assumptions, 111–12
background, 108–9
company objectives, 109
overview, 107–8
recommendations, 115
results, 113–14
risk management approach, step by step, *109*
strategy application, 114–15
and interest rate and inflation risk, 53–166; *see also main entry*
literature on case studies of, xxi
literature on, xx–xxi
and M&A-related risk, *see* M&A risk
and managing FX risk with dynamic option strategy 227–37
background, 229
company objectives, 229–30
overview, 227–9
recommendations, 235–7
and Merton's model, optimal debt duration via 33–40, *39*
and monetising deferred consideration, *see* deferred consideration, monetising
and netting FX risk, 185–98, *187*, *189*, *190*, *191*, *192*, *193*, *194*, *195*, *196*, *197*
analysis, 186–7
background, 186
company objectives, 186
and earnings-at-risk calculation, 190–3
and individual transaction exposures by subsidiary and currency, 189–90
overview, 185–6
recommendations, 197
step-by-step process of, 187–97
and obtaining credit rating, 9–18, *10*
Step 1: forming initial rating expectations 12–13
Step 2: introductory agency meetings, 13–16
Step 3: preparing for management presentation 16–17
and optimal deposit composition, 263–76, *265*, *268*, *269*, *270*, *271*, *272*, *273*, *274*, *275*
analysis, 264
background, 263–4
company objectives, 264

overview, 263
recommendations, 274
step by step, 264–74
practice of, literature on, xxi
and prehedging credit risk, 277–83, *279*, *281*, *282*
analysis, 278–9
background, 277–8
call spread, 281–2, *282*
company objectives, 278
hedging strategy, 280
overview, 277
recommendations, 282–3
straight call, 280–1, *281*
and prehedging interest rate risk, 117–25, *119*, *120*, *124*
and accounting treatment, 122–4
analysis, 118
background, 118
and bond issuance, step by step, 118–24, *119*
company objectives, 118
overview, 117–18
recommendations, 125
solutions, designing, 120–1
and uncertain maturity, 124
and uncertain starting date, 124
and prehedging, when to, 127–39, *128*, *129*, *130*, *131*, *132*, *133*, *134*, *135*, *136*, *137*, *138*
background, 127
company objectives, 128
cost analysis, step by step, 129–38, *129*
cost, forecasting from distance to local minimum, 134–6
cost, one into five years, 130–1
and dynamic of past swap rate hikes, 137–8
future cost, steepness as indicator of, 133–4
market background, 128–9
overview, 127
recent cost, comparison of, 131–2
recommendations, 138–9
step-by-step process of, 230–5, *231*
Step 1: evaluating credit use of static strategies 230
Step 2: evaluating credit use of dynamic strategies, 230–4
Step 3: comparing cashflow volatilities of dynamic strategy versus CSA, 234–5
Step 4: tactical considerations, 235
surveys of, literature on, xxi
theory of, literature on, xxi
and translation risk, managing, 215–25, *218*, *219*, *220*, *221*, *223*
analysis, 217–18, 218–24, *218*
background, 217
company objectives, 217
overview, 215–17
recommendations, 224
cost drivers, funding, 41–50, *43*, *44*, *45*, *46*, *48*
analysis, 42–3
background, 42; *see also* funding
company objectives, 42
recommendations, 48–9
step-by-step process of, 43–8, *43*
Step 1: historical analysis and peer benchmarking 43–6
Step 2: selecting main drivers, 46–7
Step 3: creating single- or multi-factor model of cost, 47
Step 4: analysing implications for company, 47–8
counterparty risk methodology, *246*, *247*, *248*, *250–1*, *252*

analysis, 246
recommendations, 252–3
and single counterparty options, summary of, 250
counterparty risk protection, 255, 255–61, *256*, *257*, *258*, *260*
analysis, 255
background, 255
company objectives, 255
overview, 255
recommendations, 260
risk management approach, step by step, 256–60, *256*
Step 1: calculating MTM distribution of derivative portfolio, 256–7
Step 2: calculating loss distribution using CDS-implied probabilities, 257–8
Step 3: exploring restructuring alternatives 258–60
covenants:
currency risk on, 207–14, *208*, *210*
and accounting treatment, 213
analysis, 209–12
and average strike call, 211
and average strike collar, 211–12
and average strike forward, 212
background, 208–9
company objectives, 209
overview, 207–8
recommendations, 213
solutions, comparison of, 213
credit rating, obtaining, 9–18
analysis, 11–12, *11–12*
company objectives, 10
introductory agency meetings, 13–16
and peer group analysis, *15–16*
recommendations, 18
step-by-step process of, *10*
Step 1: forming initial rating expectations 12–13
Step 2: introductory agency meetings, 13–16
Step 3: preparing for management presentation, 16–17
see also funding
credit risk, 241–83
and counterparty risk methodology, 245–53, *246*, *247*, *248*, *250–1*, *252*
analysis, 246
background, 245
company objectives, 246
overview, 245
recommendations, 252–3
and single counterparty options, summary of, 250
and counterparty risk protection, 255, 255–61, *256*, *257*, *258*, *260*
analysis, 255
background, 255
company objectives, 255
overview, 255
recommendations, 260
and optimal deposit composition, 263–76, *265*, *268*, *269*, *270*, *271*, *272*, *273*, *274*, *275*
analysis, 264
background, 263–4
company objectives, 264
overview, 263
recommendations, 274
step by step, 264–74
prehedging, 277–83, 279, *281*, *282*
analysis, 278–9
background, 277–8
call spread, 281–2, *282*
company objectives, 278
hedging strategy, 280
overview, 277
recommendations, 282–3
straight call, 280–1, *281*

risk management approach, step by step, 246–52, *246*
Step 1: identifying risky positions and possible actions to limit risk, 246–7
Step 2: calculating credit risk from each counterparty, 247–8
Step 3: suggesting optimal allocation under a portfolio approach, 248–52
Step 4: reducing and managing portfolio risk, 252
section overview, 241–3
credit valuation adjustment charge, increase in, xxvii
currency risk, 169–237
and commodity-linked costs, 353–9, *354*, *355*, *356*, *357*, *358*
analysis, 354
background, 353
company objectives, 353–4
overview, 353
recommendations, 358
results, 358
risk management approach, step by step, 354–8, *354*
and commodity-linked revenues, 345–52; *see also* commodity-linked revenues and currency risk
analysis, 345–6, *346*, *347*, *348*, *349*, *350*, *351*
background, 345
company objectives, 345
overview, 345
recommendations, 352
results, 351
risk management approach, step by step, 346–51
on covenants, 207–14, *208*, *210*
and accounting treatment, 213
analysis, 209–12
and average strike call, 211
and average strike collar, 211–12
and average strike forward, 212
background, 208–9
company objectives, 209
overview, 207–8
recommendations, 213
solutions, comparison of, 213
and credit risk, 241–3, 241–83
and counterparty risk methodology, 245–53
and emerging-market currencies, 199–206
background, 200
company objectives, 201
and econometric signals of Kaminsky and Reinhart, 201–3, 204–5
and market-based signals, 203–5
overview, 199–200
recommendations, 205–6
and FX hedging policy, how to develop, 175–84, *176*, *179*, *180*, *181*, *183*
analysis, 176–8
background, 176
and budget rates, 181–2
company objectives, 176
and hedging products, 182
how much to hedge, 178–81
overview, 175–6
recommendations, 184
risk management approach, step by step, *176*
which currencies to hedge, 182–4
managing, with dynamic option strategy, 227–37
analysis, 230
background, 229
company objectives, 229–30
overview, 227–9
recommendations, 235–7

netting, 185–98, *187*, *189*, *190*, *191*, *192*, *193*, *194*, *195*, *196*, *197*
analysis, 186–7
background, 186
company objectives, 186
and earnings-at-risk calculation, 190–3
and individual transaction exposures by subsidiary and currency, 189–90
overview, 185–6
recommendations, 197
step-by-step process of, 187–97
section overview, 169–72
and translation risk, managing, 215–25, *218*, *219*, *220*, *221*, *223*
analysis, 217–18, 218–24, *218*
background, 217
company objectives, 217
overview, 215–17
recommendations, 224

D

debt duration:
and cost of fixing, 71–2
and fixed–floating mix, 69–92
analysis, 70
background, 69
company objectives, 69–70
recommendations, 89–91
Fortune 500, study on, 33
optimal, via Merton's model, 33–40, *39*
analysis, 35–8
background, 35
company objectives, 35
recommendations, 39; *see also* funding
optimisation approach, step by step, 70–89, *70*
Step 1: changing treasury policy, 70–7
Step 2: reducing hedging cost, 77–9
Step 3: monitoring risk impact, 79–84
Step 4: tactical considerations, 84–9
optimisation of, versus VaR, 154–5
and perfect timing, value of, 84–7, *85*, *86*, *87*
and possible ways to reduce hedging costs, 73–7
increasing probability of saving, 75–7
reducing duration, 74–5
reducing fixed proportion, 73–4
reduced fixed proportion, *80*
strategy, current versus reduced duration, *78*
strategy, current versus reduced fixed, *80*
strategy, reduced duration, *79*
swaption strategy, 90–1, *90*
debt, inflation-linked, 107–16, *109*, *111*, *112*, *113*, *114*
analysis, 109
assumptions, 111–12
background, 108–9
company objectives, 109
overview, 107–8
recommendations, 115
results, 113–14
risk management approach, step by step, *109*
Step 1: quantifying interest rate and inflation risk, 110
Step 2: determining optimal liability composition, 110
strategy application, 114–15
deferred consideration, monetising, 317–21, *318*, *320*
analysis, 318
background, 317
company objectives, 317–18
overview, 317
pricing, 319–20
recommendations, 320
results, 318–19

financing SPV in capital markets, 319
optimal structure, 318–19
derivatives risks:
counterparty, 61
liquidity, 61
settlement, 61
valuation, 60
derivatives scandals, rarity of, xxiii
Dodd–Frank Act, xxviii
dynamic hedging, limits on, 64–5
dynamic option strategy:
and managing FX risk, 227–37
analysis, 230
background, 229
company objectives, 229–30
overview, 227–9
recommendations, 235–7

E

emerging-market currencies, managing, 199–206
background, 200
company objectives, 201
and econometric signals of Kaminsky and Reinhart, 201–3, 204–5
and market-based signals, 203–5
overview, 199–200; *see also* currency risk
recommendations, 205–6
equity:
higher cost of, 102–4
reducing risk of, 163–4
European Market Infrastructure Regulation (EMIR) xxviii

F

fair-value risk, 148
fixed–floating mix and duration, improving, 69–92, *70*, *71*, *72*, *73*, *74*, *75*, *76*, *77*, *78*, *79*, *80*, *81*, *82*, *83*, *85*, *86*, *87*, *88*, *89*, *90*
analysis, 70
background, 69
company objectives, 69–70
optimisation approach, step by step, *70*
see also debt duration
foreign exchange (FX) risk, *see* currency risk
forming initial rating expectations, 12–13
Fortune 500 Company list, 33
funding, 3–50
cash tender offer, 27–32
background, 27
company objectives, 28
market background, 29
results, 31
solution, 29–30
structure summary, 30–1
cost, creating single- or multi-factor model of, 47
cost drivers, 41–50, *43*, *44*, *45*, *46*, *48*
analysis, 42–3
background, 42
company objectives, 42
recommendations, 48–9
step-by-step process of, 43–8, *43*; *see also* cost drivers, funding
intermediated exchange, 19–25
background, 19
company objectives, 20
execution of operation, 24
market background, 20–1
principal benefits, 22
pros and cons of different approaches, 22–3
recommendations, 23
results, 24
solution, three options, 21
step-by-step transaction structure, *23*
and Merton's model, optimal debt duration via, 33–40, *39*
analysis, 35–8
background, 35

company objectives, 35
recommendations, 39
obtaining credit rating, 9–18, *10*
analysis, 11–12, *11–12*
background, 9–10
business profile, *13*
company objectives, 10
recommendations, 18
Step 1: forming initial rating expectations, 12–13
Step 2: introductory agency meetings, 13–16
Step 3: preparing for management presentation, 16–17
and peer group analysis, *15–16*
section overview, 3–7
FX risk, *see* currency risk

H

hedging costs, reducing:
possible ways of achieving, 73–7, *77*
simplified strategy for, 77–9, *77*
hedging policy, developing, 57–68, *61*, *62*, *67*
analysis, 58–60
methodology, 58, *58*
summary, 58
background, 57
benchmarking, 66
company objectives, 57
derivatives risks, 60–1
for foreign exchange risk, 175–84, *176*, *179*, *180*, *181*, *183*
analysis, 176–8
background, 176
and budget rates, 181–2
company objectives, 176
and hedging products, 182
how much to hedge, 178–81
overview, 175–6
recommendations, 184
which currencies to hedge, 182–4
for foreign exchange, risk management approach, step by step, 176–97, *176*
and optimum fixed–floating mix, 66–8
performance measures, 65
processes and organisation, 60
recommendations, 68
risk management approach, step by step, *58*
sector case studies, 58–60
aggressive approach, 59
conservative approach, 58–9
dynamic approach, 59
hedging uncertain exposures, 323–35, *325*, *326*, *327*, *328*, *329*, *330*, *331*, *332*, *333*
analysis, 325
background, 324
company objectives, 324–5
and duration optimisation approach, step by step, 325–34
Step 1: scoring deal sensitivity to FX (transaction occurs), 325–7
Step 2: scoring unwind P&L (transaction fails), 327–8
Step 3: scoring post–hedge rate, 328–31
Step 4: applying FX distribution, 331–3
Step 5: applying deal likelihood, 334
overview, 323–4
recommendations, 334
historical analysis and peer benchmarking, 43–6

I

inflation-linked debt, 107–16, *109*, *111*, *112*, *113*, *114*
analysis, 109
assumptions, 111–12
background, 108–9

company objectives, 109
overview, 107–8
recommendations, 115
results, 113–14
risk management approach, step by step, *109*
Step 1: quantifying interest rate and inflation risk, 110
Step 2: determining optimal liability composition, 110
strategy application, 114–15
initial rating expectations, forming, 12–13
interest rate and inflation risk, 53–166
and asset and liability management, 147–57, *148*, *149*, *151*, *152*, *153*, *155*, *156*
analysis, 151–2
background, 150
overview, 147–50
recommendations, 156–7
risk management approach, step by step, 151–6
and company valuation, impact of fixed–floating policy on, 93–105, *95*, *96*, *98*, *99*, *100*, *101*, *103*, *104*
analysis, 94
and back-testing, 100
background, 94
company objectives, 94
and consensus forecasts, 98
discounted cashflow methodology, 96–7
and equity, higher cost of, 102–4
overview, 93–4
recommendations, 104
and share price, step by step, 95–104
and valuation, 98–100
and WACC calculation, 98
and constrained maturity optimisation, 141–6
analysis, 142–5
background, 141–2
company objectives, 142
recommendations, 145
and cost of fixing, 71–2
and fixed–floating mix and duration, improving, 69–92, *70*, *71*, *72*, *73*, *74*, *75*, *76*, *77*, *78*, *79*, *80*, *81*, *82*, *83*, *85*, *86*, *87*, *88*, *89*, *90*; *see also* debt duration
analysis, 70
background, 69
company objectives, 69–70
optimisation approach, step by step, *70*
and fixed–floating mix, optimum, 66–8
and hedging policy, developing, 57–68, *61*, *62–3*, *67*
analysis, 58–60
background, 57
benchmarking, 66
company objectives, 57
derivatives risks, 60–1
dynamic, limits on, 64–5
mitigation, 62–5
performance measures, 65
processes and organisation, 60
recommendations, 68
risk management approach, step by step, *58*
and inflation-linked debt, 107–16, *109*, *111*, *112*, *113*, *114*
analysis, 109
assumptions, 111–12
background, 108–9
company objectives, 109
overview, 107–8
recommendations, 115
results, 113–14
risk management approach, step by step, *109*
strategy application, 114–15
and possible ways to reduce hedging costs, 73–7
increasing probability of saving, 75–7

reducing duration, 74–5
reducing fixed proportion, 73–4
prehedging, 117–25, *119*, *120*, *124*, *128*, *129*, *130*, *131*, *132*, *133*, *134*, *135*, *136*, *137*, *138*
and accounting treatment, 122–4
analysis, 118
background, 118, 127
and bond issuance, step by step, 118–24, *119*
company objectives, 118, 128
cost analysis, step by step, 129–38, *129*
cost, forecasting from distance to local minimum, 134–6
cost, one into five years, 130–1
and dynamic of past swap rate hikes, 137–8
future cost, steepness as indicator of, 133–4
market background, 128–9
overview, 117–18, 127
recent cost, comparison of, 131–2
recommendations, 125, 138–9
solutions, designing, 120–1
and uncertain maturity, 124
and uncertain starting date, 124
when to, 127–39; *see also* prehedging
section overview, 53–6
intermediated exchange, 19–25
background, 19
company objectives, 20
execution of operation, 24
market background, 20–1
principal benefits, *22*
pros and cons of different approaches, 22–3
recommendations, 22–3
results, 24
solution, three options, 21
step-by-step transaction structure, *23*
introductory agency meetings, 13–16

K

Kaminsky and Reinhart (KR) method, 201–3, *203*, 204–5
see also currency risk

L

liability and asset management, 147–57, *148*, *149*, *151*, *152*, *153*, *155*, *156*
analysis, 151–2
assumptions, 151–2, *152*
methodology, 151
background, 150
overview, 147–50
recommendations, 156–7
risk management approach, step by step, *151*
Step 1: optimising fixed–floating mix versus VaR, 153–4
Step 2: optimising duration versus VaR, 154–5
Step 3: evaluating cashflow-at-risk impact, 155–6
liability and asset management, pension funds, 159–66, *160*, *161*, *162*, *163*, *164*, *165*, *166*
analysis, 160
background, 159–60
company objectives, 160
and equity risk, reducing, 163–4
and interest rate risk, reducing, 163
overview, 159
recommendations, 164
risk management approach, step by step, 160–4, *160*

Step 1: calculating asset and liability sensitivities and distribution, 160–2
Step 2: determining breakdown of risk to surplus by asset class, 162
Step 3: exploring ways to reduce risk to the surplus, 163–4

M

M&A risk:
and bond documentation, 313–16, *315*
analysis, 314
background, 313
company objectives, 313–14
consent solicitation overview, 314–15
overview, 313
recommendations, 315–16
results and outcome, 316
and deferred consideration, monetising, 317–21, *318*, *320*
analysis, 318
background, 317
company objectives, 317–18
overview, 317
pricing, 319–20
recommendations, 320
results, 318–19
and hedging uncertain exposures, 323–35, *325*, *326*, *327*, *328*, *329*, *330*, *331*, *332*, *333*
analysis, 325
background, 324
company objectives, 324–5
and duration optimisation approach, step by step, *325*
overview, 323–4
recommendations, 334
management for, 299–311, *301*, *303*, *304*, *305*, *306*, *308*
analysis, 300–2
background, 299–300
capital structure, 303–7
company objectives, 300
currency cashflow mix, 303
deal parameters and timelines, 300–1
financials: assuming all-debt financed, 303
optimal debt structure, 307
overview, 299
recommendations, 310
and total debt, optimal currency split of, 307–9
understanding transaction, 300
and rating impact of an acquisition, 293–8, *295*
analysis, 294
background, 293
company objectives, 294
overview, 293
recommendations, 297
risk management approach, step by step, *see* rating impact of an acquisition
section overview, 287–91
event-specific, 288
Step 1: rating impact of an acquisition, 289; *see also* M&A risk: and rating impact of an acquisition
Step 2: addressing ALM considerations, 290
Step 3: finding optimal debt composition, 290–1
Step 4: assessing risk and finding hedging solution, 291
strategic, 287–8
transforming, 288
uncertainty, 288–9
sources of, 309
management presentation, preparing for, 16–17
Markets in Financial Instruments Directive (MiFID) Review, xxviii

mathematical assumptions and required knowledge, xxv–xxvi
maturity optimisation, constrained, 141–6
  analysis, 142–5
    methodology, 143–5
  company objectives, 142
  recommendations, 145
mergers and acquisitions, risks related to, *see* M&A risk
Merton's model, optimal debt duration via, 33–40, *39*
  analysis, 35–8, *38*
    of debt structure, 37–8
  background, 35
  company objectives, 35
  generalisation, 35–6
  illustration of, *37*
  recommendations, 39; *see also* funding
monetising deferred consideration, 317–21, *318*, *320*
  analysis, 318
  background, 317
  company objectives, 317–18
  overview, 317
  pricing, 319–20
  recommendations, 320
  results, 318–19
    financing SPV in capital markets, 319
    optimal structure, 318–19

N

netting FX risk, 185–98, *187*, *189*, *190*, *191*, *192*, *193*, *194*, *195*, *196*, *197*
  analysis, 186–7
  background, 186
  company objectives, 186
  and earnings-at-risk calculation, 190–3
  and individual transaction exposures by subsidiary and currency, 189–90
  overview, 185–6
  recommendations, 197
  step-by-step process of, 187–97
    Step 1: evaluating net economic risk to the group via an EaR measure, 187–93
    Step 2: separating between transactional and economic exposures, 193–5
    Step 3: looking for offsets between two sets of exposures and proposing residual hedge, 195–7
new bonds, three main questions concerning, 41

O

obtaining credit rating, 9–18
  analysis, 11–12, *11–12*
  company objectives, 10
  introductory agency meetings, 13–16
  and peer group analysis, *15–16*
  recommendations, 18
  step-by-step process of, *10*
    Step 1: forming initial rating expectations, 12–13
    Step 2: introductory agency meetings, 12–13
    Step 3: preparing for management presentation, 16–17
  see also funding
optimal deposit composition, 263–76, *265*, *268*, *269*, *270*, *271*, *272*, *273*, *274*, *275*
  analysis, 264
  applied to derivatives exposure, 274–6
  background, 263–4
  company objectives, 264
  overview, 263
  recommendations, 274
  step by step, 264–74, *265*

Step 1: simplified conservative model, 264–7
Step 2: full conservative model, 268–71, *268*, *270*
Step 3: strategic model, 271–4

P

peer benchmarking and historical analysis, 43–6
peer group analysis, *15–16*
pension funds:
asset and liability management for, 159–66, *160*, *161*, *162*, *163*, *164*, *165*, *166*
analysis, 160
background, 159–60
company objectives, 160
and equity risk, reducing, 163–4
and interest rate risk, reducing, 163
overview, 159
recommendations, 164
risk management approach, step by step, 160–4, *160*
Step 1: calculating asset and liability sensitivities and distribution, 160–2
Step 2: determining breakdown of risk to surplus by asset class, 162
Step 3: exploring ways to reduce risk to the surplus, 163–4
prehedging credit risk, 277–83, *279*, *281*, *282*
analysis, 278–9
background, 277–8
call spread, 281–2, *282*
company objectives, 278
hedging strategy, 280
overview, 277
recommendations, 282–3
straight call, 280–1, *281*
prehedging interest rate and inflation risk, 117–25, *119*, *120*, *124*
and accounting treatment, 122–4
analysis, 118
background, 118
and bond issuance, step by step, 118–24
Step 1: deciding whether or not to hedge, 118–20
Step 2: designing solution, 120–4
Step 3: testing flexibility of solution, 124
company objectives, 118
overview, 117–18
recommendation, 125
solutions, designing, 120–1
and uncertain maturity, 124
and uncertain starting date, 124
prehedging, when to, 127–39, *128*, *129*, *130*, *131*, *132*, *133*, *134*, *135*, *136*, *137*, *138*
background, 127
company objectives, 128
cost analysis, step by step, 129–38, *129*
Step 1: defining measure for prehedging cost, 130
Step 2: estimating historical prehedging cost, 130–2
Step 3: finding moments when prehedging cost is lowered, 133–6
Step 4: tactical considerations, 136–8
cost, forecasting from distance to local minimum, 134–6
cost, one into five years, 130–1
and dynamic of past swap rate hikes, 137–8
future cost, steepness as indicator of, 133–4
market background, 128–9
overview, 127

recent cost, comparison of, 131–2
recommendations, 138–9
preparing for management presentation, 16–17

R

rating impact of an acquisition, 293–8, *295*
analysis, 294
background, 293
company objectives, 294
overview, 293
recommendations, 297
risk management approach, step by step, *294*
Step 1: assessing business profile, 294–5
Step 2: peer group analysis, 296–7
Step 3: assessing execution-related issues, 297
risk:
cashflow, 148
commodity, 339–59
and commodity-linked revenues and currency risk, 345–52
section overview, 339–43
cost versus, on liability side, *148*
counterparty, 61
credit, 241–83; *see also* credit risk
and counterparty risk methodology, 245–53
and optimal deposit composition, 263–76; *see also main entry*
section overview, 241–3
currency, *see* currency risk
derivatives, 60–1
fair-value, 148
foreign exchange, *see* currency risk
interest rate and inflation, *see* interest rate and inflation risk
liquidity, 61
M&A-related, *see* M&A risk
roles and responsibilities for management of, *61*
settlement, 61
structural, 170
to surplus, determining breakdown of by asset class, 162
transaction, 171, 187–8, 299
translation, 170–1, 187, 299
translation, managing, 215–25, *218*, *219*, *220*, *221*, *223*
analysis, 217–18, 218–24, *218*
background, 217
company objectives, 217
overview, 215–17
recommendations, 224
valuation, 60
ways of mitigating, 62–5
risk management approach, step by step, to surplus, exploring ways to reduce, 163–4
risk management performance, benchmarking of, xxiv–xxv
risk management roles and responsibilities, *61*

S

structural risk, 170
swaptions:
Bermudan, 121
for floating debt, 90–1
strategy for, *90*

T

transaction risk, 171, 187–8
FX, 299
translation risk, 170–1, 187
FX, 299
managing, 215–25, *218*, *219*, *220*, *221*, *223*

analysis, 217–18
background, 217
company objectives, 217
overview, 215–17
recommendations, 224
risk management approach, step by step, 217–18
Step 1: defining scope of analysis, 218–19
Step 2: simulating market variables, 220
Step 3: determining efficient frontier, 221–4
Step 4: tactical considerations, 224

U

uncertain exposures, hedging, 323–35, *325*, *326*, *327*, *328*, *329*, *330*, *331*, *332*, *333*
analysis, 325
background, 324
company objectives, 324–5
and duration optimisation approach, step by step, 325–34
Step 1: scoring deal sensitivity to FX (transaction occurs), 325–7
Step 2: scoring unwind P&L (transaction fails), 327–8
Step 3: scoring post–hedge rate, 328–31
Step 4: applying FX distribution, 331–3
Step 5: applying deal likelihood, 334
overview, 323–4
recommendations, 334

V

value-at-risk (VaR):
and duration, optimisation of, 154–5
limitations of, xxvi–xxvii
scenario analysis, including duration split, *155*